Property Rights and
form in China

DATE DUE FOR RETURN

Property Rights and Economic Reform in China

EDITED BY JEAN C. OI

and

ANDREW G. WALDER

Stanford University Press, Stanford, California   *1999*

Stanford University Press
Stanford, California
© 1999 by the Board of Trustees of the
Leland Stanford Junior University

Printed in the United States of America
CIP data appear at the end of the book

1002659131

To
Gregory Oi Walder

Acknowledgments

The essays in this book originated as papers for a conference at the Hong Kong University of Science and Technology in 1996 on "Property Rights in Transitional Economies: Insights from Research on China," funded by a grant from the Henry Luce Foundation to the John King Fairbank Center for East Asian Research at Harvard University, where we were faculty members at the time the conference was conceived. We would like to thank two successive directors of the Fairbank Center, Roderick MacFarquhar and James Watson, for making these funds available to us. We are also indebted to the Hong Kong University of Science and Technology, where we were privileged to teach for two years, for giving us access to superb conference facilities, and to the university's Division of Social Science, which provided tireless and efficient help in organizing the meeting.

Most of all, we are indebted to the volume's contributors, who drew upon their recent research to respond to the questions that defined the conference, and who shaped their papers into finished chapters without delay. Several others presented papers at the meeting and made important contributions: Scott Rozelle, Albert Park, Scott Wilson, and Susan Young. Muriel Bell of Stanford University Press has our gratitude for her strong support in bringing the results to publication.

This book is our second attempt at coauthorship. We dedicate it to our first.

J.C.O. AND A.G.W.

Contents

Figures and Tables

Contributors

CHIH-JOU JAY CHEN received his Ph.D. in Sociology from Duke University and is currently Assistant Research Fellow, Institute of Sociology, Academia Sinica, Taiwan. He is the author of *Markets and Clientelism: The Transformation of Property Rights in Rural China* (1999).

CORINNA-BARBARA FRANCIS is Assistant Professor of Political Science at the University of Missouri–Columbia. She received her Ph.D. from Columbia University and is the author of articles in *China Quarterly, Asian Survey,* and other journals.

XIAOLIN GUO is Assistant Professor in the Department of East Asian Studies, University of Aarhus, Denmark. She received her Ph.D. in Anthropology from the University of British Columbia. During the 1997–98 academic year, she was a postdoctoral fellow at the Fairbank Center for East Asian Research, Harvard University.

JAMES KAI-SING KUNG is Assistant Professor in the Division of Social Science at Hong Kong University of Science and Technology. He received his Ph.D. in Economics from the University of Cambridge. His articles have appeared in the *Journal of Comparative Economics, World Development, Journal of Development Studies, The China Journal,* and elsewhere.

NAN LIN is Professor of Sociology and Director of the Center for Asia-Pacific Studies at Duke University. His articles have appeared in the *American Journal of Sociology, Theory and Society,* and other journals.

YI-MIN LIN is Assistant Professor in the Division of Social Science, Hong Kong University of Science and Technology. He received his Ph.D. in Sociology from Yale University. His articles have appeared in *Studies in Comparative Communism* and other journals.

JEAN C. OI is Associate Professor of Political Science and Director of the Center for East Asian Studies at Stanford University. She is the author of *State and Peasant in Contemporary China: The Political Economy of Village*

Government (1989) and *Rural China Takes Off: Institutional Foundations of Economic Reform* (1999).

GREGORY A. RUF is Assistant Professor of Anthropology and Chinese Studies at the State University of New York–Stony Brook. He is the author of *Cadres and Kin: Making a Socialist Village in West China, 1921–1991* (Stanford, 1998).

EDUARD B. VERMEER is head of the Documentation and Research Center for Contemporary China at Leiden University. He is the author of *Economic Development in Provincial China: Central Shaanxi Since 1930* (1988) and editor of *Cooperative and Collective in China's Rural Development: Between State and Private Interests* (1998).

ANDREW G. WALDER is Professor of Sociology and Senior Fellow, Institute of International Studies, Stanford University. He is the author of *Communist Neo-Traditionalism: Work and Authority in Chinese Industry* (1986) and the editor of *The Waning of the Communist State: Economic Origins of Political Decline in China and Hungary* (1995), *China's Transitional Economy* (1996), and *Zouping in Transition: The Process of Reform in Rural North China* (1998).

DAVID L. WANK is Associate Professor of Sociology in the Faculty of Comparative Culture, Sophia University, Tokyo. He is the author of *Commodifying Communism: Business, Trust, and Politics in a Chinese City* (1998).

SUSAN H. WHITING is Assistant Professor of Political Science and International Studies at the University of Washington, Seattle. She received her Ph.D. from the University of Michigan and is the author of *Power and Wealth in China's Rural Industry: The Political Economy of Institutional Change* (1999).

ZHANXIN ZHANG is a Ph.D. student in the Division of Social Science, Hong Kong University of Science and Technology.

Property Rights and
Economic Reform in China

Chapter 1

Property Rights in the Chinese Economy: Contours of the Process of Change

ANDREW G. WALDER AND JEAN C. OI

It is widely believed that a market economy requires property rights that are defined with sufficient clarity and enforced with sufficient predictability to encourage individuals and firms to expend effort, plan, invest, and bear risks. These general tenets have not been seriously disputed in the spirited debates about economic institutions in transitional economies. The real disagreements are about specifics. How clear is clear enough? How predictable is predictable enough? What institutional arrangements are capable of ensuring the requisite clarity and predictability, and how do we create them? The sharpest disagreements are about government officials: should those who operated a failed command economy be granted asset ownership in any form? This question leads directly to another: how closely must economic institutions conform to models provided by Western European or North American capitalism (or textbook versions thereof)?

At one end of the spectrum are those who advised postcommunist regimes to make a clean break with past failures: sell off unproductive state assets to clearly designated private entities and establish administrative regulations and legal guarantees that support private enterprise against interference by government officials.[1] For these writers, government ownership is the core of the problem and should be avoided even in transitional forms. The economic institutions of North Atlantic capitalism are the logical model for transitional economies to emulate. Half measures are ineffective compromises; advocacy of alternative institutions is wishful thinking.[2]

At the other end of the spectrum are those who argue that rapid privatization cannot work because functioning economic systems cannot be created "by design."[3] These critics point out that the economic institutions of Western capitalism emerged through a long process of evolution.[4] Those who seek to remake entire economies on the model of Western Europe, they contend, are making the same mistake made earlier by central planners—the wholesale transformation of an economy based on untested theory and a healthy dose of ideology.[5] Rapid privatization cannot work in the absence of a preexisting regulatory and legal framework— something that cannot be created as quickly as firms can be sold. The alternative, they argue, is gradual experimentation with hybrid property forms that would compete and evolve through time, an evolutionary process of competition and selection based on the recombination of previous organizational routines and practices.[6] While these arguments are appealing on intellectual grounds, the earlier failure of such evolutionary reforms in Hungary justified skepticism about calls for gradual reform.[7] Those who have championed evolutionary processes have yet to specify what institutional arrangements lead to an invigorated mixed economy instead of the stagnation and corruption so often feared. Until they are able to do so, they are critics without an alternative analysis.

While the debate pitted those whose reasoning was founded in marginal analysis and equilibrium models against those who derived insights from institutional economics, economic history, or sociological analysis, *neither* side has an explicit theory about the transition from one economic system to another.[8] Worse, the debate was not based on evidence from a transitional economy that in fact had enjoyed rapid economic progress. The *real* disagreements about privatization raised empirical issues about which evidence of any kind was very scarce:

How far and how fast can privatization realistically proceed in the absence of legal and regulatory enforcement mechanisms that cannot be created quickly?

Does "privatization" require the outright sale, auction, or gift of government enterprises to private entities; or can effective arrangements be created by sharing government property rights with private actors who contract or lease the assets?

How clear do property rights have to be before they are "clear enough"? If changes stop short of outright privatization, will they fail to offer strong enough incentives?

Are there effective transitional substitutes for systems of civil law and independent, impartial courts and regulatory agencies? Are financial incentives for government agencies and officials, bribes, and kinship or other social ties sufficient to guarantee the predictability or trust necessary for investment and risk-bearing?

To the extent that governments must exercise property rights over public firms, can incentives be created to make government officials behave in ways different than in years past?

This last question is fundamental. In practice, government bureaucrats control key economic resources at the outset of reform. Their behavior as economic actors will therefore have an enormous impact on the direction of change and the performance of the economy as it moves away from Soviet institutional forms. Reform thus involves the design of incentives, not only for firms, but for governments as well.

The Relevance of China

For almost two decades, China has spurned ambitious privatization programs, yet it has been one of the fastest-growing economies in the world. China's relevance, however, is clouded by conflicting and sometimes confusing claims about the property rights that exist in different sectors of its economy. The confusion is most pronounced in the massive literature on the rapidly growing industrial enterprises in rural townships and villages, a once-marginal sector that now produces more than half of China's industrial output. What explains the rapid growth of these rural industries? Some argue that it is the clarification of village and township government's rights to income flows from local public enterprises that gave local officials unambiguous control over them and the incentive to manage them in an entrepreneurial fashion.[9] Others argue to the contrary that underneath the seeming reality of government ownership and control, there is a hidden process of privatization in which local enterprises have been sold, leased, or contracted to private entrepreneurs, and that this hidden privatization is what really explains rapid growth.[10] The first argument emphasizes that these firms are still publicly owned and operated, while the second claims that in fact they are private firms, or very nearly so.

Others view ownership in village communities in a way that implicitly denies the terms of this dialogue. Some argue that clear property rights are not necessary in China's cultural context.[11] Others argue that whether enterprises are owned and operated by the village government, by families, or by some arrangement in between, the owners of the important assets are always members of the local elite, tied together by kinship and friendship.[12] Therefore what appears to be "public" village property is in fact essentially the property of the lineage or political clique that dominates the village. Public village property is inseparable from the property of local elites: they do not formally own it, but they benefit disproportionately from it. Moreover, the process of "privatization" through contracting, leasing, or selling public firms to families is nothing more than a process whereby these local elites share out benefits to their own families and friends.

Wide disagreements about the nature of rural enterprise in China have encouraged fundamentally opposed inferences about the issue of privatization. While some have used China to argue that it is not privatization but competition in the context of gradual institutional change that is essential for effective reform, those who have argued for rapid privatization in Eastern Europe point to China's rural industrialization in support of *their* arguments.[13]

Such confusion is unnecessary. The issues of contention are empirical questions about what actors exercise what kinds of rights over what kinds of productive assets. They are also empirical questions about the pattern of change in the Chinese economy, how early various changes have occurred, how fast the pace of change has been, how far property rights have evolved. These questions apply, not only to the rural industrial sector, where disagreements have been most pronounced, but to the rest of the Chinese economy as well. Part of the problem is that property rights per se have not usually been at the center of analyses of reform in China. Instead, they are addressed in passing in studies of reform policies or institutional changes, or they are background assumptions that are props in analytic exercises, but are themselves unsupported by any evidence.[14]

The purpose of this volume is to directly address questions about property rights in the Chinese economy. To this end, each author was asked to describe and document the evolution of property rights in regions or sectors in which he or she has conducted research, and to state the implications for recent analyses of the Chinese economy. The property rights, not reform policies and their outcomes, are the focus.

Property as a Bundle of Rights

Property rights in emerging market economies have long been referred to as "hybrid" forms that combine features of private and public property.[15] Our task is to explore the properties of such ownership forms in different settings and, more important, to document and account for variation across regions and sectors, and through time. This empirical and explanatory focus demanded that our authors agree upon a single set of definitions at the outset; we could not proceed if there was confusion and disagreement about how to define the phenomenon of interest.

Harold Demsetz's notion of property as a "bundle of rights" was ideal for our purposes.[16] It disaggregates the notion of property into three kinds of rights—control, income, and transfer—and explicitly acknowledges that there are a variety of ways in which such "rights" might be enforced, ranging from formal law to social custom. It is therefore a flexible tool for the more precise description of variation in economic institutions; and it permits us to set aside questions about how a property form should be classified and labeled in favor of an empirical focus on the real issues at hand: who exercises what rights, how they do so, and what the associated incentives and risks are.

Demsetz's framework posed the following questions for our authors:

Who exercises managerial control? Who decides how an asset shall be used in production—whether it shall be used, what should be produced, and how it shall be produced. Who makes major decisions regarding production and investment? Who makes day-to-day decisions about operations and methods? How clear are such rights in practice? If such rights are shared, how are they shared?

Who has a right to income flows? Who can claim shares of the income from the assets? What are the claims of the government, the enterprise, or the employees of the enterprise? If these claims are shared, what is the sharing arrangement? How clear are these claims and how stable is the exercise of such rights? If there are losses, who bears responsibility for them?

Who has the right to assign ownership to other parties? Who has the right to decide to transfer the above rights to other parties, either through some kind of contract or partnership, or through outright sale? Who enjoys the income, and who bears the loss, from such a transfer?

How are the above rights specified and enforced? Are there *ex ante* agreements that are respected in practice? Is the government a reliable and impartial enforcer of such rights? Do the rights rest on kinship, personal networks, or some other kind of private and personal arrangement?

These questions are derived directly from the conception of property as a bundle of rights. They demand from authors factual description, and they provide a platform for asking the questions about variation and change that are the key concern of this book: *How have property rights varied across regions and economic sectors, and how have they changed over time? What are the reasons for such variation and change?*

It should be evident that our approach is empirical and historical. We seek to understand actual practices and their consequences in the Chinese economy over the past 20 years, and we seek to uncover and analyze patterns of variation and change. We have used our research findings to clarify confusion, adjudicate differing claims, chart the observable contours of change, and reflect critically upon some of the discussions about economic policy in transitional economies.

It should also be evident that our approach is descriptive and inductive rather than axiomatic and deductive. Those who counsel the systematic and early privatization of government assets base their arguments upon a deductive exercise that identifies a narrow range of property rights arrangements as theoretically optimal. Implicitly, this means that the only acceptable "bundle of rights" is one where a private entity exercises control rights, where income flows to the private owner are subject only to limited and predictable taxation, where the private owner has relatively unimpeded rights to reassign or sell the assets, and where these rights are enforced through impartial administrators or courts—the logical opposite of the command economies formerly characteristic of these countries. From this vantage point, "partial" reforms—all the potential property rights arrangements that lie between these extremes—are suboptimal and flawed. Any halfway measures are compromises that have little prospect of real success and will only stall truly effective changes.

In contrast, our approach accepts that what is optimal in theory is not necessarily attainable in practice. Efforts to move quickly to the theoretically optimal condition may entail unacceptable social and political costs. Existing social structures, organizational practices, and personal networks may alter and subvert privatization programs in ways not envisaged. In China, where the Communist Party is still firmly in power, and intent on staying there, change will come gradually, through myriad "suboptimal" forms, if it comes at all.

Reform as a Reassignment of Property Rights

Extensive reassignments of property rights can alter ownership in an economy without wholesale privatization. Agency theory is founded on the idea that variations in the assignment of such rights within organizations can have an important impact on incentives and behavior in organizations.[17] Compared to the massive changes involved in the sale of state assets, the reassignments of rights usually analyzed by agency theorists are relatively minor. Yet it is understood that such reassignments can have a significant impact on performance.[18]

For almost 20 years, reform in China has proceeded through the gradual reassignment of specific property rights from higher government agencies to lower government agencies, or from government agencies to enterprises, managers, families, or individuals. This has occurred gradually, and different ownership forms have held sway in different parts of the economy at different times. As the chapters in this volume make clear, the outright sale of public property to private entrepreneurs or families played a relatively minor role throughout the 1980s in most areas of China.[19] Only in the 1990s has the privatization of public firms gained momentum, a trend that first manifested itself in the rural industrial sector.

To illustrate the varieties of property rights reassignments characteristic of China's reforms and provide a vocabulary to refer to changes described in the following chapters, we outline five types of ownership arrangements that define a continuum from traditional state enterprise to the recognizably private. The three intermediate types—the reformed public firm, contracted public firms, and leased public firms—are defined by the progressive reassignment of property rights away from traditional state or collective ownership toward private ownership forms.

TRADITIONAL STATE OR COLLECTIVE OWNERSHIP

This is the socialist firm analyzed critically by János Kornai and many others. Government agencies decide what the firms will produce, supervise their activities in detail, make investment decisions, and decide when to change product lines. The prototype is the large urban state-owned enterprise, but the commune and brigade industries of the Mao period— the forerunners of today's township and village enterprises—operated under essentially the same arrangements.[20] Government officials decide what to produce, how, and to whom the products are sold; they appropriate all profits or make up all losses; and they arrange all financing for the firm. Enterprise managers are paid employees who are hired, fired, and promoted by government officials acting on behalf of the government as owner.[21]

THE REFORMED STATE OR COLLECTIVE FIRM:
MANAGEMENT INCENTIVE CONTRACTS

This differs from traditional state or collective ownership by the partial reassignment of control and income rights to the firm and its managers. Managers are still government employees, but they are given greater incentive to improve enterprise performance, and they bear greater responsibility for it. Managers gain new rights of control: decisions about production processes, product lines, the marketing of products, and the purchasing of supplies. They also gain new income rights. While the forms of profit-sharing have varied widely, the central principle is that firm managers work under *ex ante* agreements about how the profits of the firm are to be divided. Typically, these agreements specify a planned amount of taxes and profits to be remitted to the government, after which point the firm is permitted to retain a specified percentage of the additional profits, if any. The percentage has varied widely in practice and has usually been implemented flexibly and readjusted annually by the government. The enterprise's retained funds have usually been subject to close regulation by the government, but permitted expenditures have included much larger bonuses and wage raises for managers and other personnel, and expenditures for new housing and services provided to employees.

These partial reassignments of property rights have long been criticized as being too limited to lead to sufficiently improved firm performance. The constant readjustment of profit-sharing arrangements and the continuing constraints on the expenditure of retained funds are seen as serious remaining flaws in the incentives for managers. They constitute a "soft budget constraint" that undermines incentives. Kornai's influential analyses of such piecemeal reforms in Hungary during the 1970s and 1980s led him to conclude that only more decisive changes in property rights would remedy the fundamental flaws of the command economy.[22] More recently, empirical work on the Chinese state sector has led some to argue that, contrary to expectations, there have been significant improvements in the factor productivity of state firms, improvements that have accelerated over time. These findings have been challenged, and debate has ensued.[23] At stake is the question of whether more extensive reassignment of property rights, if not outright privatization, is necessary.

THE CONTRACTED PUBLIC ASSET:

GOVERNMENT-MANAGEMENT PARTNERSHIPS

While incentive contracts have dominated in the reformed urban state firms, partnership contracts have been extensively employed in rural industry since the mid 1980s. When a public asset is "contracted," more extensive reassignments of control and income rights are assigned to the manager than in the reformed public firm. Because the scale of the enterprise is typically small, and the amount of fixed capital investment by the government relatively modest, the manager will have even greater freedom to change product lines, and will bear even greater responsibility for finding market outlets for products. Managers also obtain more extensive income rights; their share of the residual (net profit) is typically larger, the shares more equal, and constraints on the allocation of retained profit (including income for the managers) fewer. There is considerable variation within this category: the more conservative forms of contracting can resemble the more liberal forms of state enterprise reform, while the more liberal forms of contracting can resemble the next form, the leasehold.

There are two ways to distinguish contracting from the reformed public firm. Conceptually, the reformed firm is analogous to an improved incentive scheme for hired professional managers whose performance is closely monitored by owners. Contracting, by contrast, is analogous to a partnership between owners (government) and managers (entrepreneurs). The manager is given extensive control over the assets, and the owner and the contractor share the rewards and risks of business. Empirically, what distinguishes the reformed from the contracted public firm is that profit-sharing arrangements are not readjusted annually. Contracts are signed for a minimum of three to five years, and the presumption is that the terms will not routinely be readjusted during that time.[24] As a result, the manager-entrepreneurs enjoy more extensive rights to residual income and can potentially enrich themselves in ways not possible in reformed public firms. At the same time, managers bear much more of the risk, and they may find themselves losing their own money and out of a job if their firm suffers extensive losses and the government is unable or unwilling to bail them out.

LEASED PUBLIC ASSETS

When public assets are leased, the leaseholder effectively assumes all control and income rights in exchange for fixed rental payments to the government for a specified period of time. Contracted public firms resemble partnerships, because risk and residual are shared: if profit fluctuates, the income of both contractor and government rises or falls. In contrast, the government's share is fixed in a leasehold: no matter how large profits become, that share will not rise; and, conversely, even if losses occur, the government must still be paid. The manager or entrepreneur therefore becomes the sole residual claimant, but at the same time bears greater risk than under a partnership. Except for contractual restrictions designed to preserve the government's fixed assets (the leaseholder cannot sell off these assets, for example), the leaseholder enjoys control rights similar to those of a private owner.

What distinguishes leaseholding from outright privatization is that it is initially still the government's investment in fixed assets that is at risk, not the manager's. Over time, leaseholds easily lead to conflicts of interest and complex contract negotiations between the government and leaseholder, especially if the leaseholder reinvests profits in capital equipment. Because of these complexities, leaseholds have been used most commonly when a local government wishes to divest itself of an unproductive asset, in which it no longer has a strong interest, but cannot find buyers with sufficient capital to purchase the firm outright. Leaseholding has often become a means of privatization whereby lease payments are effectively installment payments on a sale.

PRIVATIZATION

Government has no effective ownership rights over this kind of firm, although, as in all economies, it may attenuate the owner's rights through regulation and taxation. The private entrepreneur is the residual claimant, and the government's claim on the business is only in the form of taxes. The entrepreneur also bears all of the risk, and there is neither obligation nor any expectation that the government will bail out firms in difficulty. The entrepreneur has the right to sell the asset or to decide to close and liquidate the firm. As later sections will make clear, this encompasses family-started firms and firms that were formerly publicly owned but were sold by local governments to entrepreneurs. This latter category comprises the cases where the government simply sells its interest in a public enterprise outright. This is the process that is generally called "privatization" in policy discussions.[25]

These categories constitute a conceptual sketch, but in practice there is much variation within them, and there are practices that fall on the borderline between two categories. Several chapters in this book make clear, for example, that shareholding arrangements may fall into any of the categories, from the contracted public firm to the private firm, depending on their actual rules. This continuum is designed to communicate the fact that in China a wide range of property forms progressively grant to managers or entrepreneurs larger and clearer claims to the residual and make them bear larger proportions of risk. While it is possible to view this continuum as one of privatization via gradations, the intermediate forms, especially the very common partnership contracts, are not "privatized" in the sense recommended by those suspicious of halfway measures. They are the prototypical half-measure, a true "hybrid" form of property.

The Contours of Change: Contributions
of This Volume

The gradual pattern of change that we observe in China has involved a steady shift from the traditional state and collective firms down toward the reformed, contracted, leased, and private types. Change has occurred in a cascading pattern, with the reformed type most prominent early on, and then a progressive shift down the continuum toward contracting, leasing, and, finally, the private firm. However, it should be noted that different forms of ownership have often existed within one locality during the same period of time.

The pattern of change has been uneven, with the large-scale state sector still dominated by the reformed public firm model, while the massive rural industrial sector shifted toward partnership contracting early on, and since the mid 1990s has been increasingly characterized by the leased and privatized forms.[26] This volume documents a steady evolution in property rights that has proceeded along different trajectories in different regions and economic sectors. It describes five separate processes through which change has occurred and offers explanations for the pace and trajectory of change.

The first process is through the contracting or leasing of public firms. Some sectors of the economy, notably large state firms, do not appear to have reached this stage until very recently.[27] Village- and township-owned enterprises, however, have moved the farthest through this process, with high proportions of public firms contracted or leased, although at a very different pace in different regions. All of the examples of this process in the chapters below are about this latter sector, where change has been most extensive, and about which there has been the most confusion.

The second process is the one most often identified with the word "privatization" in policy discussions. This is the outright sale of government assets to private individuals or families. This occurred only rarely in China during the 1980s, and it was employed primarily in small-scale enterprises. But several chapters below indicate that this process has accelerated in many rural areas during the 1990s.[28] Again, the trend appears most pronounced in the rural industrial sector, and it appears to occur at the end of a long trail of local experience with various forms of direct government management and contracting. The chapters by James Kaising Kung and Susan Whiting document this evolutionary trend and specify the reasons for it.

The third process is a more ambiguous one, whereby government officials and their associates begin to reap such private benefits from their domination of public firms that public firms begin to shade gradually into a form of local elite privatization. In the village analyzed by Nan Lin and Chih-jou Jay Chen, the shareholding system is being used as a vehicle for the massive, formal transfer of a large industrial base, long operated as reformed socialist firms, into a corporate empire owned by local elites.

The fourth process occurs when state agencies or enterprises invest public funds in new enterprises that operate independently as private firms. Capital is thereby diverted from the government budget or from state firms into the private economy. Government agencies or enterprises are "owners" of these private firms in ways that parallel institutional ownership of private firms in market economies. This is analyzed in the chapters by Yi-min Lin and Zhanxin Zhang and by Corinna-Barbara Francis.

A fifth process of change occurs through the start-up of new private enterprises by individuals and families, and their subsequent growth. To the extent that new firms increase in number and grow in size, the proportion of the economy that is private grows, and the economy as a whole becomes, in the aggregate, more private.[29] In China as a whole, this has been a gradual process, starting first in the small-scale services sector and gradually spreading beyond it. However, in some coastal regions, such as the county examined by Chih-jou Chen in Chapter 3 and one of the counties examined by Susan Whiting, this process of privatization occurred very early and has dominated the local economy.

Therefore, despite the fact that China's leaders have resisted calls for the systematic outright privatization of public enterprises through the kind of sales, auctions, or shareholding schemes proposed to postcommunist regimes, ownership has evolved decisively, if gradually, away from traditional forms of state and collective ownership toward a mixed economy pervaded by contracting, leaseholding, and various forms of private enterprise—the family firm, the elite industrial empire, and the private companies owned by government agencies and enterprises. We shall see, however, that the nature of these ownership types is not always what they appear, encompassing different configurations of property rights. As the chapter by Xiaolin Guo on two townships in Yunnan shows, the labels "collective" and "private" may tell us little about the actual property rights relationships. Nonetheless, in a way that parallels what Barry Naughton calls "growing out of the plan," China's economy as a whole has evolved far from the state ownership once characteristic of communism.[30]

Regional Variation in Property Regimes

This evolution, however, has proceeded along different paths in different economic sectors and regions. One striking conclusion to be drawn from these chapters is that much of the confusion about property rights in the huge rural industrial sector has simply been because property rights in the most rapidly growing regions have varied in fundamental ways. Markedly different regional property regimes emerged during the 1980s, and they have evolved continuously. The chapters in this volume describe two different property regimes—government-centered and entrepreneur-centered—both of which, despite their differences, supported rapid growth for well over a decade. The authors clarify the differences between these regional property regimes, explain them, and specify the reasons for their subsequent patterns of evolution.

DIFFERENT STARTING POINTS AND THEIR CAUSES

The rural case studies in this book describe two starkly different patterns of rural industrial growth. The first is decidedly government-centered, in which village and township officials played an active entrepreneurial role, and industrial enterprises were government-owned and from the outset operated by hired managers under various incentive contracts. This is the pattern of rural industrialization that has so often been referred to as a form of "corporatism," in which the rural government is likened to a business corporation and the individual enterprises to the corporation's manufacturing plants.[31] This property regime is richly elaborated in Gregory Ruf's study of Qiaolou village in Sichuan; James Kung's study of Wuxi County, famous as the heartland of rural public enterprise; Nan Lin and Chih-jou Chen's study of Daqiuzhuang in Tianjin Municipality, and Susan Whiting's study of Songjiang County, near Shanghai.[32]

The second pattern is very different. It is decidedly entrepreneur-centered, and rural officials are not involved in manufacturing, marketing, investment, and hiring decisions in the way that is typical of the corporate pattern. Existing village enterprises, which were few in number, were sold or leased at the outset and rural officials subsequently primarily played a supporting role in facilitating investment and growth in private enterprises. This "littoral" pattern appears to be common along the coastal fringe of southeastern China. Chih-jou Chen's case study of two rural counties near Quanzhou on the coast of Fujian is a clear example, as is Susan Whiting's study of Yueqing County in the Wenzhou region of Zhejiang, long famous for this pattern of rural development.[33]

Why such strikingly different starting points for rural industry? The analysis is made explicit in Whiting's comparison of Songjiang and Yueqing, and it is supported by the arguments made by Ruf for his Sichuan village and Chen for his Quanzhou townships. The answer is that differing resource endowments and opportunities pushed economic growth in different directions.

"Corporatist" regions often had a base of commune- and brigade-operated rural industries as a legacy from the Mao period. This concentrated capital, existing enterprises, and, to a considerable extent, business expertise, in the hands of local officials when reforms began. Collective agriculture was abandoned, and farming was turned over to families.

However, rural officials retained the commune and brigade enterprises as their power base, which they sought successfully to expand by using their position to mobilize capital within their own communities and their connections in towns and cities to arrange sales and subprocessing contracts. Managers were hired to operate the enterprises with liberal incentive pay or management contracts, but the more liberal forms of contracting and leasing, in which managers would have significant claims to residual income and bear significant amounts of risk, were generally shunned at the outset.

The littoral regions had no significant rural industrial base at the start of reform. While this difference is striking, it is not the only explanation for regional differences. Also important is access to capital. In many corporatist regions, officials enjoyed preferential access to public finance and local banks, and they could thus draw on larger sources of capital and credit than family-run firms, which could only rely upon the initially meager savings of their owners or the latter's relatives or neighbors.[34] This difference in access restricted the family firm to subsidiary markets and small-scale enterprise in most areas of China throughout the 1980s.

What is distinctive about the areas studied by Whiting and by Chen is the extraordinary access to capital and credit enjoyed by the private sector. In these coastal areas, local governments were neither financially prepared nor inclined to challenge the private sector when the reforms began. During the first 30 years of the People's Republic, coastal links to the world economy were severed, but for most of this same period, local families continued to receive remittances from overseas relatives. Once the reforms began in earnest, the number and amount of such remittances quickly grew. People in these regions had been deeply involved in commercial activities prior to the collectivization of the 1950s, and they had a long history of large-scale migration overseas. These were the regions that had populated Chinese communities in Southeast Asia and beyond, and these same ties of kinship and dialect also tied them to Chinese across the Taiwan straits and in Hong Kong.

As Chen describes in his chapter on the Quanzhou region, local officials encouraged family enterprise and other forms of private investment as a way to draw on the capital that could flow into the locality through ties of kinship and native place. For private entrepreneurs, the political risk in exceeding legal restrictions on private enterprise was lower than in the inland regions. Instead, private business worked together with local officials to shield the essentially private nature of local industry and commerce by designating private firms as "collective" or publicly owned. In addition to overseas remittances, families also received remittances from members who had migrated to work in more prosperous regions. Peasants around

Wenzhou, as Whiting shows, actively sought opportunities for wage labor in other parts of the country. The result was a rapid surge of growth based essentially on private enterprise—growth that led to massive increases in the revenues at the disposal of local officials (and to increases in their personal income). Consequently, officials driven to increase local revenues via industrial growth did not choose a corporatist strategy, where local officials undertook the entrepreneur's role, but permitted the private sector to take the risks, while they played a supporting part.

REGIONAL PATTERNS OF EVOLUTION

AND THEIR CAUSES

Another striking finding of these rural studies is that neither the "corporatist" nor the "littoral" property regimes were static. They both evolved under pressures exerted by the twin forces of economic growth and increased competition, which eventually forced major readjustments. By the mid 1990s, the governments of corporatist regions began to divest themselves of unprofitable enterprises by leasing them or selling them at accelerating rates, while the governments of littoral regions developed new forms of shareholding to mobilize investments beyond the capacity of relatively small-scale family firms.

The pressures for change in the corporatist regions are analyzed by James Kung and Susan Whiting, and they are illustrated prominently in Gregory Ruf's account of Qiaolou. Growth brings change by expanding the local economy beyond the point where officials can effectively monitor the performance of hired managers, creating incentive problems. This gradually forces more liberal incentive and contracting schemes for local public enterprises. Growth, moreover, forces change by increasing competition in many product markets and forcing down profit margins. This has resulted in fiscal crises in many rural communities, which have in turn spurred local governments to divest themselves of the liability for financially troubled firms by leasing them or selling them off.[35]

These competitive pressures hit with full force in the early to mid 1990s. In Ruf's Sichuan village, the small industrial complex that had emerged rapidly under village management during the 1980s faced a crisis that was resolved only by contracting or leasing out most of the village enterprises. In the more highly industrialized villages surveyed by James Kung in Wuxi County, village leaders began selectively to sell or lease the least profitable firms, while developing enhanced incentive schemes for managers in the remaining village-run enterprises. In Songjiang County, Susan Whiting found that rural governments, no longer enjoying the budgetary surpluses that permitted rapid investment in their firms throughout the

1980s, turned to new shareholding arrangements that diluted government ownership in an effort to attract increasingly scarce capital from new sources. In the last two cases, two rural regions that have long been in the "corporatist" heartland are rapidly evolving into mixed economies with a greater variety of ownership forms.

At the same time, the property regimes of the more heavily private littoral regions have evolved due to the challenges of growth and competition. These regions labored under two competitive disadvantages. First, private firms could not grow very large without attracting the negative attention of higher officials outside the locality. For these firms to grow, their true property arrangements had to be masked for political reasons. Second, the small scale and predominant family ownership of these local economies made the mobilization of capital difficult, and these small firms did not fully enjoy the advantages of the public firms of other regions: preferential investment and taxation, political backing, and extra-regional business connections provided by local officials. The solution to both of these problems has been to organize shareholding cooperatives in which these essentially private enterprises mobilize investment from both government and private individuals within an ownership form that is touted as "socialist." This created stronger incentives for local officials to support these firms and helped mobilize more capital in a politically legitimate way. Thus, in Whiting's analysis, shareholding cooperative reforms in both types of regions are solutions to different problems and have different intents: in the corporatist region, they are intended to solve capital shortages for public firms; in the littoral region, they are intended to solve capital shortages and political problems for private firms. Her analysis is supported by Eduard Vermeer's study in Chapter 6, which traces the historical evolution of the shareholding system and the conflicting agenda embodied in the different policies governing it. Examining the implementation of shareholding cooperatives in several rural regions, Vermeer found that the form masked the domination of a variety of different owners. He views this kind of shareholding cooperative as temporary and unstable.

The rural changes described in these chapters are a dramatic illustration of the macroeconomic trends highlighted in Barry Naughton's work on the Chinese economy. He argues that the spectacular growth of rural industry during the 1980s was owing to its ability to take advantage of product markets left unexploited by the state sector in the period when it held an industrial monopoly and served producers' rather than consumers' needs.[36] Small firms with low initial investment and much lower labor costs than state industry were created rapidly by rural governments and enjoyed high profitability and spectacular growth rates. However, with the entry of countless new producers, competition increased, and the profit rates in the old state sector and the newer rural collective sector converged as profits fell. Naughton has argued that intensified competition has pressured both the state sector and the rural collective sector to consolidate and reorganize.[37] The rural case studies in this book show the consequences of these pressures for the property regimes of the industrialized rural regions.

The Hollowing Out of Public Ownership

Yet another pattern of evolution represents a "hollowing out" of public property. This is occurring through two distinct processes. In the first, elites who control public property transform it imperceptibly into an asset that takes on the features of family property, or the property of a network of closely connected elite families. In the second, public bureaucracies and state enterprises invest in the creation of "private" firms that are registered and operate as such. The first process hollows out public ownership by shifting public assets to personal control and benefit; the second does so by diverting capital from the public to the private sector and by making public entities themselves important institutional stakeholders in the private economy.

The first pattern is illustrated in the chapters by Gregory Ruf, Nan Lin and Chih-jou Chen, and David Wank. Ruf's study of the rise of managerial corporatism in Qiaolou village makes clear that the rise of village-owned industry was paralleled by a rise in the fortunes of the families that held village political office. Drawing historical analogies to corporate property found in villages dominated by one lineage earlier in this century, Ruf points out that in the village setting, it is hard to disentangle "public" property from the kin relationships that are so prominent in village social structure.[38] Lin and Chen's portrayal of Daqiuzhuang, a heavily industrialized village in a county adjacent to the large metropolis of Tianjin, presents a similar analysis. Lin and Chen look in detail at this famous national model of a successful "corporatist" village, in which a massive industrial empire was built on public ownership. The village's Party secretary, Yu Zuomin, ruled this empire with an iron hand, and tracing the personal networks among the key players, Lin and Chen conclude that Daqiuzhuang's "public" village property was in fact a personal empire controlled by Secretary Yu, his family, and his longtime friends and associates. In an exaggerated case of the situation described in Qiaolou by Ruf, literally every one of the key enterprise management posts was filled by someone with a close personal relationship to the Party secretary.

The interesting twist in the story of Daqiuzhuang is that Secretary Yu was imprisoned for abusing his power and challenging higher-level authorities. He and his son were put in jail, the village industrial empire was broken into four parts, and the county reorganized the village government into a town, enabling it to appoint all future leaders. One would have predicted that Yu's personal empire was at an end. However, Lin and Chen show that the remnants of Yu's elite network remained highly cohesive and in control of the local economy. Those of his associates untouched by the scandal remained in their positions and began to implement shareholding cooperative reforms that will permit them to transform these public enterprises into legally recognized family ownership within a few years.

David Wank's study, based on close observation of the private sector in the coastal city of Xiamen, echoes some of these same themes. He describes the close association between the larger private entrepreneurs and urban bureaucrats, tracing the ways in which public property finds its way into the private sector. Wank's study specifies the ways in which personal networks serve as bridges for this continuous invisible transfer of rights.[39] His findings are particularly significant in that they provide a clue to why the private sector has continued to grow at such rapid rates in the absence of what many would consider secure property rights. Wank's work suggests that the social regulation of property rights in China is effective, at least in this transitional period.

The second pattern is analyzed in the chapters by Yi-min Lin and Zhanxin Zhang and by Corinna-Barbara Francis. Both describe the massive transfer of public property and funds to private enterprise. Despite the scale and importance of this process for ownership in the Chinese economy, it has received only a small fraction of the scholarly attention devoted to the rural industrial sector. Lin and Zhang provide an overview and analysis of this process. They specify the policy changes and the incentives that have driven public agencies and enterprises, from the ministry level down to the grass roots, to establish separate enterprises that they own. They document the ways in which these private ventures are established and show the futility of efforts by the central government to restrict the process and control the corruption that has often resulted. They also show how the budgets of state agencies and enterprises, the income and living standards of their employees, and the personal wealth of officials have all become increasingly dependent upon this "private economic backyard" of the public sector. This leads to a situation where free riders are rewarded for their passive acceptance of the benefits from these firms in exchange for their silence and turning a blind eye. This trend is more often associated with corruption than with reform, but it represents a striking evolution away from the state ownership that characterized China's planned economy 20 years ago.

In her chapter on the private high-technology firms that have been created by state agencies and educational institutions in Beijing's Haidian District, Francis closely examines one corner of this nationwide process. As these firms have grown and become prominent in their markets, the vague nature of the ownership claims by the state entities that created these "spin-offs" can produce serious conflicts over control and income flows. Examining the development of individual firms, Francis shows how in some cases continuous bargaining over property rights has led to their clarification in favor of the entrepreneurs who run these firms. The leverage a spin-off has depends on the size and type of initial investment made by the parent firm and the nature of the product being sold. Francis argues that over time the entrepreneur has advantages in the bargaining process that permit the firms to be spun off into increasingly autonomous private entities that have diminishing obligations to their original founders. While Lin and Zhang emphasize the potential corruption inherent in this phenomenon, Francis shows the contribution of these same practices to the creation of a competitive private sector that still has roots in state agencies.

A Dynamic Perspective on Evolutionary Change

It is clear from these chapters that tentative initial changes in property rights at the outset of China's reforms began a sustained evolution away from the property forms common 20 years ago. It is also clear that these changes have occurred only partially as a result of explicit reforms of ownership, and that they have continued without repeated intervention by central officials seeking to implement a reform blueprint. This volume seeks to describe and explain these changes, but it also points to a dynamic perspective on the evolution of property rights—an understanding of the processes that drive forward further change.

PUBLIC OFFICIALS AS ECONOMIC ACTORS

Strong critiques of partial reform are founded on the conviction that the behavior of socialist bureaucrats is decisively influenced by the rents that they receive from their interference in, or predation upon, profit-generating enterprises.[40] This suspicion is based on long and accurate observation of official behavior in communist regimes. Partial reform is therefore seen as an invitation to obstruction, as bureaucrats seek to maintain their hold over the economic assets on which their traditional privileges rest, and to a stagnant economy, as needed reforms are blocked. This not-unfounded fear led to a logical argument in favor of rapid, decisive, and coordinated change.

The pattern of change described in this book contrasts sharply with the predictions based upon such fears. The evolution of the Chinese economy, especially in rural areas, shows that initially small changes in property rights and their associated incentives for bureaucrats can lead to major changes in bureaucratic behavior.[41] Regardless of the region described, incentives for bureaucrats are central to the story. Xiaolin Guo's study of adjacent rural communities in northwest Yunnan, for example, shows that the different opportunities created for minority and nonminority areas by central government policy did not only lead rural bureaucrats to structure property rights differently and exert claims of ownership over local enterprise. The benefits embodied in being a "minority and poverty-stricken county" relaxed the fiscal constraints to the point where officials in these localities did not even bother to assert their ownership rights over enterprises that elsewhere would certainly be classified as public or collectively owned. The underlying significance of Guo's comparison is that even in these poor mountainous regions in China's interior, rural bureaucrats respond flexibly and pragmatically to the particular constraints and incentives created by the upper levels of government and the opportunities available in their local economy. The same findings are underlined in Susan Whiting's careful comparison of corporatist and littoral regions of Songjiang and Wenzhou: she shows that local officials consciously responded to the opportunities and constraints they faced at the outset of the reforms. In one region, it led to a corporatist strategy; in another, to a strategy that centered on the promotion of family and private enterprise. Both Whiting's and Guo's studies warn that ownership labels, such as "collectively owned" or "private," may reflect strategic decisions and existing incentives more than actual property rights.

These comparisons, and the related case studies in the other chapters, show that the role of local officials is central to the process of growth and change even in those areas that emphasize private enterprise. Regardless of the degree of involvement that officials subsequently assume in the economy, their power and preferences at the outset of reform have a decisive impact on the direction of change. Even in regions where local officials do not assume commanding roles in corporate economic structures, their active support of private economic activity is essential for it to develop. Chen's study of the Quanzhou region in Fujian emphasizes the essential support provided by local officials in permitting private economic activity to move forward, and in actively colluding with local entrepreneurs to mask the private nature of their enterprises and circumvent the central regulations designed to inhibit their growth. The same role is evident in Whiting's portrayal of Yueqing, where local officials provided political protection to private firms from the outset and later cooperated actively with them in creating shareholding cooperatives designed to overcome emerging local shortages of capital—again masking the essential ownership relations, circumventing official restrictions, and avoiding censure from above.

These studies all support a central point: seemingly small initial changes in the opportunities and incentives for bureaucrats lead them to behave in ways assumed to be highly unlikely by those critical of "partial" reform. In some instances, public officials behave like growth-oriented executives; in others, they invest in the private sector or spin off private firms; in still others, they step back from public ownership and actively support the development of the local private economy. In all of these instances, the incentives and opportunities facing bureaucrats have an important initial impact on the character of emerging property regimes. Bureaucratic behavior is not static and immutable, and analysis of economic change therefore requires an understanding both of officials as economic actors and of the varying incentives, constraints, and resources that shape their opportunities and choices.[42]

GROWTH AND COMPETITION AS FORCES FOR CHANGE

However important officials may be as economic actors, the direction of economic change is nonetheless not the sum of bureaucratic preferences. The dynamic element, as emphasized by William Byrd, Barry Naughton, Thomas Rawski, and others, is economic growth and competition.[43] Whatever officials' initial preferences may have been, once local enterprises begin to participate in competitive markets whose boundaries are far beyond local political jurisdictions, officials, like managers and entrepreneurs, must respond to competitive market pressures or suffer the financial consequences.

This point is illustrated repeatedly in the parallel accounts of crisis and change in local corporatist economies by Ruf, Kung, and Whiting. Ruf describes how Qiaolou village was forced to contract, lease, or sell virtually all of its village-owned enterprises to private entrepreneurs after accumulating heavy debts in the early 1990s. Kung analyzes the same process in more highly industrialized villages in Wuxi County, where the result was the selective leasing and sale of the less profitable local public industrial plants. Whiting shows that in Songjiang, parallel to this selective divestment of public firms, local officials began to contemplate shareholding, and the potential dilution of traditional public ownership, as an answer to the financial pressures of the more competitive 1990s.[44] What-ever their rhetoric about the socialist road may have been in earlier years, and whatever dreams these local officials may have had about the futures of their publicly owned corporate empires, they are forced to adjust to competitive pressures and market forces that are beyond their control. As a direct result, property regimes continue to evolve. A dynamic perspec-tive on this process of change flows from understanding this interaction between official preferences and the rise of competitive forces.

Conclusions

This book contributes in two ways to discussions about the role of prop-erty rights in economies, like China's, that are moving decisively away from economic institutions derived from the Soviet model. The first is a set of factual findings about the evolution of property rights in China— findings that should serve to clarify the confusion apparent in writings on the subject, and therefore better specify China's potential implications for more general discussions. The second is a set of implications for the way that we analyze the process of economic change.

CONTOURS OF THE PROCESS OF CHANGE

Property rights in the Chinese economy have moved decisively away from traditional state ownership through five different processes—the contracting or leasing of public assets, the sale or outright "privatization" of those assets, the illicit transfer of ownership to elites, investment by state entities in private enterprise, and the creation of new family or other private businesses. These piecemeal changes have proceeded over a pe-riod of almost two decades, and they have led to major changes in the way the Chinese economy operates and performs. Emblematic of these changes is the way in which the behavior of public officials has been transformed by participation in market competition.

The rural case studies in this book help greatly to clarify existing con-fusion about property rights in the important rural industrial sector. The confusion stemmed in the first place from the fact that the most rapidly growing rural regions appear to have operated with one of two starkly opposed local property regimes. Both the corporatist and littoral patterns have had remarkable success.[45] "Privatization," in the sense in which the word is usually employed in policy discussions, has played a limited role in both regions until very recently. The littoral pattern did not begin with extensive privatization, because there was very little industrial base at the outset of the reforms in those regions. This pattern grew through the start-up and expansion of new private enterprises, often disguised by invented ownership forms. In the corporatist regions, not until after a decade of rapid growth has privatization begun to play an important role in the process of change.

A second source of confusion was the fact that both corporatist and littoral property regimes have evolved considerably since their inception. Even the regions famous for rural corporatist growth in the 1980s are rapidly evolving in the 1990s into mixed economies as portions of these public industrial empires are leased or sold in response to financial pressures. And the littoral regions, hampered by small enterprise scale and capital shortages, have implemented new shareholding arrangements with participation by local government.

Did the rapid growth of the corporatist regions occur through extensive use of liberal contracting arrangements or through leaseholds—that is, through partial and hidden privatization? There is little evidence for this view in these chapters, because the changes in this direction did not become important until the 1990s. The fact that, along with the sale of firms, these more liberal property forms became a response to financial pressures in such areas as Wuxi and Songjiang only in the 1990s indicates that throughout the "take-off" period of the 1980s, rural industry in these regions was operated variously in the shape of reformed socialist firms or through conservative forms of contracting. "Hidden privatization" analogous to the disguising of private enterprise commonly observed in the littoral regions appears to have been rare in the 1980s. Only in the 1990s has the corporatist heartland begun to feel this trend.

However, it is less clear that publicly owned enterprises, especially at the village level, are not somehow "private" in the sense that local elite families dominate them and benefit disproportionately from them. Both Ruf's Qiaolou and Lin and Chen's Daqiuzhuang show the ambiguity of the boundaries between village ownership and elite family ownership. However, these accounts also suggest that the kind of legal maneuvers referred to in Eastern Europe as "*nomenklatura* privatization," where officials transfer legal ownership to themselves as part of a transition to a market economy, have not been common.[46] Lin and Chen suspect that Daqiuzhuang's political elite, through new shareholding forms, are now in the midst of transferring formal ownership to themselves, but even here the process is not complete.

These findings help dispel confusion exhibited in past writings, but they are not definitive. They serve to reshape the questions to be asked in future research. Debates about the nature of China's rural enterprises should henceforth be about variations in the nature of enterprises across and within rural communities. We still have at best a sketchy understanding of the economic geography of property regimes. The case studies in this book show that it is no simple matter to divine property arrangements from official ownership categories. Still ahead is the task of explaining the emergence of different property regimes across regions, and of demonstrating the relationship between property arrangements and economic growth.[47]

THE UTILITY OF SUBOPTIMAL SOLUTIONS

The main underlying theme of this book is the utility of solutions that are suboptimal in theory. Theories that proceed by identifying deviations from the theoretically optimal leave open the empirical question of how far institutions may deviate from their optimal forms and still lead to positive outcomes. They also evade the practical dilemmas involved when the optimal solution cannot be attained within existing political arrangements, or when entirely new administrative and legal edifices must be constructed in order for them to work. The studies collected here suggest that small initial changes can have a large impact, and that theoretically flawed and suboptimal solutions may nonetheless have highly beneficial results. They may also be the only feasible solutions, given that political and administrative arrangements are far less malleable in reality than in theory.

These points are fairly evident, and they have been made before.[48] But if institutions that are suboptimal from the perspective of one theory nonetheless seem to work, how can we explain their effects? Most of the chapters in this volume are indirect answers to this question, but David Wank is the only author to make the argument that partial reassignment of property rights has advantages that are absent when rapid privatization has occurred. Wank sees the informal social ties that bind officials and entrepreneurs as co-owners as providing means to specify and enforce property rights in ways that would not otherwise be possible in the absence of an effective system of government regulation and civil law. He points to other societies that have experienced rapid privatization in the absence of such formal regulatory guarantees—Sicily in the nineteenth century and contemporary Russia—and suggests that economic stagnation and private protection rackets are the common result.[49] This argument reminds us that the task of specifying the properties of informal social arrangements and "halfway measures" that will lead to a vibrant economy rather than stagnation and corruption is still far from complete. The task requires good theory, to be sure—but theory that is grounded firmly in an understanding of the behavior of real-world economic actors.

PART ONE

Enterprise Ownership in Village Communities

Chapter 2

Collective Enterprise and Property Rights in a Sichuan Village: The Rise and Decline of Managerial Corporatism

GREGORY A. RUF

This chapter is a case study of a Sichuan village where nonagricultural collective enterprises established during the 1980s led to a dramatic rise in administrative revenues, family incomes, and living standards. While in many parts of China collective enterprises were leased to individual entrepreneurs, leaders in Qiaolou village kept their enterprises under "collective" management and operation; none were contracted out to private managers. But if privatization is critical to efficient economic management, as many theories maintain, how can one account for the successes attained in Qiaolou? What might such explanations suggest about the way property relationships are being expressed and practiced in rural enterprises?

Here I explore some of the social relations and rhetorical claims involved in the exercise of property rights in collective village enterprises. I examine how control of these enterprises has been shaped by interfamily relationships. After a brief statement of the theoretical framework of this study, I introduce the village, its achievements in rural enterprise development, and a subsequent dramatic reversal of fortunes. In the next section, I offer a description of local property relations in the past, before the advent of communist rule in 1949 and during the era of Maoist collectivism. Then I recount the establishment of collectively owned village enterprises during the early 1980s and discuss the role of shareholding in a local property rights regime of managerial corporatism. Finally, I describe the economic crisis that developed in the mid 1990s, and how this has altered property relations.

Property Rights and Social Relations
in Transitional Economies

The concept of property entails a social relationship between two or more people, usually mediated through an object. "Property" in this sense is not the reified object itself, but rather the relationship that is constructed between the social actors concerned, be they individuals or organized groups. The "rights" that are established in property relations involve the expression and enforcement of claims to relative exclusivity. For the purposes of this study, these claims may be regarded as the control of decision-making power over the disposition of "collectively owned" productive assets and the revenues they generate.

Reductionist dichotomies of private versus public ownership offer limited insight into how such relationships are constructed and modified over time.[1] A more useful analytical framework conceives of property relations as a "bundle" of rights involving control over the use and transfer of productive resources as well as the income generated from them.[2] Such an approach directs attention to the actual control of resources, rather than privileging formalistic notions regarding written or legal codes of ownership.

Much of the debate over the structuring of property rights to rural enterprises in contemporary China is about the extent to which such control or power is held securely by a well-defined principal owner or operator. Many rural enterprises established early in the post-Mao era were collectively owned and operated. Fiscal reforms hardened budget constraints for local government authorities, providing an incentive for local leaders to seek new sources of revenue to fund their administrative operations, investments, and social welfare programs.[3] At the same time, marketing channels remained relatively underdeveloped in many parts of the country during much of the 1980s. This placed a premium on the political and social ties that local leaders had to elites in other areas as a means of obtaining raw materials, power, and other inputs, as well as for purposes of marketing.[4]

More recently, organizational forms in Chinese rural industries have diversified. Most commonly cited are profit-sharing partnerships between local governments and individual entrepreneurs, joint-stock or shareholding cooperatives, or businesses leased to private managers for a fixed fee. Regardless of the organizational form, the economic interests of managers have become increasingly tied to issues of performance and productivity. But does this imply that property rights in Chinese rural enterprises are evolving toward a single model of capitalist private ownership? Or are the property rights exercised by managers shaped by other considerations, such as aspects of social organization and local family alliances, that may provide the foundations for alternative forms of ownership?

Kinship is, among other things, about property rights.[5] It provides an ideological framework for structuring access to and control over resources, including the transmission of such privileges across time (through generational inheritance and succession) and space (through marriage, ritual "godparentage," and sworn brotherhood). Although, as I shall show, kinship has been an important factor in the management of collective enterprise in Qiaolou, it has not been the sole determinant of the restructuring of property rights.[6] Nevertheless, various aspects of social organization, such as ties of descent, marriage, and personal alliance, have provided an organizational nexus through which village managers have lowered enterprise "transaction costs," as well as the costs of monitoring and enforcing the compliance of their labor force.

While some have argued that property rights practices in rural enterprises are best interpreted as an expression of vaguely defined notions of communalism or cooperation embodied in Chinese tradition,[7] this study suggests that such assumptions are more evocative of notions regarding an "Asiatic mode of production" than reflective of the historical realities of property relations in China. An ethnography of the historical development of property rights in Qiaolou may offer insights into how property relations have been organized, structured, and transformed throughout the twentieth century. It may also suggest how and why rural enterprises have proven so productive during the post-Mao era of transition.

A "Civilized Village" on the Socialist Road

Qiaolou village is located in Meishan County, Sichuan, roughly midway between the cities of Chengdu and Leshan. Situated amid "shallow hills," just off the western Chengdu plain, it lies less than ten kilometers from the county seat, a major north-south provincial highway, and the Chengdu-Kunming railway line. With a population of roughly 350 families in 1991, Qiaolou is one of sixteen administrative villages that, together with a small rural market town and administrative center, comprise the rural township of Baimapu. Both Qiaolou and the township market settlement that it abuts sit astride an asphalt road linking Meishan and the basin floor with the towns of Danling, Hongya, and Ya'an in the "deep hills" to the west.

During the 1980s, Qiaolou earned regional acclaim as the site of a successful rural industrialization program initiated by village authorities. By the mid 1990s, a cumulative list of its enterprises included a fruit orchard, a distillery, a transport team, three brick kilns, a zinc refinery, and a tire factory. All of these enterprises were collectively owned, funded, and operated by village authorities; at the time of my original research in Qiaolou, none of these facilities had been contracted out or leased to individual or private entrepreneurs. In fact, as an administrative entity, the village was organized and run much like a corporation, directed by a strong and active Party branch secretary who had been in power since the Cultural Revolution. For present purposes, Qiaolou may serve as one example of a wide variety of firms and institutions often referred to as "township and village enterprises" (TVEs).[8]

The success of rural industrialization in Qiaolou contributed to its selection by provincial and local authorities as the site of my research in 1990–91.[9] During the 1980s, Qiaolou had repeatedly received official acclaim as an "advanced civilized village" (*xianjin wenming cun*), where the "spiritual" values and material benefits of Chinese socialism had been combined in exemplary ways. When I arrived in August 1990, Qiaolou owned five of the eight major nonagricultural enterprises in the township.[10] While the other three, all owned by the township government, had been contracted out to individual entrepreneurs, all Qiaolou enterprises were described as under "collective ownership" (*jiti suoyou*) and "village operation" (*cunban*). These included an orange orchard, two brick factories, a distillery, and a transport team with five large vehicles. When I left Qiaolou in the summer of 1991, plans were well under way to convert the village's two brick factories to new lines of production: one as a zinc refinery and the other as an automobile tire factory.

All of Qiaolou's enterprises had been run by village administrators or their appointees, and major decisions concerning these collective assets were made ultimately by the village Party secretary. Fiscal decisions, labor allocations, and production plans were centrally coordinated.[11] Revenues funded not only enterprise operations but also village administration, an investment account, and a range of social benefits. While the distribution of family income in Qiaolou was by no means equal or egalitarian, each family did receive certain advantages unavailable to those in neighboring villages. Residents of Qiaolou enjoyed a level of material prosperity that was unparalleled in the township.

In what was at the time still a relatively cash-poor local economy, families in Qiaolou enjoyed rare wage labor employment. Revenues from village enterprises also supported family tax subsidies. Not only did Qiaolou authorities avoid assessing village residents with local administrative levies (*tiliu*) to finance administrative operations, but they also covered all or part of similar surcharges imposed on village families by the township government. Moreover, basic health care was provided free of charge through a lay pharmacist (the former brigade "barefoot doctor," whose salary was now paid by the village), with additional funds available to defray the cost of emergency hospitalization. A new primary school was also built, and several supplemental (*minban*) teachers were hired by the village to assist the state-assigned (*guoban*) core faculty. Electricity was wired to every family home, and village roads and paths were paved or resurfaced. Rising living standards were reflected in accumulated family savings, as well as in investments in or purchases of new amenities, from electrical water pumps and television sets to new homes and elaborate tombstones.[12] While Qiaolou still had poor families, even they enjoyed more security than their counterparts in neighboring villages.

When I returned to Qiaolou during the winter of 1994–95, I was surprised to find that the threat of bankruptcy loomed over this model of socialist rural development. Village enterprises with the greatest profit potential now sat idle or faced closure, and roughly one-third of the village labor force had been laid off. The long-incumbent Party secretary, who had a reputation as a militant collectivist and an ardent advocate of self-reliance, was seeking to attract foreign investors. Meanwhile, declining village revenues had led to the elimination of many benefits Qiaolou families had come to enjoy during the previous decade. Only those still employed in village enterprises retained free access to the pharmacist. New tuition charges had been assessed for children attending primary school. Most unpopular had been the termination of subsidies that once covered local administrative levies; families now faced new *tiliu* charges imposed by both township and village authorities, fees that often surpassed state agricultural taxes.

Dramatic changes were also evident in the control and management of village enterprises. Both brick factories, as anticipated, had exhausted their clay supplies and ceased operations. But a much-lauded joint venture with Chengdu-based investors to establish a zinc refinery had collapsed after only a few years, and Qiaolou managers were struggling to reestablish supply and marketing networks. Construction of the new tire factory had exhausted village capital, and the imported Italian machinery sat idle for lack of operating funds. The distillery had been leased to one of its former managers, who replaced village workers with new outside laborers he hired himself. In teashops throughout the local market town, residents spoke in hushed whispers of how a young man with ties to a sworn brotherhood organization had coerced Qiaolou authorities into leasing him several rooms in the village office building for use as a restaurant and private karaoke club. Clearly, the corporate village collective faced an uncertain future.

Managing Property Relations in
Twentieth-Century Qiaolou

To understand contemporary property relations in Qiaolou, it is useful to examine the historical antecedents out of which they developed. Even during the most radical periods of Mao-era collectivism, land and other forms of property continued to hold strong familial associations. Political control of productive resources was exercised through local patterns of family alliance, based largely on relations of patrilineal descent, marriage, ritual kinship, and personal friendship. Moreover, notions of identity and descent, residential settlement and native place continued to find expression in the named topography of the area, even after private ownership of land was effectively abolished. Social organization provided the principal framework through which property rights were claimed, exercised, and interpreted, both before and after the communist revolution.

During the 1940s, the decade prior to the advent of communist rule in Qiaolou, most land, businesses, and other forms of property in the area had been owned by individual families. Although the collective ownership of the Maoist era has often been contrasted with the private property rights of the past, it is important to note that families rather than individuals had been the principal property-owning units in the early twentieth century. In a few instances, families grew to unusual size and complexity. One such case involved a large joint family of more than thirty people living as a single, but diversified, economic unit. The elderly parents, together with their five married sons, daughters-in-law, and grandchildren (one of whom eventually became Qiaolou's Communist Party secretary), owned only less than half a dozen mu (one mu = 0.1647 acres) of land themselves, but rented an additional forty mu from local rentiers, maintained a large number of hogs (mostly for the organic fertilizer they produced), and operated a cloth-weaving cottage industry out of their home.

Family property (*jiachan*), be it animals, furniture, labor, land, or tools, was owned collectively by a family as a corporate group, and its sale or transfer required the formal authorization of the family head (*jiazhang*), or senior male. Although their seal or signature was affixed to all contracts, deeds, and other legal documents, such men were not the owners of family property, but merely its officially recognized stewards. A family head's transfer rights over, or authority or power to sell or otherwise dispose of, family property was restricted under a system of equal partible inheritance. All (recognized) sons were equal shareholders in their natal family estate, and their acquiescence was needed before a father could divest family holdings. Although women had few formal property rights in this context,[13] many nevertheless did exercise day-to-day control over family labor, land, and finances by virtue of their position as family managers (*dangjia*).[14]

In addition to individual families, there were also several institutional corporate property owners in 1940s Qiaolou, including patrilineal ancestral associations, schools, temples, religious societies, and sworn brotherhoods, membership wherein was based on shareholding principles.[15] The aggregate total holdings of these institutional property owners, however, represented less than 5 percent of land in the village, the bulk of which was held as individual family property.[16] While most families owned at least some land, only about 30 percent had holdings sufficient to meet their subsistence needs. Roughly 60 percent of the land in Qiaolou had been owned by half a dozen families: rentier-merchants who also possessed commercial holdings in the local market town. This class of local notables, many of whom came from the largest descent groups to have settled in the area in the mid to late nineteenth century, dominated administrative posts in the rural township government and militia organization.

The land reform of the 1950s abolished the property base of ancestral associations, temples, and other corporate organizations, redistributing land ownership rights (including transfer rights) to individual families. With the subsequent collectivization campaign, agricultural collectives held formal ownership rights to land, although the state government continued to exercise practical control over the use and transfer of land, including rights of eminent domain.[17] "Peasants" were administratively bound to their local collective, and physical mobility was severely curtailed and regulated by the household registration system of state government. In the countryside, production teams, the lowest level of the commune-brigade-team system, were the most significant units of political organization. While use rights to local land were often determined within the context of the production team, state authorities continued to hold ultimate authority over issues such as crop selection, production targets, distribution of inputs, and price determination, and distribution and marketing continued to be controlled by the state.[18]

Yet even in the most tumultuous periods of agrarian radicalism, the existence of family property (*jiachan*) continued to be recognized, mainly in the form of accumulated workpoints, household furniture, and "private plots."[19] Production team leaders (and team accountants, who kept tallies of the workpoint earnings of each family member) often mediated family division (*fenjia*) settlements, extending a practical political recognition to family property.[20] Moreover, common descent, affinal relations, matrilateral ties, and personal alliances continued to have major influence on the exercise of practical property rights within production teams.[21] Job assignments and workpoint assessments, for example, were often influenced by favoritism.

In fact, the interpersonal alliances around which local political power was restructured during the Cultural Revolution were deeply influenced by relations of descent, marriage, and friendship. Qiaolou's current Party secretary came to power at that time, mobilizing support from patrilineal kin, marital affines, former youth league members whom he had tutored, and childhood friends with ties to the Red Guard organizations of the local commune and to the PLA. By and large, this group of families continue to constitute the managerial elite of Qiaolou today. While kinship was not the sole determinant in their rise to power during the collective era, it was nevertheless a principal idiom through which they—and others—not only endeavored to mobilize resources but also interpreted the changes affecting their lives.

Redefining the Collective in the Post-Mao Era

The era of post-Mao reform brought a significant restructuring of property relations in Qiaolou, as the village leadership attempted to redefine the economic and political basis of the village collective. With the decollectivization of agriculture, the restoration of rural markets, and changes in the grain-procurement system, many rural cadres have seen the power and influence of their formal positions decline.[22] Since the former production brigades and teams of the collective era were abolished, their reform-era successors at the village and subvillage levels have been largely removed from—or at least marginalized in—agricultural production, planning, and appropriation.

The contract-responsibility system formally gave individual families decision-making power regarding land use, labor allocation, and the distribution of revenues. State authorities, to be sure, continued to set mandatory production quotas for families that contracted land, but families became the financial risk bearers in their agricultural activities. While the Land Management Law of 1984 moved formal ownership and transfer rights to land from teams to villages, political intervention in production, investment, marketing, and consumption was sharply reduced. Families acquired succession rights and limited transfer rights over the land they farmed, determining its redistribution in family division settlements and even subcontracting use and quota obligations to other families.

Agricultural reform reduced village leaders' control of labor and land use, as well as of income from farming. Pressed for revenues to finance cadre salaries or social services, local administrators in many parts of the country have raised *tiliu* levies, a practice that has been unpopular. In some villages, accumulation, production, or social welfare funds have been depleted or abolished. "In our village, the collective has become an empty shell [*kong ke*]," the Party secretary of a peri-urban village elsewhere in Meishan County lamented to me. In Qiaolou, by contrast, the development of collectively owned (*jiti suoyou*) nonagricultural enterprises helped village leaders recast the village collective as a managerial corporation.

Qiaolou had been the last of sixteen villages in the township to implement agricultural decollectivization. The village Party branch secretary had delayed implementation of state-mandated reforms for several years, as he endeavored to establish a new nonagricultural collective sector in the village economy.[23] This local initiative was financed in part through a capital accumulation fund established previously by the brigade under the commune system, and through state loans on preferential terms. The accumulation fund, like similar ones sanctioned during the Maoist era, appropriated investment capital through involuntary withholdings from agriculture.[24] These funds were augmented by revenues from a brigade construction team, established in 1974.[25]

In 1976, the brigade leadership invested its capital savings in the purchase of 3,000 tangerine saplings.[26] Transplanted into two separate "brigade orchards" (*dadui guoyuan*), in northern and southern Qiaolou respectively, the saplings were later grafted with sprouts from more expensive and profitable types of oranges and produced their first harvest in 1982. Also in that year, Qiaolou opened its first "collectively operated" (*jiti bande*) village brick factory. Becoming operational the same year that agricultural production was finally contracted out to individual family households, the "No. 1 Brick Factory" was to become Qiaolou's first successful industrial enterprise. More significant, the organization and management of the production relations at the brick factory contributed to a major shift in local perceptions of "the collective" (*jiti*). Once an agricultural production unit that was part of the people's commune system, it came to be regarded as a relatively autonomous village corporation, in which nonagricultural production, wage labor, investment strategies, and revenue distribution were centrally coordinated.

The consciously constructed collective character of this enterprise drew support from county authorities, who arranged deferred interest loans of approximately Y 300,000 for the village from the Agricultural Bank.[27] Moreover, the village was granted a one-year tax exemption by the state authorities for its effort to promote collectively operated, rather than privately contracted, rural enterprises. According to village cadres, the collective basis of the factory also enabled them to circumvent legal restrictions on the number of hired employees that could be taken on by private entrepreneurs or contractors. Established just as the house-construction boom of the early reform era was getting under way in this part of Sichuan, the brick factory proved to be a phenomenal success. The village repaid its state bank loan in full within three years, avoiding interest charges and improving Qiaolou's credit standing with county officials. A large proportion of factory income, however, was appropriated by the village leadership for further enterprise development, which included a five-vehicle truck and transport team (established in 1983), a second brick factory (in 1984), and a sorghum distillery (in 1985), all similarly owned collectively by the village.

Shareholding in the Collective

The larger and more capital-intensive of these ventures, namely, the brick factories, were also financed in part through the compulsory purchase of Y 100 "shares" (*gufen*) by each family in Qiaolou. Families without ready cash to buy shares had their income from compulsory state grain sales withheld by the brigade leadership at the year-end distribution.[28] Yet the shareholding character of these factories has been largely nominal. Shareholders have had little influence over decisions regarding village enterprises. Daily operations were overseen by enterprise management committees, appointed by the village administrative council. While most council members have been elected by fellow villagers, there has been no proportional balloting for larger shareholders.[29] Moreover, the managerial heads of various enterprise staff in Qiaolou have generally been council members themselves.[30] However, this is not to say that nonofficials have had no voice or influence in the management of the village or its enterprises. As I describe below, they sometimes have, but not because of their shareholding status per se.

What, then, was the character of shareholding in Qiaolou enterprises, and what has shareholding meant in this local context? As noted above, the notion of shareholding rights to corporate property was well developed by the early twentieth century and continued to find (limited) expression through the decades of collectivized agriculture. The creation of shareholding rights to the new collective village enterprises had important symbolic value. It not only resonated with established cultural practice, but also ostensibly preserved the socialist principle of each village family's equal right to collective property. Moreover, the sale of compulsory shares to all village families helped village leaders raise venture and working capital with which to pursue their enterprise plans. Yet by retaining direct "collective" control over these new industrial assets, rather than contracting out enterprises to private managers, Qiaolou cadres were better positioned to lobby county superiors for lower tax rates and deferred-interest loans from state banks.[31] Creating jobs, raising living standards, encouraging local residents to remain in the village, generating new tax revenues, and enforcing compliance with birth planning all reflected favorably on the "performance criteria" of village officials. In form, if not in practice, these enterprises and their revenues were managed in a manner that generally conformed with guidelines for "shareholding cooperatives" promoted by national authorities in the 1980s.[32]

At the same time, centralized corporate management over village enterprises strengthened the local power of the former brigade leadership. The economic empowerment of the village collective in the post-Mao era lessened the dependency of village leaders on the party-state as their source of political legitimacy. Qiaolou's leaders repositioned themselves as job-providing patrons representing the interests of the Qiaolou collective and its "big family" (*da jiating*) of villagers.[33] As a notion with relevance to state agendas, local corporate interests, and established cultural practice, shareholding became a central—if largely symbolic—feature of the managerial corporatist regime created in Qiaolou under the post-Mao reforms.[34]

It should also be noted that such "shares," like most other forms of property in Qiaolou, were owned by families rather than individuals. As many Qiaolou residents saw it, a "share" represented each family's entitlement to employment in a village enterprise. Decisions regarding which family member would be employed in such jobs were left to individual families, usually to a family manager. Families also had the authority to transfer employment status from one family member to another, although such "rights of succession" (*jieban quan*) did not guarantee new employees the same job at the same enterprise. In fact, employment at particular jobs on different pay scales, or for more than one family member, were issues left to the discretion of enterprise managers and, ultimately, the village Party secretary.[35]

Qiaolou's Party secretary was the principal architect of the collective enterprise development plan, and has remained active in asserting his influence and power as the head of the village corporation. To date, he alone has had the authority to transfer collective village assets. He appointed, or approved other village cadres' nomination of, enterprise managers and staff to oversee the daily operations of Qiaolou's collective enterprises. While enterprise assets were operated by enterprise managers, all production targets, budgetary allocations, and revenue projections for each enterprise were set at an annual meeting with the Party secretary and the village accountant.[36] Managerial staff have had only limited control over fiscal flows at the enterprises they run. The Party secretary has repeatedly appropriated revenues from one enterprise to subsidize a less productive one.

Unbundling Property Rights in Corporate Qiaolou

The village corporation established by the Party secretary reflected his vision of the long-term economic development of Qiaolou. While promoting an ideology of corporate inclusiveness that rhetorically portrayed the village collective as one "big family," his enterprise scheme has also produced concrete material benefits for individual families.[37] Average per capita income in the village has become the highest in the township; more than 90 percent of village homes have been converted from mud-brick, thatched-roof structures to fired-brick, tiled-roof houses; most families now own a variety of popular consumer goods and electrical appliances; and the value of dowries has risen dramatically in the past decade.[38] It was a strategy that encouraged farming families to remain resident in the village, while simultaneously strengthening the position of the Qiaolou political elite at a time when the raison d'être of village cadres in some regions was being questioned.

Although the "bundle" of key property rights relating to the use, transfer, and income from collective enterprises was apparently controlled by the village Party secretary, there remains the question of how he constructed and maintained this dominance. Delineation of such a "bundle" of rights is better set in the context of social relationships and alliances among village families. Who, precisely, were the other administrative officials of the village, and what was their relation to enterprise managers and production-line workers? How have specific families and individuals positioned themselves in the village corporation, obtained jobs for multiple family members, or secured more influential and better-paying positions as managerial staff? Such issues are relevant, not only to assessing productivity in rural enterprises, but also to an understanding of "actually existing" property rights and social stratification in Qiaolou.

Qiaolou's Party secretary pursued his development agenda by staffing collective village enterprises with competent, trustworthy staff, chosen disproportionately from among allies, kin, and marital affines. While his descent group is the largest in Qiaolou (comprising roughly 28 percent of all registered village families in 1989), these kin have been disproportionately represented in the upper echelons of enterprise management, holding nearly half of Qiaolou's 40 enterprise staff positions in 1990 (see Table 2.1). Another 28 percent of salaried office staff were men or women married to his patrilineal kin. Of the ten remaining staff positions, half were filled by men with marital ties to families whose long-standing personal and political ties to the Party secretary date back to the Cultural Revolution or earlier. Nearly all families that have employed two or more members in a village enterprise have come from this privileged group of kin and allies.

The distribution of jobs at particular enterprises was also revealing. The management staff of the village orchard, a key enterprise that has consistently turned an annual profit, was similarly dominated by relatives and personal allies of the Party secretary. So, too, was employment with the transport team, long regarded as among the most coveted work in Qiaolou.[39] Employment at the village distillery was also highly desired in the late 1980s and early 1990s. The work was not very physically demanding and afforded much leisure time (usually spent playing cards), in addition to such side benefits as free alcohol, hot baths, and access to fermented sorghum, reputed to be excellent hog feed.[40] The manager appointed to run the No. 1 Brick Factory was the popularly elected village head (*cunzhang*), while the No. 2 Brick Factory was managed by a brother of a villager turned state cadre.[41]

The use of kinship and personal or particularistic ties to control labor, and to supervise the management of collective village enterprise, was instrumental to the success of the corporate endeavor in Qiaolou. The Party secretary and his managerial allies have kept down the costs of monitoring labor discipline through a combination of material incentives and punitive sanctions, coupled with appeals to normative sentiments of affect, propriety, and reciprocity embodied in concepts such as *ganqing*, *renqing*, and *guanxi*.[42] Bonuses and promotions were offered to productive workers, while employees frequently absent, tardy, or unconscientious in their work have been admonished by relatives on the enterprise staff for causing the latter to "lose face." In more serious cases, wages have been withheld or workers even suspended in order to enforce labor discipline. But most minor infractions have been dealt with indirectly, often with the concerns of enterprise managers brought to the attention of a worker's family by a friend or relative.

Yet the very same social relationships that have been a source of empowerment to some families have contributed to the alienation of others, particularly those who have come to feel relatively marginalized in the village collective. Domination based on control of corporate resources frequently fosters the development of rigid social hierarchies in which opportunities for social and economic mobility are restricted.[43] As one

TABLE 2.1

Qiaolou Enterprise Management Committee Staff, 1991

Enterprise	Staff position	Relationship to Party secretary or other noteworthy status
No. 1 Brick Factory	Factory head	Village head; Party member
	Assistant factory head (production)	Nephew; former village head; Party member
	Assistant factory head (finances)	Daughter-in-law; Party member
	Accountant	Affine of early land reform activist
	Treasurer	Son of former women's cadre, who was the first villager to join CCP
	Storage supervisor	Nephew; Party member
	Purchasing and sales agent	Nephew
No. 2 Brick Factory	Factory head	Brother of state cadre
	Assistant factory head (production)	Nephew of former women's cadre, who was the first villager to join CCP
	Assistant factory head (finances)	Party member
	Accountant	Nephew; son of township credit cooperative director
	Treasurer	Nephew
	Storage supervisor	Cousin; Party member
	Purchasing and sales agent	Son of former team leader
	Pharmacist	PLA veteran; former team leader
	Tea water attendant	Wife of village head
Orchard	(Former orchard head)	(Brother; now deceased)
	Orchard head	Security chief; Party member; affine of Party secretary
	Assistant orchard head	
	Accountant	Cousin
	Treasurer	PLA Korea veteran; Party member; former team leader and brigade security chief; lifelong friend of Party secretary
	Storage supervisor	Uncle; former brigade accountant
Transport Team	Director	[Qiaolou Party secretary]
	Accountant	Uncle; former brigade treasurer
	Driver 1	Son

TABLE 2.1

(*continued*)

Enterprise	Staff position	Relationship to Party secretary or other noteworthy status
	Driver 2	Nephew
	Driver 3	Nephew of former Party secretary; affine of current Party secretary; Party member and former deputy Party secretary
	Driver 4	Son of former women's cadre
	Driver 5	Neighbor
Distillery	Distillery head	Nephew; Party member; currently deputy Party secretary
	Assistant distillery head (production)	Neighbor; Party member; affine of Party secretary
	Accountant	Cousin
	Storage supervisor	Cousin
	Treasurer	Cousin; brother of former team leader and military policeman
	Purchasing and sales agent	Affine of village accountant, who was longtime ally of current Party secretary

villager characterized Qiaolou's managerial elite, "They are like a [political] party. They have their own organization and discipline, but they take care of their own before they take care of others." By the early 1990s, when enterprise revenues began to drop and wages fell, a sense of divisiveness arose as the contours of privilege received heightened contrast. Villagers not closely associated with or related to allies of the Party secretary complained of being relegated to relatively low-wage jobs, with little hope of moving up to staff or management positions. Many had come to feel increasingly uncertain about the security of their current village jobs. The search for a "road out" (*chu lu*), an exit, from dependency on the Qiaolou collective became a popular topic of discussion in family courtyards and market-town teashops.

The Crisis of Managerial Corporatism

During the 1980s, collective enterprises in Qiaolou were highly successful, tapping growing markets for popular products. Qiaolou fired bricks for a booming construction market, produced an award-winning banquet alcohol (*qujiu*), and harvested oranges for export to the Soviet Union and Japan. Employment was steady and work often not too strenuous. Productivity was up, as were receipts. Visiting delegations toured village enterprises and were fêted in a reception hall, the walls of which were adorned with an impressive array of framed awards and embroidered banners of achievement. Village leaders could recite a growing list of consumer goods, from bicycles, furniture, and washing machines to refrigerators, color televisions, and VCRs, that marked the material prosperity of families and the contribution of the village to the development of the "petty commodity economy."

While the growing variety of goods and services circulating in local and regional markets presented new opportunities to villagers who had previously enjoyed few other options, by 1990 markets for products from Qiaolou collective enterprises had tightened. New housing starts had slowed, while new kilns in neighboring townships using better-quality clay presented serious competition. At the No. 2 Brick Factory, production was scaled back, halted, and restarted again on a limited basis as the factory ran short of storage space for unsold bricks.[44] A proliferation of distilleries throughout Sichuan in the late 1980s and early 1990s depressed alcohol markets and led to forcible government closure of many facilities. Although the Qiaolou collective distillery had its license renewed, it continued to operate at a loss and amassed a large backlog of unsold alcohol. Large numbers of farmers enthusiastically followed the successful introduction of orange cultivation, until it became a nearly universal subsidiary family enterprise in the area. Prices dropped as supply outpaced regional demand.[45] As growing difficulties began to overshadow Qiaolou's collective enterprises, bonuses were cut, and in some cases wages were even suspended for a month or more. Workers (but not managers) whose families were judged by village officials to be not as needy of cash jobs were laid off, as the labor force was retrenched to save costs. At the distillery and the No. 2 Brick Factory, production was halted completely, dramatically reducing the income of roughly one-third of village families.

Growing concern over the future of the brick factories prompted Qiaolou's Party secretary to seek a joint venture with a private group of Chengdu technicians to convert the No. 2 Brick Factory into a zinc refinery.[46] After lengthy negotiations, a contract was signed, the terms of which suggested the importance of technical expertise in the development of new industrial product lines. The technicians, including scientists from a state research institute, provided design plans for a high-temperature smelting furnace, specialized knowledge to operate the facility and to train a local workforce, and marketing contacts for both low-grade (input) and refined zinc. Although they invested no capital in the venture, the urbanites received 60 percent of profits. They had no rights of transfer over the fixed assets of the refinery; the village paid for the equipment and retained exclusive possession of it.[47] Operations were managed by the technicians (or their agents), who controlled use of enterprise assets, with Qiaolou appointees serving—and learning—as their deputies. Managers had authority over decisions regarding supply, production, and marketing, but the village was responsible for personnel matters. Workers were selected from among the most experienced employees at both brick factories, were directly overseen by Qiaolou supervisors, and were paid wages from the village's share of profits. Both parties provided an accountant to cross-check bookkeeping.

The joint venture offered an attractive deal to the technicians, since it cost them little or nothing.[48] This arrangement operated for more than a year before the agreement began to fall apart, reportedly over disputes concerning fiscal management. It was alleged that the Party secretary had wanted to use refinery revenues to subsidize the costs of retooling the No. 1 Brick Factory, a move that was strongly opposed by the technicians. Qiaolou managers charged that the urbanites were refusing to share their market contacts. Other recriminations followed. The joint venture was abandoned, and the technicians returned to Chengdu. Village staff at the refinery, freed from the tutelage of their former supervisors, took up the latter's previous responsibilities and pursued both existing and new contacts.[49] Apparently, despite the terms of the contract, real powers of use, income, and transfer had been effectively retained by the village Party secretary. Qiaolou emerged from the joint venture in debt, but with an overhauled industrial infrastructure producing a marketable commodity.

The refurbishment of the No. 1 Brick Factory, whose clay supply had been of a higher quality and lasted slightly longer, began only after the refinery went into operation. Once again, through use of contacts and political capital with county authorities, village leaders obtained another low-interest loan, which they used to purchase imported Italian machinery for manufacture of automotive tires and other rubber products.[50] By 1995, this new "modern" facility was ready, but it sat idle for lack of operating capital. Faced with mounting debts, costly product lines, and discontent among laid-off families, the Party secretary decided to solicit new outside investment. In a dramatic departure from his earlier self-reliant stance, he now sought a foreign partner to invest U.S.$1 million, which he claimed was necessary to get production rolling at the tire factory. Potential investors in this 50:50 profit-sharing partnership would be welcome to participate in marketing. But Qiaolou would have all managerial authority over use of enterprise assets, retain full rights of transfer over the enterprise, and reserve the right to practice cross-asset subsidization (using residual revenues from the factory to support ailing collective enterprises).

During the refinery's first months of independent operation, production lagged as the enterprise struggled to secure new sources of low-grade zinc, the basic input. Although the novelty of the refinery positioned it to sell highly refined zinc to large state-run industries, markets for material inputs were still rudimentary. In hopes of regaining revenue flow, the village government decided to invest in the construction of yet another brick factory, Qiaolou's third. Once again, "shares" were sold involuntarily to all village families to subsidize construction costs. On this occasion, however, shares were also offered publicly in the local market town. For the first time, nonresidents of Qiaolou could become shareholding members of a collective village enterprise.[51] As had been the case in earlier "share" offerings, purchasers willing to forgo dividend payments were assigned jobs at the new No. 3 Brick Factory.

The manager appointed by the village to run the enterprise was the deputy Party secretary, son of the Party secretary's deceased elder brother, who was given the authority to hire and fire workers.[52] His position as a gatekeeper to wage labor has enabled him to construct his own patronage relations with young people of his generation in the township, and he has hired many workers from outside Qiaolou. A young man in his late thirties with extensive experience in enterprise management, the deputy Party secretary has acquired a reputation for being more concerned with economic development than with politics, to the chagrin of his uncle, who has groomed him for succession. Leading his agenda for the future is a reduction of social and economic inequalities between rural and urban areas, and to this end he has voiced his conviction that Qiaolou's collective enterprises must ultimately be "privately contracted" (*siren chengbao*) to individual entrepreneurial managers to secure managerial efficacy, high productivity, and profitable returns.

Conclusions: A Lease on the Future

While it seems unlikely that all of Qiaolou's collective enterprises will be contracted out to independent entrepreneurs as long as the current Party secretary remains in office, managerial corporatism in Qiaolou clearly faces a precarious future. In fact, several collective assets have already been contracted out or leased to private operators since the mid 1990s. The distillery, which for several years had been operating at a loss, was effectively leased to its production supervisor, who had worked at the enterprise since its establishment in 1985. The young man, a Party member of good standing with affinal ties to the Party secretary, was an ambitious entrepreneur with a reputation for diligent work and a mind for business.[53] This watershed transfer agreement in 1994 represented the first time a particular family or individual, acting in a nonofficial capacity, acquired relatively exclusive control over a collectively owned village asset.[54]

Paying a one-time fee, the new manager was given a multi-year lease with authority to run the distillery as he wished, to select and hire new workers, to set employee wages and bonuses, and to retain all revenues after taxes.[55] He and his wife ran the enterprise together, raising capital through a successful family fruit business and by borrowing money from associates and kin. They entered into a partnership with a technical expert (and his wife) from the county seat, another young man who had worked at a highly reputable state-run distillery in Meishan. As was the case with the refinery, this outsider partner brought technical expertise to improve product quality, but invested no capital. Yet profits were split evenly.

One other significant change in property rights to collective village assets in Qiaolou was the leasing of several street-front rooms in the village office building to another private entrepreneur and his wife. The couple also paid a one-time fee for a multi-year lease, then refinished the rooms and opened a small restaurant and karaoke club, using investment capital from associates in other parts of the county and even as far away as Chongqing. This enterprise was the topic of much popular discussion when it opened a week before the 1995 Lunar New Year. The proprietor was a young Qiaolou man in his late twenties who had spent several years in prison. Following his release and return to the village in 1991, he became active in a sworn brotherhood organization allegedly engaged in both legal and illicit entrepreneurial activities. A reputable source close to the Qiaolou leadership confirmed rumors that the Party secretary had been unwilling to grant the young man the contract he sought and did so only after the latter threatened that his associates would "blow up" (*zha*) the village office building.[56]

These developments raise serious questions regarding the future of managerial corporatism in Qiaolou, as well as for the structuring of property rights to collective village enterprise in general. Do they represent a gradual trend toward private ownership as China moves toward capitalism? Or are they the consequences of a retrenchment strategy that has "downsized" the village corporation in an attempt to restructure and reconcentrate collective resources on more profitable product lines? Do they suggest that the market-oriented reforms of the post-Mao era have given rise to new postsocialist entrepreneurs who are willing to use violence in predatory pursuit of profit? While a single case study is too limited to construct broad generalizations, several tentative conclusions might be suggested.

The administrative elite of Qiaolou that gained ascendancy during the Cultural Revolution had, by the mid 1980s, transformed themselves into a local managerial class. This group of allies, affines, and kin controlled "collectively owned" production assets in the village and dominated the social relations that determined the organization of work in—and the distribution of material benefits from—Qiaolou's enterprises. Having once derived their power as administrative agents who brokered the flow of goods and services between the state and the local collective during the Maoist era, they had become local patrons in their own right: executive managers of village-owned and village-operated enterprises who controlled a powerful economic base largely autonomous from the state government. More than mere "transaction managers," they were uniquely positioned to mediate the general relationship between the village, its resident families, and the state authorities.

Qiaolou's managerial elite expressed their claims to local property rights through the rhetoric of self-reliant struggle against hardship and notions of a corporate community based on idioms of kinship. They exerted their decision-making power over the use and transfer of village assets (as they defined them), as well as over the distribution of revenues from collective enterprises. Although they styled themselves representatives of the interests both of the village collective and of village families collectively, they also demonstrated an ability to position their own descendants, relatives, and friends as privileged successors. While the image of collectivism no doubt appealed to the political sensitivities of Party-state authorities in the post-Tiananmen period, the local power and legitimizing authority of the Qiaolou managerial elite derived, not from their links to government superiors, but rather from the autonomous economic base they created and controlled. The era of collective agriculture had ended, but "the collective" had been given a new lease on life, so to speak, by the former brigade leadership.[57]

Changing economic conditions in the region and the country created a growing crisis for the corporate village collective and the image its leaders projected of a familylike social welfare community. Attempting to achieve a rapid transition to profitable new product lines, the managerial elite of Qiaolou apparently overextended collective investments in capital construction, leaving village accounts with funds inadequate to operate the refinery and tire factory effectively.[58] "Spinning off" less profitable enterprises such as the distillery and offering "shares" in the No. 3 Brick Factory to nonresidents of Qiaolou were short-term tactics in a more pro-tracted strategy of corporate restructuring. The consequences of such de-cisions, however, may yet prove more profound than the village Party secretary and his allies anticipated.

The contracting or leasing to independent contractors of use rights to smaller, less profitable and capital-intensive collective assets, such as the distillery or rooms in the village office building, may be only temporary. In no instance did contractors acquire rights of transfer over these assets, although they did obtain control of residual income generated by their enterprises. Qiaolou's most expensive and sophisticated enterprise assets have remained under the control of the village collective and its Party secretary, who seemed determined to retain the power to use revenues from profitable enterprise to subsidize other collective ventures. Control over a collective aggregation of assets had been instrumental in generat-ing the capital and other resources to incubate rural enterprises in the area. As village factories shift to larger-scale, more capital-intensive pro-duction of commodities, economies of scale may remain crucial.

However, as local markets for other goods and services continue to develop, and growing numbers of village families find themselves obliged to search outside the collective for new avenues of mobility, families have become less dependent on the village collective for their economic se-curity. Since the early 1990s, young and old alike have turned increasingly to new opportunities offered in the market economy. By 1995, more than a third of village families had members living outside Qiaolou, some in distant provinces. Many families with members still employed in village enterprises have turned those jobs over to women, particularly young wives and daughters-in-law, while men seek alternative sources of income both near and afar. Yet as the young thirst for profits, the elderly search for security.[59] Both envisage an uncertain and indeterminate future.

A new generation of young pioneers is coming of age, and they are asserting their own claims to property rights in the corporate village col-lective. While it may be premature to conclude that Qiaolou is experi-encing a trend toward capitalist private ownership, many of these heirs apparent to the village managerial elite have come to regard collective enterprises as a means through which to pursue their own individual and family interests. The more "enterprising" among them use their jobs to cultivate contacts and relationships with associates elsewhere in the hopes of one day striking out on their own.[60] Most lack the ideological commit-ment to collectivism that has guided the current Party secretary's corpo-rate strategy and the memories of past hardship and scarcity that fuel the anxieties and concerns of older villagers. There are, however, other young people who continue to express dedication to the future of the collective, such as another nephew of the Party secretary who recently completed study at a provincial institute for rural enterprise management, funded by a village scholarship.[61] The future of property rights and management practices in Qiaolou enterprises will be shaped by the relationships that develop between these administrative successors in the coming years.

Chapter 3

Local Institutions and the Transformation of Property Rights in Southern Fujian

CHIH-JOU JAY CHEN

To a large extent, China's dramatic economic growth since the late 1970s has been fueled by rural industry. The gross output value of rural industry (township, village, and private enterprises—TVPs) jumped from 9.8 percent of the country's total in 1980 to 44 percent in 1994, while employment climbed from 9.4 to 33 percent of the total rural labor force.[1] With the adoption of the household responsibility system and the consequent removal of agricultural assets from government control, local industrial enterprises have become the government's most reliable source of income and have also directly contributed to local development. The analysis of property rights arrangements and the evolution of TVPs therefore provides insight into China's rural transformation and the changing economic, political, and social dynamics of Chinese society.

As reform proceeds, the question of ownership becomes critical for understanding economic institutions and organizational features in China's rural economy. Eirik Furubotn and Svetozar Pejovich suggest that property rights include the right to use an asset, to appropriate the returns from an asset, and to transfer an asset to others. In essence, they refer to the use of, derivation of income from, and sale of assets.[2] Scholars also extend the notion of property to include all sorts of valued resources, ranging from objects (e.g., garments, machines) and assets to information and personal abilities.[3] Variations in bundles of property rights therefore serve to define important organizational differences among firms.

Studies of the Chinese economy have drawn different pictures of economic institutions and property rights in rural China. Oi and others, for example, stress the continuity of cadre power and redistributive corporatism in the rural reforms.[4] While the reforms decentralize power to regions and localities, cadres have been able to retain power by controlling resource allocation and redistribution, playing a key role in economic decision-making. One of the most important institutional changes to buttress the continued authority and autonomy of local government is fiscal reform, which provides strong incentives for local government to become entrepreneurial.

Another perspective suggests that China's reforms can best be understood as a transition from a redistributive command system to a market system.[5] This means that power shifts from redistributors (i.e., cadres) to the direct producers (i.e., entrepreneurs). Meanwhile, human capital will be more salient than political capital in seizing economic gains, and thus inequality of opportunity and rewards will be reduced. This argument predicts a decline in the power of cadres, a corresponding gain in the power of producers, and lessening inequality in the distribution of resources and rewards.

A third view focuses, not on state bureaucracy or market penetration, but on indigenous social institutions.[6] Local institutions, based on such sociocultural elements as kinship, serve to shape the trajectory of change. Therefore, market transition and bureaucratic corporatism are not the only mechanisms that coordinate economies in Chinese reforms. The operation and legacies of native institutional arrangements should be taken into account as well.

Each of these perspectives, which represent different research emphases, provides useful insights into the process of institutional transformation. Nevertheless, their arguments and findings raise the issue of regional variation and highlight the necessity of examining local institutional arrangements in detail. Considering the fact that various types of property rights and economic institutions may coexist in different regions across China, the critical issues are: Why did state policies bring about different economic forms across rural regions? How should regional variation be explained? How do local variants evolve over time?

To address these questions, this chapter draws on field research in southern Fujian to provide insight into one type of economic organization in one of China's rapidly developing coastal areas. It first identifies the characteristics of economic organizations and property rights arrangements in an area where individual and joint-household management is widespread. Then it examines the local social institutions in which economic institutions are embedded. Finally, it studies the role of local government in reforms and shows how it both facilitates and benefits from the booming local economy. I argue here that while economic policies at the national level began the process of reforms, differences in social and political institutions in each locality dictate variations in economic organization and property rights. Local officials in different regions adapt national policies to local social and economic realities. They are constrained by their respective local institutions and thus cannot fully implement policies passed down from above. On the other hand, open-door policies and market forces indeed promote economic production and market transactions, but these proceed within the institutional arrangements of bounded rural communities. If the particular characteristics of local institutions in each area are overlooked, one is likely to exaggerate the effect of market forces and central policies and thus misunderstand the reforms' transformative mechanisms.

Property Rights Arrangements in Southern Fujian: The Jinjiang Model

Jinjiang is located in southeastern Fujian, south of the estuary of the Jin River, which empties into Quanzhou Bay, an inlet of the Taiwan Straits. Before it was renamed Quanzhou prefecture in 1984, Jinjiang prefecture included today's Quanzhou, Jinjiang, and Shishi City. Shishi (Stone Lion) used to be one of Jinjiang's eighteen townships before it was amalgamated with three nearby townships to establish Shishi City in 1989. Although the administrative boundaries were redrawn several times, Jinjiang has long been known as the region of today's Jinjiang City (consisting of fourteen townships) and Shishi City (consisting of four townships), with a land area of 903 square kilometers and a population of 1.25 million.[7]

Located within the "Minnan Golden Triangle" (the prefectures of Quanzhou, Zhangzhou, and Xiamen), Jinjiang achieved fame as the "Jinjiang Model" (*Jinjiang moshi*) soon after reforms began in the late 1970s. It is one of the most developed areas in rural China. In the general achievement (*zonghe shili*) rankings of rural China's more than 2,000 cities and counties, Jinjiang City entered the top 100 (ranked fifty-fifth) in 1991. It jumped to twenty-fourth in 1992 and to fifteenth in 1995.[8] Per capita incomes of the rural populations of Jinjiang (Y 3,358), the Shanghai suburbs (Y 3,436), and Suzhou (Y 3,090) are as much as 2.5 to 2.8 times the national average (Y 1,223). In 1994, Jinjiang's per capita gross national product (GNP) reached Y 13,040, slightly higher than Suzhou's Y 12,639 and far ahead of the Shanghai suburbs' Y 7,200 and Y 3,679 yuan for China as a whole. Suzhou and the Shanghai suburbs each have a large industrial base, and the volume and value of their industrial products are much higher than those of Jinjiang, which tends to concentrate on low-value products such as garments, foodstuffs, and footwear. In 1994, the per capita gross value of industrial output (GVIO) in Jinjiang reached Y 18,449, lower than the

TABLE 3.1

Per Capita Economic Indicators, 1994
(yuan)

	Jinjiang	Shanghai suburbs	Suzhou	Fujian	All China
Per capita net income, rural population	3,358	3,436	3,090	1,578	1,221
GNP per capita	13,040	7,200	12,639	5,454	3,679
GVIO per capita[a]	18,449	22,084	42,036	7,203	6,417

SOURCES: *Fujian tongji nianjian 1995* [Statistical yearbook of Fujian, 1995] (Beijing: Zhongguo tongji chubanshe, 1995), pp. 367–94; *1995 Shanghai jiaoqu tongji nianjian* [1995 Statistical yearbook of the Shanghai suburbs] (Shanghai: Statistical Bureau of Shanghai City, 1995), pp. 6, 19, 23; *Suzhou tongji nianjian, 1995* [Statistical yearbook of Suzhou, 1995] (Beijing: Zhongguo tongji chubanshe, 1995), pp. 18, 27, 198; *Zhongguo tongji nianjian, 1995* [Statistical yearbook of China 1995] (Beijing: Zhongguo tongji chubanshe, 1995), pp. 32, 279, 375.
[a] Gross value of industrial output.

TABLE 3.2

Scale of Rural Industrial Enterprises, 1984 and 1994
(average GVIO, Y 10,000, at original value)

	1984			1994		
	Jinjiang	Suzhou	Shanghai suburbs	Shishi[a]	Suzhou	Shanghai suburbs
Township-run	25	122	163	206	2,636	1,333
Village-run	19	28	49	99	809	428

SOURCES: Calculated from data in *Jinjiang xian guomin jingji tongji ziliao, 1984* [Statistical material on the national economy, Jinjiang County, 1984] (Jinjiang: Statistical Bureau of Jinjiang, 1985), p. 220; *Shanghai jiaoqu nianjian, 1949–1992* [Almanac of the Shanghai suburbs, 1949–1992] (Shanghai: Shanghai renmin chubanshe, 1994), pp. 655–56; *1995 Shanghai jiaoqu tongji nianjian*, pp. 111–12; *Suzhou nianjian, 1984* [Suzhou almanac, 1984] (Suzhou: File Office of Suzhou City, 1986), p. 383; *Suzhou tongji nianjian 1995* [Statistical yearbook of Suzhou 1995] (Beijing: Zhongguo tongji chubanshe, 1995), pp. 197–98; *Shishi shi shehui jingji tongji nianjian, 1994* [Yearbook of social and economic statistics of Shishi, 1994] (Shishi: Economic Bureau of Shishi City, 1994), pp. 193–95.
[a] Data for Jinjiang are not available for 1994, but Shishi was under Jinjiang's administration before 1987, and their industrial sectors shared similar characteristics.

Shanghai suburbs (Y 22,084) and Suzhou (Y 42,036), but still much higher than the national average (Y 6,417) (Table 3.1).[9]

The different industrial structures of Jinjiang and the Yangtze Delta region are also reflected in the scale of local enterprises. The average firm size is small in Jinjiang, relative to Suzhou and the Shanghai suburbs. In 1994, the average GVIO of township- and village-run enterprises in the Shanghai suburbs was roughly five times that of Jinjiang, and Suzhou's was roughly ten times larger (Table 3.2).[10]

Since the 1970s, state-owned enterprises' share of industrial output in Jinjiang has declined sharply, from 38 percent in 1970 to 2 percent in 1992. On the other hand, enterprises run by villages and joint-household and individual enterprises have increased their share of industrial output from 36 percent in 1970 to 91 percent in 1993 (see Table 3.3). It is clear that state-owned enterprises, mostly under the jurisdiction of the prefecture and the county, have been driven out of the picture. Equally important, the official statistics indicate that rural enterprises are overwhelmingly under the ownership and administration of village governments or lower (joint households or households), with little contribution from county- or township-run enterprises.

Nevertheless, the statistics tell only part of the story regarding property rights in Jinjiang industry and need to be interpreted with caution. It is clear that ownership of industrial assets has shifted downward in the hierarchy of government jurisdiction from county to village and household, but the actual property rights arrangements in different rural enterprises, mostly registered as village-run (*cunban*), joint-household (*lianhu*), or individual, cannot be divined from official statistics. Specifically, does classification as "village-run" necessarily entail cadre involvement and government intervention? If not, how are the bundles of property rights arranged? Also, "fake collectives" (*jiajiti*) and "wearing red caps" (private enterprises with collective licenses) have been reported in other regions,[11] suggesting that the property rights of "village-run" enterprises deserve closer examination.

The following data on economic organizations and local institutions in

TABLE 3.3

Sectoral Share of Industrial Output in Jinjiang, 1970–1993[a]
(Y million; percent of total GVIO)

Year	GVIO[b]	State-owned enterprises		Township-run enterprises		Village-run and below	
		Amount	Share	Amount	Share	Amount	Share
1970	45.9	17.4	38%	12.2	27%	16.3	36%
1975	60.8	17.9	29	19.8	33	23.1	38
1980	189.6	40.1	21	58.8	31	90.8	48
1985	636.1	66.4	10	91.3	14	478.4	75
1990	2,341.2					1,891.5	81
1991	3,595.6	115.8[c]	3			3,054.6	85
1992	7,064.0	134.1[c]	2	221.2[d]	3	5,499.8	78
1993	14,270.3			96.0[d]	1	12,996.3	91

SOURCES: *Jinjiang xian guomin jingji tongji ziliao*, various issues; *Fujian jingji nianjian*, 1991, 1992, 1993, 1994 [Economic yearbook of Fujian, 1991, 1992, 1993, 1994] (Fuzhou: Statistical Bureau of Fujian, 1991, 1992, 1993, 1994).
NOTE: The data for 1970–85 are at 1980 prices, and for 1990–93 are at 1990 prices. After 1990, some types of ownership (e.g., foreign joint ventures) are not included in any of the three categories, and thus the sum would be less than the total GVIO.
  [a]Includes Shishi, unless otherwise indicated.
  [b]Total gross value of industrial output, in million yuan.
  [c]Shishi data are unavailable and not included.
  [d]Calculated from related data.

TABLE 3.4

Basic Data on Field Sites in Fujian, 1994

	Population	No. of industrial enterprises	GVIO[a] (Y 10,000)	GVIO per capita (yuan)
Jinjiang[b]	1,245,500	—	2,297,822	18,449
Chendai Township	72,050	2,118	251,566	34,915
Yangcun Village	6,298	238	23,000	36,520
Pingcun Village	2,008	103	8,370	41,683
Hanjiang Township	46,931	754	111,500	23,758
Hancun Village	5,264	98	23,600	44,832
Fujian Province	31,268,700			7,203
All China	1,198,500,000			6,417

SOURCES: Information from fieldwork; *Zhongguo tongji nianjian, 1995* [Statistical yearbook of China, 1995] (Beijing: Zhongguo tongji chubanshe, 1995); *Fujian tongji nianjian, 1995* [Statistical yearbook of Fujian, 1995] (Beijing: Zhongguo tongji chubanshe, 1995).
[a] Gross value of industrial output.
[b] Includes the administrative divisions of Jinjiang City and Shishi City.

Jinjiang were collected during fieldwork in 1995–96. Research was mainly conducted in Yangcun and Pingcun villages of Chendai township, Jinjiang City, and Hancun village of Hanjiang township, Shishi City.[12] Chendai is the richest township in Jinjiang.[13] In 1994, the township had a population of 72,050, divided into 26 administrative villages. In 1984, it became the first township to produce an industrial output of more than Y 100 million in Fujian Province. Within Chendai, Yangcun is one of the most prosperous villages. In 1991, Yangcun became the first "Y 100 million village" (*yiyuancun*) in Fujian, and in 1994, its production value topped Y 230 million. In that year, Chendai's industrial production value grew to Y 2,515 million; of the 26 villages, 10 had production values above Y 100 million.[14] Although the production output of Pingcun village reached only Y 84 million in 1994, its per capita industrial output (Y 41,683) exceeded even Yangcun's (Y 36,520) (Table 3.4). The most developed village in Hanjiang township is Hancun village, about 25 kilometers from Chendai. Its production output grew rapidly from Y 18 million in 1991 to Y 236 million in 1994. Overall, Yangcun, Pingcun, and Hancun are among the most advanced and industrialized villages in Fujian, and in fact in all of China. The main features of the property rights in these villages are summarized below.

PRIVATE OWNERSHIP FROM THE OUTSET

During the later period of the Cultural Revolution, a number of Jinjiang's joint factories or partnerships (*hezuo qiye*) resumed operation, meeting pent-up demand for household commodities among urban residents.[15] By the end of 1978, Jinjiang had 1,141 township and village enterprises, of which 143 were registered as township-owned and 998 as village-owned.[16] The output value of the 998 village-run enterprises amounted to Y 31.3 million, even higher than that of state-owned enterprises (Y 29 million).[17] Compared with other coastal regions, Jinjiang was still at a low level of industrialization in the later 1970s. In 1978, industry in Jinjiang accounted for 37 percent of its total social product, much lower than Suzhou's 65 percent.[18] Similarly, the Yangtze Delta region's industrial output largely outperformed Jinjiang's. In 1978, for example, Jinjiang's per capita GVIO (113 yuan) equaled only 10 percent of that in Suzhou (967 yuan) and 17 percent of that in the Shanghai suburbs (651 yuan) (Table 3.5).

Starting from a modest industrial base, the ownership of Jinjiang's rural enterprises was collective in name but private in nature. With few exceptions, most of these enterprises either adopted the "leaned-on" (*guakao*) strategy, namely, obtaining a false collective registration for individual or partnership business, or operated as cooperatives (*hezuo jingying*), jointly managed by the collective and peasants. It was rare for enterprises to be established by collective funds and run by government officials.[19] At the time, private business was still gravely prohibited, and local entrepreneurs therefore had no choice but to operate under the umbrella of the collective (i.e., township or village government).

In the early 1970s, Shishi, a harbor township of Jinjiang, experienced a revival of small factories and petty private businesses. During the Cultural Revolution, more than 30 household hardware factories were engaged in producing "Chairman Mao" pins.[20] In 1974, there were 918 vendors and shops in this small town, selling various articles smuggled from Hong Kong and Taiwan.[21] Most of the factories and shops were independently or jointly run by different households, which obtained business

TABLE 3.5

Gross Value of Industrial Output in Various Rural Regions, 1970–1980
(yuan per capita)

	1970	1975	1978	1980
Shanghai suburbs[a]	190	478	651	945
Suzhou[b]	373	677	967	1,419
Jinjiang[a]	55	68	113	191
Jinjiang[b]	60	69	98	196

SOURCES: Calculated from data in *Shanghai jiaoqu nianjian, 1949–1992* [Almanac of the Shanghai suburbs, 1949–1992] (Shanghai: Shanghai renmin chubanshe, 1994), pp. 589–601; *Suzhou shi shehui jingji tongji ziliao, 1949–1985* [Statistical material on society and economy, Suzhou City, 1949–1985] (Suzhou: Statistical Bureau of Suzhou City), p. 5; *Zhongguo guoqing congshu: Jinjiang juan* [Chinese national conditions: Jinjiang volume] (Beijing: Zhongguo dabaike quanshu chubanshe, 1992), pp. 50, 106–7.

[a] 1998 prices.
[b] 1980 prices.

licenses by "attaching" their businesses to the collectives. The booming market activities and household factories were attacked as the "restoration of capitalism" (*ziben zhuyi fubi*), periodically provoking crackdowns by the government in Beijing.[22] After 1978, as the political climate improved, the local economy regained its momentum and the once repressed commercial activities in this small township were revived and expanded. Shishi was called "little Hong Kong," attracting many outside traders, merchants, retailers, and vendors from all over the country, who came for goods unavailable or in short supply elsewhere, including electronic appliances, pornographic materials, and fancy clothes. The shops were surreptitiously run by individual households, either without any registration or with collective licenses issued by the government.[23] In the early 1980s, a booming garment industry developed, further increasing the scale of local market transactions in Shishi.

In nearby Chendai, Yangcun village first established factories for agricultural machine repair, grain processing, straw-weaving, and hardware processing in the mid 1970s, all in the guise of village-run enterprises. In fact, they were also individual or partnership enterprises run independently by villagers. Local cadres rarely participated or intervened in the day-to-day management of the firms. By the early 1980s, a large number of joint enterprises were registered under collective licenses, and such registration became the major organizing principle for township and village enterprises in Jinjiang. In 1980, Chendai had 20 enterprise licenses but more than 190 "leaned-on" factories. From 1978 to 1983, Yangcun village registered seven enterprises with the township's Office of Enterprise, but by 1983, there were actually 80 "leaned-on" factories, in which a number of firms shared one license under the collective.[24] Most of these enterprises were suboptimal in scale. In Jinjiang, the average value of industrial output per unit in 1984 amounted to 250,000 yuan for township-run enterprises and 190,000 yuan for "village-run or below" enterprises, less than half their counterparts' size in Suzhou and the Shanghai suburbs (Table 3.2).

In practice, the collectives (township and village governments) offered some conveniences to local enterprises. For example, Yangcun village implemented a "five uniform, six self-managed" (*wutongyi, liuzizhu*) policy.[25] The "five uniform" principle applied to uniformity in licensing, in invoices, in tax collection and administration fees, in seal-stamping administration, and in bank accounts.[26] The "six self-managed" principle applied to investment and partnership, production and marketing, leadership, management, labor employment, and profit distribution. In general, the administrative fee was about 3 percent of gross income, of which 2 percent was paid to the village, and 1 percent to the township. Since the village government controlled access to and use of bank accounts and invoices, it could monitor the businesses' cash flows, enabling it to assess management fees accurately. By 1990, each enterprise had received its own license, albeit a "fake collective" one, and the management fee was then changed to a fixed annual remittance.

In 1984, a set of state regulations was announced for rural individual businesses employing no more than seven workers; private enterprises employing more than seven workers were not granted legal status until as late as 1988, after the passing of a constitutional amendment.[27] The 1984 regulations legitimized individual and private enterprises in the countryside. Nonetheless, this policy did not substantially change the collective registration of private enterprises in Jinjiang. According to the 1994 records of the Chendai township government, among the 2,118 industrial enterprises, 1,241 (59 percent) were registered as township- or village-run, 646 (31 percent) as private or individual, and 231 (11 percent) as joint ventures.[28] In fact, the nominal category generally did not refer to any specific property rights arrangement, with the registration of enterprises as township- or village-run demonstrating conformity to older institutional arrangements. According to an enterprise manager in Chendai, when all village enterprises renewed their business licenses in 1992, despite the fact that all of the enterprises were privately run, higher-level authorities demanded that 60 percent of the enterprises be registered as collective and 40 percent as individual. "So," as the interviewed manager noted, "the township government grouped the enterprises with larger scope and assets as collective (township or village-run), and the smaller enterprises as individual or private."[29]

Local officials and enterprise managers have no doubt that the enterprises are privately owned. In interviews, local entrepreneurs showed no hesitation in labeling their factories as privately run (*siying*) or private individual (*siren*). Only asking specific questions such as "Under which ownership type is this enterprise registered?" would reveal the nominal ownership category.[30] It was also unthinkable for the local government to claim any kind of property rights over these "collective" enterprises. Instead of propagandizing about the collective economy, the government's materials and reports like to use the term "people-run" (*minying*) enterprises to describe the booming economy of the region.[31]

Among Hancun village's 98 enterprises in 1994, Lin Shuipong's factory was a typical household business. In 1982, Lin went into partnership with his nephew and started his firm. They bought local seaweed and transported it to Guangdong for sale. The business was operated under the umbrella of the Hanjiang Township Sea Products Collection Station, which received an annual administrative fee of 2 percent of the sales income. In

1987, Lin's wife became a partner with two other housewives and started a garment factory. Three years later, the partnership broke up and Lin started his own children's garment factory with a labor force of 20–30, licensed as a village-run enterprise.

SHAREHOLDING INVESTMENT AND FAMILY MANAGEMENT

Although labeled village- or township-run enterprises, rural enterprises in Jinjiang were organized with investments from the individual residents, with limited contributions from local government or collective investment. Inasmuch as household savings were limited, partnerships and shareholding came into fashion in the 1970s and 1980s. The four factories in Yangcun village that were originally set up in 1976 all obtained investments from and sold shares to villagers, who thus became the firms' shareholders. A firm's biggest shareholder usually served as the factory director. The shoe plant (originally a hardware-processing plant) was opened with an original investment of 20,000 yuan contributed by nineteen shareholders. On starting work at the factory, each worker also paid a deposit of 300 yuan, which was to be returned after one year of employment.

At the end of 1980, joint-household (*lianhu*) enterprises, along with township-run and village-run enterprises, became recognized as "non-private" enterprises by the county government.[32] Two or more households could organize themselves and register as a joint-household enterprise. By maintaining the "cooperative" form, these enterprises avoided the danger of being tagged as "tails of capitalism." This type of enterprise subsequently mushroomed in Jinjiang. One source states that in 1985 more than 34,600 households—16 percent of all households in Jinjiang—were engaged in such enterprises.[33] In 1984, joint-household firms in Jinjiang accounted for 44 percent of the employment and 52 percent of the output value of total TVPs. In that year, the share of joint-household enterprises in the national TVPs sector accounted for only 10 percent of employment and 7 percent of output value. By 1992, this gap had not narrowed significantly (Table 3.6).

In fact, village-run and joint-household enterprises had converged such that villagers individually or jointly invested in and managed their enterprises, periodically submitting management fees to the village. Joint-household management was intended to accumulate assets, particularly start-up capital, and to reduce risk. Over time, as assets increased, experience accumulated, and differences emerged in management and distribution of profit, these joint-household enterprises tended to collapse and be replaced by individual enterprises or regrouped households. In the

TABLE 3.6

Ownership Structure of Rural Enterprises, 1984 and 1992

	1984		1992	
	Jinjiang	China	Jinjiang	China
Employment (percentage)				
Township-run	21%	36%	8%	25%
Village-run	24	40	34	24
Joint-household	44	10	45	7
Individual	11	14	13	44
Output Value (percentage)				
Township-run	13%	48%	16%	37%
Village-run	25	38	38	30
Joint-household	52	7	41	6
Individual	10	7	5	27

SOURCES: *Jinjiang xian guomin jingji ingji tongji ziliao, 1984; Jinjiang shi zhi*, pp. 307, 1434; *Zhongguo xiangzhen qiye nianjian, 1993* [China's rural enterprise yearbook, 1993] (Beijing: Nong-ye chubanshe, 1993), pp. 143–47.

late 1980s, Chendai showed an annual failure rate of 20 percent of joint-household enterprises, and marginally more in the case of new start-ups. Since the early 1990s, as individual households have accumulated assets, family enterprises have increasingly emerged.

A recent survey reports that 76 percent of the village households in Jinjiang operate their own family businesses, of which 37 percent manufacture garments, 29 percent produce shoes, and 34 percent engage in commerce or service.[34] About 29 percent of the sample enterprises involve partnership in investment and management, with cooperation primarily linked by kinship ties. In Yangcun village, which had 238 registered enterprises in 1994, one-third of them were run cooperatively by siblings.[35] Equally important, often all members of the family are mobilized in the management of these enterprises. A significant portion (81 percent) of village enterprises employ fewer than 30 workers and are usually located in the courtyards of the villagers' residences (Table 3.7).

Chendai Garment Company provides another model of shareholding management in Jinjiang. Originally the Yangcun Shoe and Hat Factory, the company was established in 1979 on a shareholding basis, licensed by Yangcun village. The original investment of 20,000 yuan comprised eleven local shares and another four shares from Hong Kong. The company hired eleven workers, all shareholders' relatives. In 1982, the village began to implement the household responsibility system in agricultural production. Some of the managers and workers were primarily occupied by their farmwork. Subsequently, the factory's production effi-

TABLE 3.7

Household Enterprises in Jinjiang, 1995

	Pingcun Village		Shantou Village		Total	
	Number	Share	Number	Share	Number	Share
Household Factory						
Yes	39	78%	37	74%	76	76%
No	11	22	13	26	24	24
n	50		50		100	
Partnership						
Yes	15	38	7	19	22	29
No	24	62	30	81	54	71
n	39		37		76	
Firm Size						
less than 10	14	36	22	59	36	47
11–20	7	18	5	14	12	16
21–30	10	26	4	11	14	18
more than 30	8	21	6	16	14	18
n	39		37		76	
Product						
Garment	12	31	16	43	28	37
Shoes	22	56	0	0	22	29
Commerce and service	5	13	21	57	26	34
n	39		37		76	

SOURCE: Data calculated from survey, "Economic Development and Women's Work in Jinjiang," conducted by Yu-hsia Lu, Institute of Sociology, Academia Sinica.

ciency decreased, even coming to a halt during the harvest. The factory eventually ceased operation, and all the assets were divided up among shareholders. The factory director, Lin Qiu, together with his brother, son, and son-in-law, then founded another factory. In 1984, with an investment of 60,000 yuan from the township government, which also provided the original license and appointed a cadre to help during the initial period, Lin's factory and three other village garment and leather factories combined to form a new Chendai Garment-Shoe-Hat Company, with Lin serving as "general representative" (*zong daibiao*). The company took the lead in negotiating with external parties for raw materials, in taking orders, and in handling financial matters. It also provided a business license, bank account, and seal for the subordinate factories, which operated independently and did their own accounting, while benefiting from the economies of scale provided by the amalgamation. By 1988, Lin Qiu's own factory was valued at 1,700,000 yuan. In 1990, Lin reorganized the company into the Dali Shoe Factory, with the other three factories contracted as its workshops, their original owners serving as managers and shareholders. So as to take advantage of reduced taxes for foreign investment, the new factory was registered as a foreign joint venture in the name of a relative of Lin's in Hong Kong.[36]

The foregoing discussion of organizational features of Jinjiang's rural enterprises highlights the dynamism of partnership, shareholding, and household management. The collective registration of private enterprises, along with investment by partnership and shareholding, is one of the strategies of individual households and entrepreneurs for gaining economic advantage within state-determined constraints. Individual households and entrepreneurs have earned substantial profits and, more important, have secured significant property rights over their enterprise assets, despite different ownership labels (township-run, village-run, joint-household, and individual) adopted. Also of note, these organizational configurations emerged as soon as reforms began, rather than evolving from preexisting collective ownership of local enterprises. There is no transfer of property rights in enterprise assets, because the original owners (individuals, families, or joint households) retain their control of and residual income from assets. In other words, there is no de facto *privatization* occurring in the course of Jinjiang's industrialization and development, partly because local governments had few collective enterprises available for contracting or leasing to individuals to start with.

Local Social Institutions: Family Coordination in Practice

The organizational features of Jinjiang's rural economy were not mandated by state reform policies, nor were they anticipated by policy makers. Instead, the local social context and institutional environment shaped the growth of enterprises in Jinjiang. What has propelled the development of the privately owned economy over the past two decades? What are the institutional forces underpinning these particular configurations of property rights (i.e., private, family-centered enterprises)? I suggest that Jinjiang's economic organizations, dominated by household and partnership management and investment, are embedded in the local institutions of family and clan. Family and clan enforce norms and standards of conduct centered on kinship principles and community identity. This promotes and constrains certain features of social relations and economic activities. Although such institutions were suppressed by the Chinese state in the Mao period, they have now revived.

LINEAGE IDENTITY AND KINSHIP PRINCIPLES

For centuries, social order and community solidarity in rural China were based on lineage organization and ancestor worship.[37] However, in communist China, the lineage group was divested of its role as a corporate group benefiting members through jointly owned property.[38] Lineage organization, ancestor worship, and regional religious cults were denounced as "feudal superstition" and banned for decades. However, in the reform era, Jinjiang's indigenous kinship institutions have gradually revived and fused with local political and economic institutions.

Since the late Qing dynasty, Hancun village has been divided geographically and socially into three neighborhoods, or "corners" (*jiaoluo*)— West Corner, East Corner, and Rear Corner. A number of *fang* (sublineage or lineage branches) occupy each "corner." In the West Corner, the major sublineages are four lines of the Lin surname, along with some other minority lineage groups, called *wei-cu-bian* in the local dialect (meaning "far behind the houses"). During the turmoil periods of the Great Leap Forward (1958–60) and the Cultural Revolution (1966–76), as elsewhere in rural China, a large number of Hanjiang's lineage halls and genealogies were destroyed. Some of them, however, were preserved. In the early 1960s, the brigade office was moved into Lin's lineage hall, preventing this ancestral shrine from being demolished. In the early 1980s, the ancestral shrine was refurbished for its original use again. One of Lin's preserved genealogies had been hidden by a *fang* member, then the father of the village Party secretary. Since the 1980s, most of the ruined ancestral shrines in Hanjiang township have been rebuilt, and the lost genealogies are being rewritten and revised.[39]

The quick revival of lineage identity and kinship principles in Hancun illustrates that, despite state suppression for three decades, these indigenous institutions are deeply rooted and were silently preserved. The kinship connections and lineage-centered social relations are most observable in social events such as weddings, the birth of children, birthday banquets, and funerals. As I observed in Hancun, these events are participated in jointly by relatives within the same sublineage and "corner" neighborhood. Kinship principles and lineage affiliation have resumed their former position as central to social norms and local institutions. They are now so deeply and widely practiced in the community that even young children were aware of the *fang* origin of each fellow villager.

Kinship networks and clan identity are particularly active and vivid in the seven Hui (Muslim) villages in Chendai. Overall, these Hui people were assimilated to southern Fujian culture as early as the Ming dynasty (1368–1644) and now no longer practice Islam or Muslim dietary restrictions or religious rituals.[40] But as verified by local genealogies and historical documents, they identify themselves as descendants of Muslims who arrived in Quanzhou—a Silk Road maritime port under the Yüan dynasty—in the thirteenth century. They organize their lineage affairs through a grass-roots Hui Affairs Association.[41] In fact, government recognition as a minority group offered the Hui community an advantageous position in consolidating its *lineage* identity (much more important than its *ethnic* identity) at no risk of political repercussion, and further mobilizing overseas resources through kinship connections. The Hui lineage successfully connected itself with overseas fellow lineage members in the Philippines, Indonesia, Singapore, and, finally, Taiwan. The mutual visits and communications between local and overseas lineage communities have been enthusiastically established and maintained.[42]

THE INFLOW OF OVERSEAS CAPITAL

Jinjiang and Shishi are among the major hometowns of overseas Chinese, particularly those in the Philippines, Indonesia, Singapore, Malaysia, and elsewhere in Southeast Asia. The massive emigration to Southeast Asia started under the Qing dynasty (1644–1912), and reached its peak in the 1930s and 1940s.[43] According to an official survey conducted in 1990, among the population of 1.25 million in Jinjiang and Shishi, nearly 70 percent were classified as either "returned overseas Chinese" (*guiqiao*) or "overseas Chinese dependents" (*qiaojuan*). Their fellow countrypeople (*xiangqin*) from Jinjiang and Shishi residing overseas numbered 1.5 million.[44] In this area, overseas connections are common in people's daily lives.[45]

Channeled through clan origin and kinship networks, the inflow of overseas Chinese capital has long been a driving force for Jinjiang's local development. Since the 1930s, overseas endowment has been a major financial source for public services (e.g., education, infirmaries, libraries, nursing homes, charity affairs, etc.) and local infrastructure (e.g., roads and bridges, tap water, electricity and street lights, etc.). The statistics in 1935, when the Nationalist government was still in power, show that the educational expenditures of Jinjiang County government amounted to 474,000 yuan, of which only 30,000 (6 percent) was derived from government allocation and the rest from overseas endowment.[46] During times of political repression, such as the Anti-Rightist Campaign (1958–61) and the Cultural Revolution, interactions between local residents and relatives abroad were limited, but foreign remittances (*qiaohui*) still continued.[47] Overseas connections and support have been a consistent and important source for household livelihood and local charity throughout most periods in communist China.[48] The reforms' open-door policies immediately saw a resurgence of homeward-bound financial assistance. For instance, up to the early 1990s, an overwhelming majority (97 percent) of today's educational institutes in Jinjiang, including 43 middle schools, 367 elementary schools, and 289 kindergartens, were originally established or partially financed by overseas donations, amounting to a total figure of 170 million yuan. In addition, another 60 million yuan was donated to finance local infrastructure, medical care, and lineage activities.[49]

Besides the financial support of local public services and individual households, the reforms further opened the door for overseas involvement in expanding foreign trade and foreign investment in Jinjiang. Since 1978, Jinjiang enterprises have enthusiastically engaged in "processing trade" and "compensation trade" in order to obtain overseas resources and business opportunities.[50] In the period between 1980 and 1987, more than 60 percent of local enterprises in Jinjiang had entered into subprocessing and assembly contracts with foreign businesses.[51] Most of these business opportunities were found through kinship or local connections with overseas fellow countrymen; contracts were signed by local government on behalf of the local enterprises.[52] In addition, between 1979 and 1987, 3,325 rural factories, accounting for 60 percent of 5,418 rural enterprises in Jinjiang, were operated by local "overseas Chinese dependents" through the investments of their overseas relatives.[53]

The early to mid 1980s saw a surge of local economic activities in processing and compensation trade, marking the first period of overseas participation in the local economic boom. From 1984 on, overseas capital began to make direct investments in the local economy by establishing joint ventures (sanzi qiye).[54] Again, most of the investment is linked by kinship. According to a survey of foreign-invested firms in southern China, foreign investment in Quanzhou, the prefecture in which Jinjiang is located, was overwhelmingly determined by local connections and kinship.[55] In 1993, the survey found, around 99 percent of foreign investors in Quanzhou were Hokkien speakers (the regional dialect), 88 percent were of local origin, and 86 percent still had relatives in the area. The investors were mainly from Taiwan and Hong Kong, who followed their local origins and kin ties in making investments and building joint ventures in the PRC. For example, most Hong Kong investors, the largest foreign venture group in this region, were not Cantonese but southern Fujianese.[56] These findings imply that the overseas Chinese found that dialect, kinship, a common origin in a clan, a village, or (if necessary) a county gave a sure footing of trust for an investment or business deal to be conducted.

Overseas connections also benefit local enterprises by offering access to establishing joint ventures, even without any foreign investment. As with the collective registration of private enterprises, a number of local enterprises obtained the title of joint venture through a nominal joint investment from overseas relatives. Such a title allowed the enterprises to take advantage of tax and other privileges accorded to foreign joint ventures. For example, the Chendai Garment-Shoe-Hat Company in Yangcun village changed from a township-run enterprise to a joint venture in 1990, while actually there was no foreign capital invested. Overseas relatives merely provided the necessary documents for processing registration as a foreign joint venture.[57]

In sum, family ties and kinship principles have formed the core axes of local institutions in Jinjiang, particularly in the post-Mao era as state suppression has gradually loosened. Local family coordination is distinct from bureaucratic and market coordination. It shapes social relations while also coordinating economic activities in the community.

The Role of Government in Local Coordination

Elsewhere in rural China, local governments establish corporate forms of economic growth and dominate economic decision-making,[58] but Jinjiang's local government has acted less like a dominant corporate authority and more like a provider of administrative services, and for a certain period, a political shelter. During the early reform period, rather than intervening in day-to-day management, local government sheltered and created a more favorable environment for privately run (household and joint-household) businesses, which were still severely constrained by central government policies. After the state policies recognized and approved individual and private businesses, political shelter became less needed, but local government's role in providing infrastructure and social welfare came to be indispensable.

LOCAL POLICY INITIATIVES AND CENTRAL REPERCUSSIONS

As we have seen, in this locality, household and joint-household factories began to emerge as early as the late 1970s. To "legalize" these private-oriented factories in the locality, local governments in Jinjiang sidestepped state policy by designating these factories as township- or village-run enterprises. The township authorities in Chendai, which were said to be very much "mentally emancipated" (*sixiang jiefang*), took the initiative to mobilize villagers' savings in investing in household factories.[59] In nearby

Shishi, whose streets were filled with vendors and shops with smuggled commodities, the township government also issued a number of temporary regulations to license small shops and tax the commerce.[60]

Jinjiang County authorities, observing practices in Chendai and Shishi, decided to take extraordinary measures to institutionalize local economic activities without support from the central government. In 1980, the county's Communist Party committee announced a series of temporary regulations, allowing villagers to establish joint-stock household enterprises and partnerships, to employ wage workers, and to earn dividends according to the number of shares held.[61] At the time, the measure was considered drastic. Not until 1984, three years later, did the central government approve joint-stock investment and partnerships among rural households.[62] During 1980–81, the number of joint-household enterprises in Jinjiang increased by more than 500, and the investment value increased by more than one million yuan, contributing one-third of the county's production output.[63]

During the early reform period, the administrative assistance and protection offered by local governments also helped local enterprises to make deals with outside parties, particularly with state enterprises and government agencies. To cope with the hostility toward private and small rural enterprises, hundreds of Jinjiang's sales agents (*gongxiao*) had been traveling on the mainland, seeking market channels for local products. They carried official introduction letters, identification cards, and official invoice books issued by local governments. This army of salespersons, under the protection of the collective's umbrella, was vital for the success of local enterprises, particularly during the period of poor transportation and limited market information. Relying on social connections (*guanxi*), banquets, gifts, and, more important, bribery, they successfully found buyers in the bureaucratic system as well as in the free market.

The policy initiative and efforts of Jinjiang's local governments to "legitimize" and support the local private economy were impressive and attracted attention nationwide. But it paid a price for fame. On July 13, 1985, a crackdown on "practicing capitalism" in Jinjiang was initiated in Beijing and propagated nationwide.[64] It rebuked the Jinjiang County government for permitting the mass production of "counterfeit drugs" by local enterprises.[65] Several work teams were sent to the locality to make a thorough investigation, and all the local factories involved in the "crime" were shut down.[66] Eighteen local officials and enterprise managers in Chendai township, including its Party secretary, mayor, and the director of the Industry-Commerce Bureau, as well as local cadres in the villages, were sentenced to terms ranging from one to eight years.

The "counterfeit drugs" episode of 1985 reflects the fact that despite its limited intervention in day-to-day economic management, local government's interests are still tightly interwoven with local enterprises. Local government and local enterprises often form a coalition and coordinate their efforts to obtain resources and to bargain and negotiate with, and sometimes to conceal information from, the central state.

THE MUTUAL DEPENDENCE OF LOCAL GOVERNMENTS
AND ENTREPRENEURS

As the national political environment has become more permissive in the 1990s, local enterprises are being granted more latitude in production and market transactions. Although political protection is less necessary, the role of local government in promoting local infrastructure and public expenditures has been strengthened. Because local governments (particularly township and village governments) are not adequately funded by higher jurisdictions, they can play a significant role in rural development only if they have sufficient revenues. Local enterprises and related economic activities have become the principal sources of these revenues.

Villages in Jinjiang extracted sizable revenues from village enterprises by collecting enterprise remittances and land-contracting payments (Table 3.8). In 1994, household factories in Hancun village employing fewer than 20 workers and registered as village-run paid annual management fees ranging from 100 to 500 yuan to the village government. Medium-sized and large enterprises, whether registered as joint ventures or village-run, paid significantly higher fees for land use (ranging from 2,000 to 20,000 yuan), based on their occupation of more land than the maximum allowed for a village household.[67] In order to satisfy an increasing land demand for private residences and factory buildings, the Hancun village administration redrew the village's land plan in 1993, converting half of its farmland to industrial and housing uses. At the same time, the village government built 150 residential and commercial units and sold them to the villagers, for a total net profit of nearly Y 3,500,000. With the development of the local economy and a corresponding rise in villagers' expectations, there have also been fresh demands for housing and factory land. As a result, since the early 1990s the Hancun village government has used its control of village lands to act as a real estate and land-contracting company and so far has obtained a substantial fund from this source for the village coffers.[68]

In Yangcun village, the primary sources of revenue were also enterprise remittances and asset management fees.[69] In 1992–93, the village government raised Y 3,200,000 by "selling" lands to the villagers for housing and factory buildings.[70] As of 1994, Yangcun village collected more than Y 1,000,000 from enterprise management fees for license registration,

TABLE 3.8

Receipts and Expenditures of Village Governments in Jinjiang
(yuan)

	Hancun Village, Hanjiang Township, 1995	Yangcun Village, Chendai Township, 1994
Receipts	4,036,357	3,293,336
Township allocation	38,315	0
Village enterprise remittances	16,700	1,084,450
Agricultural land contract payment	—	220,000
Village collective enterprise profit	—	102,522
Village management income	3,712,562	1,834,138
Factory land and buildings	1,126,125	—
Residential land	2,152,404	—
Other land income	434,033	—
Other revenues	268,780	52,226
Expenditure	619,225	3,563,435
Special construction project	—	1,593,777
Infrastructure	44,757	35,000
Tap water	1,717	—
Seaside dike	38,498	—
Tree planting	4,542	—
Public restroom construction	—	35,000
Village administration costs	98,385	235,000
Cadre wages	42,800	165,600
Official travel	4,080	—
Official receptions	51,505	—
Welfare, culture, and education	402,691	451,000
Pension payments	183,450	—
Public safety	31,483	145,000
Sanitation	44,062	130,000
Village elementary school	6,580	150,000
Family planning	36,168	12,000
Subsidies for military dependents	21,841	—
Remittances to town government	0	605,690
Other	52,584	642,968
Village assets	869,447	9,560,231
Real estate	—	6,988,220
Cash and bank deposits	—	791,824
Other	—	1,780,187
Funds from overseas donations	4,355,080	1,500,000

SOURCE: Fieldwork.

land use, and public services. The village government also built and leased commercial buildings to villager-merchants, making an annual profit of more than 1,000,000 yuan.

Revenues collected in the villages are used for village infrastructure (e.g., road and bridge construction, tap water, farmland irrigation, etc.), the administration of village governments (e.g., cadres' salaries, hospitality, etc.), and social services (e.g., pensions, education, sanitation, public safety, family planning, etc.) (Table 3.8). These two rich villages spent considerable sums on infrastructure and social services. In 1994, Yangcun village spent 1,563,435 yuan to replace tap water pipelines connected to each village house. In 1992–93, it spent 3,700,000 yuan paving a village road and building 30 public rest rooms. Between 1982 and 1992, Yangcun invested more than 5,000,000 yuan in constructing village school buildings and hiring more teachers. It is also interesting to note that part of Yangcun's income was turned over to the township.[71] In contrast, Hancun obtained financial support from the township government.[72] Finally, both villages hold large sums of village funds received from overseas villagers' donations for social services.[73]

This self-reliance in village affairs emphasizes the centrality of village government in supplying social services and infrastructure construction to the community, using financial resources drawn from village enterprises and related rent payments, as well as donations by overseas villagers. Village governments can profit considerably by transferring use rights over land and buildings to entrepreneurs in return for rents. Consequently, a "secondary market" in use rights and rights to income over productive assets is created.[74] As the local economy prospers, the role of village government as collective property manager and provider of administrative services continues to expand.

Conclusions: Property Rights in the Villages

This analysis of economic development in Jinjiang suggests an evolving process of change in property rights. In the course of development, the main actors in property rights arrangements—local governments, private entrepreneurs, and overseas investors—hold various rights. There has been literally no privatization in which assets previously owned by communes or brigades were transferred to individuals. Early in the reforms, local government's chief asset was bureaucratic facilitation (e.g., license registration, provision of official business documents, and transaction services, such as banking and invoicing), which enabled local enterprises to participate in direct production and market transactions. Meanwhile, foreign relatives and fellow villagers offered their financial resources, information, and technology to their families and clan members. With these facilities and resources, local entrepreneurs and households established individual or joint-household firms, with property rights to these enterprise assets under their control.

As reform proceeds and the local economy expands, the property rights arrangements in local society also change. As the local economy prospers, local government benefits from the growing revenue base. The local government can draw income by controlling access to the most valued productive asset, land, thereby improving its capacity to offer services and resources to the community. Local enterprises have been participating in direct production with limited intervention from government; however, they rely on the infrastructure facilities and administrative services provided by the local government.

It is worth emphasizing that property rights arrangements in Jinjiang have been rooted in a local environment in which family ties and kinship principles play the core role. This points to the importance of local history and indigenous institutions. Owing to its location on the front line in any potential conflict with Taiwan, Jinjiang was earlier starved of central government investment and, consequently, had only a modest industrial base. Kinship principles and clan consciousness survive to this day and provide a basis for the expansion of the local economy. This family and clan coordination also constrains the operations of local government, which has enabled but not directed the development of the economy.

State policies and market penetration may account for some aspects of the reform process, but local institutions shape the local economy's organizational features and power structure. While the Jinjiang model is not typical of the Chinese countryside, it does illustrate how local family coordination (displayed in clan identity, community solidarity, kinship networking, etc.) provides a foundation for economic organization and property rights.

It is reasonable to speculate that more diverse and heterogeneous variations of property rights arrangements and economic organizations will develop in the future. Such variations, I have argued, result from variations in local social structure and institutions. Research documenting such variation and change will continue to provide valuable data and inform theoretical analyses of the ongoing transformation of China's society and economy.

Chapter 4

The Role of Local Government in Creating Property Rights: A Comparison of Two Townships in Northwest Yunnan

XIAOLIN GUO

R egional differences, economic diversity, and local politics across China have yielded a great variety of property forms, only some of which are compatible with what is conventionally perceived as public or private ownership. This is related to what has been referred to as the "real world variability in the assignment and exercise of each of a number of relevant rights," allowing for a variety of forms.[1] The local contexts of various property rights and the social and political constraints that shape them are at the center of this study. It examines the role of local governments in the formation of property rights in two townships—Jinguan and Yongning—in northwest Yunnan. As is typical of this part of China, in both townships there is little local industry; land is still the main source of livelihood. Yet each exhibits different property rights regimes in land and in township enterprises.[2]

Government interference in the economic activities of peasants has been greatly reduced since the shift to household agriculture and the development of household enterprises. Because they still control the land and economic enterprises upon which peasants depend to varying degrees, however, local governments in northwest Yunnan continue to have substantial potential to control local production and property management. Under these circumstances, the more dependent peasants are upon land for their livelihood, and the more developed township industry is, the more powerful the local government is.

Yet the power of local government is not necessarily manifest in its interference with production. Study of these two townships shows that government behavior does not follow a single pattern. The local government in Jinguan puts economic pressure on the local community and gets directly involved in the management of land resources and the organization of township enterprises. In Yongning, however, the local government is only minimally involved in both land management and township enterprises. Variation in the degree of government economic involvement and the degree to which local government asserts its ownership rights in the two communities is ultimately owing to variations in the economic status of each community and the social and political relationship of each local government to the state.[3] Jinguan township is located in a county with a Han majority population, with no special designation. By contrast, Yongning is in a county designated as both minority and poverty-stricken. The ethnic and poverty-stricken status of the latter yields special social and political conditions that affect the economic performance and incentives of local officials, which in turn generate different government claims on property rights and thus differences in local property relations.

Land Contracts as Bundles of Rights

The implementation of the household responsibility system is sometimes referred to (in and outside the China field) as de facto privatization.[4] In theory, land contracts adopted in the household responsibility system may well qualify as de facto privatization, in the sense that the cultivator appears to enjoy almost all the rights equivalent to an owner except for the right to sell the assets. However, the real practice of property rights varies significantly. The discussion of land contracts that follows illustrates how the property relationship between the state, the collective, and individual households under the current household responsibility system is defined, enforced, and modified by the township government and the village administration. In the local practice of property rights, as we shall see, conflicts between public ownership and the individual user's rights pertaining to the land contract arise from administrative interference by the township government and the village collective. The local practice of property rights related to the land contract in the two townships under study shows that the household responsibility system in Jinguan (the Han community) is far from de facto privatization, while the situation in Yongning (the ethnic minority community) is in fact close to privatization. These differences are socially and politically determined and associated with the absence or presence of ethnic and poverty statuses.

The household responsibility system was implemented in Jinguan township in 1983, about one year later than in most other townships in the county. The delay was due to extreme caution on the part of the county government—Jinguan is one of the three townships that constitute the county's most important grain-production base. The basic unit for land allocation at the time was the production team; and the amount of land allocated to individual households was determined by the size of the team. The land was divided into three grades: "good," "medium," and "poor," and each household drew a "lot" from each category. The average portion of land per person was 1 mu. After 1983, the land contract in Jinguan underwent adjustment twice, once in 1985 and once in 1989. These two adjustments were, according to the local cadres, mainly intended to adapt to changes in household size. However, these two adjustments may have reflected major policy adjustments regarding land contracts. In 1984, one year before the first adjustment, it was stipulated that the land contract would be extended from the initial 3–5 years to 15 years;[5] and in 1988, prior to the second adjustment, the revised Land Administration Law formally and specifically endorsed the user's right of transferability.[6] Since 1989, the land contract has not been further adjusted, which is apparently in accordance with the central policy to ensure the stability of land contracts.[7]

Land in Yongning was contracted to households in 1980–81, two to three years earlier than in Jinguan, which is some 200 kilometers to the north. The method of land allocation employed in Yongning was similar to that used in Jinguan, but the land area in Yongning was much larger. In the hamlets inhabited by Mosuo (the majority ethnic population in Yongning), the amount of land under household contract was about 3–4 mu per person, which was two to three times more than in Jinguan. Moreover, while the land contracts in Jinguan have undergone adjustment twice after 1983, they have remained unchanged in Yongning since 1980. Compared to Jinguan, there is much less pressure on land in Yongning, given the greater availability of land in relation to the small population. However, the varying pressure on land does not sufficiently explain the degree to which the government administration interferes with local production. Rather, the fundamental difference between the two government administrations lies in the way the property rights linked to the land contract are formulated and articulated by the two local governments.

Land Contracts in Jinguan and Yongning Compared

In both communities, ownership of land is clearly defined as public in the land contracts. But the rights encompassed in the land contract in Jinguan are more explicitly stated than in Yongning. According to the Jinguan township land management officer, land management consists of the "three rights system" (*sanquan zhi*): state ownership (*guojia suoyou quan*), collective ownership (*jiti suoyou quan*), and individual user's rights (*geren jingying quan*). This local interpretation of the "three rights system" derives from the public ownership of land by "all people" and the collective, and from the individual user's rights as expressed in the Land Administration Law.[8] The principles of collective ownership had been drawn up by the central government in the early 1960s.[9] Currently, the collective owns all arable land (including private plots and residential sites), roads, and ditches in the village.[10] Mountains and forests are owned by both collective and state. Since the production team was abolished, collective property has been managed by the village administration; the township government manages state property. The use of collectively owned land, and any change in it, must be approved by the township government. In addition, the appropriation of collectively owned land by the township government must be compensated at a rate equivalent to 20 times its annual output value, according to the Jinguan township land management officer.[11] Under public ownership, the land contract allocates user's rights to the peasants. These are known as the right to cultivate, the right to dispose of the product from the contracted land, and the right to retain profits from production.

Some have argued that public ownership conflicts with the user's rights and constitutes an obstacle to investment by peasants, and that it is this insecurity of user's rights that has generally been responsible for the agricultural stagnation in the second half of the 1980s.[12] This does not seem to be the case in Jinguan, however, where grain output has continued to rise since 1983, although the biggest leap took place in 1984–85, immediately after the land was contracted to the households. In 1980, annual per capita income in Jinguan was Y 167 and per capita grain distribution amounted to 302 kg per capita; by 1991, per capita income was Y 543 and grain distribution totaled 635 kg per capita (Jinguan township statistics). This continuous growth can be traced to the rights to manage production and the rights to the return from the land. Because the land contract connotes "assuming sole responsibility for one's own profits and losses" (*zifu yingkui*), public ownership of land does not necessarily decrease the incentives for peasants in production. Land in this area is the vital source of livelihood for peasants who simply do not have any choice but to carefully invest in it. "Though the land is not mine, nobody else can take it away either," Jinguan peasants say. This local understanding of the relationship between public ownership and user's rights has, in fact, had a fairly positive effect on the peasants' incentives in land management.

However, the notion that "nobody else can take it away" applies only to other individuals of equal status, that is, other villagers, but not to the township government or the village collective, whose powers override those of individuals. Because the village collective owns the land, it is understood that its use and any change in the contract are subject to the will of the village collective. It is taken for granted by the township government and village leaders that the peasants are obliged to comply with government production plans. In this property relationship, while public ownership is not necessarily an obstacle to incentives in production, it bears directly on the management of land use.

The property rights over land jointly held by the village collective and peasant households actually constitute a bundle of rights, which can be divided into the right to residual income, the right of transferability, and the right of control. The *right to residual income* is generally at the disposal of the peasants under the land contract, although they are simultaneously subject to the fulfillment of public duties.[13] The *right of transferability* belongs to the state. The Land Administration Law strictly prohibits individuals from selling land, although subleases (*chuzu zhuanrang*) are permitted as long as the public duties specified by the three-land system are fulfilled. There are only a handful of sublease cases in Jinguan, and the subleasers are mostly elderly, infirm, or people engaged in other occupations away from the village. Sublease contracts are arranged between households on shorter or longer terms. The rent is paid either in cash or in kind, in which public and collective duties are sometimes included and sometimes not.

By comparison, the *right of control is* probably the most complicated of all in the implementation of property rights regarding land. The formal constraints (or administrative interference) under which the village collective and farming households share property rights generate ambiguities with respect to control. These ambiguities give the local government considerable leeway to manipulate and impose conditions on the land contracts. The enforcement of tobacco production in Jinguan is an example of government interference with property rights in land management.

Tobacco is a crop widely grown in Yunnan. The highland climate in many parts of the province provides suitable conditions for growing tobacco. The tobacco industry makes a significant contribution to Yunnan's economy and is promoted by local governments. Estimates show that the profit tax (*lishui*) from the tobacco industry between 1980 and 1994 increased from Y384 million to Y27.68 billion, and the tobacco industry provided up to 70 percent of the total revenue of the province.[14] Beginning in the 1980s, the provincial government of Yunnan exempted the new tobacco-growing counties from provincial taxes on cured tobacco leaves in the first five years of production. The incentives to increase local revenue and the favorable conditions provided by the revenue-sharing system motivated the county government—under which Jinguan township is administered—to embark on tobacco production. It was advocated for the first time in 1985, but remained only an experiment on a voluntary basis until 1991, when tobacco cultivation was made compulsory. Eleven out of eighteen townships in the county were assigned tobacco-growing areas; only the townships in mountainous areas were spared, since they lacked the necessary conditions, such as mild temperature and secured grain output.

The implementation of the tobacco policy encountered a great deal of resistance from the peasants in Jinguan, however, where land resources are scarce and rice is regarded as essential for economic security. Tobacco production conflicted with their economic interests. Owing to their lack of experience with the crop and primitive technology, tobacco provided less income on average than grain grown on the same land,[15] and the labor input in tobacco cultivation is about three times as high as in rice farming. More important, in a local economy dominated by the principle that "one produces what one consumes and consumes what one produces," tobacco (compared to grain crops) offers little subsistence value to peasants. Despite the small area designated for tobacco cultivation (about 5 percent of the total arable land in 1991 and 10 percent in 1992), peasants in Jinguan expressed considerable resentment toward tobacco cultivation from the very beginning.

But for the county government of Yongsheng, tobacco is profitable, because it bears the highest tax of all agricultural products, amounting to 38 percent. Moreover, through its purchasing agencies in the townships, the county government has a monopoly on the sale of tobacco; there is no tobacco market outside government channels. This monopoly eliminates commercial competition and guarantees the control of profits by the local government, but it also has resulted in low peasant incomes from tobacco. In order to encourage township governments to implement the tobacco production policy, the county government provided economic incentives for the township government through a revenue-sharing arrangement. The county government allowed the lower level to retain a larger portion—up to two-thirds—of the tobacco revenue (see Table 4.1). In order to accomplish the task assigned to them by the county government, the township cadres in turn have resorted to coercive means and have issued strict quotas from the village down to households. When necessary, they have ordered that grain crop seedlings be pulled from the fields.

In some villages, the quotas were evenly distributed among all the households, while in others, the tobacco-growing area was concentrated in selected fields. In these cases, where the households with assignments did not want to grow tobacco, they were requested to turn over their plots designated for tobacco to the village. The plots were then recontracted to

TABLE 4.1

Jinguan Township Tobacco Income, Revenue, and Revenue Share, 1991
(yuan)

Gross income from tobacco	470,000
(as % of gross income from agriculture)	(1.6%)
Revenue from tobacco	150,000
(as % of total revenue from agriculture)	(32%)
Tobacco revenue retained at township	100,000
(as % of total revenue from tobacco)	(67%)
Revenue turned over to county	50,000
(as % of total revenue from tobacco)	(33%)

SOURCES: Jinguan Township statistics, 1992; interviews in 1992.

other households (who do not mind growing tobacco on extra land, since their own grain security is not affected). The recontracted plots involved various arrangements for rent (or fee) payments between the village, the subleasers, and the subleasees.

In 1992, the tobacco-growing area assigned to Jinguan was raised to 3,300 mu, which was more than double that of the previous year. In 1993, the assignment was further raised to 6,500 mu. While the local government seemed to be determined to further promote tobacco production, the campaign took a dramatic turn at the end of 1993, following a poor tobacco harvest caused by drought and pests. When the harsh terms set by the government agency on the purchasing price for tobacco brought further agony to the peasants, a number of them staged a public protest that disgraced the local authorities. In the following year, compulsory tobacco production was abandoned.[16]

In the course of the enforcement of tobacco production, property rights under the land contract were adjusted, and the rights of decision-making and management that it assigned to the household had restrictions imposed upon them. On the surface, this may only suggest a breach of contract on the side of the village collective. But with public ownership, ultimate control of land is vested, not in the village collective, but in the higher levels of government, and the rights of the village collective itself are often restricted.

The role of the village collective in the local implementation of tobacco policy in Jinguan shows the "fictitious" character of collective ownership; in fact, as Louis Putterman notes, "state and Party [exercise] real control over the management of 'collective' assets."[17] Because of its semicollective and semi-governmental nature, the village administration is subject to formal constraints imposed by the township government. Despite being bound by contract with the households, the village collective is obliged to breach those contracts when under pressure from the higher level of government, which reserves the power to appropriate collectively owned land through administrative decrees, if not by negotiation, regardless of the terms specified in the contract. Given that the village leadership is appointed by the township government and village leaders are on the township government's payroll, the village administration is unlikely to disobey orders from above.

Among the three categories (township government, village collective, and peasant households), the peasant households are the least powerful in the property relationship. Because land ownership is public, all parties understand that the use of land and any change in the land contract are subject to the will of the village collective. Such formal constraints are especially effective in that the legacy of socialist collectivization provokes uncertainty among the peasants about the land contract and fear of recollectivization.[18] The enforcement of tobacco production especially caused many peasants in Jinguan to wonder how long the household responsibility system would remain in force.[19]

Land contracts in Yongning contrast sharply with those in Jinguan. There the outcome can indeed be described as de facto privatization. Peasants in Yongning enjoy greater rights of control (in terms of decision-making and management) than those in Jinguan, without being subject to interference from either the township government or the village collective. On paper, however, land contracts look much as they do in Jinguan. The "three rights system" (state ownership, collective ownership, and individual user's rights) applies, and the need to meet subsistence needs and public and collective levies is specified. But in Yongning the delineation of these rights and responsibilities does not seem to be an issue, because most public duties are not enforced, and neither the township government nor the village collective seeks to impose constraints on land management. In fact, public duties were almost nonexistent in the early 1990s. Since Ninglang (under which Yongning is administered) had been designated an ethnic autonomous and poverty-stricken county, the agricultural tax exemption was implemented in 1985. Moreover, there was no enforcement of state grain procurement,[20] and the household contribution to collective funds was minimal.[21]

The absence of government control of land resources is not only reflected in the use of arable land per se, but also in the management of other collectively owned land resources, such as residential sites. In the 1960s, peasant residential sites (except for the property on the site, including house, shed, sty, coop, and plants) were defined as collective property owned by the production team.[22] This was reinforced by the Land Administration Law in the 1980s, which stipulates:

Rural residents shall use original house sites and idle lots in villages to build residences. If cultivated land needs to be used, the matter shall be subject to the examination and verification of people's governments at the township level and the approval of people's governments at the county level. Use of original house sites, idle lots and other land in villages shall be subject to approval of people's governments at the township level. . . . The land that rural residents use to build residences shall not exceed the standards set by provinces, autonomous regions, and municipalities directly under the Central Government.[23]

In Jinguan, the official standard for a residential site is 233 square meters (although in reality the average residential site may be larger, up to 350–400 square meters), and the peasants must apply to the village collective for permission, which has to be approved by the township government. In Yongning, the average peasant residence (in the Mosuo hamlets) is much larger than that in Jinguan.[24] According to the Yongning township cadres, there is a rule on the size of residential sites but it is not enforced. As a result, there is neither any procedure for peasants in Yongning to apply for permission nor any restriction on the size of the residential site they may choose to appropriate.[25]

The reduced public duties in both state taxes and collective funds and the absence of government control of land resources together contribute to the situation of de facto privatization in Yongning. In addition, owing to the special settlement pattern in Yongning, where homesteads are much dispersed around the basin, the village organization (*xingzheng cun*) is less effective in administration and management of local resources than in Jinguan. In the latter township, village administrations seem to have taken over the function of the previous production teams (which was more or less that of a hamlet or "natural village" [*ziran cun*]) in terms of resource control. In contrast, in Yongning, the hamlet remains the holder of the collective property and enjoys more rights of control than its counterpart in Jinguan. As a matter of fact, the hamlet leadership in Yongning exercises substantial rights of control over local resources, including allocating logging quotas, leasing mountain slopes for developing apple orchards, redistributing state subsidiary materials, organizing cooperative farming, and enforcing economic sanctions on households that violate local rules. Because it is elected and paid by the local residents, the hamlet leadership is not immediately subordinate to the township government. The social distance creates a space between the collective owner and the local government, which in a way makes the collective ownership less "fictitious."

Because there is little interaction between the local government and households, the land of ordinary peasants in Yongning is more their own than it is for peasants in Jinguan. The availability of land resources and the degree of government interference in the two townships are in sharp contrast. In Jinguan, where there is greater pressure on land resources, there is greater government interference with property rights in the community. In Yongning, where there is less pressure on land, there is an absence of government interference in the management of public resources in the community. While the degree of competition for the land must be taken into consideration, the degree of government interference in the two localities largely depends on the particular relationship between the state (the higher level of government) and the local government, and between the village and households, and on the incentives embedded in those relationships for the local administration. Such differences in local government behavior are also seen in the administration of township enterprises, as discussed below.

Township Enterprises and Their Political Jurisdictions

The economic development of northwest Yunnan is different from that in other parts of China in the sense that the output value of nonagricultural enterprises constitutes only a small portion of total output value. The national average output value of rural enterprises in 1992 amounted to 64 percent of the average gross output value of rural society, while the corresponding figure for Yunnan Province was 29 percent.[26] Northwestern Yunnan lags behind this provincial average. Neither Jinguan nor Yongning has any significant development of rural enterprises. In Jinguan in 1991, the gross income from local enterprises made up 10 percent of the total income of the township.[27] In Yongning, the gross income from local enterprises in 1991 corresponded to only 1 percent of the total income of the township.[28] While the development of local enterprises can hardly be considered economically important in this area, the government's involvement in local enterprises becomes more of a significant issue here.

The term *xiangzhen qiye* translated literally means "township enterprise," but it is commonly used to denote an entire category of nonstate enterprises, including those run by a collective (*jiti*), a private individual (*geti*), or joint households (*lianhu ban*).[29] Local governments have played a very important role, in one way or another, in the development of rural enterprises. However, the scale of the government's involvement and the means that the local government employs vary greatly from place to place. It has been argued that township (and village) enterprises in China have been largely government-owned and operated,[30] largely because of the government's role in local enterprises as investor, manager, and market regulator. But in neither Jinguan nor Yongning does the township government have the financial means to embark on such undertakings, given their poor economic conditions, and government involvement in local enterprises there assumes a different form.

Like the land contract, the issue of ownership involved in local enterprises is a matter of formal jurisdiction. In the two townships, differences in government administration result in different property relationships between township governments and local enterprises. In one place, the township government plays an active role in asserting its ownership of local enterprises, while in the other, the township government shows little interest in having anything to do with the local enterprises in either name or jurisdiction. The ownership of local enterprises either asserted or rejected by the township government illustrates from yet another angle how local authorities can manipulate economic resources, and how such manipulation serves the political careers of local officials. The central question concerning property rights in township enterprises discussed here is why de facto private and cooperative enterprises are categorized as township enterprises in one place, while in the other, de jure township government–owned enterprises are not. This chapter shows that the fundamental difference is rooted in what is locally called *zhengfu xingwei*, or "government behavior," which often implies "government interference," in other words, the formal jurisdiction of government.

In this area, each level of government administration has a specified category of *xiangzhen qiye*: there are county-run enterprises (*xianshu xiangzhen qiye*), township-run enterprises (*xiangzhenshu xiangzhen qiye*), and village-run enterprises (*cunshu xiangzhen qiye*). The modifying prefixes (*xianshu, xiangzhenshu,* or *cunshu*) indicate the involvement of government administration at different levels. Despite the statistical definitions and the actual management of enterprises (collective, private, or joint-household), the category of township enterprises often demonstrates certain flexibilities. The formal jurisdiction of the township government selectively includes some enterprises and excludes others. This local practice of property rights is directly related to the incentive structure determined by particular economic and political conditions.

Rural enterprises in different localities are treated differently by the government in accordance with their social and economic status. Yunnan is one of the "eight minority regions / provinces," which enjoy preferential treatment from the state in economic development.[31] Consequently, the development of rural enterprises in this area is likely to receive more state support from "specially earmarked funds" (*zhuanxiang bokuan*) and "taxation favors" (*shuishou zhaogu*). The "specially earmarked funds" used to

support rural enterprises include the *zhouzhuan jin* (circulating fund) obtained from loans granted from the higher level of government's extra-
budgetary funds, state development funds (known as centrally subsidized loans), and state financial subsidies to peripheral regions, especially
ethnic minority areas.[32] "Taxation favors" consist of tax reductions and
exemptions granted to rural enterprises in poor areas, especially in counties designated as poverty-stricken.[33] Obviously, not all rural enterprises
enjoy preferential treatment, given the limited funds available, and township enterprises are subject to selection by the local government for both
subsidies and tax breaks.

Unlike the enforcement of tobacco production discussed earlier, the
claim to township enterprises by the government works in the interest
of both parties. The relationship between the local government and the
township enterprises selected is based on mutual gain. While the government acquires administration fees (*guanli fei*) as a source of revenue, the
enterprises gain administrative support in their economic activities. Under these conditions, the enlisting of a township enterprise is sometimes
initiated by the government (interested in profitable enterprises as potential revenue sources) and sometimes by the enterprise itself (interested
in receiving preferential treatment). Once enlisted, township enterprises
are no longer considered private businesses in official terms. In this respect, the government administration is considered to have ownership,
which in many circumstances is not merely nominal. The selection of
enterprises to become township enterprises seems primarily based on
the economic concerns of the local government. Consequently, different
government administrations under different economic pressures under-
standably make different choices in their involvement with their so-called
township enterprises.

The official statistics show Jinguan with five "township enterprises"
(*zhenshu qiye*) in 1992, including a construction firm, a power station, a
machinery workshop, a garment manufacturer, and a zinc-smelting plant.
Although the township government had nothing to do with either the
management of production or the hiring of workers, all of these concerns
came to be designated as township-owned in one way or another.

The township construction firm was actually a privately managed business set up by a local entrepreneur in 1985, but became a "township enterprise" under an agreement with the township government, which charged
it an annual administration fee (Y 1,000 in 1992, increased to Y 3,000 in
1995). Construction workers were hired on a temporary basis whenever
there was a project, so the number of employees varied from year to year.
In 1992, the firm employed as many as 100 workers, including 5 or 6
managerial personnel.

In exchange for the administration fee it paid, the construction firm had the privilege of engaging in business in the name of the township government—for example, using the township government's official stationery for contracts. According to the township head, this gave it a competitive edge.

Apart from the administration fee, the construction firm was not subject to taxation. It is unclear whether the tax exemption was part of the preferential treatment received from the government as part of the agreement—Jinguan is under the jurisdiction of a financial deficit county. The township chief's explanation was that it was difficult to estimate the firm's income because most of its projects were contracted outside the township. In 1993, the construction firm grew larger and split into two. The newly established construction firm had the same agreement with the township government, except that it paid a bigger administration fee, perhaps arising from a more profitable business.

The power station was set up in 1965. The initial investment came from state-appropriated funds, but the enterprise has been cooperatively run. It has a dozen employees, and electricity charges are the major source of their income. The power station pays an annual administration fee (Y 1,000 in 1992, raised to Y 5,000 in 1995) to the township government and is thus classified as a township enterprise. Because this enterprise operates locally, there is no use of the official township letterhead involved, but given the importance of the enterprise, its construction and maintenance certainly require support from the township government, which has the power and the means to allocate subsidized materials and loans.[34]

The machinery workshop was first organized as an artisan association at the time of collectivization. The workers had urban household registration and received commercial grain rations. It had continued as a collective enterprise until the mid 1980s, when its business began to decline. The workshop was then dissolved, and the workers went into production on an individual basis. However, their incomes remained listed in the government statistics under the category of township enterprises. Because the sale of farm tools (the main product of the machinery repair shop) was never profitable, and the workers worked on an individual basis, there were neither any administration fees payable to the township government nor any subsidies or loans to individual workers. In 1996, the former employees of the machinery workshop requested that the assets of the workshop be auctioned off to provide pensions for the former employees (who have no land contract). Upon the approval of the township government, the transaction went through. Because the machinery workshop was a township enterprise in name, the township government took part in the sale by repossessing the premises of the former workshop.

The organization of the garment workshop is similar to that of the machinery workshop. It was established in 1956 as a collective enterprise and originally had some 100 workers. At the time of decollectivization, the workshop was dissolved and production was contracted to individual workers. Sewing machines were then allocated to the workers under contract. Though the production and distribution were no longer under the collective accounting system, the income of the individual workers was still included in the category of township enterprise in the government statistics. Because the income of the workers was low and individual garment production required little investment or subsidy, there was no administration fee charged by the township government. By 1995, there were only some 30 workers left. With the approval of the township government, the assets of the workshop (larger than those of the machinery workshop) were auctioned off to provide a pension fund for the workers. The total sale price was Y 120,000, from which the township government extracted Y 2,000, while the rest was allocated among the former workers.

The zinc-smelting enterprise was established in 1990–91. Seven households jointly organized the production. The workshop consisted of several crude smelting kilns built on publicly owned premises.[35] The land lease was a lump sum payment of Y 1,500 to the township government as a security deposit in case the land could not be recultivated when the zinc-smelting workshop was dissolved. In addition, there was an annual administration fee of Y 1,000 paid to the township government. In 1995, the zinc workshop applied for a change of status from a household jointly run enterprise to a township enterprise. In this deal, the township government acquired an annual administration fee of Y 5,000. In exchange, the zinc enterprise gained material supplies and market opportunities from the township government, in addition to "taxation favors."

The enterprises that are not categorized as township enterprises are called village, joint-household, or private enterprises. Village enterprises are those that lease land, hill slopes, fishponds, mountain woods, and so on from the village collective. Because of the nature of such collective enterprises (mainly engaged in agricultural production), these village enterprises are generally not subject to taxation. But they must pay administration fees (*guanli fei*) to the village administration for using the collective property. The joint-household enterprises are mostly brick kilns. The private enterprises are household-based and include transportation and grain-processing businesses, restaurants, and grocery stores. These two categories are subject to a business tax, usually a lump sum annual payment based on profit estimated by the township tax office. Because their production is independent and does not involve collectively managed resources, they normally do not pay administration fees to either the village collective or the township government.

While the statistics for Jinguan showed that the number of township enterprises expanded over the years, the 1992 township government statistics for Yongning show no township enterprises. Yet, in fact, there were two enterprises that were more qualified as "township enterprises" than any of the five enterprises in Jinguan, in terms of property management.

One of the enterprises is a yak farm established in 1958. The livestock were originally confiscated by the township government from the former Mosuo *tusi* ("aboriginal governor") and his wealthy relatives (locally called *sipi*), who were the biggest landowners next to the *tusi*. Under the ownership of the township government, the yak farm was operated under a collective accounting system, although yaks were at the time distributed to and raised by individual households living in the mountains. The yak farm was the only township enterprise in the government statistics until 1980. When the household responsibility system was implemented, the collective accounting system of the yak farm was dissolved, and the township government leased all 824 yaks to sixteen households. Under the present contract, the township government still owns the original 824 yaks and collects a rent or administration fee of Y 4 apiece each year, while profits from their reproduction belong to the lessees.

Another enterprise in Yongning, not listed as a township enterprise, but that provides the township government with a significant source of revenue, is the government guesthouse. It was built partly from the special development fund appropriated by the county government and partly from a central government interest-subsidized loan. The guesthouse has some two dozen rooms. Four of them are reserved by the township government for receiving official guests, and the rest are leased to a migrant worker from Sichuan, who has turned them into a public hotel. The lease specifies that a monthly rent/administration fee of Y 400 be paid to the township government. Together with the guesthouse, the township government has also leased out its canteen—an annex to the guesthouse—built from a separate fund of Y 30,000 appropriated by the county government, to the same entrepreneur, who has made it into a street restaurant. The canteen lease consists of a monthly rent/administration fee of Y 500 payable to the township government. These two leases together bring the township government more than Y 10,000 a year (twice as much as the highest administration fee extracted by the Jinguan township government from its most profitable enterprise).

One might argue that since the yak farm no longer had anything to do with the township government after its livestock were contracted out to herding households and production was organized on an individual basis, it should no longer be considered a township enterprise. But the yak herd is no less a township enterprise than the machinery and garment workshops in Jinguan (listed as township enterprises but with nothing to do with the township government in either contract or production). One might similarly argue, too, that the guesthouse is a government-run *jingji shiti* (economic entity), which is different from a township enterprise. In terms of the right to residual income, right of transferability, and right of control, however, the Yongning township government seems to have a lot more to do with the ownership of the guesthouse than the Jinguan township government does with any township enterprise there.

In 1995, two new township enterprises (*xiangshu qiye*) suddenly appeared for Yongning in the Ninglang county statistics, but no one in the county bureau of township enterprise management could tell what exactly they were. Presumably, one is the yak herd, and the other may be either the government guesthouse or a newly established firm. Questioning these two new entries, county officials concluded that the statistical inclusion of the two township enterprises by the Yongning township government may have been an administrative maneuver to acquire interest-subsidized loans from the higher level of government.

The different forms of government administration of local enterprises in the two townships have implications for local property rights. In the special arrangement between the Jinguan government and township enterprises, we see that the bundle of rights is somewhat modified. Like a household under land contract, a township enterprise has the right to dispose of residual income (paying wages, negotiating fees, and making investments). In terms of transferability, the rights become tricky. In theory, a township enterprise has the right to transfer or sell its own assets (which is different in nature from the property right in land). But, in reality, the township government must approve any large transaction of assets. This can be seen from the property settlements of the Jinguan machinery and garment workshops. In both transactions, not only did the decision to sell have to be made through the township government; it also took a share of the profits. As for the right of control, the township government basically does not interfere with the actual management of production (in contrast to its actions with regard to the land management). However, it may directly or indirectly affect the production management of the enterprise through its power to decide the amount of subsidies and other social and economic resources that an enterprise receives. It is therefore fair to say that in the management of township enterprises in Yongning, as in Jinguan, the township government partially holds the right of transferability as well as the right of control, two of the three components of the bundle of property rights. The relationship between the government and township enterprises is premised on this sharing of rights.

In a way, the relationship between township governments and enterprises can be described as a patron-client one.[36] It is an asymmetrical relationship where the dominant party—that is, the local government—is in a position to impose constraints. Because the county government issues loans and subsidies for township enterprises to the township government, it is up to the township government to decide which enterprises qualify as township enterprises and which receive loans and subsidies. At the same time, the patron-client relationship is one of exchange, in which mutual gains are acquired through negotiation, including special revenue for the local government and access to loans, market information, and tax breaks for the enterprise.[37] The amount of administration fees is determined each year through negotiations between the township government and enterprises.

Why does the local government choose to offer tax breaks, on one hand, and to collect administration fees, on the other? In other words, what difference does it make for the government to collect taxes or to collect fees? The answer lies in the way local government controls revenue. Although each category constitutes a source of government revenue, the channels for controlling taxes and fees are very different. Taxes, when imposed, are collected by the tax office and turned over to the higher levels of government, and only a certain specified amount (over-quota or according to a tax division arrangement) is allowed to be retained by the lower level of the government (although in some places where there is a financial deficit, certain percentages of taxes may be returned to make up the revenue insufficiency). While taxes are turned over and shared between the lower and higher governments, administration fees are retained at the local level and the income goes directly into the extra-budgetary funds at the disposal of the local government.

The incentives for the local government's involvement in township enterprises are further reflected in the change of status of township enterprises. Because there is economic interest involved in the government selection of township enterprises, under certain circumstances, it is in the interest of the government to recruit profitable enterprises while contracting out unprofitable government-owned enterprises.[38] Driven by the need to generate revenue, the amount of fees that an enterprise can afford to pay obviously becomes important. As a result, the focus of the government search for "township enterprises" is on those that are profitable. In the selection of township enterprises, the nature of ownership (collective, private, or government) is not really relevant.

In 1995, Jinguan township had some 900 enterprises in all categories.

Six of them were listed as "township enterprises" (*zhenshu qiye*).[39] The two unprofitable enterprises—the machinery and garment workshops—were no longer listed among the township enterprises when the number of profitable enterprises rose. The township enterprises included only three construction firms,[40] the power station, the zinc-smelting workshop, and an electroplating factory that was a private enterprise, which was formerly listed as a village-run enterprise. The annual administration fee that each of these enterprises pays to the township government is now 3–5 times the amount paid in 1992.

Aside from the acquisition of administration fees, the inclusion of the enterprises in statistics by the Jinguan township government to some extent also serves the career interests of local officials. Under the government administration responsibility system, the performance of township cadres is rated by their fulfillment of assigned quotas. Government statistics are a formal measure of how well their tasks have been completed. Specific categories such as "income from township enterprise" become an index demonstrating local economic growth. To ensure that they get good ratings on their administrative tasks, local governments have found it in their interests to manipulate their local statistics.

By comparison, in Yongning there is less administrative pressure on the local administration from the higher authorities. Local cadres are relatively secure in their positions, and punishments are rarely imposed. There is thus little need for cadres to worry about administrative achievements. The failure even to list existing township enterprises in Yongning is not necessarily an administrative strategy to maintain its poor economic status or to avoid taxes—its poverty status is unlikely to change for a long period of time. The relaxed administration of the Yongning township government is more directly related to the availability of state support for ethnic and poverty areas. Local officials there have little need to strive for revenue because insufficient revenue in the government budget is subsidized. These subsidies sometimes even extend to extra-budgetary funds, which in most other localities must be generated locally through the revenue-sharing system and by collecting fees.[41] The special treatment given to Yongning thereby eases the burden on the local government administration to generate revenue. Even if the township government needs to generate some extra-budgetary income, public resources (for example, the guesthouse funded by the state development funds) can always be exploited.

The administrative involvement of the local government in township enterprises suggests that our understanding of property rights needs to take the variation in ethnic status and poverty situation into consideration. With this variation, the availability and the degree of state support to a great extent affect the local notion of property rights. As the behavior of officials in Yongning suggests, this special designated status has an impact on the incentive structure for local officials, which further impinges upon local property rights. The following section will further detail how social and political factors have affected the forms that local property rights take.

Determinants of Variation in Property Rights

The success of the economic reforms in the rural sector has often been attributed to the incentives that fiscal reforms give local governments. Revenue-sharing has led to an expansion of the power and autonomy of local governments, giving them unprecedented control over resources.[42] The base of government power, however, varies across regions. In the wealthier coastal regions, local governments have been strengthened through the accumulation of revenue generated by rapidly developing local industry. In the poorer hinterlands, local governments have relied on state financial support; and in those areas where state support is limited and the development of local enterprises does not provide sufficient revenue, the local government resorts to exploiting the resources available— usually land—in a desperate attempt to generate revenue. In short, the economic behavior of government varies with the social and economic circumstances of the locality.

Different statuses—social and economic—determine the degree of autonomy with which local government can manipulate resources to its advantage. Jinguan and Yongning townships are both located in financial deficit counties, which constitute the majority of counties in Yunnan.[43] While in theory both county governments receive millions of yuan each year in "fixed amounts of financial subsidy" (*ding'e buzhu*) from the state to remedy budget deficits, the county designated autonomous-ethnic and poverty-stricken is entitled to additional preferential treatment. Owing to its special status, the "fixed amount of financial subsidy" does not apply in practice to Ninglang county, of which Yongning is a part, and its financial needs are instead generally met by negotiation, with the result that it receives more state support than the non-ethnic-poverty county.

As seen in Table 4.2, the state financial subsidy per capita in the ethnic-poverty county is almost twice as much as in the non-ethnic-poverty county. The larger amount of state subsidies also explains the higher government spending per capita in the ethnic-poverty county. This is why the government seat of the ethnic-poverty county is a modern town compared to that of the non-ethnic-poverty county; and why the ethnic minor-

TABLE 4.2

State Subsidies, Local Revenue, and Local Expenditure, 1991
(yuan)

	County with no special status	Ethnic-poverty county
State subsidies	23,410,000	26,210,000
Per capita	65.5	128.2
Locally generated revenue	14,940,000	8,000,000
Per capita	41.8	39.1
Local expenditure	41,450,000	34,170,000
Per capita	115.9	167.2

SOURCE: Interviews in both counties in 1992.

ity autonomous county government possesses more and fancier motor vehicles than any other county in the prefecture, despite being the only state poverty-stricken county in the prefecture.

In addition, being both an ethnic minority autonomous county and a state poverty-stricken county, the county in which Yongning lies receives a series of relief funds from the state to which non-ethnic-poverty counties are not entitled. These special funds include the "aid to developing areas fund" (*zhiyuan bufada diqu zijin*),[44] "operation expense subsidy to border regions" (*bianjing minzu shiyefei*),[45] "aid to work as relief" (*yigong daizhen*),[46] "development fund for the old-minority-border-poor areas" (*laoshaobian-qiong diqu fazhan zijin*),[47] and centrally funded interest-subsidized loans (*zhongyang tiexi daikuan*), which sometimes are known as "low-interest loans" (*dixi daikuan*).[48] From 1980 to 1996, the total amount of state relief funds appropriated to the ethnic-poverty county exceeded Y80 million.[49]

Apart from financial subsidies, the ethnic-poverty county also enjoys reduced public duties, as discussed earlier in the section on land contracts. Aside from the exemption from agricultural tax and nonenforcement of state procurement, the ethnic-poverty county receives a larger amount of state-resold grain.[50] The agricultural taxes paid and state-resold grain subsidies received by Jinguan township (in the non-ethnic-poverty county) and Yongning township (in the ethnic-poverty county) respectively are illustrated in Table 4.3.

In the autonomous-ethnic, poverty-stricken county, increased production inputs for meeting state procurement quotas, such as chemical fertilizer, go along with lower taxes. In Jinguan township, 8 kg of chemical fertilizer at the state-subsidized price is supplied for every 100 jin (50 kg) of grain procured; in Yongning, almost twice as much—15 kg—is supplied for the same amount of procured grain. In addition, there is an extra supply of 2 kg per person with contracted land and 7.5 kg per mu of area sown in corn.[51] These two subsidies are not available to Jinguan peasants. Moreover, these subsidies are granted in Yongning regardless of whether the grain procurement quota is met or not.

The special status of the ethnic minority and poverty-stricken county gives the local government a special relationship with the state. This affects the availability of state support and the behavior of the local government. Different incentives lead to different behavior. While the ethnic-poverty county can rely on the state to make up for its inadequate revenues, the non-ethnic-poverty county has to depend more on itself. Because the non-ethnic-poverty county cannot expect a high degree of state support, it exercises firm control over local resources. Under such circumstances, it puts pressure downward onto the village and households. As land is the major source of income, it is not only vital to the peasants as subsistence security, but also important to the local government as a source of revenue. In a predominantly agricultural area like Jinguan, growing cash crops presents an alternative way of increasing revenue income. This is why tobacco growing was made compulsory notwithstanding that this infringed upon the individual user's rights prescribed by the land contract.

Together with the fiscal reform that has provided the incentives for the local government to generate revenue, the administrative "responsibility system," called the "target administration system" (*mubiao guanli zerenzhi*), forms a concurrent impetus to the economic performance of the local officials. It contains two major tasks—"ideology" (*sixiang*) and "economy" (*jingji*). One hundred points mark the full accomplishment of the tasks in each category. Bonuses are awarded for high points, and salary cuts are imposed for low points. This provides tangible incentives for the compliance of local officials. In the countryside, where the main economic

TABLE 4.3

Agricultural Tax, Grain Procurement, and State-Resold Grain Subsidy
(kg)

	Jinguan	Yongning (in ethnic-poverty county)
Average agricultural tax[a]	40–50	exemption granted[b]
Total state grain procurement	2,527,513	344,867
Average grain procurement[c]	74	20
Total state-resold grain subsidized	17,835	190,385
State-resold grain per capita	0.5	11
State-resold grain in proportion to grain procurement	0.7%	55%

SOURCES: Jinguan Township statistics, 1992; Yongning Township statistics, 1992.
[a] Portion imposed on every mu of land under contract.
[b] Before the exemption, the average rate was 1 kg per mu of land.
[c] Portion contracted for every mu of land in Jinguan; no contract enforced in Yongning.

resources for the majority of the population are land and agriculture, the position of a government employee means privileges in both political and economic terms (not to mention leisure and comfort compared to farming); and the state payroll provides social security and welfare. Within this institutional framework, local officials are interested both in holding on to their jobs and in receiving bonuses.

The administrative responsibility system is supposedly implemented in both townships, but it has little effect in Yongning, which enjoys preferential treatment from the state. Instead of putting demands on villages and households to solve revenue shortages, the township government turns to the higher authorities for help, and it is therefore less motivated to extract revenue from land and develop township-owned enterprises. Shifting the burden upward yields better rewards with less effort than the strategy of putting pressure on the local community. So long as the county retains its ethnic minority status, preferential treatment in taxation and subsidies will continue, even if its poverty-stricken status is lost.[52] With the benefits that its dual status brings, local problems in Yongning are to a large extent taken care of by the higher authorities.[53]

The local officials in the non-ethnic-poverty county, on the other hand, are under greater pressure to achieve their economic goals for the sake of their careers. This pattern of behavior finds expression, not only in the government's direct interference in the management of land, such as by imposing tobacco quotas, but also in its relationship with the township enterprises. Although there is no coercive force used, the official claim on the township enterprises is an act of formal jurisdiction, wherein the actual ownership itself becomes irrelevant. By exerting administrative control over township enterprises, two purposes are achieved by local government: generating revenue and fulfilling assigned tasks under the administrative responsibility system.

The ability of the township government to mandate tobacco production and interfere with land contracts is a result of the expansion of local autonomy brought about by the economic reforms. The first year tobacco production became compulsory, a group of peasants in Jinguan lodged a complaint with the provincial government and pleaded for it to intervene. But the provincial government turned the case back to the county government and requested a local settlement. Although the petitioners were not subjected to any punishment (other than being forced to grow tobacco), the policy of the county government prevailed. The tobacco incident in Jinguan shows not only how much local government can interfere with the life of the local population, but also how much the behavior of local government is tolerated by the higher levels of the state.

Conclusions

Decentralization in the course of China's economic reforms has created a structure that is "small at both ends and big in the middle." This image reflects the relatively insignificant roles played by the central state and individuals in contrast to the powerful role assumed by government at the local levels. The land contract and the ownership of local enterprises in the two townships studied here have shown that the decisions made by local government are the main factor determining the implementation of property rights. This is an immediate consequence of the expansion of local autonomy. The power of local government presents itself in the claims, respectively, on the state, the collective, and individuals. As a consequence, administrative interference constrains property rights in various ways. Between the two townships, the differing levels of constraints determine the actual degree of the de facto privatization of land and the nature of the relationship between the local government and township enterprises.

As we have seen, in the local implementation of land contracts and statistical categorization of township enterprises, the allocation of rights is sometimes inconsistent with the actual ownership of property and management of resources. The inconsistency is mainly caused by administrative constraints on property rights, and as a result, ambiguity emerges. This is why in the implementation of land contracts in Jinguan, the administrative constraints assumed the form of coercion, and under such constraints, the collective ownership of land became irrelevant. Because the administrative constraints cause ambiguity in property rights, a series of rights contracted to the peasants were subject to redefinition and adjustment in the case of tobacco production. As this study has shown, what really matters in property rights is not ownership per se but the jurisdiction of the local government that serves as the legitimate base for economic intervention.

Local categorization of township enterprises is also subject to administrative manipulation. In both Jinguan and Yongning, the local categorization of township enterprises is nothing but an expression of government jurisdiction. As regards local property rights in township enterprises, the incentive system works both ways. To the government, the recruitment of township enterprises means an increase in revenue, in addition to fulfilling administrative tasks and passing administrative performance reviews. To the individual enterprises, inclusion in the category of township enterprise means special privileges—social and economic—that are not available through the market. In this relationship, both parties have something to offer and something to gain.

Our comparison of two localities has shown the ways in which local governments shape property rights in response to two kinds of incentives: administrative pressure and the availability of state support, both related to the presence or absence of ethnic poverty status. When such state support is unavailable, this puts greater pressures on local government: therefore Jinguan township exerted more control over land and township enterprises, while Yongning township seeks resources from above and allows local communities greater autonomy in developing local resources. As a result, different patterns of property rights have emerged in the two localities.

Paradoxically, the involvement of government administration does not seem to have presented an obstacle to the local development of township enterprises. This, however, does not address the issue of whether government control, or partial control, of property rights creates efficiency or not. "Institutions are not necessarily or even usually created to be socially efficient; rather they, or at least the formal rules, are created to serve the interests of those with the bargaining power to create new rules," Douglass North argues.[54] The present study of land and township enterprises has illustrated how the incentive structure in rural China has created a framework of new rules for local government to interfere with property rights, and how the new rules have created a new form of power for local officials.[55]

In this view, the claim that transition to a market economy has changed the sources of power and privilege needs to be modified.[56] Although it is in general true that government control over economic resources declines with a shift to a market economy, one still needs to explain the varying continued roles played by government in the market economy.[57] The analysis of local property rights in land and township enterprises in this chapter suggests that the bureaucratic system continues to play an important role in regulating local economic activities, and clearly there is an incentive structure for it to do so. With the involvement of local government and its decisive role, competition among enterprises exists not only in the market but also in striving for preferential treatment from the government administration.

While ownership is not a simple dichotomy of public and private in China's transitional economy, ownership in Yongning and Jinguan has yet to evolve into forms that can be clearly defined. This study of land contracts and township enterprises suggests that whatever ownership form exists, the reality is that government and individual / private management play a joint role.

Chapter 5

The Evolution of Property Rights in Village Enterprises: The Case of Wuxi County

JAMES KAI-SING KUNG

The ownership of China's township and village enterprises (TVEs) has recently been a subject of immense interest to those concerned with the relationship between property rights and economic development. Although lacking the exclusive private rights allegedly required for successful economic development, the strong interests that local government officials have in generating revenues from TVEs has arguably powered the engine of growth of these community-based enterprises.[1] Drawing on a small sample of sixteen villages in Wuxi County, a site where most, if not all, of the village enterprises are genuinely owned and controlled by the village government, this chapter confirms, with survey data, earlier claims about the active role of village officials in enterprise development.[2] For example, it shows that while cadres are not directly involved in managing the village enterprises, they appoint the managers in the majority of instances, decide their incomes, assist the enterprises in procuring loans, and are at least partially responsible for enterprise investment decisions. My findings detail how property rights are partitioned between the main actors involved in the enterprise relationship.

But the allocation of rights is not static: it changes in response to changes in the overall business environment. Indeed, a striking feature of the evolution of property rights in the sixteen sample villages is that the majority, 75 percent, have in recent years privatized their smaller, marginally profitable, if not unprofitable, enterprises, transferring the right to claim residual profits to individuals.[3] Such a high incidence of privatization must further be seen against the background that Wuxi is, by Chinese standards, the heartland of local state corporatism. It is a county that has, at least up to the late 1980s, put great emphasis on the development of collective enterprises.[4] This chapter examines the main reasons behind these villages' decision to privatize some of their enterprises and the characteristics of the enterprises that have undergone privatization. It considers whether the observed phenomena can be adequately explained by available economic theory.

Where markets are underdeveloped, as was the case in rural China during the 1980s, access to resources is determined primarily by personal connections, or *guanxi*, rather than by impersonal, arm's-length transactions. That being the case, local cadres are thus in an advantageous position vis-à-vis enterprise managers with respect to both procuring scarce production factor inputs and marketing the output.[5] This explains why strategic decisions, according to the results of my survey, are typically made by the local officials, whereas routine managerial responsibilities are delegated to the enterprise managers. But the development of markets in an increasingly competitive business environment has altered this status quo, leading to an unambiguous trend of privatization.

As markets develop, the relational-specific *guanxi* input formerly supplied by local cadres has become less important as it is gradually replaced by arm's-length transactions undertaken by the enterprise manager. And as competition intensifies and the number of village enterprises multiplies and businesses expand, sound enterprise performance relies increasingly on the efforts of the manager. Where these changes have been most profound, they significantly undermine the cadres' role in enterprise management, as they become less knowledgeable about the enterprises' true capabilities. But with managerial compensation held in check by powerful egalitarian social norms embedded in the village community and the perception that the villagers are owners, local cadres have been constrained to remunerate enterprise managers proportionately to the latter's contribution, as is evidenced in the narrow spread of incomes—a ratio of less than three—between managers and workers. As will be seen later, many enterprise managers therefore sought to maximize their own nonpecuniary benefits rather than profits, eventually leading many village authorities to give up their claim to residual profits from smaller enterprises, while retaining ownership and control of the larger, strategic ones. In addition to shedding light on the decision to privatize, the second, more important objective of this chapter is thus to shed light on the evolution of property rights in village enterprises in Wuxi over time.[6]

The Sample Villages

Wuxi County was chosen primarily because it epitomizes an important rural development model in post-reform China, one that relies heavily on the collective initiatives of local officials in spearheading township and village economic growth (the "southern Jiangsu model," or *sunan moshi*). The predominance of collective enterprise ownership in this particular region allows us to rigorously test the issues pertaining to enterprise behavior under government ownership.[7]

There are altogether thirty-five townships in Wuxi County, of which four were selected as field sites. Since one of my objectives was to cover as many institutional variants as possible, the four townships we chose loosely represent the top, middle, and bottom performers in Wuxi County. Table 5.1 gives a crude picture of how these townships performed in 1993 on the basis of eight economic indicators.[8] Luoshe township, which lies to the west of the main railway line, is clearly the top performer in my sample, with Gangxia township, located in the northeastern corner of the county, following closely. Further down the hierarchy of economic performance is Qianqiao township, an average performer by the county standard, al-

TABLE 5.1

Township Rankings According to Economic Indicators, 1993

	Qianqiao	Luoshe	Gangxia	Luqu
GNP	22	2	5	31
(in million yuan)	(256.53)	(758.58)	(590.23)	(187.36)
Per capita GNP	25	7	6	28
(in million yuan)	(77.18)	(140.91)	(142.75)	(70.95)
Gross output value of industry and				
agriculture	12	2	7	31
(in million yuan)	(1369.02)	(2670.73)	(1861.47)	(604.49)
Gross industrial output value	12	2	7	31
(in million yuan)	(1349.07)	(2637.24)	(1817.76)	(578.99)
Gross industrial sales revenue	11	3	7	30
(in million yuan)	(1328.90)	(2331.06)	(1509.82)	(537.40)
Gross profits and taxes	35	11	5	29
(in million yuan)	(−10.54)	(79.49)	(115.76)	(24.04)
Industrial net output value	18	3	1	26
(in million yuan)	(191.98)	(483.93)	(516.25)	(134.39)
Ratio of sales to output value	28	5	11	15
(as percentage)	(90.11%)	(95.95%)	(93.73%)	(92.75%)

SOURCE: *Wuxi xian tongji nianjian, 1993* [Statistical yearbook of Wuxi County, 1993] (Wuxi: Wuxi County Statistical Bureau, 1994), pp. 662–72.
NOTE: There are altogether 35 townships in Wuxi County.

TABLE 5.2

Selected Indicators of Village Enterprise Economies in Four Sampled Townships, 1994

Township	Village	(1)	(2)	(3)	(4)	(5)	(6)	(7)	(8)	(9)	(10)
Qianqiao	Shengfeng	184.78	183.68	1,713	13	1,430	1,040.00	6,071.20	4,026.00	15,000.00	3.73
Qianqiao	Xizhang	177.60	175.35	2,760	19	1,200					
Qianqiao	Xiaoxing	59.00	56.87	1,902	20	811	488.00	2,565.70	3,158.00	9,205.00	2.91
Qianqiao	Weihua		100.56	1,898	10		756.00	3,983.00			
Luoshe	Bingkou		285.29	2,295	13	1,418	1,365.00	5,947.70	7,503.00	28,961.00	3.86
Luoshe	Qianxiang		150.00	1,991	11	828	543.00	2,727.30			
Luoshe	Xinkaihe	147.65	146.00	2,357	6	1,221	2,358.00	10,004.20	6,077.00	27,880.00	4.59
Luoshe	Hongmin	163.63	161.05	2,647	9	825	1,889.00	7,136.40	5,397.00	25,000.00	4.63
Gangxia	Lujiatang	55.60	52.81	2,297	8	408	270.00	1,175.40	3,678.00	6,605.00	1.80
Gangxia	Chenxu	137.09	135.00	2,973	3	1,080	753.00	2,532.80	4,100.00	2,100.00	0.51
Gangxia	Shanqian	42.00	40.55	2,040	4	841	205.00	1,004.90	3,276.00	5,810.00	1.77
Gangxia	Zhangmiaoshe	204.98	202.58	2,451	8	1,500	1,075.00	4,386.00	4,500.00	5,800.00	1.29
Luqu	Zhuji		20.55	2,314	8	396	202.00	872.90	3,380.00	18,000.00	5.33
Luqu	Yinzheng	17.04	15.47	1,788	6		222.00	1,241.60	5,000.00	9,500.00	1.90
Luqu	Huayuan	47.60	46.50	1,452	9	440	320.00	2,203.90	6,000.00	15,000.00	2.50
Luqu	Shengan	38.00	35.00	453	3	280	355.00	7,836.60	6,800.00	10,000.00	1.47
Mean		106.25	118.17	2,083	9	717	740.06	3,552.20	4,193.00	12,360.06	2.79
Standard deviation		68.72	82.74	593	5	520	137.06	0.23	2,151.41	9,652.95	1.50

NOTE: Column heads are (1) gross output value of village economy (million yuan); (2) industrial enterprise output value (million yuan); (3) population (number of persons); (4) number of enterprises (n = #); (5) number of enterprise workers (n = #); (6) village enterprise profits (10,000 yuan); (7) per capita village enterprise profits (yuan); (8) mean wages of enterprise workers (yuan); (9) mean income of enterprise managers (yuan); and (10) ratio of enterprise manager's-to-worker's income.

though it is conveniently located near the county seat. Luqu township's performance pales in comparison with the economic progress of the other three sample townships, a result to some extent attributable to its remote location on the border of Wuxi and neighboring Wujing County. A total of sixteen villages were in turn chosen from the four sample townships. Based on the same economic indicators used in the township ranking, data for these villages confirm the above pecking order (see Table 5.2).

Property Rights in Wuxi Village Enterprises

Rather than referring to official ownership categories, a more fruitful approach to the study of property rights in China's village enterprises is to examine in empirical detail the bundle of rights held by different parties to the various aspects of control that collectively define the firm's ownership. A salient feature of the institutional arrangements of village enterprises in Wuxi has been the substantial retention of control rights by village Party secretaries over the strategic aspects of enterprise management. In addition to directly appointing enterprise managers and deciding on their incomes, these senior village officials play a key role in the decision-making process pertaining to enterprise investment and loan procurement, among other managerial responsibilities. In short, although cadres are not directly involved in day-to-day enterprise management, the latter still demands a lot of direct effort from them. For the more troublesome, less profitable enterprises, which contributed little revenue to the village coffers, the amount of effort incurred by these senior leaders is not justified from the standpoint of organizational efficiency. It was the high costs of monitoring enterprise managers that predisposed village authorities to shed these unprofitable enterprises. As a prelude to understanding how problems pertaining to managerial supervision have led to privatization, the remainder of this section looks at how much control of enterprise management village Party secretaries initially exercised.

The first question is whether village leaders are directly involved in managing their enterprises, in the same manner as capitalists would monitor their own firms. To the extent that the answer is negative, it implies the need to assign some management rights to the manager, in which case the village authority will likely face the classic problem posed by the separation of ownership and control. Table 5.3 (panel a) shows that this is indeed the case, as the majority of village Party secretaries, twelve, or 75 percent, are not ordinarily involved in managing the enterprises,[9] but delegate such responsibilities to the chosen managers instead.[10] Since the majority of enterprise managers, 81 percent (Table 5.3, panel b), are directly

TABLE 5.3

Allocation of Control Rights Between Village Cadres and Enterprise Managers

a. Do cadres directly manage the village enterprises?

		n	%
i.	Yes	3	18.8
ii.	No	12	75.0
iii.	No answer	1	6.3

b. How are enterprise managers chosen?

		n	%
i.	Directly appointed by the Party branch secretary	13	81.3
ii.	Elected by villagers	1	6.3
iii.	By competitive bidding	0	0.0
iv.	Both (i) + (iii)	2	12.5

c. Who decides enterprise managers' income?

		n	%
i.	Village cadres	14	87.5
ii.	Enterprise employees	1	6.3
iii.	The enterprise manager herself	0	0.0
iv.	Both (i) + (iii)	1	6.3

d. Who makes decisions regarding major enterprise investments?

		n	%
i.	The enterprise manager	3	18.8
ii.	Village cadres	5	31.3
iii.	Enterprise employees	0	0.0
iv.	Both (i) + (ii)	8	50.0

e. Who is responsible for obtaining credit for the enterprise?

		n	%
i.	The enterprise manager herself	6	37.5
ii.	The village authority	4	25.0
iii.	Contributions from enterprise employees	0	0.0
iv.	Both (i) + (ii)	6	37.5

f. Personnel decisions are usually made by:

		n	%
i.	The enterprise manager	13	81.3
ii.	Village cadres	2	12.5
iii.	Both (i) + (ii)	1	6.3

g. Who makes decisions about employment and wages?

		n	%
i.	Village cadres	2	12.5
ii.	The enterprise manager	8	50.0
iii.	Both (i) + (ii)	6	37.5

TABLE 5.3

(*continued*)

h. Who do you consider the owner of village enterprises?

		n	%
i.	The village government	3	18.8
ii.	All the villagers	11	68.8
iii.	Cannot say for sure	1	6.3
iv.	Both (i) + (ii)	1	6.3

NOTE: The Party branch secretaries of sixteen villages were asked the above questions in a questionnaire in November 1995.

appointed by the Party branch secretary, who also determines managerial income in most instances (88 percent) (Table 5.3, panel c), he is undoubtedly the most powerful person in the village community.[11]

To see why market competition would create pressures to change enterprise ownership, it is important to recognize the inherent tensions or constraints the Party branch secretary faces in setting the enterprise manager's income. On the one hand, the village Party secretary needs to consider carefully the opportunity costs facing the enterprise manager, which have risen in an increasingly liberalized economic environment. On the other hand, he needs also to balance this concern for managerial incentives against informal constraints. Managerial income is powerfully checked by villagers' perceptions of fairness.[12] This kind of informal constraint exacerbates the classic principal-agent relationship and predisposes village authorities to sell their unprofitable firms.

Although the Party branch secretary has delegated management rights to the enterprise manager, he is not completely divorced from managing the enterprises, especially with respect to procuring bank loans and making major investment decisions (Table 5.3, panels d and e). The finding that in half of the reported cases investment decisions are made jointly by the enterprise manager and the local Party boss can be explained by the peculiar nature of ownership in village enterprises; namely, that the former is not the residual claimant in terms of financial risk-bearing. This also explains why, in the remaining cases where such decisions were made by only one party (31 percent, *n* = 5), it was usually the village Party secretary rather than the enterprise manager.

Further inquiry reveals that these villages are either among the largest industrialized village economies in my sample in terms of enterprise output value—such as Bingkou (first) and Shengfeng (third)—or, at the other extreme, among the smallest—such as Huayuan (twelfth), Yinzheng (sixteenth), and Lujiatang (eleventh). This finding is not surprising given that it is easier in smaller than in bigger village economies to retain tight control over enterprise management. It would be more instructive to examine the manner in which control rights are exercised in the big industrialized villages, which can be illustrated by the interesting, if atypical, case of Bingkou.

Bingkou is unusual in that its village economy is managed by a native entrepreneur, who first started a number of industrial enterprises in the 1970s and later founded the Yaxi Conglomerate, of which he is director. And yet these enterprises are not regarded as private, but as owned collectively by the entire village community. Of the Y 285 million worth of industrial output value produced in this village in 1994, this giant conglomerate accounted for Y 200 million, or close to 80 percent. In this village, new investment opportunities were mostly identified with Zhu *laozong* (or chief executive officer, as he is respectfully addressed), the local entrepreneur. Zhu appointed competent supervisors from existing enterprises he founded to become managers of new ventures. This allowed the number of enterprises in the village to multiply and become independent profit centers, resembling those of a multi-divisional firm, in the thriving local economy, as well as leaving Zhu in overall control.[13]

An interesting aspect of the development process in this village is that Zhu has recently been nominated to become a Communist Party member and, in fact, the Party branch secretary. Amazingly, Zhu had remained politically independent notwithstanding his phenomenal business success. However, according to a township cadre who accompanied us on the village visit, "it would be more convenient for someone like Zhu to acquire a formal [meaning political] status" for legitimacy's sake. Indeed, with business and communist politics so closely linked, the wearing of a "red hat" can confer tremendous, although intangible, political security to an entrepreneur.[14] But this political "baptism" benefits the Party, too, in that it now "internalizes" scarce entrepreneurial talents, and possibly wealth, like Zhu's. Such entrepreneurs are thus included among the Party's valuable assets.

As with enterprise investment decisions, credit market imperfections have similarly obliged the village Party secretary to play an active role in loan procurement (Table 5.3, panel e).[15] Although only a quarter of my subjects are assuming this critical function in isolation, the magnitude soars to 63 percent if we include cases in which both parties jointly carry out this function. In the six cases where the enterprise manager is the only party responsible for obtaining credit, only one, Zhuji village, is located at the bottom of the hierarchy in terms of enterprise output value. The remaining ones—Chenxu, Xizhang, Xinkaihe, Zhangmiaoshe, and Qianxiang—are big industrialized village economies with sizable enterprise output value (see Table 5.2). The precise reasons why these radically different villages are clustered together with respect to this particular function are not entirely clear. One possibility is that managers of large enterprises in these wealthier villages may behave more like private entrepreneurs than their counterparts in smaller enterprises do, because they may have acquired greater independence in obtaining inputs, such as credits from local financial institutions. For example, in Xinkaihe, there are only six enterprises, but in 1994 they collectively employed 1,221 workers, averaging well over 200 employees per enterprise. In addition, the enterprise manager-to-worker income ratio there was the second highest among the sample villages that year. Both these indicators tend to lend support to the foregoing conjecture. We may reasonably expect village cadres to typically assume the gatekeeping role in small, tightly knit communities, where managers of village enterprises directly approach their superiors for the required funds.

In addition, smaller, less industrialized village economies such as Yinzheng and Zhuji, located in the less affluent township of Luqu, are, according to their cadres, often forced to rely on their own savings and investments to finance development. The main reason they do not find it as easy to obtain credit as their more industrialized counterparts, I surmise, is that being small and presumably less competitive, they are regarded by financial institutions as carrying greater credit risks—a phenomenon some economists call "credit rationing."[16] (Although intuitively plausible, however, this explanation must be treated as speculative.)

If village cadres are heavily involved in enterprise management, what then is left of the dimensions over which enterprise managers are able to exercise control? Are they allowed to make decisions pertaining to personnel management, for instance? The fact that 81 percent of the enterprise managers were found to be in sole charge of this function (Table 5.3, panel f) suggests that this may indeed be the case. However, such a finding is deceptive. First, the overall enterprise wage bill is determined at the outset by the local Party boss based on such major enterprise indicators as profits, sales, output value, and tax remittances. Second, to the extent that village enterprises are genuinely owned by the village authority, local cadres are typically responsible for assigning jobs among villagers, who, under ordinary circumstances, are eligible for employment in these non-agricultural enterprises. These arrangements are partially reflected in Table 5.3 (panel g), which shows that in half of the cases, decisions concerning employment and wages were, at best, jointly made by the village Party secretary and the enterprise manager, suggesting that the independence of enterprise managers from their local Party bosses, even in this less strategic respect, may be more apparent than real.[17]

Summing up, enterprise managers are largely in charge of day-to-day operations, leaving the key control rights, as well as right to dispose of residual profits, in the hands of village officials, in particular the Party branch secretary. Although such property rights arrangements prove to work well when competition is limited and business transactions rely heavily on the input of village officials, this kind of highly centralized institution nonetheless requires substantial supervisory effort from them. This explains why village officials are predisposed to shed some of their smaller, especially poorly managed enterprises when things have taken a turn for the worse. The best way to motivate managers to work hard without personal supervision by village Party secretaries is to sell them the right to residual profits.

Social Norms and Property Rights

Privatization is also a response to village social norms and the "collective" nature of village enterprises. The preference of villagers for a "fair" or equal income distribution scheme has limited the ability of village officials to remunerate managers according to their contributions to enterprise performance, and the perception that villagers are the nominal owners of the enterprises in which they are employed has made it difficult for village officials and enterprise managers to discipline the workforce.

While we may regard the social norm of egalitarian income distribution as simply a product of the Maoist legacy,[18] it is deeply embedded in the ownership structure of village enterprises. Seeing themselves as the nominal owners of these "collective" enterprises, villagers have refused to accept large income differentials between the manager and themselves. Although village officials have control rights over enterprise management, they are nonetheless constrained by these perceptions, which have effectively resulted in property rights being split between village officials and villagers. The Party branch secretary of Shengfeng village eloquently states the constraining effects of these powerful social norms:

> Enterprise managers' incomes are constrained by people's perception of fairness. You cannot reward managers simply on the basis of how much profit they bring in; to do so straightforwardly would invite suspicions, if not outright criticisms, that we must have been part of an illegitimate plot to siphon money from the village's coffers into our own pockets. This is an issue that we need to deal with very carefully.

In point of fact, the income spread between managers and workers in the majority of villages was rather narrow, amounting to an average of less than 3:1, and in the case of smaller, presumably less affluent townships such as Luqu, it was even narrower (see Table 5.2, col. 10).

Similarly, the "collective" nature of village enterprises has made workforce discipline a serious problem. As an informant explained, an important reason why some workers are predisposed to shirk on the job is because "they see themselves as owners of the collective firm, a status that accordingly gives them the inherent right to be employed; poor work attitude and performance, in other words, cannot therefore be a cause for dismissal as long as these enterprises are owned by the village."

That villagers regard themselves as owners of village enterprises is well corroborated by the evidence of how the village Party secretaries view the ownership issue. In responding to the question of who owns the village enterprises, the majority of respondents, 69 percent, refer to "all the villagers" (*quanti cunmin*) instead of the village government as owners, despite their own heavy involvement in enterprise management (Table 5.3, panel h).[19] Although this is doubtless the politically correct answer to give, such perceptions may be partially explained by the fact that, unlike the township administration, the village is basically a self-governing organization, a semi-governmental body with no formal authority to pass local legislation, and no budget that is subject to fiscal scrutiny from above.[20]

Such differences are further reinforced by the much larger size of townships. Consisting of thousands of households, a township is hardly a community with the organic cohesiveness of a typical village, in which job entitlement is a public good desired by everyone. This is partially responsible for the different perceptions of job entitlement in townships. "The relationship between a township enterprise manager and workers is a much more straightforward one, involving little more than the provision of and response to pecuniary incentives," an informant remarked. "After all, before they have their household status [*hukou*][21] changed, many township residents have, until recently, been villagers."

Last, but not least, while the manager of an unprofitable township enterprise may be assigned to a less preferable job, he is at least spared the peer pressure that the village Party secretary has to bear from villagers who have lost their jobs. The same informant put the difference succinctly in perspective once again:

> True, the township enterprise manager may have to face the grim prospect of job reassignment, but that is precisely what saves him from having to live with the unceasing pressure that the village Party secretary will inevitably face in the event a village enterprise goes under, in which case the burden falls disproportionately upon him. Unlike the township enterprise manager, the village Party secretary is usually a native villager and a permanent resident in his home village, and as such he is subject to villagers' collective judgment even after he steps down as village leader.[22]

This picture of village Party secretaries as prisoners of their own villages helps capture the subtle behavioral differences that must be noted in distinguishing township from village enterprises and is basic to understanding the nature of property relations in China's village economy. These constraints on village Party secretaries go a long way toward explaining why, in choosing among institutional alternatives, cadres have increasingly opted for privatization as opposed to the shareholding system.

The Evolution of Property Rights: Agency Problems and Privatization

As mentioned earlier in the chapter, the high incidence of privatization in the sixteen sample villages, as summarized in Table 5.4, must be viewed in the context of the fact that Wuxi is, by Chinese standards, the heartland of local state corporatism and famous for concerted development of collectively owned enterprises.

A good starting point for understanding the main reasons behind such privatization is to examine changes in the macroeconomic environment within which village enterprises operate. In seeking to explain the success of township and village enterprises in the 1980s, many see as pivotal

TABLE 5.4

Privatization of Enterprises in Sixteen Sampled Villages, 1994

Township	Village	Privatization[a]	Total (n)	Nature of ownership		
				(1)	(2)	(3)
Qianqiao	Shengfeng	Yes	11	11	0	0
Qianqiao	Xizhang	Yes	19	13	0	6
Qianqiao	Xiaoxing	Yes	20	0	16	4
Qianqiao	Weihua	Yes	10	0	8	2
Luoshe	Bingkou[a]	Yes	13	13	0	0
Luoshe	Qianxiang[a]	Yes	11	0	11	0
Luoshe	Xinkaihe[a]	Yes	6	6	0	0
Luoshe	Hongmin	Yes	9	8	0	1
Gangxia	Lujiatang	No	8	0	8	0
Gangxia	Chenxu	No	3	3	0	0
Gangxia	Shanqian[a]	Yes	4	4	0	0
Gangxia	Zhangmiaoshe	No	8	8	0	0
Luqu	Zhuji	Yes	8	0	5	3
Luqu	Yinzheng	Yes	6	0	4	2
Luqu	Huayuan	Yes	9	4	0	5
Luqu	Shengan	No	3	3	0	0

NOTE: Numbered column heads are (1) collectively owned and managed; (2) collectively owned but leased out for management; and (3) private enterprises.

[a]Privatization in Bingkou, Qianxiang, Xinkaihe, and Shanqian occurred in 1995 and is therefore not reflected in 1994 statistics.

TABLE 5.5

Profit Rates in Sixteen Sampled Villages, 1981, 1988, and 1994

Village	1981	1988	1994
Shengfeng	.20	.16	.06
Xizhang			.00
Xiaoxing	.06	.15	.09
Weihua	.22	.06	.08
Bingkou		.07	.05
Qianxiang	.10	.04	.04
Xinkaihe	.10	.11	.17
Hongmin	.09	.12	.12
Lujiatang	.00	.02	.05
Chenxu	.10	.15	.06
Shanqian	.24	.33	.05
Zhangmiaoshe	.10	.11	.05
Zhuji	.09	.13	.10
Yinzheng	.15	.18	.14
Huayuan	.10	.02	.07
Shengan		.09	.10
Mean	0.12	0.12	0.08
Mean output value	1.19	17.90	112.70
Correlation coefficients between	.0737	− .3563	− .3583
enterprise profit rates and output	(.811)	(.192)	(.173)
value (level of sig.)			

the ability of TVEs to respond to market needs, on the one hand, and their institutional advantages over privately owned enterprises, especially with respect to obtaining credit, on the other.[23] The unambiguous effect of the growing importance of this nonstate sector on state-owned enterprises, according to Barry Naughton,[24] is the erosion or equalization of profits. History, it seems, *does* repeat itself. What happened to the SOEs in the 1980s is now happening to township- and village-owned enterprises, as the competitive pressures emanating from the rural private-sector economy increasingly confront them. This argument will be borne out by both statistical analysis and the verbal comments of village cadres detailed below.

Table 5.5 shows the profit rates, obtained by dividing enterprise profits by their output value, of all the enterprises in the sixteen sample villages for three selected years. The aggregate data unambiguously show that villages on the whole were able to maintain overall profit rates of roughly 12 percent up to the year 1988, but subsequently dropped to single-digit profit rates by 1994. With the exception of Xinkaihe village in Luoshe township, which experienced robust growth in profit rates even after 1988, we otherwise see a basically similar pattern when we disaggregate the data at the village level. In order to ascertain if differences in profit rates between the three time periods are statistically significant, an F-test was performed. The results, reported also in Table 5.5, are consistent with what one would intuitively expect: there is no difference in profit rates between 1981 and 1988, but significant variations are found between 1981 and 1994, and, more relevant, between 1988 and 1994. Many of the sample villages were unable to maintain the double-digit profit rates they had previously enjoyed.

Ironically, this secular trend of declining village enterprise profits occurred against a background where enterprise output value continued to increase in absolute terms. In 1981, the mean enterprise output value was just under Y 1.2 million, but by 1988, it had soared to almost Y 18 million, and in 1994, to almost Y 113 million (Table 5.5, penultimate row).[25] Since expansion in an increasingly competitive market environment might be an important reason for dwindling enterprise profits, a correlation coefficient analysis between the two variables, namely, profit rates and output value, was done for the three selected years, which showed that they correlated with one another positively in 1981, but negatively in both 1988 and 1994 (Table 5.5). Although the results are statistically insignificant, owing perhaps to the small size of the sample, this may nevertheless be taken to support my conjecture. Albeit anecdotal, the following remarks made by the Party branch secretary of Shengfeng, a village whose profits were severely eroded between 1988 and 1994, corroborates this: "Market competition is the main force driving down village enterprise profits in recent years. To be sure, output value has increased, but there has not been comparable growth in profit rates."

Why the expansion of village enterprise business should have led to declining profit rates is not clear. Diminishing returns to management as the size of the operation increases may be one cause, and increasing competition from private enterprises may be another. Available village-level evidence indicates that the smaller, ill-managed enterprises were the targets of privatization. As cadres in Hongmin and Yinzheng villages separately explained:

> The two enterprises that we have sold were not actually operating in the red, but they were not particularly well managed either. The dealings involved did not amount to much. What was worse, since transactions were usually in cash, it was very difficult for us to know the accurate profit figures. These enterprises were making profits of a little more than Y 100,000, of which enterprise managers were remitting a meager Y 40,000 to Y 50,000 to us. After they've turned private, the land use and management fee alone would amount to Y 80,000, almost double what they were paying.[26]

> There were two reasons why we decided to sell the two small enterprises in 1994. First, they were only making negligible profits, about Y 20,000 to

¥ 30,000 each. So these enterprises were making little, if any, contribution to the collective. Second, their books were rather messy. Since the collective wasn't able to get much benefit out of them, we decided to get rid of them instead. The result? We now get more revenue in the form of [fixed] rental income and management fees than before, as a result of keeping both the land and the factory premises.

Owing to an increase in both the number of village enterprises and the growing volume of business transactions, village cadres have experienced increasing difficulties in managing all their enterprises. This is another important factor behind the privatization drive. In Qianxiang village, for instance, only the largest, "backbone" enterprise, a factory producing die-sel engine frames for tractors, remains in the hands of the village author-ity; the other nine enterprises were sold in early 1995 to the incumbent managers for precisely this reason (see Table 5.6): "Some enterprises are rather small, so that village officials have to spread their efforts thin in managing them. But if we sell them, our leaders [*lingdao*] can focus their energies on the 'backbone' enterprises [*gugan qiye*]."

As can be seen from Table 5.6, none of the enterprises sold were in fact showing losses, although a couple of them had relatively low profit mar-gins (enterprises nos. 6 and 8). Note, however, that profit rates—whether calculated using actual realized sales or output value as the denominator—do not appear to have been the guiding criterion for privatization (Table 5.6, cols. 11–12). The village has sold some highly profitable enterprises, most notably enterprises nos. 3, 4, 9, and 10. With the exception of enter-prise no. 3, which is a relatively large establishment, the other three are rather small firms, as indicated by the absolute figures for gross profits, sales, and output value (Table 5.6, cols. 1–3). On the contrary, although the enterprise over which the village authority has retained ownership and control was performing slightly below the mean average profit rates, 9 per-cent, as opposed to 10 percent in 1994, it nonetheless accounted for almost half the output value and sales revenue of all the village enterprises taken together, 49 percent and 48 percent respectively; 45 percent of the enter-prise gross profits; and, perhaps most important, 32 percent of remitted taxes; moreover, it employed 37 percent of the village's nonagricultural labor force.

From the village leader's standpoint, the retention of ownership and control over this particular enterprise is likely motivated by the strategic importance of a firm of this size for the local economy. Most significant are the proportionately large contributions it makes to tax revenues and non-farm employment respectively.[27] In absolute terms, the total wage bill of the largest enterprise in Qianxiang was four times bigger than that of the second largest enterprise and almost twenty times more than that of the

TABLE 5.6

Main Enterprise Indicators, Qianxiang Village, Luoshe Township, 1994

Nature of enterprise	(1)	(2)	(3)	(4)	(5)	(6)	(7)	(8)	(9)	(10)	(11)	(12)
1. Diesel engine frames	568	6,147	7,479	865.80	217.30	298	7,290	39,628	133	515.5	0.09	0.08
2. Vacuum cleaners	112	1,454	1,570	198.88	50.88	90	5,653	12,978	58	90	0.08	0.07
3. Gearwheels	288	2,320	2,624	445.60	107.60	148	7,268	22,828	94	244	0.12	0.11
4. Crane machinery	41	315	476	90.30	23.30	53	4,388	8,598	13	54	0.13	0.09
5. Electrical appliances	52	470	620	120.80	34.80	70	4,973	9,848	23	63	0.11	0.08
6. Automatic control devices	19	537	575	82.00	18.00	45	4,000	7,518	64		0.04	0.03
7. Farm machinery	72	878	1,115	120.80	30.80	51	6,042	9,868	5	85	0.08	0.06
8. Paper cartons	2	128	114	21.70	6.70	20	3,370	5,898	14	1	0.02	0.02
9. Electronic control devices	24	200	176	57.90	14.90	30	4,966	7,328	7	36	0.12	0.14
10. Walking tractors	70	360	500								0.19	0.14
Total	1,250	12,809	15,249	2,004	504.28	805	47,950	124,492	411	1,089	0.10	0.08

SOURCE: Author's fieldwork, 1995.

NOTES: Column heads are (all units 10,000 yuan unless otherwise indicated): (1) gross profits; (2) sales revenue; (3) gross enterprise output value; (4) net enterprise output value; (5) total wage bill; (6) number of employees; (7) average wages of workers (n = #); (8) enterprise manager's income; (9) tax remitted to village authority; (10) net asset value; (11) profit rates (profits/sales); and (12) profit rates (profits/gross enterprise output value).

TABLE 5.7

Net Output Value of Village Enterprises in Qianxiang, Luoshe Township, 1994
(all values Y 10,000,000 unless otherwise indicated)

Nature of enterprise	Net output value	Wages (%)	Tax remitted to village authority (%)	Net asset value (%)
1. Diesel engine frames	8.66	2.17 (25%)	1.33 (15%)	5.16 (60%)
2. Vacuum cleaners	1.99	0.51 (26)	0.58 (29)	0.90 (45)
3. Gearwheels	4.46	1.08 (24)	0.94 (21)	2.44 (55)
4. Crane machinery	0.90	0.23 (26)	0.13 (14)	0.54 (60)
5. Electrical appliances	1.21	0.35 (29)	0.23 (19)	0.63 (52)
6. Automatic control devices	0.82	0.18 (25)	0.64 (78)	
7. Farm machinery	1.21	0.31 (25)	0.05 (4)	0.85 (70)
8. Paper cartons	0.22	0.07 (30)	0.14 (64)	0.01 (5)
9. Electronic control devices	0.58	0.15 (26)	0.07 (12)	0.36 (62)
10. Walking tractors				
Total	20.05	5.05 (26)	4.11 (21)	10.89 (53)

SOURCE: Author's fieldwork, 1995.

smallest one in the same village (Table 5.7). Furthermore, a large strategic enterprise may also enhance cadres' bargaining power vis-à-vis their township superiors in terms of credit provision and assignment of other resources, because enterprise status has long been tied to output value, sales revenue, and gross profits. Finally, it is highly unlikely that private entrepreneurs would be willing and able to finance the purchase of enterprises with net asset values as large as that of the largest enterprise in Qianxiang village (Table 5.7). Thus, unless the profits of an enterprise are substantially below average, the preference of cadres to retain ownership and control over large, strategic firms rather than smaller ones is readily understandable.

The anecdotal evidence cited above suggests that in addition to the erosion of profit rates in the case of some village enterprises, the rise of the private sector or entrepreneurship is likely to have adversely affected village enterprise managers' incentives in the following two respects. First, while certain major enterprise parameters, such as output value, profits, and tax remittances, are being stipulated in the contractual arrangements between the village authority and enterprise managers, it is unlikely that enterprise managers would regard these targets as binding, given that they are not the residual claimants in terms of financial risk-bearing. These predetermined targets serve merely to provide rough guidelines for evaluating enterprise performance in general and managerial performance in particular. That being the case, it would certainly be in the interest of enterprise managers not to remit the predetermined portion of enterprise profits when the projected profits have failed to materialize. This is precisely what some villages have inadvertently experienced. Take the cases respectively of Shengfeng and Xiaoxing, as described by informants:

> Competitive pressures in the market have substantially squeezed enterprise profitability, leading in some cases to the unwillingness of enterprise managers to submit the predetermined profits to the village. They won't, however, be able to do that after these enterprises have become private, because they must pay the *fixed* rental and management fee respectively charged for the use of land and factory premises, which remain owned by the village [emphasis added].

> Although the incentive system adopted is based primarily on the achievements of certain predetermined target quotas, such as output value, profits, and tax remittance, they are indicative rather than fixed [*bushi baosi*], particularly in recent years, owing to wide fluctuations in the economy.

The potentially most effective approach to resolve this managerial problem, from the standpoint of alleviating the costs of monitoring, is to assign the rights to claim residual profits to the party that directly manages an enterprise. It is by this criterion that village enterprises in Wuxi are regarded as having been privatized. Because village authorities are prohibited by law from selling the collectively owned farmland to private enterprise operators, they continue to own the land and factory premises, although they have sold the other assets,[28] an arrangement that enables the authorities to receive what are basically land rents.[29] It is important to note that these land rental payments have made far greater contributions to local revenues than the profits of the enterprise formerly did.[30] In Xinkaihe, for example, close to one-fifth of the revenues received in 1995 were in the form of land rents.[31] Moreover, these revenue streams are likely to represent stable, long-term income for the village authorities insofar as the private enterprises are able to make profits. Finally, as a result of this change in residual claimancy, an additional benefit that privatization has allegedly brought to village authorities (but certainly not to the enterprises being privatized) is that the authorities now levy a wide array of "regulated fees" (*guifei*) on these enterprises for the express purpose of subsidizing public services such as education (including adult education in some villages), welfare for the aged, a cooperative fund earmarked for agricultural investments and flood prevention, and so forth.[32]

This change in enterprise ownership and rights to residual claims has fundamentally altered the relationship between the village authorities and the enterprise manager in a direction that is likely to benefit both, but especially the former. In the past, although the village authorities were the legal residual claimant, their ability to claim residual profits was constrained by the selfish behavior of the managers, who possessed superior information regarding enterprise capability and performance but failed to maximize profits. By changing institutional arrangements in the manner described above, the village authorities now simply receive a fixed rent, which the "tenant"—the private entrepreneur—must pay regardless of profit fluctuations. In particular, by retaining ownership of specific assets, land in this case, the village authorities are in a position to terminate the tenancy agreement with the private entrepreneur should the latter fail to pay the rent, a threat that is far more credible than what would have been elicited under a profit-sharing contract, especially when the enterprise manager did not bear the financial risks.

A second, related way the rise of the (albeit nascent) private sector economy has affected village enterprises is the demoralizing effect it has had on enterprise managers. As seen above, even in a situation where the village Party secretary still controls major enterprise decisions, powerful social norms exist in the village to constrain the income of village enterprise managers. This can be gauged from Table 5.2 (col. 10), which shows a narrow spread in income between enterprise managers and workers. While we do not have systematic income data for private enterprise managers, anecdotal evidence appears to suggest that their incomes are higher than those of village enterprise managers. In order to minimize this income gap, it seems, village enterprise managers attempt to maximize non-pecuniary benefits, such as by indulging in conspicuous consumption. The following excerpts of commentaries made by various village leaders provide some support for this conjecture.

> The difficulties involved in monitoring enterprise managers is something we have experienced only in recent years, only after our government has liberalized the economy [*fangkai yiqie*—literally, "opened up everything"]. Frankly, you cannot blame enterprise managers for comparing their earnings with those of their private counterparts, when they discovered that the "private bosses" [*siren laoban*] were making so much more than they did. For them, such a reality is indeed disturbing and demoralizing, because they had never expected that to happen. [Yinzheng]

> Unlike the situation back in the past five to six years, enterprises have now become increasingly difficult to manage. The main reason, if you ask me, is the emergence of private enterprises, which have been flourishing in recent years, and they all seem to be able to make money so easily. . . . Few people now, as a consequence, have a good sense of responsibility, many are simply not interested working for the collectives. [Chenxu]

> Enterprise managers are not as obedient as before; in the past they would seek approval before they sought to spend money, now they won't. They have recently begun to indulge in lavish consumption; in our village, one enterprise manager spent Y 40,000 last year on cigarettes alone! [Xiaoxing]

> Managers see the enterprises they manage as belonging to the collective; they therefore think that it is the Chinese Communist Party's money when it comes to spending, [and] they are *very* spendthrift indeed. [Bingkou]

> The fundamental reason why it is difficult to discipline enterprise managers nowadays is that they see these enterprises as belonging to the collectives; that their financial performance has little to do with their own personal welfare. [Yinzheng]

A related reason why village cadres overwhelmingly wish to get rid of the inefficient enterprises is the difficulty of disciplining workers. As the Party secretary in Shengfeng village lamented:

> For one thing, you cannot dismiss them (meaning those native villagers) even when they frown upon their work because they think the enterprise is theirs.[33] For another, wages keep going up, and if you are unable to keep pace with the market rate, you'll easily lose the best workers; their sense of loyalty is weak and they have become exceedingly footloose nowadays.

The village Party secretary in Xiaoxing concurred:

> The other problem is that people think differently these days. Peasants used to be very proud when they first took up factory work, and they all used to work very hard; it wasn't just for the money.[34] Now, they all shy away from hard and dirty work, which has to be done by the non-locals. What is worse, they all want pay raises, and if you refuse their demand, they shirk on their jobs. What if the enterprise manager tries to fire them? Well, they'll sure come to me and make a big fuss, this much I can guarantee you.

Even smaller villages are not immune to this problem. Although Yinzheng has only a handful of small enterprises, the autocratic village Party secretary there has nonetheless experienced problems of a similar sort. It may be argued that such a problem may be more severe in villages like Yinzheng because almost all the enterprise workers there are native villagers, who tend to perceive themselves as having a share in these enterprises, and as such are not subject to dismissal by their appointer, the enterprise manager, regardless of the reason. The difficulty of managing village enterprise workers was further emphasized by the Party secretary in Chenxu village, who likened the prevailing situation in village enterprises to that of state-owned enterprises:

> The problem of "eating from one big pot" is essentially the same for both village enterprises and state-owned enterprises. The situation in township enterprises is somewhat better, and that is because, although township residents regard township enterprises as collective, they do not evidently see themselves as having a share in these enterprises. But that is not how villagers see things. "Collective" to them means that they are not merely hired employees, but are instead stakeholders by virtue of their status as villagers,

and, accordingly, the perception that "You cannot fire me because the enterprise is not private" means that you don't want to cross them too often, at least not to the extent that you won't talk to each other anymore; after all, you still see each other every day, and you just don't want that to happen.

Up to this point in the analysis, we have seen why village leaders want to sell those enterprises that both are difficult to manage and have failed to turn in handsome profits in recent years. Let us now turn to two remaining issues. First, who would buy the unprofitable enterprises, and how do they finance the purchase in a rural credit market that is far from perfect? Second, why should cadres go for outright privatization instead of a less radical institutional alternative, such as the "cooperative shareholding system" (*gufen hezuozhi*), which is essentially a joint-stock system?

The Process of Privatization

The privatization process is essentially similar in all the villages under observation, with slight variations over the period of repayment and the source of financing. The village authority would first of all have the Township Economic Management Bureau evaluate the net asset value of the enterprise destined for privatization, followed by court notarization. Depending on the selling price (or asset value) of the privatized enterprise, obtained by deducting its bad debts from the original gross asset value, the new owner is typically required to pay the capital to the village authority over a period of from one to three years. In the case of Qianxiang, for example, the stipulated rule is that for enterprises with a net asset value of Y 500,000 or less, the capital must be paid within one year. For enterprises worth Y 1 million, the new owner has an additional grace period of half a year. In the case where the enterprise has an asset value of Y 2 million or more, the repayment period is extended to two years.[35]

Since prospective enterprise owners are unlikely to have accumulated enough savings to meet even the first installment of the required payment, how do they come up with the necessary capital? According to my findings, many villages have assisted new enterprise owners in financing their purchases. First, entrepreneurs may borrow from local credit institutions, with the village authority serving as the guarantor and the enterprise as collateral. Second, special endeavors have been made by the authorities to collect outstanding debts. Third, some villages even allow the new owners to write IOUs, so that they are required only to meet the payment out of future profits over several installments. If these measures, taken together, still prove insufficient, perhaps because the net asset value of an enterprise is simply too high, as in the case of a machine tool factory in Xinkaihe, the net asset value of which was Y4.16 million at the time of privatization, existing workers may be invited to purchase shares in the enterprise as an additional source of financing (in which case ownership is certainly diluted).

Whether or not the new owner will be able to have majority control over decision-making depends eventually on the relative share contribution and the corporate governance structure set up. Where capital financing does not pose intractable problems for privatization, the organizational change typically results in the kind of economic institution that resembles the classical capitalist firm with single residual claimancy, in which ownership and control reside in one person. Where this proves impossible,[36] the new owner, middle management, the workers, and, in some cases, parties that have business relations with the enterprise, the "stakeholders" as it were, may be called upon to enter into a shareholding system based on their respective contributions.[37]

One possible means whereby village officials may privatize an enterprise is to announce their prices and invite interested individuals to bid. But in virtually all the villages where privatization has occurred, enterprises were invariably sold to the original managers.[38] Why? According to the Party branch secretary of Xiaoxing village, "you have to sell it to the original enterprise manager, because a different party will most likely refuse to take over existing liabilities." The cadre of Qianxiang offers a different answer: "The incumbent manager is the one most familiar with the enterprise. Besides, he has also acquired a reputation that allows him to command due respect from the existing workers." While this may be part of the truth, my conjecture is that the incumbent manager has a competitive edge over his outside competitors with respect to knowledge of the enterprise in which he has worked (knowledge that, according to Oliver Williamson, arises from the idiosyncratic association with the work environment, organizational culture, physical equipment, and so forth).[39]

In a highly influential paper, Armen Alchian and Harold Demsetz explain why market competition is unable to resolve the problem of shirking when individuals work in a team context, the major reason being that outsiders are unlikely to know who is shirking and how much.[40] Should such knowledge be freely available, existing team members would be able to correct the problem.[41] The incumbent manager is also likely to have a good idea of the comparative advantages of each individual worker, although as a nonresidual claimant, he is unlikely to have the same incentive to monitor workers as a residual claimant. Compared with outsiders, the incumbent manager thus clearly possesses superior knowledge of the capability of the enterprise, which he has managed, and should be in the best position to ascertain whether it will be able to make a profit after the ownership change.

The very fact that incumbent managers are willing to buy up enterprises that were previously showing either losses or only marginal profits also implies that there was X-inefficiency in these enterprises,[42] and that these managers genuinely believe that as owners, they will be able to turn them into profitable entities. In the case of the machine tool factory in Xinkaihe village that became privatized, the new management immediately laid off 37 workers out of an original 147, or roughly 25 percent of the workforce, as the first step toward enhancing organizational efficiency.[43]

The new owner of a factory producing curtain fabric in Shanqian village is reportedly adopting similar measures. Established in 1992, this enterprise had suffered losses amounting to roughly Y 500,000 each year for three years in a row, and had over the years accumulated a debt of Y 2.3 million. After it was sold to the incumbent manager, the new owner closed down the factory temporarily for three days to give himself time to decide who to retain and who to dismiss. The most critical decision he made was perhaps to sack three (out of four) generously paid marketing managers. As each of these middle-level managers had previously been receiving an annual salary of around Y 50,000, the new owner immediately saved Y 150,000. In addition, by laying off twelve workers, the new owner streamlined assembly production and saved another Y 50,000. He also adopted measures to improve cash flow so as to reduce interest payments on bank loans. The result? The enterprise no longer operates in the red; the new owner now projects that the enterprise is expected to earn net profits amounting to Y 200,000—a respectable feat to say the least.

The final issue that I want to address is why these villages have invariably opted for outright privatization instead of resorting to a less extreme solution, such as opting for a shareholding cooperative or joint-stock system, with the village authority, enterprise manager, middle management, and workers all subscribing to shares. The rationale, according to the Party secretary in Qianxiang village, where nine out of ten enterprises were being privatized in 1995, is simply that the costs of decision-making involving several residual claimants are likely to be high. But it is a story told by the Party secretary in Shengfeng village that is most revealing, since it makes clear the kinds of problems that halfway solutions to institutional reforms such as cooperative shareholding may potentially encounter.

This village, according to the Party secretary, had already begun contemplating the adoption of a cooperative shareholding system as early as 1993. The rationale for so doing, at that time, was to invigorate workers' participatory incentive. In particular, it was hoped that, upon becoming partial residual owners of the enterprise, workers would have strong incentives to monitor the manager, especially the latter's deployment of funds for nonproductive purposes, a notable example being entertainment expenses. The scheme did not work, however, because workers either (a) did not have the funds to buy the shares; (b) did not trust their enterprise managers, or, if they did, feared possible personnel changes; (c) did not think their enterprise could make a profit; or (d) saw this as an unattractive venture when prevailing interest rates were sufficiently high and risks comparatively low, preferring to put their money in financial institutions instead.

In light of the failed attempt to sell workers shares, the village Party secretary decided in 1994 to purchase shares for the villagers using the collective funds. He presumed that villagers would be pleased to be simply given free shares in enterprises in which they were employed, and that these shares would boost their morale. Things did not work out quite as expected, however. Because dividends were paid out of the shares owned, workers simply received more income, regardless of their effort levels. Unfortunately, some workers who were given enterprise shares chose more leisure instead of working harder—behavior that economists refer to as a backward-bending labor supply curve, or simply an effect of substitution between income (disutility) and leisure (utility). In principle, this would not inevitably reduce work incentives if there were no corresponding changes occurring in other behavioral respects. Unfortunately, however, that was not the case. Because the remuneration scheme employed by enterprises in this village is primarily based on piece rates, a worker's income is intimately tied to his or her effort, which means that those who worked less after having been allotted the free company shares were now receiving less than those whose effort had remained unaltered. Dissatisfied with the growing income disparity arising basically from varying effort contributions, these workers took the issue to the enterprise manager and the village Party secretary.

In light of this perverse outcome, it dawned on the Party secretary that perhaps the only solution to the incentive problem afflicting both enterprise manager and workers alike would be a thoroughgoing privatization; any institutional alternative short of that would likely get them stuck in the middle of a no-man's-land. In the case of large village enterprises, of which there are three in Shengfeng, the village Party secretary intends to contract out the management rights using a payment scheme that will allow for the transfer of fixed assets over a period of two to three years. When asked why he considers it necessary to gradually alienate the fixed assets of these large enterprises, his answer, interestingly, resembles the theoretical justification given by Alchian and Demsetz,[44] namely, that in using a (rented) piece of equipment or asset, a renter will not exercise the same degree of care as an owner. What, I asked, if the contractee eventually failed to pay the entire capitalized value? In that case, the Party secretary said, previous payments would be treated merely as interest paid for the use of capital, which would be set aside as depreciation funds, while the village authority continued to own the enterprise.

In sum, monitoring problems have driven the institutional choice of privatization. Fairness perceptions restricted cadres from adopting incentive schemes that would most adequately motivate enterprise managers. Widely held social norms that villagers, as nominal owners, are entitled to employment in collectively owned enterprises severely constrained cadres in effectively managing village enterprises. The change in enterprise ownership—from collective to private—is seen as an effective way to alter these relationships. This is amply demonstrated in the instance where the private owner of a previously collective enterprise was able to streamline staffing by sacking some of the (presumably less productive or uncooperative) employees, including middle-level managers, in a manner that village cadres were unable to do, insofar as the villagers were the firm's nominal owners. Indeed, the right to alter a firm's membership—presumably by hiring and firing—is precisely what the residual claimant is empowered to do when he is owner of the firm.[45]

Conclusions

Earlier theories have attempted to explain the phenomenal growth of China's TVEs on the basis of the "revenue incentives" with which local government officials are strongly provided, thanks to fiscal reform, making these officials the de facto residual claimants to the revenue streams profitably generated by these "collective" firms. Drawing upon the survey results of villages in Wuxi County, which has had a strong tradition of official-led rural industrial development, this study depicts the specific roles of local officials and enterprise managers in the process of local industrial development. My findings have revealed the strategic role actively played by village cadres, and the limited role assumed by enterprise managers during the early phase of village enterprise development. This "division of labor" has to be appraised within an institutional context in which markets—in particular factor markets—are yet to be adequately developed, such that business transactions have to be carried out via "relational-contracting" rather than arm's-length market exchange. It is in such circumstances that local officials are to be regarded as playing a uniquely important role in providing a wide array of factor inputs critical to the success of these unconventional enterprises, as well as in marketing the products.

But competition and the development of markets have altered this status quo. Whereas competition results in the erosion of (above-normal) profits, the development of markets reverses the respective roles of the cadre and the manager; as business development no longer relies on personal connections, "entry barriers" break down and competition intensifies. To stay competitive, the enterprise manager must now take greater initiative and be prepared to bear greater financial risks. But such self-initiative cannot be effectively induced under a compensation scheme that does not adequately reward entrepreneurship and financial risk-bearing.

• First, it has been demonstrated that in the presence of powerful informal constraints, income differentials between managers and workers have remained exceedingly narrow. Second, the perception that the villagers are owners of the local enterprises has given rise to the problem of labor discipline. Taken together, these constraints have powerfully motivated village officials—in other words, the Party, which had hitherto controlled both enterprise management and alienation of enterprise ownership—simply to transfer the bundle of rights associated with ownership to the managers.[46] By and large, the change in ownership may be regarded as driven primarily by the officials' concern for economic efficiency, and their belief that the local coffers will benefit from the fiscal contributions made by the private enterprises under the new institutional arrangements; it is a change that they judge is likely on the whole to benefit the entire village community.

Owing mainly to capital constraints, small and poorly managed firms have been the initial targets of privatization. On the other hand, village authorities have striven to keep their large enterprise(s), especially given the latter's strategic contributions to both local coffers and nonfarm employment. While the secular trend of privatizing small and poorly managed enterprises is likely to continue as China's economy undergoes further reform, the growing number of private firms will most likely coexist with and perhaps be dominated by larger "collective" enterprises that remain owned and controlled by the local authorities. Whether what we now see marks the beginning of an important wave of change that will eventually transform the ownership of TVEs in the heartland of local state corporatism or is merely a concerted, strategic response by local officials to "agency problems" during the development process is still too early to tell, although economic theory is predisposed to believe that property rights will eventually gravitate toward private ownership with economic development.

PART TWO

Rural Shareholding Reforms and Their Impact

Chapter 6

Shareholding Cooperatives: A Property Rights Analysis

EDUARD B. VERMEER

Over the past decade, the shareholding cooperative system (*gufen hezuozhi*; hereafter SHCS) has been advocated within China as a solution to ownership and management problems of rural industries. Its development across regions has varied, but 12 percent of all enterprises run by townships or villages (*xiangcun qiye*) had officially adopted this system by 1995. In the absence of adequate national regulations, many local forms have emerged. The introduction of the SHCS has been monitored in three experimental districts, giving rise to extensive domestic commentary and analysis. Because these cooperatives were advocated by the central government, almost all commentators have been very positive about their results. Advocates claim that they are a mechanism for promoting managerial independence, financial responsibility, and employee incentives.[1] However, the arguments and evidence presented are not convincing, and the legal status of such cooperatives is quite vague, a fact underlined by their omission from China's largest compendium of policies and regulations for management of township and village enterprises (TVEs).[2]

In this chapter, we shall consider the political and economic factors responsible for the development of the SHCS, its intended and perceived consequences for the ownership and management of rural collective enterprises, and its effect on property rights. My analysis is based on Chinese analysis and commentary and a survey of 36 converted industrial enterprises in two districts in Shandong and Hebei.[3] First, I shall outline some relevant aspects of ownership and management in China's TVEs in general. Next, I present a history of the original objectives of the policy and how it was implemented. I shall show that its many forms and uneven

spread—many inland areas have been very hesitant to adopt the SHCS—
were owing to several factors: differences in original ownership structures;
choices by local authorities that reflected different economic circumstances
or dominant political currents. Managerial preferences and evolution of
ownership and management practices in rural areas also played a role. The
name SHCS suggests, and Chinese scholars have claimed, that it is a combination of a *shareholding* company and a *cooperative*. I argue that SHCS is a
misnomer; at least in converted collective enterprises, it is a hybrid form
that lacks most of the attributes of either.

Subsequently, I shall describe the process whereby collective enterprises
are converted into shareholding cooperatives, and the consequences for
ownership and management. Ownership rights were changed by a new
valuation of assets, allocation and / or sales of different types of shares, and
new rules for decisions about profit retention and distribution. There is
considerable divergence between the original policy intentions and the
eventual outcomes of these conversions. This divergence is evident from
employee perceptions of ownership and management under the SHCS,
but also from shifts in managerial control. Finally, I shall try to establish
how far the SHCS has achieved a clarification of property rights, which was
one of its intended goals.

Political Objectives and Implementation
of Shareholding Cooperatives

The shareholding cooperative system has developed over a decade, and
the name is applied rather loosely to very different enterprise organizations. The term is confusing because SHC enterprises lack many of the
attributes of either an ordinary shareholding company or a genuine cooperative. The State Statistical Bureau is unsure how to categorize them.[4] The
1994 law on shareholding companies does not apply to SHC enterprises,
and most larger ones are not voluntary associations. There are some su-
perficial similarities with the U.S. employee stock ownership plan (ESOP):
both are usually adopted by small companies in order to increase their
liquidity (by providing stock instead of cash wages or bonuses to their
employees), enjoy certain tax breaks (notably for company savings), and
foster employee cooperation.[5] However, the differences are much greater.
China's SHCs are exclusively rural, often mainly or partly collectively
owned; most have issued employee shares only once, at the moment of
their establishment; most shares are purchased and carry voting rights;
and SHC tax breaks do not apply to sales of shares or deductibility of loans
used to fund company stock, but only to company profits. The SHCS is a

hybrid economic form, the product of mixed political signals from the central government and a range of local survival or development strategies of entrepreneurs and rural governments.

The Central Committee of the Chinese Communist Party advocated the shareholding system for TVEs in its January 22, 1987, decision "On Deepening the Reform." It noted that some private enterprises had already adopted employee shareholding, payment of labor dividends, democratic management, contribution to public funds, and other features that gave them a transitional character. However, a survey had revealed a lack of enthusiasm at the local levels of government, and some developed areas opposed such measures. The State Council accordingly decided to experiment first with enterprise ownership and management in three districts,[6] which were supposed to reflect different types of development and varying local experiences with shareholding: Zhoucun in Shandong, Fuyang in Anhui, and Wenzhou in Zhejiang (the latter case is examined in Chapter 8). Experiments were to focus on a number of questions: shareholder rights, asset management, profit distribution based on shares *and* labor, the authority of *xiang* and *cun* administrative organizations, responsibility for losses and in the event of bankruptcy, and share markets. Local authorities were to adopt model regulations based on their experience. The Rural Experimentation Center under the Ministry of Agriculture and its provincial and local experimentation offices monitored these local experiments and summed them up. Soon, however, marketing of shares ran into political opposition and was called off.[7]

One of the reasons why the term SHCS came into use was that the term "cooperative" was meant to signal a drawing of private enterprises into a public ownership system.[8] Thus, it reflected a "left" policy of gradual collectivization of rural private enterprise. However, to independent entrepreneurs who ran into the legal limit of eight employees, it offered a way forward, political protection, and the favorable tax treatment of collective enterprises. The allocation of shares fit well with the policy of providing more bonuses to workers. It could also be used to circumvent the new individual income tax and official regulations about the remuneration of directors of TVEs not exceeding the average worker's wage more than fivefold,[9] and (as in the capitalist world) to distribute stocks to supplement managerial salaries. Perhaps most important, issuing shares provided new risk-bearing capital, which village authorities and entrepreneurs badly wanted. Different interest groups thus had different, even conflicting, motives for supporting the SHCS.

The leftist political motive appeared most clearly in Wenzhou, China's foremost "capitalist model" city, which in 1988 started formally using the term "shareholding cooperative system" and recognized it as a special economic form. The leftist objective was to contain privatization and to lead individual and private enterprises down the road of the socialist collective economy. The Wenzhou regulations were adopted with minor changes in the national regulations of 1990. Reflecting the restrictive post-Tiananmen political climate, they expressed the idea that collective interests should dominate over private interests, and labor over capital. The 1990 regulations, which still apply today, limited the rights of shareholders in many ways. In the disposition of enterprise profits, they must follow the rule for ordinary TVEs, which stipulates that 60 percent of profits after taxes should be retained and no more than 40 percent distributed as wages and benefits. Distribution should be "mainly on the basis of labor." Generally, only one half should go to dividends, and the other half to collective welfare funds and bonuses; rates for each should be laid down by county, town, and township enterprise bureaus.[10] Furthermore, they stipulated that voting should follow the cooperative principle of one-man one-vote, and not be based on number of shares. Shares could not be withdrawn in principle, and transfer was possible only with permission from the shareholders' meeting. Collectives could sell only a minority share of 30 percent or less to management and employees. In the restrictive political climate of 1990–91, some counties abandoned shareholding altogether and ordered rural cadres to return their shares and dividends and dissolve SHCs.[11]

SHC enterprises were accorded the tax rates and preferential treatment of collective enterprises.[12] This constituted a considerable advantage over private enterprises, particularly because an SHC was permitted "to include in its production management costs that part of its dividends that corresponds to the interest on savings." The deduction of dividends from pre-tax enterprise profits, as if they were interest on loans, gives a sizable advantage to shareholders, particularly in years of high inflation and interest rates. Moreover, SHCs paid lower management fees, viz., 0.5 percent of turnover instead of 2 percent. According to this and earlier surveys, without such favorable tax treatment many enterprises would have opted to remain private.[13]

In 1992, policies became more liberal again. The SHCS was allowed to diversify, without much attempt at standardization.[14] It covered a variety of different economic forms and sizes of enterprises, such as combinations of TVEs with state enterprises, township- or village-run enterprises with employee shareholders, and private partnerships.[15] A fourth form, the "community SHC" (*shequ gufen hezuoshe*), which appeared in Guangdong, put all collective assets under the control of one company, shares in which were allocated to the resident population; it has the character of a *xiang*- or *cun*-run financial holding company rather than that of an enterprise.[16] The second group (township- or village-run enterprises with employee shareholders) was by far the largest in terms of industrial output, employment, and number of shareholders. In December 1992, new directives dropped the minimum founding requirement of "three or more working farmers" and the obligation to accept guidance by the state plan.[17] The SHCS was also stimulated by trials of the shareholding system at state-owned enterprises. Even if, with few exceptions, rural enterprises did not meet the requirements of the 1994 Company Law (i.e., a minimum share-capital of Y 500,000 and a maximum of 50 shareholders), many of the regulations passed by *xiang* governments since 1992 were inspired by it. Several provinces set up experimental districts of their own, some of which defied the 1990 rules. For example, Mixian county declared that "if shareholders really are masters of the enterprise, one should not have restrictive policies for profit distribution. So we allow enterprises to deviate from the rule of 60 percent accumulation and 40 percent distribution." While some areas had forbidden leading Party members and cadres to take shares, out of fear of corruption, Mixian actively encouraged them to do so.[18]

The 1990 regulations were never revoked, but they became increasingly obsolete. Local rules, practices, and adoption rates have continued to diverge. Officials from the relevant departments recommended a flexible application of the rules on the size of the collective share, distribution mainly according to labor, and the one-man one-vote principle. The SHC should be suitable for all China. They expressed a major concern of government and the Communist Party ever since the contracting of TVE enterprises by their managers: "[A]n important objective of the SHCS is to solve the problem of 'gray' privatization of the enterprise assets through appropriation by their present bosses."[19] With this new objective in mind, political support for conversion of TVEs to SHCs was stepped up in 1994, despite widespread local resistance to the adoption of SHCs for TVEs, inspired by what came to be known as "the three fears": township and village cadres feared the loss of power and profits, enterprise managers feared being restricted, and the people feared the risks. However, no uniform model of the SHCS was intended, because of large regional differences.[20] This political support has not yet translated itself into national legislation, most likely because of a lack of consensus about privatization of rural collective assets.

The very different adoption rates in different regions show the continued dependence of the SHCS on state propaganda for its spread. By the end of 1993, more than 20,000 township- or village-run SHC enterprises had been established in Shandong and Zhejiang (where Zhoucun and Wenzhou were models), but fewer than 8,000 in Jiangsu, and fewer than 500 each in Jilin, Shanghai, and Shaanxi. In the interior regions, adoption rates were much lower than in eastern China.

TABLE 6.1

Township and Village SHCs in Six Provinces, 1994
(year-end)

	Number (1,000s)	Labor (1,000s)	Capital (billion yuan)	Percentage of stock ownership				
				Collective	Individuals	"Legal Persons"[a]	Foreign	State
China	204.1	7,998	105.7	49%	26%	17%	5%	3%
Hebei	13.3	554	7.8	47	28	16	6	4
Shandong	27.2	1,575	19.7	59	21	13	6	1
Jiangsu	14.1	1,056	14.8	65	17	14	4	1
Zhejiang	24.7	950	12.5	26	49	21	4	1
Anhui	7.9	318	3.3	39	29	22	7	3
Fujian	4.2	195	3.2	27	22	21	27	2

SOURCE: *Zhongguo qiye guanli nianjian, 1995* [Yearbook of China's enterprise management, 1995] (Beijing: Zhongguo Qiye, 1995), pp. 232–33, 362–63.
[a]"Legal persons" are other government agencies or other enterprises.

In 1994, the number of SHCs increased from 133,000 to 204,000, or 12 percent of all TVEs. Employment increased from almost 5 million to 8 million, 13.6 percent of the labor force.[21] By 1994, 49 percent of share capital was owned by township or village collectives. Managers and employees increased their holdings to 26 percent, and other companies held 17 percent. Foreign and state participation each remained below 5 percent. Collective ownership of shares was most prominent in Jiangsu and Shandong, individual ownership in Zhejiang, and foreign ownership in Fujian. Share ownership by "legal persons," that is, other organizations or government agencies, was most common in Gansu, Guangxi, Sichuan, and other western regions. Such differences in stock ownership can be explained by prior differences in the organization of rural enterprises and the political orientation of rural governments, and the relative strength of state enterprises in the inner provinces, and are reflected in the various "models" (see Table 6.1).[22]

Paradoxically, the shareholding cooperative system may be popular as a method of preventing government meddling in business and also as a way for cadres to profit from privatization of collective assets. Which side will prevail depends to a large extent on the strength of local political institutions and on the influence of shareholders on boards of directors. This survey indicated that shareholder control is weakly developed. Although the SHC has a shareholders' representative meeting that should decide all major issues and appointments, in actual practice the president of the board of directors and all managers are usually appointed by local government and Party cadres, and sometimes they are in fact cadres themselves.[23] The gray zone between government and business shows no sign of disappearing in these cases. Entrepreneurs push the form in order to buy political protection, while cadres use the form to create companies that escape higher-level supervision.

"Neither Donkey nor Horse": Shareholding Versus Cooperative Ownership

Should the shareholding cooperative system be considered a transitional form that will ultimately lead to privatization or a long-term, viable system of its own that combines collective and private ownership and goals? If one argues the latter, as some Chinese economists do, one has to believe in the compatibility of its rules and in its proper combination of the interests of different types of shareholders. The charters of SHC enterprises never mention a future conversion to a private company. Other Chinese scholars are undecided about the nature of the SHCS, and while some believe that its lack of a definite form is a positive characteristic in times of rapid economic and institutional change, others doubt whether this hybrid can survive.[24] In this section, I identify the conflicting ideologies and interests in various types of SHCs and argue that the present SHC system cannot last, because of fundamental contradictions and unclear collective ownership and management rights.

The conceptual and legal differences between shareholding companies and producers' cooperatives are well known (see Table 6.2). The SHCS has tried to bridge some of these fundamental differences by devising compromise rules, and its proponents have allowed actual SHCS practice to diverge from ideology and regulations if found too restrictive. Western cooperatives consider their assets to be owned by individuals and allow shareholders to return their shares, but not to transfer them to others. In China's SHC enterprises, ownership may be diverse and institutional, and returns or transfers of shares are either restricted or forbidden. The ratio of

TABLE 6.2

Features of Shareholding Companies and Producers' Cooperatives

	Shareholding Company	Producers' Cooperative
Purpose	profitable capital use	profitable labor use
Ownership rights	transferable shares	partly indivisible
Profit distribution	based on shares	based on labor
Risks	limited to share	equal, limited if legal entity
Dissolution	sale of shares	withdrawal, with conditions
Decision-making	one share, one vote	one person, one vote
Management control	directors, shareholders	democratic, workers

income allocated to labor versus shareholders has been an issue in both the West and China. Dividends are limited to half the profits in Italy, to below 6 percent in France, and to 8 percent in Japan and the United States. Chinese rules limiting dividend distribution to 20 percent of the profit after taxes are no longer respected; Wenzhou put the limit at 25 percent, Zhoucun at 30 percent to 40 percent, and some areas apply no limits at all. Most SHCs have limited shareholder risks by guaranteeing dividends above bank interest rates.

As for decision-making and control rights, Western cooperatives stress the equality of all their members. The Chinese SHC has the unique problem of a dominant third organizational element: the collective ownership and control exerted by township and village authorities. Partly because of their authoritarian collectivist ideology, the egalitarian premise of the SHCs as genuine producers' cooperatives did not have a chance to develop, and it seems much less alive than in the West now. Only 10 percent of my respondents in Zhoucun said that all categories of employees should have the same number of shares, while 78 percent said they should not. In Zunhua, many common workers evaded the question. Most felt that differences in shareholding should not be too large. Almost 80 percent felt that they should be less than triple the workers' share in the case of technicians and workshop heads (actual differences were mostly lower than that), and 40 percent thought so for managers as well.

The closed character of the Chinese village and township, both of which are strong economic units to which residents belong by birth, affects not only SHCs but *all* enterprises in the community. Individual and enterprise ownership rights are weak because of the pervasiveness of and dependence on the authorities—government cadres, Party secretaries, clan elders, and family heads—who control allocation of resources. The dominant economic role of the rural authorities has enabled them to spread risks and guarantee stable dividend payments to employee shareholders almost irrespective of enterprise performance; moreover, they are subject to considerable political and social pressures from the workforce. My interview data show, and enterprise charters confirm, that shareholders' rights in SHCs to a predictable and often high income stream from their shares (risk-bearing or not) are substantial and secure. Because of their closed character, small size, and strong informal control, many SHC enterprises seem more comparable in organization and economic behavior to family firms than to the ideal-type shareholder-controlled limited company or producers' cooperative.

In my survey I found that most managers and employees had mixed feelings about their ties to the township or village leadership. On the one hand, the close relationship between the enterprise managers and the local leaders of the township or village was perceived as an advantage. The leaders were seen as instrumental in reducing transaction costs in dealings with the tax bureau, the police, the communications department, the environmental protection bureau, banks, and so on. On the other hand, almost all managers of SHC enterprises indicated that adoption of the SHCS had shifted decision-making to the enterprise, away from government interference, and affirmed their independence. Managers emphasized that their enterprise had more freedom of management than other enterprises that did not have shareholding, although half of the Shandong managers said that the difference was not large. Most employees indicated that in order to improve management, more authority for the manager was still the top priority. They indicated that, as shareholders, they had little if any influence on management decisions themselves; the perceived threat was from above.

The lack of marketability and transferability of shares in most SHCs raises the question of their real value. Transfers to other partners occur in partnership-based SHCs; in SHCs converted from private companies, large shareholders can usually sell their shares to outsiders, as long as the board of directors agrees. Managers may try to resell their shares to the collective. However, the vast majority of shareholders, the ordinary employees, are usually not permitted to sell, not even to other employees. None of the shareholders I interviewed had ever transferred or sold shares; 70 percent said they did not have the right to do so, and 83 percent believed selling them to be unprofitable, and preferred to hold on to them. One might conclude that the real test of employees' right to sell their shares is still to come. If failure to pay promised dividends later creates strong demands to sell, one may doubt whether local authorities or managers will be able to withstand the pressure.

One may conclude from the above that the cooperative character of the SHC is not firmly rooted or strong enough to guarantee sustained development of an enterprise as a cooperative. Its embeddedness in an eroding rural power structure inherited from China's collective past hampers development of the rules and management practices of a shareholding company. If local authorities cannot back up their guarantees of dividends and shareholders want out, the entire structure of the SHCS might collapse.

However, some SHCs have taken on the thorny issue of how to combine the interest of the collectivity of the enterprise with that of the rural community (which is the theoretical owner of the collective shares) one step further. The SHCS has infused a new element into the simple dichotomy between "closed" cooperative/collective and "open" shareholding. Previously collectively owned enterprises sold collective or individual shares to all employees collectively, formalizing the community of interests among the employees, who thus became joint owners of a property separate from that of the township or village collective.

Effects of Shareholding Conversions on Various Stakeholders

From the beginning, clarification of property rights has been put forward by Chinese economists as a main reason for converting collectively owned enterprises to SHCs. The same claim is not made for the SHCS when applied in other types of enterprises. The SHC has an ownership structure more complex than that of a partnership or private company, because it introduces a collective stakeholder (and sometimes shareholder) whose rights (as we saw above) lack definition and legal restraint. Also, shareholders in an SHC do not enjoy similar protection to those in companies established under the 1994 Company Law. However, most often the SHCS is adopted in township- and village-run enterprises. They reduce the collective stake and express the remaining participation of township or village authorities in terms of shares, the rights of which are defined in the company charter. The other stakeholders in the SHC and sometimes also new investors receive similarly defined shares. Conversion thus demands a change in and consolidation of the property rights of all stakeholders.

Township and village authorities that want to raise cash (for a company or other purposes) are not permitted to issue shares of their collectively owned enterprises on the open market. They may sell a sizable share in an enterprise to a contracting manager or to one or more large investors from outside, whose participation will be noted in the company charter, but for legal and economic reasons, share sales are usually limited to the employees and managers of the enterprise. For that reason, the property rights of most SHC shareholders are not only restricted by official regulations and company charters but also linked intricately with their rights as resident villagers or employees and their ability to effectuate those rights against village government, managers, or other large shareholders.

Several questions deserve our attention: Did conversion make property rights clearer for those with a stake in the company? Has management improved and profit distribution become more accepted as a consequence? Did share issues go beyond a consolidation of existing stakes or did some existing or new stakeholders manage to capture a much larger share than others? Was the conversion beneficial to all, or have there been winners and losers in the process? In order to be able to answer these questions, we need to consider four factors: the valuation of assets at the time of conversion, the transaction price, the allocation of shares to different stake-holders, and the distribution of enterprise profits.

VALUATION OF ENTERPRISE ASSETS

Once an enterprise has obtained approval from the collective govern-ment or village committee to adopt the SHCS, the first step is to have its assets valued. This should be done by an independent county accoun-tancy office, but because of their limited capacity, it may also be performed jointly by the township economic committees and the enterprises con-cerned. Accounting practices have improved in recent years, but systemic problems such as administrative intervention, accounting company mo-nopolies, and covering up of asset losses still remain.[25] Valuation may be based on age-related original value and net value, replacement cost, ca-pacity to generate profits, and other factors.[26] Inflation has rendered the traditional method based on historical price minus depreciation totally inadequate. Yet it was the preferred method in my surveyed districts.

As for fixed assets, the Fuyang accountants used a combination of book value and replacement value. Their guiding principle was that the valua-tion should be acceptable to both sides.[27] Zunhua did not take immaterial assets into account, and in Zhoucun it was highly unusual to do so. Zhou-cun used the method of historical price minus depreciation until 1993, and since then has used the actual price method as well, even though they are mutually contradictory. The first method was mainly used for the SHCS, because it depressed value and therefore favored the employees who were to purchase shares. Collective enterprises usually did not accept any valuation of immaterial assets. The eventually determined fixed asset value was the result of a negotiation process between the accountants and the enterprise.[28]

Evaluation of financial assets is less problematic. Conflicting claims to ownership by different bureaus or collective levels are settled with the founding of the new SHC enterprise. The status of loans for working capital from the township or village must be specified; under the SHC they will no longer be interest-free or subject to arbitrary withdrawal. SHC charters often stipulate that the previous collective owners are no longer responsible for their debts, which suggests that some debts were cleared before the conversion. Evaluation problems lie mainly in the as-sessment of the quality of loans and debts, the choice of interest rates, and entitlement to money transfers immediately before the conversion. If eval-uation is not performed by independent accountants, the township or village authorities have a great influence on its outcome.

Land may be an important part of the collective share in a company. It belongs to the township or village unless stipulated otherwise by government. If ownership or use of collective land is transferred, a price has to be set. Theoretically, this price should depend on its use; industrial land commands much higher prices than agricultural land. In practice, the government has allowed land to be leased to rural industries at the low agricultural price. Land allocated to village- or higher-level collective enterprises in the past cannot be transferred at will and is protected by law against usurpation by rural governments in the same (not always effective) way as other enterprise assets. SHCs have three options for the valuation of land. First, the land may be considered as a collective input into the enterprise, and take the form of a collective share held by village government. Second, the land lease (if cheaper than the market price) may be booked as an immaterial asset. Third, the land may be excluded from valuation and leased to the SHC under a new contract. The second option is hardly ever used, and the third is becoming more common as collective governments reduce their enterprise share. More often than not, land is leased to the SHC at the old rate for agricultural land. Both undervaluation of land and cheap leases are hidden subsidies by *xiang* or *cun* to the SHC, which benefit its shareholders. By demanding more or less compensation for its input of land, the *xiang* or *cun* may manipulate its share in the SHC enterprise or its fixed production costs. One way or the other, local governments thereby influence the profits of the SHCs.

Adoption of the SHCS thus presents an opportunity to the collective owner and new shareholders to reassess the value of an enterprise's fixed, liquid, and immaterial assets, including the price and utility of its land. This assessment has to be approved by independent accountants and is legally binding once establishment of the SHC enterprise has been approved. More important, employees and managers express their acceptance by taking shares. The partial privatization results in much more strictly defined ownership rights and virtual exclusion of any claims by non-shareholding employees or members of the collective.

WAS THE TRANSACTION PRICE RIGHT?

Above, we noted the undervaluation of existing assets at the expense of the original collective owner and to the benefit of the new SHC shareholders. The employees received undervalued shares, while investors got a disproportionate share, because the latter's new investment or technology was converted into shares at current prices, while existing assets were converted at lower historical prices or subsidized prices. National and provincial figures for the total nominal value of SHC shares correspond fairly closely to the original value of their fixed assets but are only weakly related to the value of their liquid assets.[29] This demonstrates, and my survey confirmed, that in general total share value was put at par with total asset value.

However, the market value of an enterprise is only weakly related to its assets. Expected profits and cash flow are much more important; when discounted at expected rates of interest (plus compensation for risk), they will yield an acceptable market value. National data on the profitability of SHCs in 1993 and 1994 show nominal capital returns of enterprises of about 20 and 26 percent, much higher than bank interest rates and also higher than the rise in the rural cost of living.[30]

My initial conclusion from interviews, company founding charters, some balance sheets, the frequent high payouts of dividends immediately after the adoption of the SHC system, and the above-mentioned 1993–94 national profitability data is that in a number of cases, collectives gave away or sold off part of their businesses at prices considerably below market value. The authorities may have felt justified in doing so for several reasons. Employees and managers held stakes in the enterprise, which ought to be recognized by giving them shares at low prices. Authorities could take comfort in the thought that as a majority shareholder and highest local authority, they could influence profitability and dividends, and thus reduce the value of the shares in the future. Most shares did not have a market value anyway, because they could not be transferred or sold. Under traditional accounting rules, and because of subsidies such as free land and cheap loans, the actual profitability of TVEs could not be determined very well, and rapid growth and market fluctuations made extrapolation of past profits a risky business. Many collective governments wanted funds badly for new economic activities. Some colluded with contracting managers to enrich themselves through private purchase of undervalued shares. The relative weight of these considerations varied between our surveyed villages and townships, and needs further research.

Of course, governments and individuals considered profitability and risks before deciding to sell or invest. New investment capital, whether from managers, employees, or outsiders, has flowed into the TVEs that were considered the best buy. This is confirmed by the higher than average profitability of SHCs. My survey showed a very positive attitude among SHC employees toward buying more shares in their company. In Zhoucun, 80 percent, and in Zunhua, 57 percent of the respondents said they would buy more shares if offered; 83 percent of all respondents thought that selling their shares at face value would be unprofitable. They saw themselves as clear winners. This does not necessarily mean that the collectives lost. Townships and villages managed to attract risk-bearing capital for their best-performing enterprises, although at a high price (through undervaluation or guaranteed high payouts). This was a recognition of the vested interests of managers and employees, but it is also owing to the scarcity of capital during most of the past decade.

SHARES: TYPES, DISTRIBUTION, AND RIGHTS

When a collective owner converts its enterprise into an SHC, it defines its ownership in terms of company shares and limits it to a definite percentage. Usually, shares are sold exclusively to managers and employees in the form of ordinary or preferred shares. Sometimes other members of the local community can purchase shares as well. In rare cases the enterprise is put up for sale at an auction, where outsiders can bid; then the new owners do not necessarily have obligations to the employees. Preferred, nonvoting shares have occasionally been used to restrain the collective government or village from interference in the enterprises. The employee share may come in any size: although districts and enterprises had stipulated that a fixed percentage of shares be distributed in advance, in many cases the eventual share depended on the financial capacity and willingness to buy of employees. Enterprises may offer additional free shares as an incentive.[31] The rules state, and my survey confirmed, that the maximum number of shares that employees are allowed to buy is based on their employment record and position in the company. The record may go back to the 1960s, the founding of the company, or the introduction of the household responsibility system. Distinctions in position may be made either between managers and all other employees, or between factory head, department head, workshop head, technician, common worker, and so on, each being entitled to a certain number of shares.

In the initial period, SHC shares often bore no risk, because the collective guaranteed that in the case of losses, they would retain their face value. Moreover, they guaranteed (and company charters confirmed) that the interest on preferred shares (and sometimes also on ordinary shares) would be increased according to increases of, and remain higher than, current bank interest rates for savings.[32] The enterprise statutes specify the different types of shares, their transferability (only to other employees or heirs), duration (some shares may be redeemed at face value after three or five years, but they are usually redeemable only when the employee leaves the company or retires), the rights of shareholders (decision on dividend; voting), and often the guaranteed percentage of the dividend.

The experimental areas adopted different methods of conversion of existing interests of stakeholders into shares. There was, and is, no agreement over the entitlement of state or collective organizations that did not invest but contributed to the enterprise by preferential policies, such as tax remission, repayment of loans before taxes, or free loans.[33] Fuyang converted all assets that had resulted from state investment, tax exemptions, low-interest bank loans, and state preferential policies into nonvoting preferred shares with fixed dividends. With its strong tradition of private entrepreneurship, Wenzhou was afraid that such state shares would go at the expense of the employees' share, and converted them into a non-interest-bearing "state support fund." The guiding principle for Wenzhou was that only the actual investor was the owner and should reap the profits. For the same reason, unlike most other areas, it allowed transfers of shares.[34]

In Zhoucun, the collectives divested only 30 percent of their enterprise ownership at first, allocating it to the employees on the basis of employment record, basic wage, and position. Most enterprises in Wangcun township applied a ratio of 40:50:10 for these three factors, reserving the 10 percent for "managing cadres."[35] Another township was less egalitarian: it allocated 60 percent of the shares on the basis of employment record, 28 percent for cadres, and 12 percent for achievement. In 1993 and 1994, Zhoucun lowered the required majority for the collective share to 51 percent, leaving this decision to the township and village level. Sales were partly forced: some of the interviewed employees still resented the obligatory purchases of shares, but indicated that their position would have suffered if they had refused. Wangcun sold 80 to 90 percent of its collective shares, a minor part of which went to outsiders. The proceeds were invested in better infrastructure and new enterprises.[36] Other townships in Zhoucun followed suit.

The Zunhua municipal government started promoting the SHCS only in 1993. It left considerable room for different practices, but ruled that shares should be distributed to employees only against payment and without obligation to buy. The collective share might be kept entirely in the hands of the collective or subsequently sold in parts (in 1995, it recommended 40 percent) to the employees.

Share ownership appeared to be widespread among SHC employees by 1995. Three-quarters of my respondents owned shares: more than 80 percent of the managers and workshop heads, and 60 to 75 percent of the technicians and accountants. Among the latter two groups, share ownership was slightly more common in Zhoucun than in Zunhua. With common workers, the difference was significant: in Zhoucun, 70 percent held shares, but only 33 percent did in Zunhua. Two explanations may be offered for the difference: the political priority given to employee shares in Zhoucun and the more recent date of conversion to SHCs in Zunhua (after some early cooperative ideals had faded). A more fundamental cause may lie in the weaker position of rural industrial workers in Zunhua, where economic growth and labor demand are not as strong as in Zhoucun.

In Zhoucun, 40 percent of the respondents owned both ordinary ("cash") shares and preferred shares, 55 percent owned only ordinary shares, and 5 percent only preferred shares. There was some indication that workers more than any other category had been obliged to purchase shares in order to obtain employment. Although this was mentioned fairly often, responses to my question "Why did you buy shares?" were ambiguous. Twenty-two percent of the Zhoucun workers said it had been necessary in order to obtain employment, 39 percent chose the answer "I imitated others," and 17 percent chose the idealistic answer "In order to become an owner." Neither of the last two answers excludes the possibility that pressure was used to get them to buy shares. Only 22 percent gave a genuine financial reason: the wish to invest, or to obtain free shares.

I registered considerable differentials in shareholding among sampled respondents, with a minimum of Y 100 and a maximum of Y 170,000 in Zunhua and Y 70,000 in Zhoucun. Average holdings per employee in Zunhua were Y 17,060, 2.5 times larger than in Zhoucun (Y 6,880). The more equal distribution of share holdings in Zhoucun (despite its being economically more developed and wealthier than Zunhua) reflects the stronger political direction and collective ideology in Zhoucun's controlled implementation of the SHCS, and its earlier date of adoption. Most employees felt that differences in shareholding between ordinary employees and managers should not exceed a ratio of one to three, but actual differences were larger than that.[37] Most managers stated that the incentive effect of shareholding could be noted only among employees who held sizable amounts of shares, but not with the other employees. Changes in the actual distribution of share ownership in rural China should give an important indication of the future direction of the SHC, but there are no data for these.

The conversion from a collectively owned enterprise to an SHC enterprise has clarified property rights to a certain degree only. Several questions remain unsolved. First, usually the collective maintained a dominant share, and the question of whether the collective government or village committee was the owner of the collective share, or only the agent of all community residents, was not solved. Second, because the required valuation of the enterprise assets at the time of conversion has often been incomplete, the ownership status of left-out assets (such as immaterial assets, bad debts, and land leases) has not been determined. As long as the collective government or village remains the majority shareholder, it is free to interpret its ownership rights and those of others according to its own interests. Third, separation between the collective government or village and the enterprise remained incomplete and ill-defined, particularly the power relations between the township (or village) economic committee, its asset management company, and enterprise management. For instance, it is generally reported, and my survey confirmed, that if the collective holds a dominant share, the township economic committee or village Party secretary has continued to appoint managers and approve contracts. Fourth, the creation of additional nominal owners, the rights of whom were not always well defined or equal (shareholders whose shares may be bought back by the enterprise at face value within three or five years probably having the weakest position), added to the complexity of relations between owners and agents. The institution of multiple ownership may be divisive, or not acceptable to all interested parties, and may fuel internal conflicts over property rights that had hitherto been dormant. Fifth, even after the collective has lost its majority stake in a company, its powers may be so extensive, and the interdependence of rural entrepreneurs, shareholders, and local officials so great, that formal rights cannot be realized. Civil law litigation is inaccessible and rare and contributes little to clarification of the ownership rights of shareholders.

On the positive side, the SHCS's primary contribution has been the demarcation of property rights of employee shareholders and managers (at the expense of the theoretical rights of all members of the collective), that is, of *nongovernmental* owners *within* the enterprise. It has done less to limit the self-proclaimed rights of government and other outside agencies. Its second main contribution has been the clarification of rights to residual income through the establishment of an explicit mechanism of distribution of dividends.

The further development of ownership in the SHC enterprise is a matter of grave concern and serious dispute for many Chinese economists and politicians. Some hold that the collective ownership share should remain dominant (as the 1990 regulations require);[38] some even deny that private shares are privately owned;[39] others believe that collective dominance can be maintained without formal share ownership, and that a 10 percent or 20 percent share will do. Some continue to defend traditional ideas about the collective and cooperatives.[40] Only a few dare advocate that a large share be held by the employees collectively—apparently, the authorities have no confidence in the collective wisdom of such autonomous groups. Alternatively, they fear that this might create a well-organized opponent of the factory management or village government and threaten its control over collective assets.

Such debates are fueled by ideological differences, and may also reflect growing disparities among regions, enterprises, and employees. From an economic management point of view, it stands to reason that differences in type and size of enterprise and different needs for capital and incentives may lead to different conclusions about optimizing the capital structure of SHC enterprises. This requires more study than can be presented here. However, one may assume, and recent history shows, that local and sectoral variations will increase when economies grow apart unless government passes proper legislation to counteract this.

PROFIT DISTRIBUTION AND DIVIDEND POLICY

The shareholders of the TVEs that have adopted the shareholding cooperative system have only limited rights to dispose of profits. As noted above, the government has set rules for profit retention and distribution in TVEs, as well as the sequence of distribution,[41] which also apply to SHC enterprises. However, in many districts, SHC enterprises no longer follow the regulations on distribution (which stipulate 6:2:2 or 5:3:2 ratios for collective accumulation, welfare, and payouts to the employees). Actual ratios that I observed varied widely: in both counties, rules were indicative rather than strictly enforced.[42] In some parts of Wenzhou, cash and stock dividends amounted to 30 to 50 percent or higher, even up to 100 percent.[43]

Such differences in payouts demonstrate the evolution of the shareholding system. Of course, different types of enterprises require different levels of profit retention. However, as local regulations apply to all local SHC enterprises, the main explanation for the growing differences should be sought in local economic policies. To the extent that the rule of retention of 60 percent of profits was devised to protect and enlarge the collectively owned assets, it made little sense after the collective had sold off most of its assets. To the extent that it was devised as a correction to the old practice of artificially boosting profits, it had to be revised as profit calculations became more realistic. However, high dividend payments represent a transfer from the collective to the private sector and speed up the process of privatization. Partly because of artificially boosted profits, annual dividends have usually been as high as 20 to 30 percent in the past few years, and in some cases even higher. Even loss-making enterprises may pay dividends.[44] During the inflation of 1992–94, only guaranteed high dividends on shares could persuade employees or outside investors to take part in shareholding schemes. To the extent that such high dividend rates have been included in company charters, establishing a custom or raising expectations, there is a real danger, now that inflation and interest rates have come down, that the financial position of SHC enterprises will be threatened by excessive payouts.

Pressure to exert the rights of shareholders is more likely to come from managers with controlling interests than from below. Asked whether they had any influence on the size of the dividend, 87 percent of shareholding respondents said they had not. Almost all laborers and technicians said they did not have any influence on the decision. The few positive answers came mainly from managers, but even among them, a majority (62 percent) gave a negative answer. Those who gave positive answers indicated that the decision about dividends was taken by the board of directors (60 percent), by the majority shareholder (13 percent), or by the shareholders' meeting (27 percent). Only 28 percent of all respondents believed that shareholders should exert their right to speak at the annual meeting of shareholders. One effect of the SHC has been, for better or for worse, to take the profit distribution issue out of the political arena, but as yet the SHC has provided neither shareholders nor employees with a level playing field for a fight about dividends or wages.

Conclusions

Introduced as an experiment in China in 1987, the SHCS has diversified and taken hold in a significant percentage of rural industrial enterprises. Its spread has been uneven, and the system has taken many different forms. It was used to convert private partnerships, collectively owned and managed industries, and enterprises contracted by their managers, as well as in newly established enterprises. Motives and objectives varied. Most collective enterprises wanted to attract new capital and create formal independence from local political leadership at the same time. Private enterprises and those dominated by their contracting managers saw the SHCS as a means to obtain political protection and draw profits in the form of dividends. Large rural enterprises used the SHCS for its tax advantages, or as a quasi-limited company, because they were not qualified to operate under the new Company Law.

Different stakeholders in collective enterprises wanted different things from the SHCS: township and village leaderships wanted to divest collective property, improve economic performance, or push for employee ownership for political reasons. Adoption of the SHCS showed their willingness to respond to political signals from above that favored it. Moreover, it protected or created the enterprise's classification as collective property, which implied that its taxes and administration fees would be under collective control. Many areas classified their rural enterprises as SHCs, even if they had only rudimentary forms of shareholding. Government and Party also wanted greater institutional control over profiteering managers. Managers appreciated the greater independence: the opportunity to provide material incentives to employees and themselves and to legalize or cash in on their stake in the company. Employees were attracted by the high dividends or wanted to keep their jobs. With such diverse motives, it may take some time and real exercise of shareholders' rights before the different shareholders have agreed on the purpose and priorities of their enterprise.

The system developed in a controlled manner in three experimental areas and more freely elsewhere. The "left-wing" national regulations of 1990 did not have much of a standardizing effect. After the 1992 liberalization, they became obsolete. Local authorities preferred to promote, or sometimes obstruct, the SHCS by rules of their own. We found that many enterprises do not comply even with these local rules. The new Company Law set an example of a formal management structure, but practices in SHCs continue to be influenced by the rules for collective enterprises, their small size, and operation in a closed community. Many remain under collective control, particularly if local government is the largest shareholder. Even when managers own a majority of the shares, their enterprise still depends on the goodwill or active support of collective government for its external relations. Employee shareholders were not seen (and did not claim) to exert any influence on decision-making.

Formal separation between collective ownership and enterprise management, and partial privatization under the SHCS, affected collective property rights in several ways. Some interviewed managers of SHC enterprises mentioned the complexity of the SHCS as a reason for not following the SHC regulations or attracting capital through share issues. Its obsolete and idealistic regulations limited its usefulness as a legal basis for combining the interests of capital, labor, and management. In general, the new management structure and procedures under the SHCS did not change operation of the enterprises or appointment of its managers very much. This may have had to do with the small size of most companies, the limited mobility of labor (including managers) and capital, and also with the combination of functions in one person. Often, the village Party secretary or township economic committee exerts ultimate control. Nevertheless, the conversion is appreciated positively by almost all managers and employees. Many reasons are given: greater financial and managerial independence; greater political support; perceived opportunities to influence the direction of the company; and more rational and accountable distribution of residual income through dividends. Also, the SHCS has a modern image, which was reinforced by the Company Law, and interviewed managers anticipated further processes of change.

The property rights of SHCs are not fully secure or unambiguous under present conditions. The question of the extent of privatization has several layers: to what extent were the collective property rights transferred, and to whom; which type of rights; and how well will they hold up in case of conflicts? The answers depend just as much on an evaluation of the scope of prior collective rights (against the claims of other stakeholders in collective enterprises) as on an analysis of the qualities of the SHCS. In my view, simple conversion from a collectively owned enterprise into an SHC with the collective as a majority shareholder does not constitute privatization per se. Below, I summarize the main answers found in this study.

1. The legal framework of the SHCS holds conflicting elements of cooperative, collectivist, and capitalist ideas. Certain rules, such as those on profit distribution and one-man one-vote shareholder representation, are held to be obsolete by most people, and are therefore ignored in enterprise charters or not observed in practice. Other rules, devised to separate ownership from management, and to regulate or exclude collectively held "common" rights of the community or employees, are only partially effective because the extent of and control over these rights has not been settled. The operation of an enterprise may thus deviate significantly from its charter.

2. Individual share ownership is restricted to employees, and in rare cases to members of the collective. Employee shareholders have a double dependency: on their employer and on the authorities of their township or village. This puts them in a position where they dare not and do not attempt to enforce their own rights against institutional and managerial shareholders. Because their shares cannot be sold, they do not have exit rights, and the value of shares is unclear. Often, shares are little more than a component of employee salaries.

3. Dividends from the SHC enterprise are a superior and accepted form of distribution of residual income. However, their usefulness for enterprise management is limited in two ways. Their size is restricted by the national standard of 60 percent profit retention, irrespective of the investment needs of the enterprise. In many enterprises, dividends are a quasi-wage, and they are therefore less flexible than if they only represented risk-bearing capital.

4. Usually, ownership and management are not fully separated. If the township or village has a majority share, or even a minority share, it may continue to control appointments and dismissals of managers, as well as commanding external resources vital to the enterprise's economic success. If the collective share is small or entirely absent, usually the contracting managers or a few partners are the major shareholders. For that reason, the formal powers of the board of directors and annual shareholders' meeting do not find much use. If the SHCS is adopted by a private company or partnership, it introduces elements of collective ownership or

claims in return for political and tax advantages, which make its property rights structure more, not less, complex and fuzzy.

5. The SHCS gives formal recognition to the claims of various stakeholders in collective enterprises, whose conversion to SHCs reduced some of the "vagueness" of collective property by establishing the value of the enterprise and converting various stakeholders into a definite number of shareholders with rights that are summed up in the company charter. The SHC legitimized or checked "gray privatization" by assessing the claims of contracting managers and employees and giving them recognition in the form of a definite number of shares and entitlement to dividends. The charters of SHC enterprises in which these rights were recognized had to pass formal political approval and constitute the legal basis for the solution of future disputes.

6. So far, the partial privatization under the SHCS has met with little opposition, either from investors (because collectives sold their most profitable enterprises first) or from the collective community (because political procedures were observed, and the community has little independent voice). However, as noted, at the time of conversion, inadequate and incomplete assessment of asset value and earning capacity was quite common. Usually, employee shareholders profited at the expense of the collective and received high dividends. Contracting managers profited most when they obtained large and legally protected shares. Because most enterprises did well, all parties seemed to be content with their share, but if the economic situation deteriorates, conflicts over ownership, share value, and entitlement to residual income will become more likely. In the light of current expectations, employee shareholders may refuse to accept a cancellation of guaranteed returns, let alone loss of share value.

One might argue that particularly in small-scale enterprises, and in periods of enterprise expansion, a certain degree of fuzziness of property rights is functional. Owners, managers, and employees are motivated by (not necessarily realistic) high expectations about their future share in earnings, and discouraged by a strict and limitative definition of their ownership or control rights. While this may be true, it is unlikely that the incentive of high expectations could be maintained in large companies and over a longer period, or in times of adversity.

Whether the SHCS will ever realize its pretense of cooperative management by employee shareholders is highly doubtful. Rather, the SHCS has been moving in the direction established by the Company Law. Its strength lies to some extent in its lack of legal clarity, which makes it useful to the Communist Party, government, managers and employees, and other stakeholders with widely divergent views in a period of economic boom and creeping transition from collective to private ownership.

Chapter 7

Local Elites as Officials and Owners: Shareholding and Property Rights in Daqiuzhuang

NAN LIN AND CHIH-JOU JAY CHEN

R ural China has been undergoing enormous institutional changes in the past two decades. Beginning with the self-responsibility system in the agricultural sector, and then extending to the nonagricultural sector, many innovative forms of organization have appeared, ranging from family and private businesses to joint-household enterprises, collective enterprises, and joint ventures involving foreign investments. A more recent form is the shareholding system (*gufen zhi*) or shareholding cooperative system (*gufen hezuozhi*). But the guidelines as to what the shareholding systems entail and how they should be run are limited. As we shall see, this vagueness and fuzziness are partly owing to multiple policy agendas. Some shareholding systems are intended to allow state enterprises to pool resources and capital, including foreign investments, and to become self-sufficient. Other systems aim to encourage households to form cooperatives instead of individual and family enterprises. Yet there is no guideline as to which existing enterprises are entitled to form a specific type of shareholding company. Given these encouraging and yet confusing guidelines and messages, many types of shareholding companies have emerged. Enormous variations can be found in (1) the existing enterprises (state, collective, households, individuals) or newly created enterprises that become shareholding companies, (2) the labels used, (3) the definition and distribution of shares, (4) the distribution of the residual income, and (5) the rights to transfer or dispose of the shares. Within the structural and policy constraints, different actors interpret these vague policies to construct rules and institutions in the creation of various shareholding companies that serve their particular interests. The critical issue, then, is which actors take advantage of such opportunities and what motivates their actions.

We argue that *shareholding systems in areas of rural China represent deliberate action on the part of local families or local elites to transfer property rights away from the state and local governments into their own hands.* The success of a particular shareholding system is, therefore, to a large extent, contingent on its usefulness to the actors involved and on the lack of clarification and enforcement of rules by the central government. So long as the state does not provide clear guidelines and shows little enthusiasm in enforcing property rights, this transfer of collective rights into private hands will continue.

This chapter begins with a description of the fuzziness and uncertainties in various state policies and classifications of shareholding systems, which enable some collective and private (family or household) enterprises to join forces as shareholding companies while holding on to their property rights in those enterprises. The focus then shifts to the case of Daqiuzhuang in Tianjin, where the local elite are turning collective firms into shareholding enterprises and transferring the property rights of the enterprises into their own hands. Such subversion of the property rights has enormous ramifications because of the huge number and assets of collective enterprises in rural China. In 1994, rural collective (village and town) enterprises accounted for 31 percent of national industrial output and 70 percent of rural industrial output. Furthermore, 79 percent of the nonagricultural labor force in rural China was employed by collective (village and town) enterprises.[1] Transfer of the property rights of collective enterprises, if carried out extensively, would have significant ramifications for the socialist nature of the rural economy in China.

Shareholding in Rural China: Policies and Practices

Official Chinese documents specify three dominant types of shareholding system: (1) shareholding cooperatives (*gufen hezuo*), (2) limited liability companies (*youxian gongsi*), and (3) joint-stock limited companies (*youxian gufen gongsi*).

The term "shareholding cooperatives" (*gufen shi hezuo*) first appeared in Central Committee document #1 of 1985, which stated:

> Some cooperative economies choose the method of shareholding management and dividend-sharing. Shares are obtained by way of investment of assets. They can also be obtained through assessment of productive materials and labor in the basic construction of the enterprise. Part of the profit can be paid out as dividends on shares. This method of management does

not change the entitlement of the property and avoids the fault of equating cooperative economy with the merging of properties and distribution of shares according to labor. Yet it merges various elements of production and more speedily establishes a new economic scale and accumulates shared assets.[2]

In other words, the state sees shareholding cooperatives as a way of allowing participating parties to invest and share profits, while allowing the state (or the "public") to hold on to the basic rights to the enterprise; namely, the rights of alienation and appropriation. The document provided general guidelines, with no specifications as to how this system could or should be implemented.

Further variations of shareholding emerged when the Company Law was approved and issued by the Standing Committee of the People's Congress on December 29, 1993, and enacted on July 1, 1994. The law identifies two types of corporations: the limited liability company and the joint-stock limited company.[3] A limited liability company involves no more than 50 shareholders, limited assets (a minimum of Y 500,000 for manufacturing or wholesaling firms and Y 300,000 for retail firms), and restricted transfers of stocks. A joint-stock limited company issues shares of equal value to an unspecified minimum number of holders, may recruit holders publicly, has more flexibility in share transfers, and has a total share issue of no less than Y 10,000,000. The shareholders may be exclusively the founding members of the corporation or include other publicly recruited holders.

Unlike the earlier regulation regarding shareholding cooperatives, which was intended to promote development of the communal form of economic organization, the limited liability company and the joint-stock limited company seem to encourage reconstitution of state-owned enterprises. The law specifically states that state-owned enterprises may become limited liability companies or joint-stock limited companies. However, the details of these transformations are unclear. It is stated that "the implementation procedures and specific measures for restructuring state-owned enterprises as companies shall be formulated separately by the State Council."[4] Moreover, "where a state-owned enterprise is restructured as a joint-stock limited company, it shall be strictly prohibited to convert the state-owned assets into shares at a depressed price or to sell off them at a depressed price, or to distribute them to individuals without charge."[5] Further, there is no information regarding how a collective (e.g., the town and village collective) might be reconstituted as a limited liability company or a joint stock company. The new forms of company thus open up the possibility of turning a collective enterprise into a stock company, but offer few guidelines as to how this should be accomplished.

As a result of the vagueness of regulations and the liberal interpretations of the documents, the actual use of a particular label, whether "shareholding cooperative," "limited liability company," or "joint-stock limited company," may bear little resemblance to its original intent. Systematic data on diverse types of shareholding enterprises are not available, but we have found four types in our fieldwork in Tianjin, Shanghai, and southern Fujian: (1) private enterprises disguised as collective enterprises (called "wearing a red cap"); (2) collective enterprises that have turned themselves into shareholding cooperatives so as to sell "social" shares to individuals; (3) shareholding companies formed by several collective enterprises, which hold shares in them; and (4) collectives labeled as shareholding companies.[6]

The first three types of shareholding enterprise represent no transformation of property rights. Shareholding is used here as a means to combine or absorb additional capital or to gain the advantages of being in the "public" sector. The original owners, whether local governments, collectives, families, or households, retain full control over the companies' assets and management, despite their nominal identification as shareholding companies. Only the fourth type shows signs of transforming property rights.

Converting Local Collectives into Shareholding Enterprises

When a collective enterprise transforms itself into a shareholding company, shares are only distributed within the enterprise. Control over assets, management, and residual income is nominally transferred to the shareholders. But because the enterprise itself retains the majority of shares, control of assets and management presumably remains in the hands of the collective, which thus retains property rights to the enterprise. The only new feature seems to be that the workers, as shareholders, are now entitled to shares of the surplus income and have greater incentives to work harder for the enterprise.

On the surface, this type of shareholding system seems similar to the first three types of shareholding. There is no actual transfer of property rights, in that the original owners (whether individuals, families, collectives, or some combination) retain control of the enterprise's resources. The key question, however, is whether the collective retains its control of the enterprise's assets and management. We argue that because of the fuzziness of the rules regarding how a collective can be turned into a shareholding enterprise, subversion of the ownership is beginning to take place in many collectives turned into shareholding enterprises. The actual control of assets and management is being transferred from the village that used to own the collective to the shareholding enterprise. The subtle aspect of this transfer is that there may not be any change in the leadership of the collective or the shareholding enterprise. The same actors who served as principal managers and Party representatives in the collective remain as chief executives and Party representatives in the shareholding enterprise. But, instead of acting as agents for the village, entrusted with the task of managing the collective, these leaders now act as members of the board of directors and chief executives on behalf of the shareholding enterprise. The village no longer commands the assets or management of the enterprise. The leaders now take action on behalf of and in the interest of the enterprise, rather than the village. The village government is now a regulatory agency relative to the enterprise, rather than the next level in the chain of command.

However, in most cases, these same leaders retain some political and social functions on behalf of the village. They remain as Party secretaries of the enterprises, and often as Party secretaries of neighborhood committees. In these capacities, the leaders remain agents of the village government. This dual role enables them to avoid criticism for turning the enterprise over to private hands and at the same time permits them to ease control of the assets of the enterprise from the public sector (the local government) into their own hands.

We hasten to add that such transformations are only one particular form of privatization, in which the enterprise is rooted in a community (cannot be relocated) and is in the hands of a few powerful members of the local elite, who also retain their nominal leadership in the Party apparatus in the enterprise. There is also evidence that the political power (state control through cadres) initially embedded in the enterprise gives way to economic and social power (local families) as reflected in the succession of the leadership in these enterprises.

Nor is this a sudden or "big bang" phenomenon. Typically, the process evolves over time, involving two stages: (1) local cadres gain control of the local economy and create enterprises that combine the features of collectives (with clear village ownership) and a market orientation (self-management and distribution of surplus value), with themselves or family members installed in the management, and (2) local enterprises are turned, by local cadres turned entrepreneurs and their family members, into shareholding companies, where they themselves obtain the majority of shares by both representing the collective shares and claiming a large portion of the shares given to the managers for their "contributions" to the enterprise. A third stage, still evolving, is a plan to accumulate sufficient noncollective capital for the shareholders in the enterprise to "buy back" the collective shares. When and if this third stage is completed, which may take years, ownership of the enterprise will have been transferred from the public sector to the private sector with the tacit consent of the state. These transformations reflect a process of interaction between what the local elite recognize and interpret as allowable by state guidelines and what rational actions they can take to acquire the property rights themselves. This process of property rights transformation is illustrated below by the case of Daqiuzhuang, regarded by some as the richest village in China until recently, when it was "promoted" to town (*zhen*) status.

Our data for Daqiuzhuang come from various sources: local informants, a participant observer, and extensive local and informal documents.[7] The senior author has visited the community numerous times (at least once a year) since 1988, most recently in the spring of 1996. During these trips, he conducted interviews with local leaders (including the village Party secretaries and heads), enterprise executives (including several directors and deputy directors of the boards and the CEOs), key actors (including Liu Wanmin, the steel worker who helped start the first plant), and workers (both local and hired hands from outside). Journals were kept for all interviews and voice-recordings were made whenever it was allowed. A key external informant was a researcher from the Tianjin Academy of Social Sciences who spent two years stationed at Daqiuzhuang conducting intensive research on the organization of and changes in the village, as well as serving as an advisor to the local leaders. He accompanied the senior author on most of his trips as well. Many figures are derived from actual documents from the village, estimates calculated by the Tianjin Academy of Social Sciences, and reports in the media. Inconsistencies were found in different documents. Most of the inconsistencies, we felt, were owing to the lack of sophistication and imprecision of calculations in the accounting system in earlier years, and the habit of using rounded numbers, rather than to deliberate falsification. In such cases, we use the figures reported in the most recent documents and estimates repeated in different documents. Errors are inevitable and the figures should be seen as illustrations of general trends rather than precise estimations. Other information (e.g., the number of hired laborers—the outside workers—and their working conditions; the actual benefits received by the top managers and relationships among them) is not documented and had to be obtained from informants who had proven generally reliable. At best, these estimates provide only the general picture and trends. In all cases, we have striven to report only reliable information.

Local Market Socialism in Daqiuzhuang

Daqiuzhuang, about 50 kilometers southeast of Tianjin, with a population about 3,886 (in 1989), became the richest village in China by the mid 1980s under the dictatorial leadership of Yu Zuomin, its Party secretary and corporate boss. In 1988, the village produced output valued at Y 403 million, equivalent then to about U.S.$100 million, resulting in a net income, after tax and deduction of costs for administration, school, materials, and depreciation, of Y 18 million.[8] Total assets stood at Y 90 million. Average household savings were about Y 7,500 annually, and total household savings exceeded Y 2.5 million in 1988. In 1990, the per capita income of Y 3,400 was ten times China's national average. By 1991, this had risen to Y 8,400. Estimates of gross output value and net income were Y 450 million and Y 25 million respectively.

The achievements were astonishing for such a small village and for such a short period of time.[9] Rumors that it had been a designated model village, like Dazhai, in which heavy state and local investments were made for the sake of show-and-tell, are false. Since details of Daqiuzhuang's rise and development are available elsewhere,[10] it will suffice to briefly recapitulate here.

It all started in 1968, when Daqiuzhuang faced starvation. Yu, the village's Party secretary, was in a desperate situation; his position was vulnerable. Through a retired villager's connection, Yu found out that Tianjin City needed bricks for construction. So he started a brickyard, with a hand-built oven and local clay, producing more than 3,000 bricks a week. In 1969, a construction team in Tianjin needed bricks worth Y 30,000, and again, through connections, Yu made a deal with the team, whereby it lent him Y 6,000 to buy a second-hand ventilation machine. As a result, production increased to several thousand bricks a day. While the brick-making business made some money, the real breakthrough came in 1977, when a local peasant named Xie started a steel-pressing business. It was a hot-pressing operation and did not make much money. Another villager, Liu Wanmin, a retired worker who had been employed by a steel mill in Tianjin, pointed out that cold-pressing would be cheaper. Yu sent him to his old factory to find out the possibilities. Then Yu and others went to Tianjin and through Liu's connections and introductions met and dined with some older workers. Upon their advice, it was decided that they could put together three steel-pressing machines with old parts for Y 300,000. Liu figured that they actually needed only Y 100,000, if he could persuade some of his old friends to work for minimum wage. Yu decided to take the risk. He collected contributions from the villagers and borrowed money from the county (through a relative's connections) and other villages. The factory was built in 1977, with an investment of Y 160,000. It went into production in 1978 and turned in an income of Y 200,000 the same year.

Yu continued to reinvest the income into other factories and imported skilled technicians and young workers. By 1989, the Daqiuzhuang Agricultural-Industrial-Commercial United Corporation owned 117 enterprises, manufacturing over 300 products in 20 industries. In 1992, Yu stepped down as the CEO (the general manager, *zongjingli*) and became the chairman of the newly created board of directors (*dongshihui*). His second son, Yu Shaozheng, took over as CEO. The corporation was split up into "Four Big Groups," each of which had its own subcompanies and enterprises.[11] Each group retained independence in management, financing, personnel, and marketing, while making annual contributions to the corporation—the village itself.

Property Rights During the Yu Era

Underneath its economic organizations, Daqiuzhuang has a social structure not unlike those of many other villages in China. Of the Four Big Groups, Liu's brother, Liu Wanquan, was the CEO of the first; Yu's cousin, Yu Zuoyao, was the CEO of the second; Yu's son-in-law, Zhao Shuzhong, was the CEO of the third; and Zhang Yannian headed the fourth. A fifth group, in charge of all agricultural production, was in the hands of the husband of Yu's niece. Yu's mistress, a woman named Shi Jiamin,[12] was the director of the administrative office, and members of her family ran the electricity office, the electronics company, and Daqiuzhuang's branch offices in Tianjin and in the Development Zone on the coast. Figure 7.1 shows these networked relationships among village and enterprise leaders.

Earlier work has characterized Daqiuzhuang as an example of local market socialism.[13] The village retained the ownership of all its enterprises, and yet allowed them to compete freely in the marketplaces of their choosing. Contributions from the enterprises were used to maintain public services and social welfare. In the final analysis, Yu was in total control, heading a local elite network dominated by his family.

In terms of property rights, Daqiuzhuang and its economic groups in the late 1980s can be characterized as follows. First of all, the ownership of the economic groups was officially in the hands of the "public"— the village. Daqiuzhuang was itself incorporated as the Daqiuzhuang Agricultural-Industrial-Commercial United Corporation, which owned all the enterprises, as well as all other units in the village. While each enterprise was allowed flexibility in the allocation of its residual income

Yu Zuomin

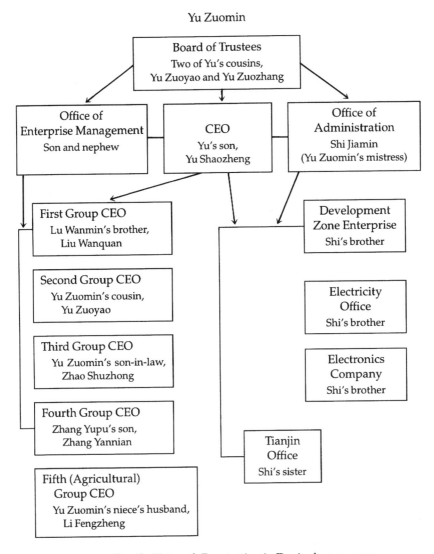

FIG. 7.1. Family Network Penetration in Daqiuzhuang, 1990

and management decisions, the assets themselves belonged to the United Corporation—and, therefore, to the village collective. Secondly, Yu, as the chairman of the board of the United Corporation, as well as the secretary-general of the local Party and village head, had supreme authority over all enterprises. To a great extent, the enterprises contributed to the redistribution process imposed by Yu for the village. A significant portion of the surplus income from each enterprise was handed over to the village for the general welfare of all residents and the village itself. All housing, schools, infirmaries, nursing services, infrastructure (e.g., roads, bridges, electricity, tap water), and other public services (scholarships for students, the security force, fire stations, retirement pensions, television and radio stations, etc.) were supported by surplus income generated by the enterprises and redistributed through the village corporation. In sum, the ultimate control of the enterprises was in the hands of the village corporation, a public, collective entity, and nominally under the continuing command structure of the state, through the county, to the village government and Party apparatus. In reality, Yu, as the local leader of the Party and village, commanded the enterprises; that is, *the political apparatus controlled economic resources.*

The Transformation of Daqiuzhuang Enterprises

DEMISE OF THE YU EMPIRE

The fortune and fame of Daqiuzhuang took a dramatic turn in 1992. It all started with the first group (Wanquan). In December 1992, a controller with the group, Wei Fuhe, was accused of doctoring accounts and was not able to explain a certain missing sum (about Y 29,000).[14] He was put under "company arrest" and subjected to interrogation and physical abuse. In the end, Wei died, probably accidentally. It was not the first time that a person had died in Daqiuzhuang under the corporation's coercive interrogation. In 1990, a man named Liu Yutian had been beaten to death.[15] However, Wei was not a Daqiuzhuang resident. His family began to investigate and pursue the matter. Rumor had it that after getting nowhere in Daqiuzhuang, they approached a relative who happened to be a police chief in a city in the northeast, who, in turn, contacted the police chief of Tianjin City. When an investigative group was sent to Daqiuzhuang, probably in February 1993, it was met and stopped by village security forces at the entrance to the village. Yu, though not personally involved in the interrogations, instructed the security forces not to allow the investigative group to enter the village. After negotiations, Yu finally relented and the investigators entered the village. However, Yu forbade villagers to cooperate with the investigators, who were then not allowed to leave the village. When the news reached Tianjin, the mayor had to intervene and demand their release. With armed police surrounding the village, Yu gave in. At this time, in March 1993, the Eighth Congress of the People's Political Consultative Conference was in session, and Yu, as a representative, appeared at the meeting. The state suppressed further reporting of the Daqiuzhuang incident while the congress was in session. Soon after the meeting was over, however, a work team from Tianjin, along with armed police, stationed itself in the village, essentially taking control. On April 15, Yu was arrested, along with several other village and group officers, including one of his sons, Yu Shaozheng, the Party secretary of the corporation.

On August 23 and 24, 1993, Yu and seven others were found guilty and sentenced to jail. Yu was convicted of concealing the four persons accused of beating Wei to death, organizing and commanding innocent villagers to interrupt legal investigations, and bribing an investigative officer. He was sentenced to twenty years in prison. His son was sentenced to ten years, and Miss Shi to one year; five others received sentences ranging from two to four years.[16] On August 27, eighteen more people were sentenced, including one with a death sentence (to be delayed for two years), two with life sentences, and others ranging from five to fifteen years in prison.

THE POST-YU TRANSFORMATION OF DAQIUZHUANG

In November 1993, Daqiuzhuang was "elevated" from a village to a town. The official explanation was that this elevation "was inevitable due to Daqiuzhuang's social, industrial and economic developments."[17] Thus, it had earned its new status. Regardless of the reason, the major political consequence is that as a town, all top officials, including the head of the village and the Party secretary, would be appointed by the county government.[18] The change in administrative status allowed Jinghai County to send in one of its vice mayors as the new town head. Moreover, it abolished the corporation, and the Four Big Groups were converted into four "administrative streets" (*jiedao*) similar to the street committees in cities and towns. On paper, therefore, by the end of 1993, local market socialism in Daqiuzhuang seemed to have received a death sentence. With the county government directly in control, the corporation gone, and the groups turned into street committees, state socialism seemed to have returned in full force.

What has happened since, however, has been a surprising process of transformation, no less dramatic than the initial rise of Daqiuzhuang. The first inkling of the survival and continued prosperity of Daqiuzhuang became public when in February 1994 *People's Daily* carried an essay entitled "Daqiuzhuang—the Charm and Color Continuing."[19] In it, the reporter described visiting teams from a Shandong Laiwu Steel Company that had just signed a joint project with Jinhai (the Daqiuzhuang fourth group) with an investment of ¥650,000,000 to produce hot-pressed steel tubes with an annual production target of 120,000 to 150,000 tons. "Every group [in Daqiuzhuang] efficiently managed its subdistrict; there was truck traffic everywhere, shops were full of goods and consumers, dance halls and karaoke clubs were everywhere in the evening, and more and more new managers and technicians are arriving every day," the article noted. "Production, from a low in July and August of 1992, started growing again, with the 1993 production target of Y 5 billion accomplished, realizing a profit of Y 430 million." Although the Four Big Groups had been reorganized into street committees, the article revealed, "all the original cadres, assets and operations were retained." Nowhere in this report were these groups identified with the local political structure.

In other words, the Four Big Groups continue to exist, despite the change of official title. Business is going on as usual. Moreover, the groups not only are now in full charge of the economic enterprises, but have also taken over administrative responsibility for the residential neighborhoods. What, then, is the role of the town government and its relationship with the Four Big Groups? Fieldwork in 1994, 1995, and 1996 (at the time of the most recent visit by the senior author in May 1996) reveals the following transformations.

Before the series of incidents in December 1992 that led to Yu's arrest, the general manager of the fifth, agricultural group (the husband of Yu's niece) suddenly died. It was discovered that the group had debts exceeding Y 300 million, since it was in the midst of constructing a number of new factories, including a joint venture with a Danish firm to build a fertilizer plant. After the reorganization, it became clear that the group could not survive without substantial infusions of capital. Yu convened the leadership of the Four Big Groups and came up with a solution: the thirty-some enterprises in the fifth group would be absorbed by the Four Big Groups, which in return would take over its debts.

Before this plan could be realized, the death of the accountant occurred that eventually led to transformation of the village into a town under the control of the county. When County Vice Magistrate Wei, who had been appointed the new Daqiuzhuang Party secretary, arrived, he was immediately faced with the problem of the Y 300 million debt. The Four Big Groups balked at keeping the agreement they had reached when Yu was in control, and the county itself was totally incapable of paying the debt. In fact, the town found itself in difficulty, because with meager county support, it could not even function properly in managing the huge, thriving industrial complex and meeting its enormous obligations in public services (maintaining schools, hospital, utilities, communications, etc.). The county and Wei realized that the only way to prevent the collapse of this system was to maintain the status quo. Wei accordingly negotiated with the Four Big Groups, which agreed to absorb the enterprises of the fifth group, as Yu had planned; furthermore, the land allocated to the fifth group would also be turned over to the Four Big Groups. The share depended on the proportion of the population under the jurisdiction of each street-group. Furthermore, all the groups would keep their original titles (Wanquan, Yaoshun, Jinmei, and Jinhai) and social and economic identity. Each street would have its own chairman (street administrator), CEO (economic head), and Party secretary.

In the end, most of the original cadres and officials except those in prison retained their positions and titles. In three of the groups, a single person became chairman, CEO (general manager), and Party secretary. In the other group, because the designated successor, a son of the CEO, was imprisoned, authority was delegated to a trusted family friend.

A brief account of these elites and the web of their social networks is useful here. In the first group, Liu continues to serve as CEO, chairman of the board, and Party secretary. (His older brother was the retired steel worker who helped start the first enterprise in Daqiuzhuang.) Liu's son, the deputy CEO, was implicated in the "incident" and sentenced to four years in prison. Zhang Yuying, who is a cousin of Zhang Yupu, a prominent figure in the village, who preceded Yu Zuomin as the village's Party secretary and was himself "rehabilitated" earlier from some "mistakes," the nature of which we never found out, serves as executive deputy CEO. This arrangement allowed the Liu family to hold on to the group, while for the time being delegating the running of the group to Zhang. Liu's son Liu Yonghua has since been released from prison and reinstated as a deputy CEO. However, as Zhang had proved his managerial skills and loyalty to the Liu family, he has continued to serve as the executive deputy CEO. The second group, the largest of the Big Four, has Yu, a cousin of Yu Zuomin's, as its CEO, chairman, and Party secretary. The third group is headed by Zhao, Yu Zuomin's son-in-law. He remains the CEO and is assisted by Li Fengzhuang, a younger brother of Li Fengzheng, who, until his death, was the husband of Yu Zuomin's wife's niece. The fourth group also retains as its CEO Zhang Yannian, son of Zhang Yupu. These networked relationships among the leaders of the groups are depicted in Figure 7.2.

With the abolition of the Daqiuzhuang General Corporation,[20] the Four Big Groups thus essentially became four independent corporations, each with its own neighborhoods, land, enterprises, and population. Each is dominated by a single family. Two of the four corporations are still connected with the Yu family, while the other prominent family in the village, the Zhangs, are involved in the two other corporations. The local familial network of elites remains strong, as does the market orientation of each corporation. Socialism has now descended from the village-town level to

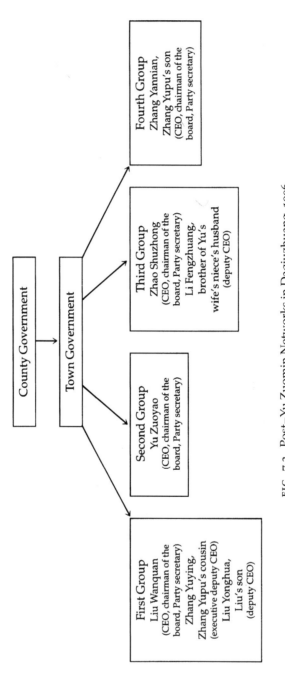

FIG. 7.2. Post–Yu Zuomin Networks in Daqiuzhuang, 1996

the corporation level. Each corporation becomes its own socialist system, responsible for the welfare of its population. Each corporation runs its own infirmary and schools (nurseries and elementary schools), cares for its senior citizens, and hires its own managers, technicians, and outside workers.[21]

The town government is responsible for security, justice, banks, accounting, auditing, environmental protection, a junior high school, utilities (electricity, water supply, heating, gas), roads, and legal services. Each corporation-street is charged an administrative fee of .30 percent of net profits, of which 33 percent is retained by the town government and the rest goes to the county government. The town government has ten cadres, five of whom are sent in by the "state" (i.e., from the county government), while the other five are from Daqiuzhuang. In addition, the county government has nineteen cadres on site. The town government, in other words, plays only a peripheral role in the social, economic, and political lives of Daqiuzhuang's inhabitants. Within a year (in April 1995), Wei was replaced as Party secretary by Wang Qingwu, another vice mayor from the county.

In the meantime, the corporations continued to grow in productivity. Production value reached Y2 billion officially (but unofficially may have reached Y4 billion) in 1992, Y4.5 billion in 1993 (unofficially Y5.6 billion), and Y7 billion in 1994 (with a profit of Y5 million). In 1995, the enterprises employed 23,000 outside workers.

Another important event in the history of Daqiuzhuang occurred in 1995: the land in the center of the town was divided and allocated to the Four Big Groups. While all the farm and industrial lands had been divided and allocated to them by 1993, the center of the town remained in the hands of the town government. In March 1995, however, it was divided into four portions and given to the four corporation-streets. The town government was left with only its headquarters, the junior high school, and the buildings occupied by the police and environmental protection agency. In essence, the four corporations have largely taken over the functions of local government, along with its land, population, buildings, residences, and industry. The town government provides only things that each corporation itself cannot, such as utilities, police, the middle school, and other functions under the direct control of the state (communication, roads, taxation).

In sum, the transfer of resources (i.e., land, population, many of the social services and social welfare functions, and the enterprises themselves) from the town to the groups represents a clear shift of property rights from government to the corporation. In contrast to the Yu era, when Yu, as the paramount Party leader of the village, exercised total control over the resources invested in and produced by the enterprises, as well as the land, the population, and all public services and social welfare functions, the town Party and government now have little control over these resources.

Practicing Shareholding and Gaining Control over Property Rights

The next question is what has happened to the enterprises within the groups themselves. Nominally, the enterprises remained collectives, and their assets, built up over the years with investments of public (village) capital, were to remain under the control of the public, which after the reorganization should have been the town. This did not occur, however, because of a transformation of property rights that began taking place in 1992, by which the enterprises in each group were turned into shareholding companies.

The evolution of the shareholding systems in two of the four groups at Daqiuzhuang is described below. Our understanding is that a similar transformation was occurring in the other two groups as well. Data are based on interviews with key administrators of each group and with informants in fieldwork conducted in 1995 and 1996. Information provided to us by officials of each group is adduced to convey the trial-and-error nature of the transformation process.

GROUP Y

In 1992, stock-sharing first appeared in Daqiuzhuang, beginning in the second group, henceforth referred to as Group Y. The largest and strongest group, with assets of 1.4 billion yuan by 1995, Group Y has 46 enterprises and a workforce of 8,000, with a production value of Y 3.6 billion and net income of Y 180 million. Group Y is proud to be recognized as the third most efficient village and town enterprise and the second-largest village and town enterprise in China, ranking 143d among the country's 500 largest industrial enterprises.

Group Y reorganized itself as a limited stock company (*gufen youxian gongsi*) in 1992. (Since the Company Law was not formally enacted until 1994, it was apparently ahead of its time.) It had two types of shares. The group held 70 percent of the shares (the collective shares, *jiti gu*), and the rest were "social" or public shares. Each share had a base value of Y 1 and was sold for Y 2. Each share earned a fixed annual dividend of 20 percent of its value. No transfer or sale was allowed. A total of 45 million shares were issued. The fixed 20 percent dividend was believed to represent little risk, because the group's profits were expanding at a much greater rate. For example, the group's assets of Y 1.6 billion in 1992 had increased to Y 2.9 billion by 1995, and thus almost doubled over a span of four years. Thus, it was simply a fixed-interest investment plan; the group generated cash and shareholders split the profits. Since the group held 70 percent of the shares, there was no transfer of property rights from the collective to private shareholders as far as the group was concerned.

Beginning in 1993, the group replaced this setup with a joint-stock company (*gufen hezuo gongsi*).[22] Again, shares were divided into two types: collective shares, accounting for 70 percent of the total, and individual shares. Individual shares, which were only available to group and enterprise employees, were further divided into two types: "position" (*gang-wei*) shares and individual or cash shares. Position shares were distributed at no cost to persons holding top managerial positions in the group and its enterprises, including the directors, the CEO, deputy CEOs, other leaders at group headquarters, and top managers in each enterprise. On average, there were three times as many position shares in each group and each enterprise as there were cash shares. Again, each share received a dividend of 20 percent of the share value each year.

The joint-stock company differs from the original limited stock company in at least two aspects. For one, the latter sold shares to the public and anyone could buy them, whereas the shares of the former are sold to local residents who are employed at the group's enterprises and to non-resident workers who are at or above the team leader level (*banzhang*). Shares can be transferred within the enterprise, but because of the guaranteed dividends, few such transactions have occurred.[23] Secondly, position shares are distributed to only a small number of high-level managers, at no cost to them. Thus, the elite of the group gained control of three-quarters of the individual shares at no cost.

Group officials claim that no transfer of ownership has occurred, because, in accordance with guidelines from the Ministry of Agriculture, the collective holds at least 70 percent of the shares. In reality, however, the collective shares are represented exclusively by group and company officials (the board of directors and top-echelon managers). Neither the town or county government nor the Party have any representation. Thus, by representing the collective shares and by holding the overwhelming majority of the individual shares, group and company officials have gained complete control of management and distribution of surplus income.

Nevertheless, the originally invested assets of the enterprises remain public. Even if state policy were to allow the group to buy back the collective assets in shares, it would be prohibitively costly. However, a plan has been set in motion that may eventually change the most fundamental property right—that of ownership. In 1992, the group reorganized itself into a so-called General Group and divided its enterprises by industry into five groups: two for steel tubes, one for other steel materials (construction materials), one for nonferrous metals (copper, aluminum, transformers), and one for light industry (e.g., foam, paint, lumber, tires, and pumps). Following the Company Law, it then "decentralized" authority to each group; the General Group only "concerns itself with macro-management, policies, and strategies, but not micro-management. It is in charge of assets, not management." In 1995, it set a production goal of Y 2 billion and a profit target of Y 120 million by year 2000 for each group. Thus, the General Group is expected to generate Y 10 billion in production value and Y 600 million in profits by 2000. In other words, the goal is to double the General Group's assets and profits in five years.[24]

While no official would reveal to us what the motivation was behind the "urgency" of doubling the assets and profits in five years, and why the decentralized system was devised to charge each enterprise with specific production and profit targets, we can offer a hypothesis: *these plans indicate a decision by the General Group to eventually "buy back" the collective shares.* Since collective assets are so enormous (representing 70 percent of current shares), they may have to be bought back in segments rather than as a whole. By allocating the collective shares down to each group and each enterprise and charging each with production and profit targets, the General Group has opened up the possibility that some groups will achieve their goals earlier than others and thus be able to buy back the collective portions of their shares sooner.

Thus, we speculate that the General Group may be preparing itself to exercise two options by year 2000: either, if state policy by then permits, buying out the original public assets so that each group, and eventually the General Group, becomes entirely private (in the hands of the individual shareholders), or, if state policy does not permit, each group returning the original assets (in equipment, capital, and other factors) and emerging as a separate privately held firm. There is no guarantee that either option can actually be exercised, since the state may not permit such options in the near future. However, the General Group leaders have set specific production goals and devised ways to accumulate capital so as to exercise these options if and when they become available. If either option is carried out, control will fall outright into the hands of the General Group elite, who hold the overwhelming majority of the individual shares in every group and enterprise.

GROUP J

For the third group, referred to hereafter as Group J, the shareholding system began to emerge in 1995.[25] According to the key administrator, Daqiuzhuang "had too many assets and too much property. It is impossible to buy it and the baggage cannot be thrown away. So we adopted a temporary measure—a contractual system for a period of five years." The group and each of its enterprises agreed to make a "risk deposit" guaranteeing the doubling of the enterprise's assets in five years. If the asset-doubling "contract" was accomplished, then returns would be doubled, trebled, or quadrupled. If it were not accomplished, the deposit would be forfeited. "And no bonuses."

The risk deposit, as far as we could find out, was roughly the equivalent of one-tenth of the assets of an enterprise. In other words, if the assets of a factory totaled Y 1 million, the risk deposit would amount to about Y 100,000. This risk deposit amount was used to calculate and claim shares. The deposit was calculated for each of the enterprises, as well as for the second-level companies. In each unit, 30 percent of the deposit was considered the collective share, and the remaining 70 percent became individual shares to be bought by the leader, managers, staff, and workers of the unit, as well as by leaders of levels above, including the leaders of the group. The principle was that the number of individual shares to be bought was calculated according to position and seniority. The group leaders (the chairman of the board–CEO, the trustees, and the deputy CEOs), holding the highest positions and being the most senior, claimed the largest shares. Leaders of the second-level company claimed the next largest shares. The leaders of the enterprise (the plant director, the station manager, and the team leader) then claimed their shares. The remaining staff and a few technical-engineering workers brought from outside who had made "significant contributions" and had "important skills" were also allowed to buy shares.

In their capacity as officials of the collective, the group leaders voted the collective shares (30 percent) of each enterprise as well as their own. Since they also received the largest number of individual shares, they held an "overwhelming majority" of the shares in each and every enterprise. The officials we interviewed refused to reveal the exact proportion to us, and none of the other informants seemed to know either.

The "contract" goal was to double assets in five years. Thus, for an annual deposit of Y 100,000, the expectation was to make Y 200,000 in annual profits. If the net profit was less than Y 200,000, the deficit was covered by the deposit. If the net profit was over Y 200,000, this surplus (over Y 200,000) was divided into two parts: 30 percent to the collective and 70 percent to individual shareholders. This plan was intended to encourage production, thus increasing the shareholders' dividends. But it would not challenge the collective ownership of the enterprises. In fact, the greater the production and profits, the stronger the collective would become, as the shares of the profits for the collective shares would increase proportionally as well.

In May 1996, when the senior author returned to Daqiuzhuang and reinterviewed the key administrator of Group J, his opinion and enthusiasm for the risk deposit system had waned dramatically. While acknowledging that it was "an extension of the self-responsibility system but with deeper practice," he saw no direct connection to shareholding.

> There were serious shortcomings and problems. Motivation was low, and mobilization insufficient. There were conflicts. The collective belonged to Daqiuzhuang. After the village became a town, the collectives belonged to the four streets [committees]. Still, it belonged to everyone and it belonged to no one. It became a state enterprise at the village [street] level, with all the interest relationships, property rights, and management problems. Under this system, the assets still belonged to the collective, which benefited. We need to find a more practical way with better effects.

In other words, the group leaders and workers were reluctant to work hard for the benefit of the collective. The risk deposit system was terminated after one year. In order to compensate for possible gains in the second to the fourth year, those enterprises suffering losses in the first year were not penalized, and their deposits were returned.

In the second half of 1995, a new system was developed. After six months of deliberations, the group leaders came up with two alternative systems: the limited liability company and the joint-stock system. After consulting with "experts from Nankai University and Beijing, and lawyers," by the end of 1995, the limited liability company system was adopted, group leaders hoping in this way "to achieve all the goals in a single step." Each enterprise became a limited liability company. The steps taken were as follows. First, a thorough accounting of assets was carried out. The accounting office, along with the county accounting affairs office, took almost six months to come up with a detailed total valuation. Second, an accounting of net assets (assets minus debts) was made. Third, the net asset value was reported to the village government (nominally, the street committee, but in reality the group), to guarantee that no assets of the collective would be lost.

After the above steps were completed, each enterprise formed a limited liability company in line with the Company Law. A board of directors was created, and the largest shareholder became the chairman of the board. The collective accounted for 25–30 percent of the shares, varying by enterprise: "The better the enterprise, the more the collective shares." The remainder were real cash shares. Total investment amounted to Y 20 million. The shares held by directors of the group represented "50, 60, or up to 75 percent" of the shares, and other individual shares were held by the enterprise's staff and employees who were Daqiuzhuang residents, as well as by some technicians who had been allowed to settle in the town. Likewise, the second-level companies would become corporations with registered cash assets of from Y 3 million to over Y 6 million. In total, fifteen limited liability companies have been established.

In the fifth and last step, the General Group signed a lease agreement with each company, on a rental basis. Each enterprise thus became an independent company, able to buy back its assets in the future, with no upper supervisory corporation: "The more independent the better."[26]

Underneath the rhetoric, and despite their seemingly different paths, Group J ended up with a system very similar to the one devised by Group Y. It has estimated its collective assets (steps 1–2), made them a matter of public record (step 3), and given each enterprise the autonomy to set production goals (step 4). However, noticeably different from Group Y, Group J estimated its collective shares at only 30 percent of all shares, making it easier to possibly buy them back, as the General Group boldly encouraged each enterprise to do (step 5). Ultimately, then, each enterprise has the option of becoming completely privatized in the future.

This does not mean, however, that the General Group has only a contractual relationship with each enterprise and merely collects rents. The leaders of the General Group in fact participate as shareholders in each and every enterprise. Directors of the General Group represent collective shares in each enterprise. Furthermore, they own individual shares. For example, Zhao, the CEO (who earned a salary of Y 760,000 in 1995), Li, the executive deputy CEO (who earned Y 200,000), and five deputy CEOs all have individual shares in each enterprise company. Because the shareholders control top appointments, the large holders (i.e., the General Group leaders) have a decisive say about management in every enterprise.

To increase the individual shares relative to the collective shares, the profits in the first three years will be turned in part into additional shares, and only a small portion of cash will be actually given to shareholders. When shares are expanded, they will proportionally go to the shareholders as bonus shares. In essence, the unequal distribution of shares between the large holders and small holders will increase over time, with the bulk of new shares going to the General Group leaders.[27]

In sum, Group J has also used the shareholding mechanism to shift the control of management and surplus income for each enterprise into the hands of the General Group elite. It has devised a plan to increase production and profits and turn the profits largely into new individual shares. The collective shares, currently standing at around 30 percent of net assets, will correspondingly shrink relative to individual shares. Given the opportunity, the General Group and its enterprises will be in a position to buy back the collective shares in the next five years or so.

Further Analyses

In retrospect, then, the demise of Yu Zuomin, instead of leading to the end of the semi-autonomous local enterprises, may have further eroded local government power. When Yu was in charge, he was a ruthless entrepreneur, but also a powerful cadre. He had absolute control over the enterprises and was known to collect money from the enterprises for specific projects at a moment's notice. The village had the best social welfare and social services in rural China, and no enterprise or CEO would have dared to think of, let alone implement, any plans or system without his approval. In other words, Yu's system was to allow some enterprises and individuals to become rich fast, and yet to maintain and enhance the collective level of well-being. In terms of property rights, the village retained ultimate control of the assets of all enterprises, and Yu, as representative of the Party and village, controlled the economic resources from his political position. In other words, *political power controlled economic and social resources.*

Now, after becoming a town, the local government has, for all intents and purposes, become a powerless and resourceless entity. It does not control the enterprises, does not manage the residents and neighborhoods, and does not even control any land. All the property rights, except those involving infrastructure and services, have fallen into the hands of the groups and their elite leaders. The town government literally lives off handouts from the corporate (i.e., group and company) leaders, who, in fact, are the same ones as when Yu was in charge. The only difference is that there is no longer any Yu to control them. They are now held together by kin and local networks.

Transformation of property rights has gone through two stages in Daqiuzhuang between 1992 and 1996. In the first stage, the Four Big Groups were able to pull resources away from the town by incorporating and dividing the population and the land. This process was possible because, first, the town was without the political or economic resources of its own to sustain the social services and welfare systems. It had to rely on the Big Four to provide the financial resources (a portion of the tax the groups pay to the county government is returned to the town government) to support town expenditure. Second, and more important, the town and the county were in no position to handle the enormous debts of the fallen fifth agricultural group and had to plead with the Big Four to assume the debts. To entice the Big Four to make such contributions, the town, in return, made the compromise of offering political (Party) and administrative (street, *jiedao*) power to the Big Four.[28] Thus, the leading actors of the Big Four (chairmen of the boards who also are the CEOs) were made the political leaders (branch Party secretaries) and administrative leaders (directors of the street committees). "There is a separation of politics and economics [*zhengjing fenzhi*] at Daqiuzhuang. The town will be in charge of politics, and will not take care of economics [*buguan jingji*]," the town's Party secretary announced. But the fact that the group leaders were also in charge of the Party apparatus and the street committees, as well as the land and the population, has left not much of the town for the town government to administer. As a result, the real economic, political, and administrative resources have clearly shifted from the town to the Four Big Groups.

During the second stage, the Four Big Groups reorganized ownership of the assets of the enterprises. Using the shareholding mechanism, the assets of each enterprise were turned into equities. Three types of shares appeared: collective shares, position shares, and individual shares. A significant portion of the shares (anywhere from 25 percent to 70 percent) belongs to the "collective" or the public. Since the corporate leaders represent the collective, they vote on behalf of the collective shares. Of the remaining individual shares, another significant portion consists of "contribution" or "position" shares distributed free to those who have made significant contributions to the enterprise—namely, for the most part, the leaders themselves. Finally, the remaining individual shares are sold to all qualified persons (usually the group and enterprise staff and workers who are local residents), proportional to their contribution and position shares. In other words, the greater their contribution/position shares, the larger the number of the cash shares they can buy. Finally, in most cases, only local residents affiliated with the enterprise are allowed to own or transfer shares. A few outside technicians who were invited to work in the enterprise have been allowed to move in with their families and to own shares. This exclusion rule inhibits possible subversion of the power of the local elite from outside. These rules seem to assure that property rights are being slowly but surely transferred from the town into the hands of the corporate leaders.[29]

Finally, we suspect that plans have been set in motion to accumulate sufficient individual shares to buy back the collective shares if the opportunity arises. The groups are dividing the collective shares down to each enterprise, where production and profit goals are set in the next five or so years to make this possible. Since the group leaders control the majority shares of each enterprise, they and their families would gain control over the assets, management, and surplus income if and when enterprises become privatized.

These local corporate elite leaders have thus molded the stock companies and interjected their own interpretations of state laws and regulations, while serving their own interests. They see and use the shareholding system as a method of diverting the rights of control and use of the collective enterprises from the town into the hands of the shareholders, even though the proclaimed reason was to provide incentives to the thousands of workers.

Furthermore, there is the process under way of transforming *the power base of these leaders from their political assets to their local and family networks.* These corporate leaders wear several hats. They are simultaneously corporate executives, Party secretaries, and village administrators. It is clear, however, their primary role is as corporate leaders. Except during the crisis period when Yu Zuomin and his subordinates were being prosecuted, political and Party ideology clearly take the back seat to running the enterprises and attending to the needs of the workers and their families. Corporate leaders are all grooming members of their families to succeed them as the next generation of leaders, working in a network of local families. These prominent families support and promote one another, as can be seen from the interlocking leadership in the various groups and enterprises, described above. Neither the county and town governments nor local residents—the other shareholders—challenge their positions. In short, the elites of the Big Four now use *their economic and social power to control political and administrative resources.*

Conclusions

Based on these observations and analyses, we argue that the shareholding system has become one means by which local elite actors have wrested control of collective assets from the public sector. It is clear that property rights subversion is taking place. Those in control of the corporations are gradually taking away the power (control of resources) from the local government and, at the same time, keeping it from the workers. At this point, the worker stockholders have little say in how the shareholding is operationalized or implemented, and the local government seems either unable or unwilling to wrest the power from the corporate elite leadership. The particular shareholding mechanisms adopted in each location are aimed at implementing this subversion.

One visible trend is the convergence of the corporate elite leaders and local elite family networks. The shift of the property rights of the corporations also signals the gaining of power by members of the local elite, who combine social and political capital rooted in their local origins and networks. Shareholding is the means by which they are shifting their power base from a largely political one (as cadres in the local government and the Party apparatus) to a largely social one (through a network of powerful families).

What remains to be seen is whether this subversion will become a stable form of control over local corporations. Our speculation is that this emerging form of property rights will remain viable if it meets the following conditions: (1) the corporate elite leadership merges with local elite families to form a strong local basis of power, (2) the corporation remains profitable, so that workers feel that there is continued improvement in their quality of life, and (3) local cadres and their families participate in the power structure and/or stock-sharing. Through this cadre-elite co-option and profit-sharing, local government will be rendered ineffective or indifferent to the erosion of the public ownership of the corporate assets.

The stage is now set for the next phase of property rights transformation for some of the local "collective" stock-sharing enterprises. Plans to quickly increase production and expand individual shares are being implemented. There will soon come a time when many of the enterprises will have the resources and strong incentive to buy back the collective shares from the state and local government. Should this occur, how would the state respond? If the state wishes to maintain the public character of these enterprises, it could face significant production slippage or even stoppage. If it permits such buyouts, then the public or "socialist" character of a huge portion of the rural economy might be lost forever. On the positive side, it would mean an infusion of substantial cash income, which the local government could probably use to meet increasing welfare and other demands. Depending on the tax revenue situation and the demands of national projects, the state government might desire such capital input as well.

The major stumbling block is the political ideology regarding the public ownership of the collective enterprises. State intervention to alter this transformation might yet occur. However, unless a better stock-sharing plan can simultaneously assure continued control and returns for the local elite leadership and cadres and the continued productivity and profitability of the corporations, the state is seen as unlikely to risk intervention where it would be met by resistance and further subversion, leading to further erosion of its command over local areas.

One scenario to preserve the socialist character of collective enterprises might be to allow the public (the state and local government) to receive full or partial cash compensation for collective assets and still retain, without cash contribution, a significant but minority portion of the shares (say, 25 to 30 percent) in a shareholding enterprise. The immediate cash inflow could come in handy as the state and local governments face increasing pressure to fund welfare and infrastructure expenditures. The public would continue to benefit from the rents (dividends) from these shares. Yet the enterprise would remain market-oriented, inasmuch as it works for the majority of the shareholders. Should the enterprise go bankrupt, the public would not need to manage issues such as layoffs and liquidations. After all, in the "socialist" market system, there is no specification of how much of a socialist character each economic entity needs to preserve.

Chapter 8

The Regional Evolution of Ownership Forms: Shareholding Cooperatives and Rural Industry in Shanghai and Wenzhou

SUSAN H. WHITING

As a major initiative in the reform of property rights in rural industry, shareholding cooperatives (*gufen hezuo qiye*) have filled the headlines of newspapers and the pages of reform-oriented journals and books in China in recent years. This chapter draws on comparative case study evidence from Songjiang County, Shanghai, and Yueqing County, Wenzhou, to analyze the significance of this reform initiative, and it makes two main arguments: First, shareholding cooperatives are a transitional form of ownership that has evolved in response to partial and incomplete changes in the legal and market environments for rural industrial enterprises. Second, local officials have used the shareholding cooperative framework to support very different combinations of public and private rights over assets.[1] The varied dispositions of local officials toward public versus private property rights can be explained by an analysis of the institutional incentives and constraints under which local officials function.

The first part of the chapter lays out the factors shaping the evolution of ownership forms in rural industry. Subsequent sections show how and why shareholding cooperatives have evolved in Yueqing and Songjiang. In Yueqing shareholding cooperatives have provided a framework in which private investors have flourished, while in Songjiang they have been used to perpetuate government dominance of rural industry. The conclusion highlights the forces driving incremental change in property rights in China's transition from planning to the market.

Factors Shaping the Specification of
Property Rights in Rural Industry

The key actors in the evolution of industrial ownership forms at the local level are local state officials and potential investors. Their actions can be understood as responses to the incentives and constraints in their institutional environment. The analysis is based on the underlying assumptions that private investors seek to maximize the value of their assets and that township and village political leaders seek to maintain their official positions in order to exercise the power and perquisites of office.[2] The actions of local state officials in particular have been critical in determining the dominant forms of industrial ownership in local communities across China.

Their actions have been shaped by the incentives contained in the two key institutions: the cadre evaluation system and the fiscal system. The criteria used to determine the income, tenure in office, and advancement opportunities for local officials highly reward the expansion and development of rural industry. Moreover, local officials are heavily dependent upon rural industry for fiscal revenue. For these reasons, promotion of rural industry has become one of the main objectives of local cadres.[3]

However, the forms of ownership that local officials chose to support in promoting rural industry at the beginning of the reform period differed markedly across regions. Choices were constrained by the financial, material, and organizational resources of each community and by the larger political and economic environment. In areas, like Shanghai, with a legacy of relatively strong commune and brigade development, local cadres exercised direct control over capital and other resources that allowed them aggressively to develop collectively owned (public) firms.[4] By contrast, in areas, like Wenzhou, with a legacy of weak commune and brigade development, local cadres lacked direct control over resources with which to develop public enterprises and tried instead to facilitate private enterprise development.

The broader legal-political and economic environments also constrained the ways in which ownership forms in industry evolved. The legal-political environment reflects the degree of legal recognition and ideological support accorded various types of ownership. The legal-political environment is shaped by official policies, regulations, and laws, but it cannot be reduced to them. As John Litwack has emphasized, legality is a social phenomenon that depends on the belief on the part of the population in the stability and enforceability of the law.[5] For example, the formal legalization of private investment in 1988 was an important milestone, but it did not suffice to guarantee the property rights of private investors in industry. As Douglass North points out, "Although formal rules may change overnight as the result of political or judicial decisions, informal constraints embodied in customs, traditions, and codes of conduct are much more impervious to deliberate policies."[6] Furthermore, contradictions and tensions are reflected in the policy decisions themselves. Despite the legalization of private enterprise, central Party documents promulgated as recently as the Fifth Plenum of the Fourteenth Central Committee of the Communist Party in September 1995 have sought to perpetuate and enforce the subordinate position of the private sector.[7] Officials at the local level, by exploiting such contradictions, have exercised significant discretion in the way they implement (or fail to implement) central policy; moreover, the principle of *yindizhiyi* ("according to local conditions") is a well-established tenet of policy implementation. Nevertheless, periodic campaigns, including those that sought to subordinate private enterprise to the Party-state, reflected the ascendance of a particular political line at a particular point in time and were forceful reminders to local officials of the limits of their discretion. Thus, the larger legal-political environment constrained but did not fully determine the choices of both officials and investors regarding the particular forms of industrial ownership they were willing to support.

Finally, forms of ownership in industry were constrained by the nature of markets for capital, land, and other inputs, as well as by the nature of markets for the sale of final products. The extent to which goods were allocated by bureaucratic decisions rather than by prices limited the ability of private investors, who functioned for the most part outside of formal bureaucratic channels, to realize the full value of their investments.[8] The distinct roles that emerged for shareholding cooperatives in Yueqing and Songjiang reflect these constraints. Subsequent sections of the chapter compare the degree to which private, collective, and cooperative shareholding forms of ownership have provided legal-political protection and access to factor and product markets for enterprises in Yueqing and Songjiang.

Private Property Rights in Yueqing

LOCAL RESOURCE ENDOWMENTS AT
THE INITIATION OF REFORM

Local officials in Yueqing were constrained in their ability to mobilize capital directly through local government-controlled channels during the

TABLE 8.1

Gross Value of Industrial Output by Ownership Type, Township Level and Below, 1978–1994

	Yueqing County, Wenzhou					Songjiang County, Shanghai[a]			
	Total	Town-run Collective	Village-run Collective	Rural Shareholding Cooperative	Urban Cooperative and Individual	Total	Town-run Collective	Village-run Collective	Urban Cooperative and Individual
LEVEL[b]									
1978	38.36	22.02	16.34			114.57	77.53	37.04	49.87
1994	7,103.30	383.39	2,638.53	2,700.00	1,381.38	11,475.57	8,420.22	3,005.48	
SHARE (percentage)									
1978	100.0%	57.4%	42.6%			100.0%	67.7%	32.3%	
1979	100.0	55.3	44.7			100.0	66.4	33.6	
1980	100.0	31.6	65.1		3.3	100.0	63.1	36.9	
1981	100.0	23.0	73.6		3.4	100.0	69.5	30.5	
1982	100.0	32.2	67.5		0.3	100.0	73.4	26.6	
1983	100.0	35.5	63.9		0.6	100.0	72.7	27.3	
1984	100.0	34.7	65.0		0.2	100.0	71.5	28.5	
1985	100.0	15.9	45.0	35.3	3.8	100.0	69.2	30.8	
1986	100.0	15.3	42.3	38.3	4.0	100.0	71.2	28.8	
1987	100.0	15.6	37.2	39.1	8.2	100.0	70.2	29.5	0.3
1988	100.0	9.9	16.1	60.7	13.3	100.0	67.7	31.9	0.4
1989	100.0	9.5	11.6	66.2	12.7	100.0	67.4	32.2	0.4
1990	100.0	11.1	11.1	64.1	13.7	100.0	74.2	25.1	0.7
1991	100.0	13.6	5.5	67.2	13.7	100.0	74.4	24.7	0.9
1992	100.0	13.6	9.7	58.3	18.4	100.0	74.5	23.2	2.2
1993	100.0	11.7	25.9	44.1	18.3	100.0	74.5	24.5	1.0
1994	100.0	5.4	37.1	38.0	19.4	100.0	73.4	26.2	0.4

SOURCES: Yueqingxian tongji ju [Yueqing County Statistical Bureau], *Yueqing sishi nian, 1949–1989* [Forty years in Yueqing, 1949–1989] (n.p., 1989); Yueqingxian tongji ju [Yueqing County Statistical Bureau], *Yueqing tongji nianjian* [Yueqing statistical yearbook] (n.p., various years); He Huiming and Wang Jianmin, eds., *Songjiang xianzhi* [Songjiang county gazetteer] (Shanghai: Shanghai renmin chubanshe, 1991); Songjiangxian tongji ju [Songjiang County Statistical Bureau], *Songjiang tongji nianjian* [Songjiang statistical yearbook] (n.p., various years).

[a] In Songjiang, shareholding cooperatives in which the township or village is the dominant shareholder are recorded under township- or village-run collectives respectively.

[b] 1978 output level reported in million 1980 yuan; 1994 output level reported in million 1990 yuan.

early years of reform. The development of the rural collective sector was relatively weak in Wenzhou during the Maoist era.[9] The earliest available comparable data on fixed assets, output value, and profits in Yueqing and Songjiang illustrate the disparity.[10] Whereas the original value of fixed assets of collectively owned township and village industry in Yueqing County was Y25 million in 1985, it was Y280 million in Songjiang. Earlier data are available to compare the output and profits generated by this sector. As of 1978, the gross value of industrial output of township and village (then commune and brigade) industry was Y38 million in Yueqing (Y47 per capita), compared to Y115 million in Songjiang (Y253 per capita) (see Table 8.1). Comparable data on gross profits as of 1980 show that gross profits were less than Y10 million in Yueqing (Y11 per capita), compared to nearly Y50 million in Songjiang (Y107 per capita).

While the weakness of Yueqing's rural collective sector left little revenue in official hands at the township and village levels, there were some financial resources in private hands even in the early 1980s. Although the sources of private capital accumulation are too numerous to list here, one example may serve to demonstrate the potential importance of mobilizing this source of investment funds.[11] One such source was cash remittances from migrant laborers. By 1983, cash remittances from these workers came to more than Y500 million for Wenzhou Municipality as a whole—or more than Y40 million per county on average.[12] This county average is greater than the total value of profits and taxes generated by township- and village-run collectives in Yueqing in that year. With relatively few resources under the direct control of townships and villages and with at least some capital resources in the hands of local residents, local officials in Yueqing sought to mobilize these alternative, private sources of investment by specifying *private* property rights.

THE POLITICAL ENVIRONMENT FOR PRIVATE ENTERPRISE

Officials in Yueqing—and in Wenzhou more broadly—were limited in their ability to specify and provide effective political support for private property rights within the existing legal-political framework. They provided informal support for private investment in a variety of guises beginning in the late 1970s and early 1980s—well ahead of formal regulations and laws designed to govern the emerging private sector.[13] Nevertheless, most of the informal arrangements for private investment in Yueqing suffered from one of two shortcomings: either they failed to provide explicit recognition of private claims to assets or they failed to provide a collective license that facilitated access to highly imperfect and heavily bureaucratized factor and product markets. Without the former, investments themselves were insecure; without the latter, the value of private investments was limited. As a result, firms were very small in scale and highly volatile.[14]

Beginning in 1987, local officials were able to address the concerns of private investors with the designation of Wenzhou as an experimental zone that would focus on reforms in ownership. Reform progressed along three tracks; the municipal government promulgated three sets of experimental regulations, one of which sought to establish a regulatory basis for outright private ownership.[15] These regulations contributed to the promulgation of national regulations governing private enterprise (*siying qiye*) in June 1988.[16]

Nevertheless, even after a constitutional amendment and passage of national regulations, both designed to legitimize private ownership, private enterprises continued to come under political attack. In particular, the rectification campaign of late 1988 through 1991, which targeted private enterprise, called into question the ability of local officials to protect investors from challenges from the center. The Fourth Plenum of the Thirteenth Central Committee in June 1989 led to an attack on "individual and private entrepreneurs who use illegal methods to seek huge profits and thereby create great social disparity and contribute to discontent among the public."[17] The Fifth Plenum, held in November 1989, determined that unspecified aspects of private development were "not beneficial" to socialism and would be limited.[18] Similarly, the Fifth Plenum of the Fourteenth Central Committee held in September 1995 reiterated the position that "[a]ny practice that shakes or forsakes the dominant position of the public sector is a departure from the socialist orientation."[19]

The lack of effective guarantees of private property rights directly affected the behavior of private investors. Entrepreneurs were uncertain as to how long their firms could continue to exist or how large they would be allowed to become. According to a study conducted by the Economic Policy Research Center of the Ministry of Agriculture, significant numbers of private enterprise owners reduced the scale of funds invested in their enterprises or even ceased operation during the economic rectification campaign of 1988–91 because they perceived that political support for the private sector was being undermined from the center.[20] Indeed, one source of uncertainty stemmed from reports that the local government in Yueqing had been given internal targets for converting private enterprises to collective ownership during the economic rectification campaign.[21] As a result of this uncertainty, the registered capital of private enterprises (*siying qiye*) in Wenzhou declined by 5 percent, and employment in private enterprises dropped by more than 10 percent in 1989 alone.[22] From the perspective of local cadres, the political environment undermined the mobilization of investment as well as the generation of revenue and employment opportunities in *siying qiye*. By contrast, total investment in the fixed assets of shareholding cooperatives (*gufen hezuo qiye*) increased in 1989 and rose increasingly sharply in the early 1990s, although employment did decline in 1989.

According to an official of the Wenzhou Municipal System Reform Commission, his office consulted directly with dozens of private entrepreneurs in order to ascertain what would encourage them to invest more actively.[23] He reported that they were most concerned about two issues: the disposition of firm assets and the determination of the "nature" (*dingxing*) of the enterprise. Specifically, the entrepreneurs wanted clear title to their firms' private assets, and yet they also wanted their firms legitimately to be considered *collective* in nature; this was seen as essential to their political security as well as contributing to their ability to participate fully in restricted factor and product markets. Registration as a *siying qiye* could meet the former but not the latter condition.

THE ECONOMIC ENVIRONMENT FOR PRIVATE ENTERPRISE

Owners of *siying qiye* faced economic as well as political obstacles. The inability of many private enterprise owners to gain access to the bank financing, land, or material inputs necessary for expansion placed an effective ceiling on their firms' development.[24]

The ability of investors to realize the full value of their assets was limited in particular by restrictions on access to capital through the system of state-run banks and rural credit cooperatives even after the legalization of private enterprise in 1988.[25] Surveys of private entrepreneurs consistently found that access to capital was a major obstacle to private development.[26] Private firms in Wenzhou did receive greater support from the state-run banking system than did private firms in the Shanghai area. As of 1992 in Yueqing County, the Agriculture Bank and the Industrial-Commercial Bank were willing to grant loans of up to Y 100,000—and in special cases up to Y 250,000—to private firms.[27] Nevertheless, loans to private enterprises and *getihu* combined represented only about 5 percent of approximately Y 18 million in total loans to industry made by the local office of the Industrial-Commercial Bank.[28] Moreover, loan requirements, including requirements for collateral and demonstrated cash reserves, were much stricter for private enterprises. Finally, alternative credit sources, such as private banks and credit clubs serving private entrepreneurs, were branded illegal and suppressed in Wenzhou during the late 1980s and early 1990s.[29]

Access to land was even more highly restricted for private enterprises.

Even in Yueqing, most private enterprise owners relied on informal, second-best solutions to meet their needs for factory space during the first decade and a half of reform. One solution was to integrate home and factory, building additional workshop space in the guise of home expansion and remodeling.[30] Another solution was to rent existing space from the village collective or from neighbors, although such space was often ill-suited to the production needs of the firm. However, during the first decade or more of reform, it was extremely difficult for private enterprises to purchase or rent land on which they could build with clear title to their assets.

Among the reasons that Wenzhou was as successful as it was in developing the private economy were the early emergence of informal, private markets for production materials and the rapid expansion of Wenzhou-based networks of private supply and marketing agents. As a representative of the Wenzhou municipal agriculture and economic commission emphasized, the growth of Wenzhou's private economy was facilitated beginning in the early 1980s by the development of specialized markets dealing in steel, lumber, cement, and other commodities.[31] Private purchasing agents specialized in acquiring scarce materials in small amounts from state enterprises around the country based on the personal networks they developed. The existence of informal commodities markets in Wenzhou was important to the development of private industry, since state enterprises could not openly sell materials to the private sector during the early years of reform. Private entrepreneurs also reported being excluded from access to the state-run transportation system. Similar restrictions prevented private firms from competing on an equal footing in product markets.

The combination of the unfavorable political-legal environment and the necessity of relying on informal market sources to obtain capital, land, and other inputs constrained the growth of the private sector. The approach to shareholding cooperatives adopted in Yueqing allowed private investors to function more effectively in these legal-political and economic environments. In this context, the shareholding cooperative framework provided greater net benefits to private investors in both political and economic terms.

THE POLITICAL ENVIRONMENT FOR
SHAREHOLDING COOPERATIVES

The *gufen hezuo* framework adopted in Wenzhou addressed the ongoing concerns of private investors about the political nature (*dingxing*) of their enterprises and official recognition of their claims to their assets. This framework had its roots in central policy statements that recognized and encouraged privately formed cooperatives as early as 1983, reflecting trends that were already emerging at the grass roots.[32] As noted above, informal cooperatives among relatives and friends engaged in household industry were found in Wenzhou as of the early 1980s.[33] Such informal cooperatives were a response both to the discrimination (*qishi*) against and limitations (*xianzhi*) on private enterprise and to the necessity of pooling capital and skills.[34] Central Committee document #1 of 1983 established that cooperative ventures were socialist in nature and could legitimately be considered part of the collective economy.[35] Building on this party decision, a 1983 State Council document on cooperatives made explicit provisions for the investment of private assets. First, the document made it clear that individuals who invested capital or other assets in a cooperative venture *retained private ownership* of those assets.[36] Second, it established provisions for investors to receive dividends on their assets (*gujin fenhong*), although dividends were not to exceed 15 percent of net profits.[37] These early provisions went a long way toward reestablishing the concept of private investment in a cooperative framework.[38]

After the designation of Wenzhou as an experimental zone in late 1986, local officials began to construct a more formal framework for the development of cooperative enterprises, building on key elements of earlier central documents. The first version of local regulations defined a shareholding cooperative as an entity with a minimum of two investors; it faced no restrictions on the number of employees but had to meet certain guidelines regarding financial accounting practices and the distribution of after-tax profits. These guidelines set a limit of 25 percent on the share of profits that could be divided among investors, required that a minimum of 50 percent be reinvested in the firm in the names of the investors, and stipulated that the remaining portion be committed to the enterprise accumulation, welfare, and bonus funds.[39] Officially, therefore, shareholding cooperatives were premised on the limited attenuation of the rights of owners to obtain income from and alienate their assets. The trade-off was that these firms would be considered part of the *collective* economy. Collective status conferred certain valuable benefits: the firms would be considered a legitimate part of the socialist political economy, would be taxed at collective rates and would be eligible for tax deductions, exemptions, and reductions, as well as for bank loans according to the guidelines governing *collective* enterprises. Additionally, collective status would facilitate access to restricted factor and product markets.

The collective legal-political status of shareholding cooperatives received official confirmation in February 1990, when the Ministry of Agriculture promulgated national regulations on *gufen hezuo qiye*. The regulations stipulated that these enterprises were collective in nature and were to be issued collective licenses.[40] A subsequent Ministry of Agriculture document emphatically asserted that regardless of whether a *gufen hezuo* enterprise was established through the conversion of assets of township- or village-run enterprises or through new private investment, all forms would fall into the collective ownership category and should receive active support.[41] Thus, the *gufen hezuo* regulations not only encouraged private investment by legitimating it within the existing legal-political framework; they also potentially increased the value of the assets, since *gufen hezuo qiye* were afforded better access to land and capital under highly imperfect market conditions.

The regulatory framework that emerged beginning with Central Committee document #1 of 1983 and the State Council document on cooperatives set shareholding cooperatives apart from "fake collectives." Like cooperatives, "fake collectives" emerged in response to the discrimination against and limitations on private enterprise; in practice, individual investors would pay the township or village either a fixed fee or a share of the profits in return for nominal status as a *township- or village-run* collective enterprise. However, "fake collectives" were frequently subject to renegotiation of the terms, and private investors had no legal recourse in fighting increasing demands from local officials. Indeed, unlike cooperatives, "fake collectives" offered no official recognition of the claims of investors to their assets. On the contrary, the assets nominally belonged to the township or village.[42] As both Chinese and Western scholars have pointed out, a change in the disposition of local officials toward these firms "could suddenly demote the founders and investors to mere employees with no right to a return on the capital that they had invested."[43] Such occurrences were not unheard of—even in Wenzhou.[44] Finally, fake collectives were particularly vulnerable to campaigns emanating from higher levels. For example, following the conservative line established at the Fourth Plenum of the Thirteenth Central Committee in June 1989, the State Council launched a series of investigations into tax evasion in the private economy, targeting all private firms but focusing in particular on those firms that continued to register falsely as collectives.[45] This campaign extended even to Wenzhou, where fake collectives were targeted for rectification, while shareholding cooperative enterprises retained their status as legitimate collectives, with all the attendant preferential policies.[46] Thus, one significant aspect of the shareholding cooperative framework in Yueqing was that it provided more formal legal recognition by the state—recognition that was politically more secure, since it provided private investors with legitimate status as members of the public sector.

THE ECONOMIC ENVIRONMENT FOR
SHAREHOLDING COOPERATIVES

For shareholding cooperatives, status as a legitimate public sector entity has also facilitated access to factor and product markets characterized by bureaucratic allocation and subject to significant political control. In Yueqing, greater access is particularly evident in restricted markets for loan capital and land, as well as in certain restricted product markets.

With respect to loan capital, local offices of the Agriculture Bank and the Industrial-Commercial Bank in Yueqing allowed shareholding cooperatives access to bank loans on the same preferential terms as township- and village-run collectives; this set shareholding cooperatives apart from private enterprises registered as *siying qiye*, particularly in the years leading up to 1992.[47] Owners of *siying qiye* and *gufen hezuo qiye* interviewed in Yueqing were unanimous in their perception that the latter enjoyed better access to fixed-asset as well as working-capital loans at lower interest rates and for longer loan periods. Evidence that between 1985 and 1994, total loans outstanding to *gufen hezuo qiye* in Yueqing increased every year except 1990—as did the average size of the loans—is suggestive (see Table 8.2). Since 1992, however, reforms in the banking system have made the state-run commercial banks more attuned to profitability; as a result, loans are increasingly allocated on the basis of creditworthiness rather than politically defined criteria, and this change may increase the availability of loan capital to *siying qiye*. Nevertheless, *gufen hezuo* status performed a key function in facilitating access to capital for private investors during the first decade and a half of reform.

Of the key factor inputs, land appears to be the slowest to develop a functioning market in Yueqing, and the absence of a commercial real estate market is a real constraint on enterprise development. The *gufen hezuo* framework plays a particularly important role in meeting the need for land on the part of privately invested firms. All land transactions of three mu or more must be approved at the county level or above; nineteen industrial parks have been established in the eight central towns in the county, and county-level officials provide *gufen hezuo qiye* with preferential access to land in these zones, while limiting the access of *siying qiye*.[48] Virtually all of the more than 600 enterprises granted approval to build production facilities in county industrial parks between 1993 and 1996 were shareholding cooperatives.

TABLE 8.2

Growth of Shareholding Cooperatives, Yueqing County, Wenzhou, Township Level and Below, 1985–1994

Level	1985	1986	1987	1988	1989	1990	1991	1992	1993	1994
Number of firms	2,311	2,224	2,261	2,947	2,959	2,723	2,770	2,972	3,636	4,370
Total employment	36,753	39,439	21,545	64,787	54,248	50,808	52,088	60,127	73,185	
Gross value of output (million yuan)	165.12	196.11	253.91	487.77	575.22	524.99	712.18	1,220.80	1,970.15	
Taxes (million yuan)	12.05	14.94	19.81	42.30	50.29	46.37	67.80	89.13	146.01	
Average net profits per firm (yuan)	3,704	4,024	5,184	11,127	11,582	12,986	17,903	24,653	45,470	
Average bank loans outstanding per firm (yuan)	1,177	4,195	4,980	8,426	9,605	8,898	17,628	30,784	45,547	45,437
Average value of fixed assets per firm (yuan)		9,159	10,398	16,430	23,917	32,956	42,368	71,174	118,328	187,526
Profitability (net profits / total capital)	0.14	0.13	0.14	0.17	0.12	0.12	0.13	0.10	0.13	

Percentage increase over previous year	1986	1987	1988	1989	1990	1991	1992	1993	1994
Number of firms	-3.8%	1.7%	30.3%	0.4%	-8.0%	1.7%	7.3%	22.3%	20.2%
Total employment	7.3%	-45.4	200.7	-16.3	-6.3	2.5	15.4	21.7	
Gross value of output	18.8%	29.5	92.1	17.9	-8.7	35.7	71.4	61.4	
Taxes	24.0%	32.6	113.5	18.9	-7.8	46.2	31.5	63.8	
Average net profits per firm	8.6%	28.8	114.7	4.1	12.1	37.9	37.7	84.4	
Average bank loans outstanding per firm	256.4%	18.7	69.2	14.0	-7.4	98.1	74.6	48.0	-0.2
Average value of fixed assets per firm		13.5	58.0	45.6	37.8	28.6	68.0	66.3	58.5
Profitability	-7.5%	4.4	20.1	-25.9	-6.9	15.2	-23.8	28.4	

SOURCE: Yueqingxian tongji ju, Yueqing tongji nianjian [Yueqing statistical yearbook] (n.p., various years).

Four of Yueqing's industrial parks, housing about 120 enterprises, are located in Hualing Town. In Hualing, *gufen hezuo qiye* are given preference in the allocation of land in the industrial parks. The first private investors to get approval to purchase land and build factory space in the industrial park explicitly linked their status as *gufen hezuo* enterprises to receipt of the necessary bureaucratic approval.[49] The owner of the largest *siying qiye* in the town, an electrical equipment factory, reported being unable to acquire the necessary approval to purchase land in the industrial park until he established a shareholding cooperative and submitted the application under its name.[50]

Status as a *gufen hezuo* enterprise also facilitated access to highly regulated product markets. Industrial production in Yueqing is concentrated in electrical components and related products—many of which are governed by production permits (*shengchan xukezheng*) issued by the Ministry of Electronics or, in some cases, by the Ministry of Posts and Telecommunications. In order to receive a production permit, a firm must meet certain standards in terms of both equipment and technical personnel, and products must meet certain quality standards. Moreover, applications for production permits must pass through an initial screening by the relevant industrial management bureaus at the county and provincial levels before going on to the central level.[51] In general, better access to capital and other inputs, as well as greater political acceptance outside of Wenzhou, all contribute to the ability of *gufen hezuo qiye* to obtain production permits.

Bureaucratically, *gufen hezuo qiye* are also better situated to receive the technical and political support necessary to obtain production permits. Unlike *siying qiye*, for which the industrial-commercial bureau serves as the supervisory bureau (*zhuguan bumen*), *gufen hezuo qiye* come under the auspices of the enterprise management office that governs all collective enterprises engaged in industry and is part of the larger industrial management structure at the county level and above.[52] Since *gufen hezuo qiye* pay a management fee to the enterprise management office, while *siying qiye* pay a management fee to the industrial-commercial bureau, the incentives are also aligned such that the enterprise management office will more actively support shareholding cooperatives.

In Yueqing, the first enterprises to receive official production permits in 1987 were *gufen hezuo qiye*.[53] Local officials were instrumental in helping these firms obtain new equipment and attract the needed technical personnel in order to obtain production permits for five types of low-voltage electrical components. Owners of shareholding cooperatives in Hualing Town described how the Hualing enterprise management office worked closely with the Yueqing County rural enterprise bureau and the Yueqing County Electronics Company in appointing technical specialists to assess

and improve the quality of products.[54] The Hualing enterprise management office also guided the applications through the approval process at
the county and provincial levels to help ensure that the central ministry
issued the permit.[55] By the mid 1990s, county officials had assisted more
than 460 *gufen hezuo* enterprises to obtain production permits and related
certifications.[56] According to an official of the Yueqing economic system
reform commission, before Deng Xiaoping's "southern tour" in 1992, no
production permits were granted to *siying qiye*; since 1992, some *siying qiye*
have also obtained production permits, but these firms account for a small
minority of permit holders in Yueqing.[57]

COSTS AND BENEFITS OF SHAREHOLDING
COOPERATIVE STATUS

Gufen hezuo reforms provided privately invested firms with greater
political legitimacy, a public bureaucratic identity, and better access to
land and capital, as well as to highly regulated product markets, contributing to the overall development of shareholding cooperatives. Table 8.2
provides statistics on the growth of shareholding cooperatives in Yueqing
since 1985. According to a representative of the system reform commission, prior to 1985, only a few hundred shareholding cooperatives existed
in the county.[58] While the number of enterprises has grown slowly since
1985, the value of fixed-asset investment has increased steadily at double-
digit rates—even during the years of economic rectification from 1989
through 1991. As noted above, the growth of shareholding cooperatives
has been supported by strong increases in bank loans. At the same time,
net profits have increased every year, and the rate of profit on capital (as
measured by net profits divided by the total value of capital) has been
steady. With the exception of 1990, output growth has been strong, and tax
receipts have continued to grow. To put the growth of *gufen hezuo qiye* in
the context of countywide industry as reported in Table 8.1, as of 1985,
these firms contributed approximately one-third of the county's total industrial output; by the early 1990s, their contribution was about two-
thirds.[59] Although employment levels have fluctuated, total employment
in shareholding cooperatives doubled in the period between 1985 and
1993 to reach nearly 75,000 people. Data reported in interviews in Hualing
Town, Yueqing, for example, show that shareholding cooperatives have
become the dominant form of ownership; as of the early 1990s, *gufen hezuo*
qiye accounted for 80 percent of all industrial enterprises in the town. By
contrast, *siying qiye* accounted for only 11 percent, while township- and
village-run collectives together accounted for only 9 percent. Overall,
these figures suggest that adoption of *gufen hezuo* status likely increased

the value of industrial assets to private investors from the mid 1980s through the mid 1990s. Moreover, local officials also reaped the benefits from *gufen hezuo qiye* in terms of revenue and employment generated.

However, as noted briefly above, the benefits to shareholding cooperatives of greater political security as well as of greater access to loan capital, land, and restricted product markets were partially offset by the limited attenuation of the rights of owners to obtain income from the use of assets and to alienate their assets. In addition, shareholding cooperatives were subject to official guidelines with respect to their corporate governance structure. In principle, the limited attenuation of rights distinguished *gufen hezuo qiye* from *siying qiye*. Nevertheless, local officials in Yueqing attempted to make registration as a *gufen hezuo qiye* as attractive as possible for private investors, and, in practice, neither limitations on the rights of owners to obtain income from and to alienate their assets nor guidelines on corporate governance were enforced. Weak enforcement had the effect of minimizing the costs to private investors of adopting the *gufen hezuo* framework, while maintaining the benefits to both local officials and investors outlined above.

For example, many firms failed to set aside enterprise accumulation funds and distributed more than the formally stipulated share of profits among investors. However, loose implementation of these and other stipulations fueled challenges by the state administration of industry and commerce to the collective status of these firms.[60] In response to these challenges, the Wenzhou municipal government issued a document in November 1989 calling for the "standardization" of cooperative stock enterprises.[61] This document reiterated the importance of maintaining enterprise accumulation funds in distinguishing "collective" from "private" firms and specified that at least 15 percent of after-tax profits must be dedicated to this purpose. In order to appease critics, a distinction was made between those enterprises that had complied fully with the standardization criteria and those that had only complied partially. The former would be registered simply as "collective enterprises" (*jiti qiye*), while the latter would be registered as "collectively owned cooperative enterprises" (*jiti suoyouzhi hezuo qiye*).[62] However, interview data suggest that the only significant effect of the challenge was that "standardized" firms enjoyed certain tax deductions and exemptions not available to other firms.[63] For example, "standardized" firms could repay bank loans from pretax profits. Nevertheless, "nonstandardized" shareholding cooperatives continued to be taxed at collective tax rates and to be eligible for bank loans at collective levels and interest rates. This suggests that owners of shareholding cooperatives in Yueqing could enjoy the benefits of *gufen hezuo* status without accepting significant attenuation of their property rights.

In principle, "standardization" also entailed the adoption of an enterprise charter (*zhangcheng*) that would clarify the rights and duties of investors, as well as the mechanisms for decision-making within the firm.[64] In reality, there was little difference in the internal management and operation of private firms before and after the transition to the shareholding cooperative framework. In most cases, there was no separation between ownership and management; owners were usually directly involved in the management of the firm. Adoption of the shareholding cooperative framework did not result in the imposition from outside the firm of a new pattern of control rights.

SUMMARY

In theory, there were certain costs associated with adoption of *gufen hezuo* status—the attenuation of rights entailed in restrictions on income from assets, restrictions on alienation of assets, and the imposition of new patterns of decision-making about the use of assets. These costs were reduced by lax enforcement by local officials. The biggest impact of *gufen hezuo* status in Yueqing resulted from legal recognition that increased the security of property rights and facilitated access to factor and product markets for private investors.

Public Property Rights in Songjiang

LOCAL RESOURCE ENDOWMENTS AT
THE INITIATION OF REFORM

Property rights in Songjiang developed in a very different direction from those in Yueqing. Local officials in Songjiang were able to mobilize capital for new investment in rural industry directly through their control over commune and brigade resources. This ability had its roots in the strength of commune and brigade development following the recovery from the Great Leap Forward in the early 1960s.[65] At the outset of reform, therefore, townships and villages in this region already had a relatively strong collective revenue base, which enabled them to invest even more in collective enterprise development. Direct investments in productive assets by township and village governance structures—particularly in developed areas like Shanghai—played their most important role during this period.[66] Table 8.1 illustrates the different levels and composition of the gross value of industrial output in Songjiang and Yueqing Counties and highlights the early strength of the collective sector in Songjiang.

While township and village collectives clearly did not enjoy the same political status as did the state-owned economy (*quanmin suoyouzhi*), their status and legitimacy as full members of the socialist collective economy (*shehui zhuyi jiti suoyouzhi*) was affirmed early in the reform process.[67] These enterprises had their origins as integral parts of the commune system, in which political and economic management were fused. Even after the transition from communes and brigades to townships and villages in 1983,[68] most rights over industrial assets remained in the hands of township or village leaders who served as representatives of the "collective"— the community composed of all local residents. Such control was consistent with the principal of "whoever invests is the owner and receives the benefits" (*shei touzi, shei suoyou, shei deyi*), because investment in the earliest collective enterprises was financed directly by commune and brigade accumulation.

Township leaders exercised significant control over both decision-making and income in the collective enterprises within their jurisdiction. In Songjiang, the appointment and remuneration of managers were determined by the office of management and administration of the township government. The same office was also responsible for setting the total wage bill for each collective enterprise. Township leaders were regularly consulted on major enterprise decisions and, more important, controlled a large portion of enterprise income. Although during the early years of reform, local leaders used these resources to reinvest in enterprise development, by the mid 1980s they increasingly used them to finance administrative expenses and public goods and services.[69] In Songyang Town, Songjiang, for example, the town leader responsible for industry reported that collective enterprises retained less than 12 percent of profits on average as of the early 1990s.[70] These enterprises received the active support and protection of local political leaders, reflecting their importance to financing township functions. Table 8.3 illustrates the growth of township- and village-run collectives in Songjiang County between 1987 and 1994.

The close ties between local officials and collective enterprises facilitated their growth and development in the incomplete market environment that prevailed during the first decade and a half of reform. The

TABLE 8.3

Growth of Township- and Village-Run Collectives, Songjiang County, Shanghai, Township Level and Below, 1987–1994

Level	1987	1988	1989	1990	1991	1992	1993	1994
Number of firms	1,913	2,142	2,251	2,278	2,332	2,322	2,390	2,197
Total employment	142,412	154,905	153,241	154,385	158,620	156,392	153,137	146,925
Gross value of output (million yuan)	1,395.64	2,016.66	2,420.31	2,815.27	3,544.86	4,823.19	7,997.99	12,647.80
Taxes (million yuan)	50.51	69.28	88.42	90.64	103.74	133.12	191.65	278.69
Average net profits per firm (yuan)	49,310	52,806	35,318	38,033	51,068	64,608	123,812	
Average bank loans outstanding per firm (yuan)	141,730	176,741	188,627				421,033	
Average value of fixed assets per firm (yuan)	326,675	330,154	397,508	465,290	553,559	692,472	853,490	1,316,532
Number of loss-making firms	144	155	206	234	209	227	250	240
Share of loss-making firms (percentage)	7.53%	7.24%	9.15%	10.27%	8.96%	9.78%	10.46%	10.92%

Percentage increase over previous year		1988	1989	1990	1991	1992	1993	1994
Number of firms		12.0%	5.1%	1.2%	2.4%	-0.4%	2.9%	-8.1%
Total employment		8.8%	-1.1	0.7	2.7	-1.4	-2.1	-4.1
Gross value of output		44.5%	20.0	16.3	25.9	36.1	65.8	58.1
Taxes		37.2%	27.6	2.5	14.5	28.3	44.0	45.4
Average net profits per firm		7.1%	-33.1	7.7	34.3	26.5	91.6	
Average bank loans outstanding per firm		24.7%	6.7					
Average value of fixed assets per firm		1.1%	20.4	17.1	19.0	25.1	23.3	54.3
Number of loss-making firms		7.6%	32.9	13.6	-10.7	8.6	10.1	-4.0
Share of loss-making firms		-3.9%	26.5	12.2	-12.8	9.1	7.0	4.4

SOURCE: Songjiangxian tongji ju, Songjiang tongji nianjian [Songjiang statistical yearbook] (n.p., various years).

benefits borne of close ties between government and enterprise are particularly clear when one compares the access to capital of collective and private firms between the early 1980s and the early 1990s. Bank loans became an important source of capital and a key source of growth for township- and village-run collectives beginning in the early 1980s.[71] Rising rural incomes led to increases in savings deposits in local branches of the Agriculture Bank and the Rural Credit Cooperative, which, in turn, fueled loans to rural industry.[72] As the share of investment financed directly by townships and villages declined, collective enterprises came to rely more heavily on privileged access to bank credit. A 1986 cross-provincial survey of 200 rural enterprises conducted by the Development Research Institute identified loans from banks and rural credit cooperatives as the single most important source of capital at that time.[73] As of 1987, the first year for which systematic data are available for Songjiang, bank loans were the single largest source of capital in township- and village-run collectives, accounting for nearly 50 percent of fixed-asset investment, as illustrated in Table 8.4.[74] They continued to be the largest source of fixed-asset investment through 1990.

In contrast, private enterprises were largely shut out of access to credit through the state-run banking system in Songjiang County during this period. Banks did not support private enterprise in principle. Access to credit through rural credit cooperatives was somewhat easier for private firms, but the scale of available capital was still extremely limited. For example, loans to private firms accounted for approximately 0.2 percent of the credit cooperative's total loans outstanding in 1991, and none of the loans exceeded Y 10,000.[75] In the context of less than fully developed capital markets, private firms suffered from lack of the close institutional ties to local officials that made access to bank loans easier for collective firms.

Relatively easy access to bank loans for rural collectives was in part a reflection of political and institutional relationships. Local state institutions, including the township governance structure and local offices of the Agriculture Bank and the Rural Credit Cooperative, along with township- and village-run enterprises, were part of a communitywide collective organizational structure, the goals of which were largely defined by township political leaders. Township leaders could influence bank officials through Party channels, since the Party affairs of township bank offices were governed at the same level. The township industrial corporation, the arm of the township government responsible for overseeing collective industry within the township, commonly served as guarantor on bank loans for subordinate enterprises. This guarantee reduced the risk borne by banks and diversified risk throughout the township. Township control of property rights over collective assets facilitated this access. When col-

TABLE 8.4

Sources of Fixed-Asset Investment, Township- and Village-Run Enterprises, Songjiang County, Shanghai, Township Level and Below, 1987–1995

Million Current Yuan	1987	1988	1989	1990	1991	1992	1993	1994	1995
Bank loans	52.51	88.34	88.55	85.57			171.79	68.39	179.99
Own funds (ziyou zijin)	20.01	31.80	32.70	31.25			247.84	270.77	373.57
Outside capital	5.12	21.39	10.39	35.56			212.18	823.40	1,391.78
Bureau grants	19.26	18.38	13.15	24.43			3.82	17.11	59.90
National support fund	2.30	3.01	4.30						
Other	8.07	7.73	17.23	13.66			106.78	225.02	260.68
Total	107.27	170.65	166.32	190.47	221.01	422.19	742.41	1,404.69	2,265.92

Percentage share	1987	1988	1989	1990	1991	1992	1993	1994	1995
Bank loans	49.0%	51.8%	53.2%	44.9%			23.1%	4.9%	7.9%
Own funds (ziyou zijin)	18.7%	18.6	19.7	16.4			33.4	19.3	16.5
Outside capital	4.8%	12.5	6.2	18.7			28.6	58.6	61.4
Bureau grants	18.0%	10.8	7.9	12.8			0.5	1.2	2.6
National support fund	2.1%	1.8	2.6						
Other	7.5%	4.5	10.4	7.2			14.4	16.0	11.5
Total	100.0%	100.0	100.0	100.0	100.0	100.0	100.0	100.0	100.0

SOURCE: Songjiangxian tongji ju, Songjiang tongji nianjian [Songjiang statistical yearbook] (n.p., various years).

lective enterprises faced difficulty in repaying loans, the township industrial corporation typically placed levies on the retained profits of the successful enterprises under its jurisdiction in order to repay the delinquent loans of enterprises that were performing poorly. This practice, referred to as *tongshou huandai*, was common in Songjiang during the 1980s and early 1990s.[76] For cases in which the township industrial corporation was unwilling to serve as guarantor, the township public finance office itself would frequently step in to back up the loan.[77] The heavy reliance on bank loans both to finance new investments in fixed assets and to provide working capital is highlighted by the experience of Songyang Town in Songjiang County. According to the report of a town government official, debt as a share of total collective industrial assets increased from 15 percent in 1980 to 40 percent in 1989, and by the latter date, the ratio of debt to assets was commonly 80 percent or higher for new enterprises.[78] During the latter half of the 1980s, the debt of town-run industrial enterprises increased an average of 25 percent per year.

The central role of township and village governance structures in facilitating access to capital for collective firms in the context of less than fully developed capital markets is reflected in the division of property rights between township leaders and the managers of the firms themselves. As reflected in the 1986 survey of 200 rural enterprises cited above, fewer than 30 percent of firm managers surveyed could make decisions regarding new investments or the expansion of production independently of the township or village.[79] By contrast, approximately 65 percent of enterprise managers surveyed could make independent decisions regarding sales strategies. The delegation of sales authority to the manager is consistent with more competitive product markets, which developed earlier than competitive capital markets for much of the rural industrial sector.[80] Indeed, a similar survey conducted five years later in 1991 by the World Bank found that fully 90 percent of township- and village-run enterprises surveyed could make independent decisions regarding sales strategies.[81] However, the percentage of firms that could make independent decisions regarding new investments had not increased compared to the 1986 survey results; as of 1991, only 25 percent of firms surveyed reported having such independent authority. The preceding analysis suggests that the continued influence of local officials over investment decisions through the early 1990s was related to their central role in the provision of capital.[82]

While the rural collective sector ranked above the private sector in the political pecking order, it ranked below the state sector. Loren Brandt and Xiaodong Zhu find that between 1986 and 1993, more than 85 percent of all new credits were extended to the state sector.[83] Moreover, during periods of economic retrenchment, such as the economic rectification campaign of 1989–91 and the renewed retrenchment of 1993, nonstate enterprises faced severely restricted access to credit through the state-run banking system. "In 1989, for example, credit to the entire non-state, non-agriculture sector through the financial system fell from 16 billion to 6.4 billion yuan, and in percentage terms from 10.5 percent to 3.5 percent [of total credit]," Brandt and Zhu note.[84] Furthermore, loans for fixed-asset investment in township- and village-run collectives were particularly tightly restricted. Data from Songjiang County show that the *level* of bank loans for fixed-asset investment increased only 0.2 percent in 1989 compared to 1988 and actually decreased by 3.4 percent in 1990. Bank loans as a *share* of total fixed-asset investment began to decline from a high of 53 percent in 1989 and fell to a low of 5 percent in 1994 (see Table 8.4). These trends, combined with the growing profit orientation of the state-run commercial banks, made it harder for local officials to provide privileged access to bank loans for rural collectives as of the 1990s.

Barry Naughton identifies a more fundamental tension in the macro-economy. The state's use of the state-run banking system to channel savings from the household sector to the state sector involves a de facto tax on the banking system.

> Depositors get less than they could earn for their funds elsewhere, and borrowers (other than favored state clients) find their access to funds obstructed. Although the bank system provides a service in intermediating funds from savers to borrowers, the transaction is highly taxed by the government. . . . As a result of this high "tax rate," *there is a strong temptation for both savers and borrowers to opt out of the formal state-run banking system and try to make deals through other kinds of institutional arrangements.*[85]

Indeed, Naughton identifies 1988 and 1992–93 as periods of particularly severe disintermediation crisis in China, when household savings deposit growth slowed while the amount of currency in circulation grew rapidly.[86] His findings suggest that a significant amount of capital is available to be tapped outside the state-run banking system. As argued below, local officials in Songjiang used the *gufen hezuo* framework to mobilize investment capital directly from local residents while maintaining their political control over collective firms.

Although rural collectives were also criticized for competing with state-owned enterprises for access to scarce inputs,[87] their inclusion in the larger organizational framework of community governance provided them with advocates within the local bureaucracy who could be instrumental in facilitating access to such inputs in an incomplete market environment. A 1979 State Council document, "Regulations Regarding Several Issues of Commune- and Brigade-run Enterprise Development," directed local planning commissions and industrial bureaus at the county level and above to extend their management to include township- and village- (then commune- and brigade-run) firms.[88] In Shanghai, these firms—together with county-run state and collective enterprises—were governed at the provincial level by the agricultural equipment industry bureau (later renamed the suburban industry management bureau) and were governed at the county level by the rural enterprise management bureau. Certain products produced by rural collectives were to be included in local economic plans either directly or indirectly (through joint production arrangements with local state-run enterprises), although other products would remain outside the local planning system. Officials of the Shanghai suburban industry management bureau, as well as officials in Songjiang and subordinate townships, emphasized the role of local government agencies in helping township- and village-run collectives gain access to scarce inputs like steel, copper, aluminum, and energy.[89]

Direct or indirect inclusion in local state plans was particularly important for the survival of some rural industries during the first decade of reform. The degree of direct and indirect linkage to the planned economy may have been particularly high in suburban counties such as Songjiang because of close ties to Shanghai's state-run industry. According to a representative of the agriculture committee of the Shanghai municipal Party apparatus, even as late as 1992 about 20–30 percent of the steel and 10 percent of the coal used by rural collectives were governed indirectly by local state plans through state-collective joint ventures.[90] As one local official put it, "there are good reasons why government and enterprise are not separate [*zhengqi bufen*]."

Indeed, by the early 1990s, the establishment of new collective enterprises was relatively well institutionalized in Songjiang. The county planning commission coordinated the necessary approvals from relevant agencies such as the land bureau, suggesting that access to land was not a major hurdle for rural collectives. By contrast, private entrepreneurs, who lacked such institutional advocates, faced much greater hurdles in gaining access to land, as well as to material inputs. According to a representative of the policy research office in Shanghai, even as of 1992 it was local policy in Shanghai to limit both the use of land and the scale of factory building for private enterprises.[91] Private entrepreneurs echoed this view themselves.[92] The contrast between collective and private firms highlights the importance of institutional ties to the bureaucracy in the context of continued bureaucratic allocation of land and other inputs.

The rapid development of rural collectives during the first decade and a half of reform was spurred by the opening of previously restricted industrial sectors to production by these firms. A resolution approved at the

Third Plenum of the Eleventh Central Committee in December 1978 established that

> commune and brigade enterprises should gradually engage in the processing of all farm and sideline products that are suitable for rural processing. Urban factories should shift part of their processing of products and parts and components that are suitable for rural processing to commune and brigade enterprises and help equip the latter with necessary equipment and technology. . . . In addition, the state should adopt a policy of allowing tax breaks or tax exemptions for commune and brigade enterprises.[93]

As Barry Naughton notes, these changes represented a crucial shift in policy orientation, which led to "the abandonment of the restrictive model of rural industrialization that had confined its growth during the 1970s primarily to a few agricultural producer goods."[94]

However, local officials in Songjiang protected their growing investments in collectively owned productive capacity by largely shutting out private producers in industry during the first decade and a half of reform. Chinese researchers have highlighted the fact that, as of 1992, the number of private firms engaged in industry in the Shanghai suburban counties overall was quite small.[95] The highest concentration of firms in private industry in the suburban counties was found in Songjiang County, with 21 percent of firms under private ownership.[96] Private enterprise owners reported that even in Songjiang, private enterprises were not granted licenses in product lines in which collective factories were already operating. The township industrial corporation, which had no interest in allowing the emergence of competition for its collective firms, exercised effective veto power over private enterprise license applications in industry.[97] Such practices perpetuated the dominance of collective property rights that had emerged as a result of local officials' direct control over relatively abundant collective resources. Even as local officials aggressively shifted production by rural collectives into new industrial sectors, they sought to restrict competition from the local private sector.

Without the close institutional ties between local officials and collective enterprises, the development of rural collectives might arguably have occurred later and more slowly in Songjiang. At the same time, local officials came to rely heavily on the rural collectives to finance and provide a wide range of public goods and services in rural communities. Thus, rural collectives bore a heavy fiscal burden imposed by local officials. As factor and product markets have become more complete, particularly since 1992, the benefits for collective enterprises of close integration with local governance structures have become less apparent. Although "the failure to separate government and enterprise" (*zhengqi bufen*) in the rural collective sector had certain benefits during the early years of reform, when factor markets were incomplete, reformers increasingly began to regard the fusion of government and enterprise as an impediment to enterprise efficiency. It was in this context that *gufen hezuo* reforms were introduced into the collective sector on an experimental basis.

THE POLITICAL AND ECONOMIC ENVIRONMENT FOR

SHAREHOLDING COOPERATIVES IN SHANGHAI

Gufen hezuo reforms were introduced in Shanghai in the context of a rapidly changing economic environment characterized by the increasing commercialization of markets for capital, land, and other factor inputs. The stated intention of *gufen hezuo* reforms in areas that were under predominantly collective ownership, such as Shanghai's suburban counties, was to further the separation of government and enterprise (*zhengqi fenkai*) in order to make enterprise managers more responsive to growing market forces. However, despite the stated intentions of the reform, local officials in Songjiang implemented *gufen hezuo* reforms in such a way as to channel new sources of investment capital into collective enterprises, while preserving their control over the collective economy. As the conclusion to this section will suggest, it was only in 1996, nine years after the first *gufen hezuo* experiments in Shanghai, and four years after the first wave of broader implementation, that the potential of *gufen hezuo* reforms to bring about the separation of government and enterprise began to be realized in Songjiang.[98]

Central Committee document #5 of 1987 on "Deepening Rural Reforms" highlighted the need to separate the government and the enterprise and to end the legacy of fused political and economic control lingering from the commune and brigade era.[99] The document explicitly identified shareholding cooperatives as a means of limiting government interference and increasing the autonomy of township- and village-run collectives from the local government. After the appearance of Central Committee document #5 of 1987, Shanghai expanded its experiments with shareholding cooperatives from one to a total of ten firms.[100]

One of Shanghai's earliest experiments with the shareholding cooperative form in rural industry began in the Chuansha Printing and Dyeing Machinery Factory in Chengzhen Township in 1989. Although the experiment was begun with the expressed goal of expanding firm autonomy, an internal report of the Chuansha County Party Committee Policy Research Office highlighted the mobilization of idle capital in the hands of enterprise employees into productive investment within the firm as a key outcome of the experiment.[101] Indeed, the experiment was begun during a period in which the firm was experiencing an acute shortage of capital because of the failure of its largest, state-owned client to make payments on completed orders.[102] Beginning in 1989, slightly more than Y500,000 in existing assets were converted into shares held by the township;[103] Y258,950 in existing assets were converted into shares held by enterprise employees and management; and Y258,950 were offered to employees and management as new shares. In 1991, an additional Y500,000 were offered to employees and management as new shares.[104] The two types of shares available to employees and management (representing existing assets and new investment respectively) were distinct. The rights conferred by holding the first type were extremely limited. These shares received dividends only; they were nontransferable and conferred no voting or decision-making rights. By contrast, new shares offered to employees were intended to offer more powerful inducements for new investment. In addition to entitling the holder to receive dividends and exercise voting rights in board elections, they offered interest payments guaranteed not to fall below the interest rate charged by state banks on working capital loans.[105] While this provision was not intended to be a standard part of future share conversions, it was seen as important for encouraging employees to invest in this early experiment. (Note that such interest payments were prohibited in *gufen hezuo* experiments conducted with private investors in Wenzhou.)[106] Together the two new share offerings to employees in 1989 and 1991 generated a total of Y759,000 in new investment—roughly Y1,500 per employee.

The report of the Chuansha County Party Committee Policy Research Office was equivocal in its assessment of the initial effect of the experiment on enterprise autonomy, since the early share offerings were structured to maintain township control over a majority of voting shares.[107] The Party branch, of which the manager was not a member in this case, continued to exercise veto power over the appointment or transfer of all enterprise-level cadres. Indeed, the firm, founded in 1969 as a commune-run farm equipment factory, had a long history of active involvement by local officials. This problem was reflected in broader criticism of *gufen hezuo* experiments in collective enterprises that they entailed "changing the path not changing the system" (*zhuan gui bu zhuan zhi*).[108]

Beginning in 1992, experiments with *gufen hezuo* forms were extended to a total of 593 enterprises in Shanghai, the majority of which were in the rural industrial sector. These experiments were explicitly intended to attract new capital investment into the rural enterprise sector by diversifying property rights.[109] Although firms in Shanghai had used a variety of informal mechanisms since the early 1980s to mobilize capital from workers, including borrowing money at interest from workers and requiring new workers to make payments of up to several thousand yuan upon receiving a job (*yizi dailao*), these mechanisms were limited in scope and did not entail any transformation of property rights. In the later experiments, most existing assets were converted into shares held exclusively by the township or village, and the practice of converting existing assets into shares held by employees and management was downplayed.[110] However, new share offerings were expanded to include not only enterprise employees and management but also individuals and units not directly involved with the firm. These experiments generated more than Y700 million in new investment capital, an average of nearly Y1.2 million per enterprise. Close to Y110 million came from individuals outside the firms (in the form of *shehui geren gu*), while approximately Y400 million in new investment capital came from enterprise employees (in the form of *qiye zhigong gu*), with an average investment of Y4,448 per employee. The remainder came from other institutions in the form of *shehui faren gu*.[111] Still, as of 1992, most township- and village-run collectives involved in *gufen hezuo* experiments in the Shanghai area had maintained local official dominance by restricting new capital sources in such a way as to preserve local officials' majority control over voting shares.

The implementation of *gufen hezuo* reforms in Songjiang was consistent with this pattern. Songjiang Party Committee document #4 of 1992, which addressed shareholding cooperative reforms as part of a larger agenda for speeding up economic development, laid down the principle that collective shares (*jiti gu*) held by the local government should constitute no less than 50 percent of the total.[112] At the same time, local documents described amassing capital (*jizi*) from local workers as the "most important function" (*zuida gongneng*) of shareholding cooperatives. As of 1996, there were 274 shareholding cooperatives in Songjiang, of which 131 were newly established firms and 143 were existing firms that underwent conversion. The latter had attracted Y77.4 million in new investment from workers and others. Of the 274 firms, the local government was the controlling shareholder in 214 (78 percent). As in the case of the early experiment in Chuansha County, *gufen hezuo* reforms were implemented in the context of what local leaders perceived to be a shortage of capital confronting the rural collective sector.

As elsewhere in Shanghai, workers who invested in shares were to receive both interest (equivalent to the rate charged by the local Agriculture Bank on working capital loans) and dividend payments (equivalent to a set percentage of profits).[113] Through dividend payments, they had a claim on enterprise profits and, in theory, shared risk. They also in theory had an indirect voice in decision-making. According to the standard shareholding cooperative charter employed in Songyang Town, workers could elect and remove the members of the board. In turn, the board, which was to convene at least twice a year, had the authority to appoint or remove the manager and to approve or reject the plan of operations and the financial report.

The experience of the collectively owned Songyang Textile Equipment Factory, a domestic joint venture between a Shanghai state-owned enterprise and the Songyang Town government, highlights some of the problems that arose in implementation. Although the shareholders went through the motions of electing the ten-member board of directors, as of 1996 it had not met formally since the conversion to shareholding cooperative status in 1993. The town leadership continued to appoint the local manager, while the town office of management and administration continued to set output and profit targets for the enterprise, to determine the salary and bonus of the local manager, and to set the total wage bill for the factory.[114] As the local manager put it, "there has basically been no change in the way the enterprise is managed" (*jingying guanli meiyou shenme duoda de bianhua*) since conversion to a shareholding cooperative. The Y900,000 in capital provided by the purchase of shares by workers was used to augment the factory's working capital. When the factory lost a substantial portion of its market to private competition from Zhejiang Province in 1995 and profits plunged, it ceased making interest and dividend payments to shareholders. As a result workers began to agitate for the return of their original share value; furthermore, precedents for the return of shares existed: as of 1996, shares had been returned to workers in 24 other enterprises facing financial difficulties throughout Songjiang County. Thus, workers who invested in the enterprise failed to gain any effective influence over decision-making and at the same time bore no risk. A 1996 report by the county executive in charge of industry assessed the implementation of shareholding cooperatives in the following terms: "Government and enterprise have still not been separated. . . . the township still holds the majority of shares, the government still directly appoints the manager and directly interferes in production and operations, and the manager still seeks political intervention whenever he runs into difficulties."[115]

POSTSCRIPT

According to official policy statements, property rights reform in Songjiang entered a new phase as of late 1996. Local leaders have put forward the slogan *zhuada fangxiao* ("hold on to the large [enterprises] and let the small ones go"), indicating their goal of maintaining control and income rights over a select group of large enterprises, while transferring property rights over the remaining enterprises to private individuals through a variety of means. These means include enterprise auctions, enterprise leases, and cooperative shareholding in which the local government no longer holds a controlling stake in most enterprises and in which control is actually turned over to the shareholders and the board of directors, and— through them—to the enterprise manager. This transition, still in the early stages in Songjiang, reflects changes in both the market and the political-legal environment. Through the early 1990s, the Songjiang government sustained a fairly stable percentage of loss-making firms, while the average size of losses and losses as a share of net profits increased sporadically. (Reported losses as a share of net profits reached a high of 20 percent in 1992.) However, as markets for both inputs and outputs have become increasingly competitive, and as the budget constraints of local governments have grown increasingly hard, in part reflecting recent changes in the fiscal and banking systems, the ability and willingness of the local government to maintain control over the property rights of all collective enterprises in this environment has waned.

Conclusions

The shareholding cooperative framework provided an institutional context that allowed local officials significant discretion in their actions. It became an umbrella that covered many different divisions of property rights between state and private actors. Local officials played key roles here; in the hands of local officials, selective interpretation and enforcement of the regulations were means by which they could affect the pace and, to some degree, the direction of change. At the same time, the direction of change in ownership forms also reflected gradual changes in the broader political and economic environments. The declining influence of ideological constraints and the development of markets for factors and products created new opportunities for private firms and new challenges for collective ones.

At the outset of the reform period, local officials sought to promote different divisions of property rights in the two communities under examination. Local officials in Songjiang promoted public forms of ownership, reflecting local government control over important capital resources, while their counterparts in Yueqing promoted private ownership, reflecting an attempt to mobilize the investment of privately held capital resources. However, during the first decade and a half of reform, the legal-political environment discriminated against openly private firms, and the incompleteness of markets for inputs and outputs made it relatively difficult for such firms to flourish. Under the same conditions, publicly owned firms benefited from their close ties to local officials. When experiments in property rights reform—specifically, the introduction of shareholding cooperatives—came onto the political agenda, local officials in both Yueqing and Songjiang exploited the policy for their own ends. Local officials in Yueqing employed the *gufen hezuo* framework to provide greater political legitimacy and better access to bureaucratically controlled factor and product markets for privately owned firms. Local officials in Songjiang, by contrast, employed the *gufen hezuo* framework to mobilize new sources of capital for the collective economy while retaining significant control over property rights.

In 1989, the State Council research office characterized shareholding cooperatives as a "transitional form."[116] Ultimately, the particular role that shareholding cooperatives have played in Yueqing may be made unnecessary by an increasingly robust market environment that does not discriminate based on the form of ownership. Similarly, in an increasingly marketized environment, the ability and willingness of local officials in Songjiang to retain their dominance over the local economy may be waning. These implications are consistent with the hypothesis that marketization drives privatization. Market reforms, like legal-political reforms, have occurred at a gradual pace in China. In this context, the significance of the shareholding cooperative framework lies in its contribution to incremental change in property rights in China's transition from planning to the market.

PART THREE

*The Transformation of Public
Property in the Urban Economy*

Chapter 9

Backyard Profit Centers: The Private Assets of Public Agencies

YI-MIN LIN AND ZHANXIN ZHANG

This chapter examines how public ownership in China's reform era is being compromised and transformed by the self-seeking behavior of state agents. Since the mid 1980s, large numbers of state agencies have engaged in and benefited from for-profit activities through economic entities that they set up, run, or facilitate outside the scope of their regular administrative functions and budgets. Mostly registered as independent public enterprises in the tertiary sector, such economic entities are managed by former or incumbent officials or persons they trust. They receive funding and favorable regulatory treatment from or with the help of their government sponsors and contribute a significant part of their revenue to the slush funds of the latter. In view of their close ties with the private interests of the individuals in their sponsoring state agencies, we call these economic entities the backyard profit centers of state agencies.

Despite its pervasiveness, this phenomenon has largely escaped close scrutiny in the existing literature on the post-Mao Chinese political economy. Starting with an account of the main organizational features of the backyard profit centers, we show that, although most of them are labeled public enterprises, their property rights arrangements are different from those in traditional state-owned enterprises and collectives. The decisions (control rights) on their formation and closure, personnel appointment, agenda setting, and budgets are all separate from the government chain of command. Their profit-making relies heavily on the allocative and regulatory favors granted by or via their sponsoring agencies, outside of their regular announced public policy agendas. Net income gains accruing to the backyard profit centers are distributed to funds exclusively controlled by their enterprise leaders and to their sponsoring agencies' slush funds for the provision of individual and collective benefits to agency members. Property rights relations in these publicly owned organizations are thus driven by the private interests of the parties concerned, embodying a process of hidden privatization. Also, by channeling state-allocated resources away from traditional public enterprises, the expansion of these organizations further erodes the remaining foundations of the state socialist economy.

To bring to light the mechanisms whereby these changes have taken place, we trace the origins of the backyard profit centers to the late 1970s and explore their path of growth up to the mid 1990s. The theme of our discussion resonates with the following observations about social action: what causes something may not be what augments, sustains, or perpetuates it; and unintended consequences may well signal cues or directions for subsequent courses of action. We illustrate that the initial impetus for the formation of backyard profit centers came from the need of the state to find expedient solutions to pressing problems after the Cultural Revolution (1966–76). But the initial problem-solving orientation of the newly formed economic subsidiaries quickly changed, because it soon became clear that they could also be used to serve self-seeking agendas. Enticed by the potential of these entities to make lucrative profits under a legitimate organizational cover, state agents availed themselves of a major avenue via which to turn the public assets and regulatory authorities under their command into capital for individual and collective gains. Their subsequent attempts to broaden this avenue have been facilitated by concurrent developments that have created more opportunities for expanding and justifying the use of public office for private gains. They include growing inconsistencies and uncertainties in the state's trial-and-error style of reform, intermittent spells of accelerated economic liberalization, and persistent strains on budgetary resources that already have to be partially financed by agency-generated funds.

Parallel to the increased opportunities for state agents to divert resources is a realignment of interests among state agents (especially between political and nonpolitical functionaries) under the mandate of promoting economic growth. This further strengthens the incentives for state agents to weaken the traditional organizational constraints of mutual monitoring based on divided interests. A commonly pursued strategy to muffle potential whistle-blowers and develop collusive ties is to share part of the gains from backyard profit centers with all members of a state agency. As growing numbers of state agents turn from disinterested caretakers to discretionary users and immediate beneficiaries of public assets that they control, more agents take on the role of player along with their role as the referee. The rules of the economic game are increasingly interpreted and redefined in the best interests of the most powerful participants. This mutation in property rights therefore indicates a fundamental change in the political process. The state apparatus has degenerated from an ideology-guided instrument of social engineering to a marketplace where public assets are increasingly "owned" by state agents and traded for private gain.

The Main Features of Backyard Profit Centers: A Peculiar Type of "Public Enterprise"

State agencies in China fall into two categories: *jiguan danwei* and *shiye danwei*.[1] The former consist of party organizations and functional departments of the government, whereas the latter include nonprofit units that have no administrative, allocative, or regulatory authorities beyond their own organizational boundaries, such as newspapers, research institutes, and hospitals. In this chapter, we mainly focus on the profit-seeking entities sponsored by *jiguan danwei*.[2] In Chinese literature, these entities are referred to as *jingji shiti* (economic subsidiaries), *gongsi* (companies),[3] or *sanchan* (tertiary sector undertakings) under the auspices of state agencies. Most of them are registered as independent, for-profit economic organizations in the public sector. Of the 27,000 such organizations investigated by the Gongshang guanli ju, or State Industrial and Commercial Administration (SICA), in 1984–85, for example, 23 percent were classified as "state-owned," 67 percent as "collective," and 10 percent as "jointly owned by the state and collectives."[4] This "public" veneer still adhered to these entities five years later. According to a 1989 report presented by the director of SICA to the Standing Committee of the National People's Congress,[5] of the 23,913 such entities investigated by the central authority in 1988–89, 43 percent were registered as "state-owned" enterprises and 53 percent as "collective enterprises." There are, however, important differences between these and other public enterprises.

First, they are not part of the vertically integrated plans of the government and have enormous autonomy and flexibility in decision-making. Unlike conventional public enterprises placed under the jurisdiction of departments in charge of economic affairs (such as the bureaus of textiles, machine-building, chemicals, and commerce), these firms can be affiliated with any state agency, including the public security office, the local Communist Party committee, and the bureau of cultural affairs.[6] Their activities often fall outside the regular administrative and regulatory functions of their sponsoring agencies. For example, a Beijing University study on a district government in a northern provincial capital[7] shows that the district headquarters of the Youth League ran thirty economic entities in 1993. Among them were a hotel, a kindergarten, a barber shop, a beauty parlor, an applied research institute, two eateries, eleven retail outlets, four trading companies, three repair centers, and five factories. None had anything to do with the political functions of the Youth League.

Second, most of these economic entities are affiliated with state agencies at administrative levels higher than the rural or urban township. Township-owned economic organizations are normally placed under the control of a unified economic authority, which assumes different names in different localities (such as township economic development corporation, township economic cooperative, or township enterprise corporation, to name a few), and are subject to close monitoring by the heads of the local government. The taxes on their proceeds constitute a major revenue obligation of township governments to higher-level authorities. In contrast, while the revenue of the backyard profit centers discussed here is subject to taxation, their sponsoring agencies are not obligated to achieve any tax target based on such revenue. On the other hand, these entities are neither eligible for the allocation of budgetary funds and other economic resources (such as low-interest loans and industrial materials at state-controlled prices) earmarked for enterprises under state budget nor subject to close monitoring by the financial authorities of the government. They receive funding and favorable regulatory treatment from or with the help of their sponsoring agencies, to which in return they contribute part of their gains. Since their entire operation lies outside the scope of the budgetary process and the *nomenklatura* at large, they are sometimes referred to as "extra-budgetary" or "extra-establishment" (*bianzhi wai*) units.[8] As will be shown below, however, this does not preclude their sponsoring agencies' diverting part of their budgetary resources to these entities, and the contributions from these entities may also be used to supplement their sponsoring agencies' needs to carry out budget-funded activities.

Third, perhaps the most important difference between these entities and other public enterprises is that, despite an initial orientation toward tackling imperative problems faced by the state, their operations have increasingly been aimed at generating profits that individually or collectively benefit the state functionaries in their sponsoring agencies. The contributions from these entities end up in the pool of discretionary resources of their sponsoring agencies, which takes two major forms: extra-budgetary funds and *xiao jinku* ("slush funds"). Extra-budgetary funds are generated from channels other than those for regular budgetary revenues (e.g., taxes) and controlled by the state agencies that generate them.[9] In 1992, the total size of such extra-budgetary funds was equal to that of budgetary funds.[10] Although there are regulations regarding the use of such funds, monitoring has become increasingly difficult.[11] *Xiao jinku* are illicit funds generated and hidden by various state agencies for their own private or parochial uses. Despite the repeated inspection campaigns launched by the financial authorities since the early 1980s, such funds remain widespread and elusive. In the directives issued by the State Council to investigate and clean up *xiao jinku* in 1989 and 1995, for example, the phrase *lujin buzhi* ("never stopped despite repeated bans") was used in the introductory sections to describe the tenacity of the phenomenon.[12] Because of the flexibility in the disposal of these slush funds, they are widely used as personal or group benefits. State functionaries in the agencies and departments that control these funds use them as bonus payments, as income supplements in kind, for housing, and for communal and office facilities.

The Initial Impetus

To trace the origins of the "backyard phenomenon" and find out why certain new property rights arrangements were allowed to develop under the exclusive purview of various state agencies, one needs to look at the initial conditions of the Chinese reform. It was the need to find quick fixes to some of the most pressing problems faced by the state after the Cultural Revolution that led to the creation of limited numbers of profit-seeking entities under the sponsorship of state agencies. These problems include severe budgetary strains on the existing operation of the state, large numbers of unemployed urban youths, an increase in redundant personnel in Party-state agencies, and a shortage of resources for financing newly added, increasingly localized regulatory functions. The common feature of the solutions is that they were all decentralized mechanisms of revenue generation and disposal. The resultant creation and expansion of an *exclusive* domain of decision-making and income rights in various state agencies marks a major crack in the traditionally centralized, highly integrated system of property rights assignment within the state apparatus.

BUDGETARY PRESSURES

A major legacy of the Mao era was a growing imbalance between limited budgetary resources and large numbers of items and projects that needed to be funded, which resulted in a large budget deficit in 1979. That year, to maintain the operation of the state apparatus under increasing financial strains, the Finance Ministry introduced a provisional administrative expenditure contract system (*xingzheng kaizhi baogan zhi*) for Party and government agencies. It placed a cap on the spending of various agencies, while granting them more leeway in the disposal of the budgetary surplus they could save, thus opening a gate for discretionary use of public resources. At the same time, all the nonprofit and nonregulatory units (namely, *shiye danwei*) were urged by the central authority to explore ways to become self-financed so as to reduce the burden on fiscal allocation.[13]

The budgetary pressure on the state was further exacerbated by two related problems. One was the lack of funds for housing construction for state agents. Spending on housing had never been a recurrent budgetary category under the central planning system. The resources used for housing were allocated mainly at the initial stage of the formation of a project or agency according to the size of the establishment. Regardless of the number of personnel added subsequently, extra funds would not be provided unless the units concerned obtained approval for a new capital construction project that would expand the current number of authorized positions. What this resulted in was a gap between the resources available for housing and the increase in the number of employees. To address this, various state agencies had to squeeze pockets of funds from other budgetary categories, which became more difficult during the Cultural Revolution, resulting in a growth of pent-up demand.

According to a report prepared by the Construction Commission,[14] at the end of 1977 the average per capita living space in urban China was 3.6 square meters, lower than the level of the early 1950s—4.5 square meters. In view of the worsening situation, in 1978, the Construction Commission, the State Planning Commission, the Ministry of Finance, and the State Bureau of Materials Allocation jointly issued a directive on using "self-raised funds" for the construction of housing for state employees. It called for joint efforts on the part of the state, work units, and individuals to solve this problem.[15] In the same year, the State Council approved and circulated a report by the Construction Commission on measures to accelerate urban housing construction, in which state agencies at various levels were urged to take active steps to raise more funds for housing.[16]

The other problem came along with the restoration of the bonus system after the Cultural Revolution—first in economic organizations, then in state agencies. Unlike public enterprises that could set aside part of their revenue as bonus funds, most state agencies had to rely totally on an increase of budgetary allocation for this purpose, which was extremely difficult given the shortage of budgetary resources. In 1978–79, while large numbers of state functionaries were given a pay raise on the standardized salary scale, on the average each employee in state agencies (including *shiye danwei*) only received a year-end bonus of Y 10.[17] In contrast, the average bonus for the employees of state-owned industrial enterprises, many of whom also received pay raises on the wage scale,[18] was Y23 per person in 1978 and Y75 in 1979.[19] To make up the gap and keep the morale of state functionaries from being affected by a sense of relative deprivation, state agencies, especially those not in charge of economic affairs, had to find ways to establish additional revenue sources of their own.

The financial authorities suggested *zengshou jiezhi*, or "increase revenue and save expenditures," as the main solution for various state agencies to cope with the shortage of funds for bonuses. Saving from the very lean budgetary allotments was virtually impossible, because it was difficult to bargain for an increase in the amount of budgetary appropriation. Increasing revenue, especially that accruing to off-budget accounts, therefore became the only viable way out. While departments in charge of state-owned enterprises could levy extra fees from those under their purview to supplement their spending needs, other agencies had to scramble for alternative means. Given the green light for turning auxiliary *shiye danwei* into self-financing units, many of these agencies started to explore revenue creation opportunities in this direction. Some started retail outlets, whereas others commercialized the services of certain auxiliary units (such as hostels, canteens, car fleets, auditoriums, and printing shops).[20]

UNEMPLOYED URBAN YOUTHS

As many state agencies were struggling to find ways to finance their basic administrative needs and keep up the standard of living of their staff, the state apparatus was confronted with another serious problem, the presence of large numbers of unemployed urban youths.

From 1966 to 1978, the government sent over 16 million middle school graduates to the countryside to do farmwork.[21] That policy was partly driven by the ideological agenda of transforming the minds of the youths through exposure to harsh working and living conditions, and partly by the practical need to reduce the unemployment pressure on the urban sector. The practice was brought to an end in 1978. In 1978 and 1979, 6.5 million sent-down youths returned to their home cities.[22] Since urban employment opportunities remained highly limited, and since newly graduated middle school students were no longer required to go to the countryside,[23] the return of large numbers of sent-down youths exacerbated the already acute situation of urban unemployment, which reached an unprecedented level of 15 million in 1979.[24] In 21 provinces, there were gatherings, demonstrations, petitions, and even harassment of government officials by disgruntled jobless urban youths, posing a serious threat to political stability.[25]

A solution adopted by the central authority was to create a new organizational form called labor service companies (*laodong fuwu gongsi*) in 1979.[26] They were organized by state-owned enterprises and state agencies to accommodate the unemployed children of their employees. Registered as independent, for-profit urban collective enterprises, they mainly operated in the then highly underdeveloped tertiary sector. Since the financial authorities could not come up with the necessary funds, the sponsoring state-owned enterprises and state agencies were urged to squeeze out some resources from their own coffers to provide the seed capital for these organizations. Tax exempt status was granted to them in the initial years of operation. Local labor departments were designated as the authority to coordinate and regulate their activities. In 1979, 4,211 labor service companies were set up; in 1985, the cumulative number reached 45,567.[27]

Regulations and stipulations existed as to how these organizations should be run as independent economic entities. For example, the rules stated that labor service companies should be self-financed and that sponsors should not use their profits. However, in practice, financial and personnel ties with their sponsors, especially state agencies, were often too close to be severed. In fact, many state agencies treated their labor service companies as their additional subsidiary units, to which they appointed key decision-makers and continued to provide financial and regulatory support after the founding stage.[28] In return, these companies paid a management fee and made additional contributions (such as in-kind benefits and "reimbursement service") to their sponsors.

REDUNDANT PERSONNEL

Immediately after removing Hua Guofeng from top positions in the Party and government in 1981 and fully consolidating his own power base in the central leadership, Deng Xiaoping initiated a cadre retirement scheme in order to make way for younger, more capable and pragmatic functionaries to assume key decision-making positions. In February 1982, the CCP Central Committee adopted a "Resolution on the Establishment of an Old Cadre Retirement System," which stipulated that cadres should retire at the age of 60, with the exception that provincial or ministerial leaders could stay on until 65. In 1983, the "blood change" was carried out in 26 provinces. By the end of 1985, nearly 2 million old cadres had been retired.[29]

Parallel to the first wave of cadre retirement was a major revamping of the state bureaucracy. Calling it a revolution, Deng Xiaoping launched a nationwide campaign in 1982–83 to improve administrative efficiency through downsizing, streamlining, and reorganizing the state bureaucracy, which had expanded enormously after the Cultural Revolution. The number of employees in various state agencies increased from 12.6 million in 1977 to 18.1 million in 1982.[30] From 1976 to 1981, the total number of ministry-level agencies under the State Council almost doubled, jumping from 52 to 100.[31] The growth at the provincial level generally paralleled that at the center. Between January 1977 and September 1981, Beijing issued over 60 directives instructing provincial governments to establish agencies corresponding to those newly added to the central government, such as the Department of Tourism, the Bureau of Higher Education, and the Science and Technology Commission. Consequently, the average number of department-level agencies in provincial governments increased from 40–50 to 80–90 within four years.[32] During the administrative restructuring between 1982 and 1983, the total number of central ministry-level agencies was reduced to 62. Provincial governments were instructed to reduce the total number of department-level agencies to 35–40. By the end of 1985, the average number had decreased to 60–70.[33]

In consequence of these concurrent moves to force out old cadres and streamline the state bureaucracy, large numbers of personnel were made redundant. Accommodating these people turned out to be a politically sensitive and financially difficult issue. Economically viable alternative opportunities had to be offered to pacify the resentment and discontent of old cadres who lost their posts and the associated petty privileges. Means also had to be sought to pay for those who were squeezed out from the state's regular, budget-funded payroll during administrative restructuring, but remained as *bianzhi wai renyuan* (extra-establishment personnel) within the state apparatus. As a solution, many former state agencies or their subsidiary units were converted into for-profit entities. Former party-state functionaries were granted tacit permission to take limited part in commercial activities. This led to an expansion of the small commercial outlets set up by state agencies in the late 1970s and early 1980s, and an enlargement of the functions of labor service companies, from helping unemployed youths to facilitating the accommodation of redundant administrative personnel and retirees. From 1983 to 1985, the number of labor service companies rose from 23,988 to 45,567.[34] During the same period, 300,000 new commercial organizations were formed, one-tenth of which had direct financial and personnel ties with various state agencies.[35]

NEW REGULATORY FUNCTIONS

As the reform process unfolded, social and economic activities soon expanded beyond the traditional domain of central planning and party-state control, entailing an addition of new regulatory functions to the state. However, the diversity and complexity of the problems encountered by authorities across the country made it extremely difficult to design a well-defined and integrated regulatory structure *ex ante*. Consequently, localization of regulation became the main mode of operation. In 1986, the National People's Congress passed a resolution to amend the Organic Law of Local People's Congresses and Governments. In that resolution, large cities were given the authority to "enact" (*zhi ding*)—as opposed to "draft" (*ni ding*), the old modus operandi—local laws and regulations provided that such enactment was to be reported to and approved by provincial authority.[36] Between 1978 and 1987, the NPC enacted 60 laws and 58 amendments, the State Council formulated over 500 administrative regulations, and provincial authorities introduced nearly 900 local laws and regulations.[37] While the central authority continued to issue general guidelines and directives, how they were interpreted, substantiated, and implemented increasingly became a matter under the purview of local authorities.

To cope with the increasing volume of localized regulatory activities, state agencies with expanded or newly acquired regulatory functions had to increase their staff, which was difficult owing to budgetary limits. The solution found by many agencies was to set up subsidiary units without budgetary funding (known as *zishou zizhi danwei*, or self-financing units) or to farm out part of the work to designated professional or specialized agencies. These operations were financed by part or all of the revenue generated from regulation-related activities, ranging from fines for environmental pollution to the charge for certified Chinese translations of joint-venture agreements.

The Bureau of Cultural Affairs, for example, used to be a propaganda agency of the government with little regulatory authority. With the commercialization of various cultural products (e.g., publication and sale of printed materials, manufacture of audio and video products, and establishment of entertainment and recreational facilities) in the early 1980s, however, the bureau started to assume the role of regulating cultural markets.[38] This function was normally assigned to a self-financing subsidiary, which derived its revenue from permit fees, fines, and management fees handed over by its own commercial subsidiaries.[39] Similar fee-collecting subsidiaries with partial regulatory functions were established under other agencies too. The Bureau of Personnel Affairs ran so-called personnel mobility service centers where state agency employees had to deposit their personnel dossiers (*dang'an*), with a fee, in the event of their leaving their work units to take employment in joint ventures or private enterprises, for study overseas, or for other purposes. The Labor Department ran labor contract verification (*laodong hetong jianzheng*) centers, which charged a fee for double-checking the contents of labor contracts and validating them. What these arrangements had in common is that they provided a legitimate avenue for state agencies to use their regulatory functions to generate revenue that was not effectively subject to the monitoring of the financial authority and could be used for purposes other than the operation of the self-financing units.

The Formation of Backyard Enterprises: Conversion, Creation, and Adoption

While backyard profit centers are sheltered by their sponsoring state agencies, property rights relations within the sheltered space do not display a uniform pattern. The control and revenue rights of sponsoring agencies are strong over some backyard profit centers but weak over others. How these rights are assigned to the parties involved depends greatly on how the backyard profit centers are formed. There are three commonly used methods of formation: conversion, creation, and adoption.

"Conversion" refers to the formation of self-financing spin-off organizations that used to be parts of state agencies. Starting from 1980, for example, increasing numbers of auxiliary units (such as hostels, canteens, car fleets, and printing shops) of state agencies have been spun off and reorganized as for-profit service organizations.[40] Although they are no longer part of the regular, budget-funded operations of those agencies, these profit centers remain under the jurisdiction of their parent agencies, with which their financial and personnel ties are not fully severed.

In 1993, the Beijing municipal government investigated 558 profit-seeking entities sponsored by 321 state agencies (at the administrative rank of county or above) under its jurisdiction. Fifteen percent of them were found to have been formed to accommodate personnel whose former agencies had been reorganized; a total of 1,625 incumbent cadres held part-time positions in the 558 entities.[41] After Beijing's vice-mayor Wang Baosen killed himself in 1995 when faced with charges of taking bribes,[42] the municipal government conducted an investigation into 169 profit-seeking entities sponsored by 42 department-level agencies. Seventy-three officials, including one with the rank of vice-mayor, 18 department directors, and 22 division directors, were found to have held part-time positions in backyard profit centers, and 3,844 of the 15,888 employees of such entities had been transferred from their sponsoring agencies.[43]

"Creation" involves a partial or full supply of resources (in addition to the provision or arrangement of regulatory support) by state agencies for the establishment of new backyard profit centers. The resources used for this may come from a state agency's budgetary funds, extra-budgetary funds, or a combination of the two. This can be seen from a breakdown of the figures on the above-mentioned 169 profit-seeking entities cited in the investigation report.[44] These entities had a total Y 1.93 billion in registered capital, which came from the following sources: Y 1 billion from bonds held by other state agencies; Y 370 million from fiscal appropriation; Y 63 million from loans from the Bureau of Finance; Y 212 million from the slush funds of various agencies; Y 62 million from bank loans; Y 56 million from shareholding; Y 40 million from fund-raising among employees; and Y 77 million from loans taken out by the entities themselves. Only Y 51 million came from the entities' own funds. Apparently, the magnitude of fund diversion was enormous. The same report revealed that the Y 20 million registration capital of a real estate company under the auspices of the Beijing Economic Commission had been diverted from the commission's low-interest loan for technological renovation and upgrading.

"Adoption" means the provision of patronage by state agencies to existing public or private enterprises. The agencies involved serve as their *zhuguan danwei* (supervising bodies), which is an institutional requirement for all organizations registered as public (i.e., state or collective) enterprises.[45] They provide the adopted enterprises with various "services," such as acquisition of resources, protection against predatory actions by other agencies, facilitation of entry and expansion, creation of monopoly positions, ad hoc relaxation of restrictions, exemption from taxes or other levies, and defusing punitive action by law enforcement authorities. In return, the latter contribute part of their revenue to the former. Decisions on personnel appointments, operations, and finances are left to these enterprises themselves. This practice is known in Chinese as *guakao* (mooring), or—less commonly—*shouyang* (adoption) and *jieshou* (takeover). A Beijing University study found, for example, that of the 30 economic organizations under the sponsorship of the Youth League in the northern political capital mentioned above, 29 took the form of *guakao*.[46]

The ways by which backyard profit centers are formed directly condition the bargaining power of the parties involved (especially the leaders of the sponsoring agencies and the enterprises), and hence the assignment of property rights. The rule of the game seems to be that the larger the share of input from the sponsoring agencies,[47] the greater their control and revenue rights tend to be.[48] It follows that those formed through conversion and creation are likely to be more fully "owned" and more closely monitored with respect to finances and personnel by their sponsoring agencies than those formed by adoption. According to the Beijing University study cited above,[49] the backyard entities formed by *guakao* had much fuller autonomy in personnel decisions, more clear-cut financial obligations to their sponsoring agencies, and simpler terms of contract than those formed through conversion and creation. The normally weak financial and personnel ties of those formed and sustained through *guakao* with their sponsoring agencies also make it easier for such entities to delink themselves from the "fee-for-service" relationship when its costs outweigh its gains.[50] In contrast, for those formed through conversion or creation, breaking away is more difficult, because their sponsoring agencies tend to regard the value added by the backyard profit centers as the return on their seed capital and therefore extend their claims to property rights over the enlarged pie.[51]

Methods of Profit-Making: Arbitrage, Monopoly, and Competition

Most of the profit-seeking entities sponsored by state agencies operate in the tertiary sector. The underdevelopment of this sector under the central planning system resulted in imbalances between demand and supply and created abundant opportunities for speculation and rent-seeking. This sector also includes many lines of activity where the costs for setup, management, diversification, and exit tend to be lower than those for production activities. Of all the irregular for-profit organizations (including those under the sponsorship of state agencies) investigated by the State Industrial and Commercial Administration in 1989, 63.6 percent undertook activities in the tertiary sector; only 25.3 percent were in "production and development of science and technology."[52] Drawing on allocative and regulatory favors from or through their sponsoring agencies, many backyard operations are profitable. In 1995, for example, the 169 profit-seeking entities investigated in Beijing made a total reported profit of Y 374 million and suffered a total loss of Y 21.7 million. Dividing the net profit by their total capital (Y 1.93 billion) yields a rate of return of 19 percent.[53] Three business methods are commonly used by backyard profit centers: arbitrage, monopoly, and competition.

State control over the prices of inputs and products, and the unevenness in the pace, scope, and degree of relaxation of such control across different economic boundaries (e.g., sector, ownership, and locality), spawn opportunities to profit from price discrepancies. According to Wu Jinglian, a leading Chinese economist,[54] the center of arbitrage gravitated toward consumer goods in the late 1970s and early 1980s; shifted to industrial materials in the mid and late 1980s, when the "dual-track price system" was adopted; and subsequently moved to land and capital in the early 1990s, when the markets for real estate and securities opened up. Connected to state agencies in control of large amounts of resources, many backyard profit centers are well positioned to reap huge gains from the practice of buying low and selling high. In an apparent move to show its resolve to curb "unhealthy trends" immediately after the Tiananmen Square events of June 4, 1989, the central authority publicized limited findings from an investigation into five large profit-seeking entities sponsored by central government ministries.[55] A common feature of their operations was that arbitrage constituted the most important means of profit-making. Among the major items they brokered were foreign currency, low-interest loans, automobiles, minerals, and industrial materials.

Many sponsoring agencies of backyard profit centers have regulatory responsibilities. They can use regulatory authority to generate exclusive rights for the provision of certain services and grant such rights to their front organizations. An example of this is the commodity markets owned and run by the local offices of the State Industrial and Commercial Administration (SICA)—the agency that issues industrial and commercial licenses and regulates market transactions—in different localities. Before the reform, free market trading activities were highly restricted by the state. This changed in the late 1970s, and since then the number of commodity markets has grown rapidly. In 1994, there were a total of 84,463 regular marketplaces in the country.[56] Sellers in these markets are required to pay a market management fee to the SICA. In addition, they need to pay a stall fee (*tanwei fei*) to the organization that owns and maintains the marketplace. In view of the stable and lucrative gains from running the marketplaces, and based on their authority in determining where the markets should be established and who should run them, many local SICA offices set up front organizations and granted them exclusive rights to build and run marketplaces, especially in prime areas. In 1995, these organizations owned 34.4 percent of the markets in Beijing, 46.4 percent of those in Henan province, 65 percent in Shanghai, and 69 percent in Hainan province.[57] Note that these figures include only the profit-seeking entities that formally listed the local SICA offices as their sponsoring agencies. Those with informal ties to them are not counted. It was not until 1995 that the national headquarters of the agency launched a campaign to sever formal (financial and personnel) ties with these entities.

Large numbers of profit-seeking entities sponsored by state agencies also engage in activities that other economic organizations undertake. Taxi service, for example, is one of the most competitive businesses in Chinese cities. It is also an area where many backyard profit centers operate. In Beijing, the agencies that have such operations range from central government departments to neighborhood committees.[58] Strong competition inevitably affects the rate of return to the players involved. But with the ad hoc favorable treatments from their sponsoring agencies in the allocation of resources and opportunities, many backyard profit centers tend to have a competitive edge over those that cannot obtain such treatment.[59] In early 1995, for example, a paging service company run by the Hubei Post and Telecommunications Department adopted a new fee scheme to compete for customers with dozens of other paging service providers. Under the new scheme, subscribers only needed to buy the pagers and the monthly fee was waived. To help compensate the company for the lost revenue and enable it to compete with its competitors, the department concurrently raised the charge for phone calls to pager carriers from Y 0.32 to Y 0.52 and transferred part of the increased revenue to the company.[60]

The Flow of Proceeds and Their Use by Sponsoring Agencies

The most common way by which backyard profit centers contribute to the discretionary funds of their supervising agencies is to pay a "management fee" or offer a direct payoff for their investment. The 1995 investigation into backyard profit centers in Beijing revealed that the city's Zoning Commission collected an annual "administrative fee" of Y 50,000–60,000 from each and every one of its backyard profit centers, while a division of the commission earned dividends on a Y 500,000 share that it held in a civil engineering company.[61] In addition, backyard profit centers may provide in-kind contributions such as cars, office supplies, living quarters, meals, entertainment, and hotel accommodations to their sponsoring agencies or foot the bills for the latter's public or private functions such as meetings, trips, and sightseeing.[62]

Although it is the sponsoring agencies rather than their leaders that "own" the backyard profit centers, these leaders play a key role in managing income flows. The funds contributed by backyard profit centers to their sponsoring agencies are used for a variety of purposes. Because of the covert nature of *xiao jinku*, the funds that enter them are more subject to the discretion of a few key decision-makers than those in the agency's extra-budgetary funds. By and large, slush funds are used in three major areas: consumption-oriented spending, reinvestment, and supplementary resources for covering the gaps in budgetary allocation.

Consumption-oriented spending is often shared—although not necessarily in an equal fashion—among the members of an agency. This can take many forms, including cash income supplements, free or subsidized consumer goods, the provision, improvement, or expansion of communal facilities (e.g., housing, kindergartens, bathhouses, canteens, and cable TV), group consumption (e.g., banquets, junkets, and entertainment), and the addition or upgrading of office property that can easily be put to private use (e.g., automobiles, telephones, fax machines, and photocopiers). Of these, cash income supplements and housing are the most important. A 1993 interview survey of state employees' incomes ($n = 611$), conducted by the Sociology Department of Beijing University and *Zhongguo qingnian bao* (China Youth Daily), shows that on the average about one-quarter of the income of state agency employees came from supplementary pay provided by their work units.[63] Also, according to statistics released by the State Statistical Bureau, staff housing construction occupied a significant portion (e.g., between 40 percent and 50 percent during 1985–92)[64] of nonproduction fixed asset investment by state agencies, which mostly comes from their slush funds.[65]

Reinvestment can be directed to any profitable activity. A major use of slush funds, along with diverted budget funds, is for the construction of hotels, office buildings, and auditoriums that can generate commercial revenues. The central authority has repeatedly imposed restrictions on the construction of these, but to little avail.[66] Since the early 1990s, real estate development has also become a major area attracting off-budget investment from state agencies. In Beijing, for example, 22 of the 42 department-level agencies that were investigated by the municipal government in 1995 for running profit-seeking entities in their backyards had set up and run real estate development companies.[67]

While it is a widely known fact that slush funds are sometimes used to supplement the financing of activities that normally lie within the scope of regular budget funding,[68] it is difficult to discern a uniform pattern of such use. One type may be driven by the need to narrow or close the spending gaps deliberately left open by higher-level authorities. A method commonly used by higher-level authorities to generate funds for new investment projects undertaken by lower levels of government is to provide only partial funding in budgetary appropriation and ask the latter to come up with the necessary matching funds. This practice is called "baiting the hook" in China's policy circles.[69] Another type is for state agencies to use slush funds to support their pet projects or for donations that add legitimacy to the existence of these funds. During the preparation for the 1990 Asian Games (an event likely to enhance the profile of the leaders of the sponsoring city), top leaders in Beijing exerted enormous pressure on various departments and agencies to make contributions—from their slush funds—to reducing the deficit in financing. After the event, the city leaders openly thanked the contributing agencies for their support.[70] In the wake of a series of heavy floods in several southern and northeastern provinces in the summer of 1991, the centrally controlled media orchestrated a nationwide campaign to solicit donations for the affected areas. Many government departments and agencies pitched in and donated large sums of money (many in the amount of millions of yuan)—apparently from their slush funds—to help the "good cause." Their names and amounts of donation were acknowledged on the front page of *Renmin ribao*.[71]

The Scope and Tenacity of the Phenomenon

The bulk of the backyard profit centers' activity takes place in the gray area of law and regulations. There are no unified, consistent, and clearly defined rules governing the scope of their functions and their relationship with their sponsors. The central authority has never categorically declared that these entities are illegal. What has been repeatedly emphasized, though, is that state agencies must sever their formal financial and personnel ties with them, which are characterized as "unhealthy trends," "improper practices," and "irregularities."

Although the profit-seeking entities sponsored by state agencies are not identifiable from official statistics, and detailed accounts of their operations are sparse, there are indications that these entities are pervasive and difficult to eradicate. In 1985, when a nationwide campaign was carried out to curb their growth and spread, 27,000 such organizations were investigated and delinked from their sponsoring agencies. In 1988–89, an additional 24,187 were screened out in a second nationwide cleanup campaign, which also uncovered extensive involvement of large numbers of state agencies and senior Party and government officials in profit-making activities.[72] Among the most salient achievements of that campaign was the closing down in 1989 of the Kanghua Company, which was the subsidiary of a ministry-level agency headed by Deng Xiaoping's eldest son, Deng Pufang. During the same campaign, 62 percent of the provincial government agencies in Liaoning were found to have engaged in profit-making activities through economic entities under their auspices.[73] Nationwide, it was reported that 37,380 Party and government officials held part-time positions, and 10,567 retired cadres worked on a part- or full-time basis in various for-profit organizations. Of the incumbent cadres involved, 246 had the rank of provincial government department heads, 2,324 held positions equivalent to prefectural department heads, and 8,193 were county chief administrators or had equivalent ranks in other government agencies.[74] In Shanghai, 85 high-ranking incumbents and 138 retired government officials at the rank of department director or above held part- or full-time positions in various for-profit organizations.[75] In 1993, a third nationwide campaign was launched to tackle the same problem, again leading to the delinking of large numbers of backyard profit centers from their sponsoring agencies.[76] In the three centrally administered cities alone, over 2,000 backyard profit centers were uncovered: Tianjin had the highest number of such entities, 886, while Shanghai had 750 and Beijing 558.[77]

Despite the magnitude of the phenomenon, few officials seem to have been subjected to punitive legal or even disciplinary action for their involvement in profit-seeking activities. Moreover, the repeated efforts made by the central authority appear to have had very limited containing effect.[78] On September 11, 1989, for example, on the same page of *Zhong-guo gongshang bao* (Industrial and Commercial News of China) that carried the report about the 1988–89 campaign, a quarter-page announcement proclaimed the establishment, with the authorization of the State Industrial and Commercial Administration—the agency directing the campaign—of a new company specializing in the construction materials trade. Ironically, this turned out to be a backyard profit center of the Ministry of Construction and was physically located in the same building as the ministry.[79] The severing of formal ties between sponsoring agencies and some of their backyard profit centers that has resulted from each of the major campaigns may be short-lived, or those ties may be replaced with ties sustained through various alternative means, such as in-kind contributions and provision of reimbursement for various expenses incurred by sponsoring agencies.[80] Less than two years after the 1993 campaign, for example, the "Wang Baosen Affair" in Beijing triggered another round of investigation into state agencies' profit-seeking activities in the capital city. According to the concluding report on the investigation,[81] 42 of the 56 department-level agencies were found to have backyard profit centers (169 in total, plus 309 subsidiaries), 78 percent of which were set up before or during 1993 and apparently survived the cleanup campaign carried out in that year. Their total registration capital amounted to Y 1.9 billion, which was equivalent to about one-fifth of the city government's total budgetary expenditure for 1995.

A major contributing factor to the persistence of this phenomenon is the efforts by state agents to justify it. Providing partial financing to state agencies' formal functions with off-budget funds, for example, has become a commonly used method to add legitimacy to the operations that generate them.[82] Many of the reports and documents about the nationwide cleanup campaigns, for example, praise the positive contributions made by some of the backyard profit centers to alleviating budgetary strains, providing employment opportunities, absorbing redundant ad-

ministrative personnel, and stimulating the economy.[83] In Beijing, after
discussing the problem of the backyard profit centers investigated in 1995,
the investigation team in its concluding report put a positive spin on the
involvement of some of the sponsoring agencies. The Beijing Higher Education Commission was praised for helping improve the living conditions
of university staff through its (improper) involvement in real estate development. The real estate development projects undertaken by subsidiaries of the Beijing Economic Commission were credited with facilitating
the strategic goal of "two steps backward and three steps forward" set by
the city government for industrial development.[84]

Other opportunities came from the inconsistencies in central policy,
which has followed a zigzagging course between liberalization and retrenchment during the reform. At the height of each spell of liberalization
(e.g., the Third Plenum of the Twelfth Central Party Committee in 1984;
the Thirteenth Party Congress in 1987; and Deng Xiaoping's southern tour
in 1992, which became the focus of a drive for economic liberalization),
backyard profit centers mushroomed. The call by central leaders to accelerate economic change was opportunely used by state agents to justify
their attempts to expand their private economic backyards as experiment-
ing with bold new measures to promote economic growth or tackling
problems in a trial-and-error fashion. In the wake of Deng's southern tour,
the State Industrial and Commercial Administration issued a document
on enterprise registration that relaxed many previous restrictions in the
name of "promoting reform and opening economic development."[85] Important modifications of previous rules include allowing financial institutions to use their slush funds to run nonfinancial subsidiaries and make
investments, and permitting *shiye danwei* to undertake for-profit activities.
Although the document was entitled "Yijian," or "Suggested Measures,"
it was implemented immediately. Despite the 1993 cleanup campaign,
those measures have survived.

Another important contributing factor is the weakening of mutual
monitoring among state agents, largely owing to the growth of shared
interests among state agents and the use of strategies for peer co-optation.
Before the reform, the scope and intensity of self-seeking behavior of state
functionaries through collective action were highly constrained by an institutional arrangement called the dual command chain, where political
organizations of the Party were intertwined with administrative hierarchies of the government. Because of the emphasis on ideologically defined
behavioral conformity in performance evaluations and the reward system,
and because of the differences in professional qualifications and functional
orientation between political and nonpolitical functionaries, there was a

deep division of interests among state agents.[86] The resultant interpersonal rivalry provided a major fulcrum for applying a checks-and-balances mechanism to control behavior through a divide-and-rule strategy.

In the reform, depoliticization of the agendas of state action has rendered the Communist Party redundant in government affairs and thus reduced the divergence in behavioral orientation fostered under the old dual command structure. As the rewards for both political and nonpolitical functionaries become increasingly dependent on their agency instead of on their individual *biaoxian* (manifest conduct), the basis for cooperative efforts to promote collective gain expands. The tendency to explore these gains is further enhanced by a widely shared sense of relative deprivation among state functionaries under mounting pressures of materialism and inflation.[87]

Since diversion of public assets for private gain involves risk, collusion between state agents is necessary for the success of this course of action. A commonly used strategy is to designate state agencies (rather than individual officials) as the immediate beneficiaries of profits from their backyard profit centers and distribute a significant part of such profits as an entitlement to all members of an agency. This not only offsets individual risk but, by making everyone share in the proceeds, creates a major disincentive for spoilers. Using public funds for various semi-open forms of group consumption—extravagant spending on wining and dining (*dachi dahe*), free junkets, and "souvenirs"—not only evades the restrictions and disciplines imposed by financial authorities, but co-opts potential whistle-blowers and thus consolidates the basis for collusive collective action.

Conclusions

Maintaining public ownership as the dominant form of property rights arrangement has been a central concern in the design of China's reform policies. From the "Four Cardinal Principles" spelled out in 1979 to the blueprint for a "socialist market economy" presented at the Fourteenth Party Congress in 1992, the communist leadership persistently emphasized the vital importance of this condition for China's institutional change. But what is called "public" ownership cannot simply be taken at face value. Ownership, as a bundle of rights, is a function of the effectiveness of the institutional and organizational constraints on infringement by excluded parties. The extent to which public property remains "public" depends greatly on the extent to which public servants are kept from diverting public assets and authorities for private purposes.

In the above account of the "backyard profit center phenomenon," we have shown an area where the boundary of public ownership has been significantly reduced by state agents' self-seeking behavior. This development can be viewed in three dimensions. First, backyard profit centers are not effectively subject to state regulation. The exclusivity of sponsoring agencies' supervision authority over the enterprises in their backyards means a weakening or even breakdown of inter-agency checks on the use of resources in these entities, leaving intra-agency mutual monitoring among state agents as the only remaining line of defense for public property rights. Second, state agents within the sponsoring agencies tend to collude in the running of backyard profit centers, rather than monitoring each other's behavior according to public policy goals. This not only turns the public ownership of these enterprises into an empty shell but also makes it a legitimate cover under which to divert the resources and authorities collectively controlled by state agents. Third, the property rights relations between sponsoring agencies and their backyard profit centers mostly follow a market rule of contract and transaction: control and revenue rights are divided according to the relative contributions of the parties involved. The more important the input supplied by one party relative to that provided by the other, the greater its share in decision-making and income, and vice versa. What shape the functioning and outcomes of such economic entities, therefore, are the exchange relations between the major players.

To be sure, property rights relations in many backyard profit centers are far from being stable and clearly defined, as suggested by a seeming increase in the number of disputes between such entities and their sponsoring agencies in recent years.[88] Moreover, before nominal public ownership is totally abandoned, its continued use will shape the evolution of backyard profit centers, casting a constraining shadow, however small, over the behavior of the parties involved and modulating their bargaining relationship. A full exposition of these issues, however, requires at least another study. Furthermore, because of the elusive nature of these economic entities, we cannot ascertain the precise magnitude of their activities in the national economy. Despite such limitations in our understanding of this phenomenon, the visible traces of the growth of backyard profit centers nonetheless point to important mechanisms of mutation in the institution of public property rights.

The first mechanism that emerges from our account is that contingencies create opportunities for institutional change. We have shown that expediency in central policy-making created a crack in the rules governing administrative financing, which was subsequently enlarged and perpetuated by opportunistic adaptations of state agents seeking to derive private gains from the public resources under their collective stewardship. Induced by the growth of economic markets and the potential gains therefrom, their attempts at this are facilitated by two additional, inter-related mechanisms: legitimation and co-optation.

Since state agents are not owners of the public assets under their control, justification is needed in order for them to divert such assets for private gain. The lower the cost of doing so, the greater their ability to lay private claim to public property. We have highlighted three strategies commonly used to legitimize this type of privatization: (1) increasing the dependence of the state's administrative functions on off-budget funds; (2) twisting or redefining the restrictions on state agents' self-seeking behavior in the name of reform; and (3) stretching the limits on discretionary decision-making and action in the gray area engendered by the uncertainties and inconsistencies in the reform process.

While the decline of communist ideology and the ascendance of the economic agenda in government decision-making have broadened the ground on which to cultivate common interests among state agents, not all state agents are equally active participants in the privatization effort. The widespread practice of sharing a significant part of the proceeds from backyard profit centers among members of the same state agency suggests that, under certain circumstances, provision of public goods to group members may be necessary to sustain collusive collective action. In the literature on collective action, free riding has been commonly treated as a threat to it.[89] This is true when collective action requires a certain level of positive contribution from all group members. But when defection is the main obstacle to collective gains, when zero effort on the part of certain group members can be valued by other members as an asset relative to such defection, and when the gains from collective action without the active participation of certain members are sufficiently large, selective incentives may be needed to create limited free-riding opportunities for potential spoilers.

Although their growing private rights over public property tend to drive state agents to search for the most gainful ways to supervise or facilitate the operation of their backyard profit centers, their action does not necessarily result in efficient use of resources. Wastage may occur in developments associated with state agents' differential treatment of economic actors, such as creation and maintenance of monopoly positions, sunk cost in speculative activities, and intensification of rent-seeking efforts. Further analysis is needed to ascertain how economic efficiency is affected by the growth of backyard profit centers. But it seems clear that along the way of such growth, the state apparatus is increasingly manipulated by special interests through exchange ties, which may compromise social justice and hamstring normal functions of the state. Also, since backyard profit centers compete with traditional public enterprises for the limited supply of state-allocated resources and regulatory favors, opportunity cost calculations by state agents make them less willing to allocate scarce resources to loss-making state enterprises that bring them little concrete gain. This may further exacerbate the difficulties faced by such enterprises and make their problems intractable, adding, in a perverse way, to the pressure for their privatization.

Chapter 10

Bargained Property Rights: The Case of China's High-Technology Sector

CORINNA-BARBARA FRANCIS

It has been a core tenet of Western economic thought, at least since the emergence of classical economics in the eighteenth century, that well-defined property rights are essential in persuading individuals to invest their time, efforts, and resources in commercial ventures and to make the most efficient use of resources.[1] Poorly, or "vaguely," defined property rights lead to inefficiencies, distorted incentive structures, and other suboptimal economic behavior. Well-clarified property rights, by contrast, "enabl(e) owners to capture the full value of their individual investments, thus encouraging everyone to put time and labor into the development of resources."[2] It is only by allowing property owners to exclude others from enjoying the benefits and income from resources that individuals are motivated to develop them to the fullest. The alleged superiority of private property stems from, among other things, its being the property form that most clearly assigns claim rights over resources to specific agents, allows for exclusivity, and thereby provides the strongest individual incentives for the proper and efficient utilization of resources.

China's transition to a market economy challenges the above premises. China has experienced persistently rapid economic growth despite a small private sector and a regime in which property rights appear to be vaguely defined and weakly enforced. This anomaly has led to heated debate and has resulted in competing explanations.[3] Three competing theories explicitly address the property rights issue. The first argues that the anomaly of China's rapid economic growth can be explained by the phenomenon of de facto privatization. A growing proportion of China's national resources have come under the effective control of individuals and other nonstate entities, despite their nominal classification as publicly or collectively owned, and are thus de facto private property.[4] This de facto, albeit hidden, privatization has been the key to strengthened individual incentives, improved monitoring, and intensified competition in the economy and thus helps explain China's rapid economic growth.

A second theory also links China's economic successes to the strengthening of property rights: the strengthening of the property rights of local governments at the expense of the higher levels of the state.[5] China's economic reforms have shifted ownership from higher levels of the state to local governments, which, owing to institutional variables, are more effective owners. Relative to higher levels of state, local rural governments exercise greater control and supervision over their enterprises, are better able to extract their legitimate share of the residual income, are less able to subsidize failing enterprises, and overall have a greater incentive to ensure the efficient utilization of their resources.[6]

A third explanation links the success of dynamic new enterprise types in China to the informal definition and enforcement of property rights. Ownership of village and township enterprises is "vaguely defined" in legal terms but effectively defined and enforced through community norms, shared societal values, and social practices embedded in local culture.[7] Chinese rural communities are characterized by a high level of trust, an "organic unity," and a community orientation that enable individuals to cooperate and to invest in long-term economic relationships and to resolve conflicts without recourse to formal legal procedures. Social norms and the tight-knit nature of local communities allow for effective monitoring of behavior such as cheating and violations of contracts. Societal norms and local culture thus perform functions that legal contracts and formal property rights perform in legally based property rights regimes.

These theories do not contradict the neoclassical assumption that clearly defined property rights are key to the efficiency of a market economy. The first two link China's economic successes to the strengthening of property rights—one through de facto privatization, the other through enhanced public ownership. The third argues that property rights within dynamic new enterprise sectors are effectively defined and enforced informally through cultural mechanisms within local communities. This accords with the view that property rights may be determined by a variety of means, including informal customs, tradition, and social norms.[8]

This chapter presents a more direct challenge to the premise that property rights that are underspecified and neither effectively defined through legal contract nor defined and enforced by informal community norms and traditions backed by the cohesiveness of local society and cultures of high trust will inhibit growth. It examines the growth of a new enterprise type, referred to here as a spin-off enterprise, which has played a key role in China's market economy. Spin-offs are defined as business ventures set up with a degree of initiative and support from government agencies and other public institutions and entities, often in conjunction with individual entrepreneurs. While parent institutions exercise significant claims over a portion of the residual profit, property rights over these commercial ventures are not legally well defined or protected and are contested by a range of actors. In practice, property rights over these resources are worked out through bargaining between the various contestants.

Contrary to neoclassical theory, which associates indeterminate property rights with suboptimal incentive structures and other inefficiencies, spin-off enterprises have facilitated the transfer of human, capital, and technological resources from the state-owned sector to more dynamic business ventures, encouraged entrepreneurship by reducing the levels of risk involved in initiating new businesses and reducing start-up costs, increased the level of competition in the economy, and contributed to hard budget constraints. "Vaguely defined" property rights have therefore helped resolve problems of entrepreneurship, resource allocation, investment, soft budget constraints, and other institutional and economic challenges to market reforms.

The argument in this chapter is in two parts. Based on a case study of high-technology spin-off enterprises concentrated in Haidian District, Beijing, I first demonstrate that property rights over spin-off enterprises are contested and determined through bargaining.[9] Second, I argue that despite the indeterminate nature of spin-off property rights, this enterprise form has uniquely contributed to the dynamism and success of China's market transition.

The Sources of Spin-off Enterprises

The decentralization of fiscal and managerial control that has come to characterize China's market transition has been accompanied by a decline in central government funding for government agencies, administrative departments, and public institutions on the premise that these entities should become increasingly self-financing.[10] Universities, research institutes, cultural and artistic organizations, and other public institutions have been particularly affected.[11]

One response on the part of public institutions to this changing environment has been to launch their own commercial ventures.[12] Spin-off enterprises have proliferated in every sector of China's urban economy. Nearly every type of public entity in China has become involved in setting up business ventures—the backyard enterprises outlined by Yi-min Lin and Zhanxin Zhang in Chapter 9. These include high-tech companies set up by universities and research institutions, manufacturing, trading, and commercial enterprises set up by the military, satellite and telecommunications companies set up by various national-level ministries, entertainment companies run by central and local public security bureaus, and taxi companies set up by municipal government departments. Even religious institutions such as Buddhist and Moslem temples have joined this trend.[13] Forming a broad and diverse category, spin-offs share the basic feature of being commercial ventures set up with input from, and sometimes at the initiative of, a government agency or public institution, over which the latter exercises a certain degree of managerial control. They are established to offer public institutions and their employees a way to channel resources to more efficient uses, to earn extra-budgetary revenue, to provide better-paying jobs for their employees,[14] and to relieve themselves of excess personnel.[15] Spin-offs receive varying degrees of financial and material support from their parent unit, typically referred to as the "leading institution" (*zhuguan bumen*). They range from small-scale, low-budget projects that involve little more on the part of the parent institution than releasing a number of employees to engage in commercial ventures, while retaining their original employment, to large-scale projects that receive large investments of capital, personnel, and technology from the parent agency.[16]

Some sectors, such as China's high-tech industries, have from their inception been dominated by spin-off enterprises.[17] The earliest high-tech spin-offs were established in the early 1980s, many of these in Haidian District, Beijing.[18] Institutes within the Chinese Academy of Sciences (CAS), national-level ministries, and Beijing University and other universities have been among the most active in setting up these businesses. By the mid 1980s, there were nearly 100 new electronics and high-tech firms in Beijing, mostly concentrated on one street in Zhongguancun, Haidian District, colloquially referred to as Electronics Street (Dianzi jie).[19] Typical of this type of ownership form, universities, research institutes, and other public institutions have played a central role in the establishment of high-tech firms. Of the more than 10,000 high-tech enterprises operating nationwide in 1993, a large number were set up with assistance from some public or governmental institution.[20]

The proliferation of high-tech spin-offs reflects declining public R&D funding, which has given universities and R&D institutes the incentive to supplement their revenues by launching their own commercial ventures.[21] In Beijing, the CAS, Beijing University, the Ministry of Electronics, and research institutes within national-level ministries such as the Ministry of Aeronautics and Aviation have been active in setting up high-tech businesses.[22] Government policy has explicitly encouraged high-tech spin-offs as a way to commercialize China's technological resources; to link producers of technology with industrial end-users; to encourage R&D institutes to transfer their technology and human resources to more commercial uses; and to overcome the socialist division between R&D and entrepreneurial activities.[23] The "Decision on the Reform of the Science and Technology Management System" by the Central Committee of the Communist Party of China in May 1985 advocated the creation of a market for technology and commercial arrangements in which industrial end-users would pay R&D institutes for the transfer of product and process technologies, technological consulting services, and contracts for the development of production technology.[24] Subsequent policies were adopted to encourage the transformation of entire R&D institutes into profit-making companies and the merging of entire R&D institutes with existing enterprises. The Torch Program launched in May 1988 by the State Science and Technology Commission finally identified spin-offs as the preferred strategy for commercializing science and technology and restructuring the existing R&D infrastructure. It provided fiscal incentives and institutional support for the establishment of new technology enterprises, high-technology zones, and policies to improve infrastructure.[25] These policies have contributed to a rapid growth of high-tech spin-offs; the total number of such enterprises in China's high-tech zones increased from 1,704 in 1989 to over 10,000 in 1993.[26]

Parent Agencies and Insecure Property Rights

Of all the high-technology firms registered in China's high-tech zones in 1989 and 1990, including enterprises officially registered as publicly owned and collective, 80 percent were found to have been launched by individual government agencies and public institutions—as opposed to private individuals, local or national government, or foreign companies. The institutions that have been most active include R&D institutes, state-owned enterprises, and individual administrative units within local government. Of these, R&D institutes accounted for 48 percent and 52 percent of high-tech firms operating in 1989 and 1990 respectively; enterprises accounted for another 22 percent; and local administrative units and other government agencies accounted for around 5 percent in 1990.[27] The role of public institutions and agencies is difficult to gauge by simply comparing the number of public, collective, and privately owned spin-offs, because they also play a key role in sponsoring high-tech firms registered as collectively owned. A fuller understanding of their involvement can be gained by looking at the two different types of collectively owned spin-offs—those that "have a supervising unit" and those "without a supervising unit." The vast majority of high-tech firms operating in China's high-tech zones registered as collectives fall into the category of those "with a supervising unit." Those "without a supervising unit" accounted for only 6 percent, 7.5 percent, and 10 percent of all such firms in 1989, 1990, and 1991 respectively.[28] This pattern is also evident among high-tech firms in Haidian District, where more than 90 percent of enterprises registered as collectively owned reported "having a supervising unit."[29]

The role of public institutions has been all the more striking in light of the minor role that banks have played in financing high-tech enterprises.[30] According to a survey of 271 public and collective high-tech enterprises in Haidian District's high-tech zone, leading institutions were the source of 54.2 percent of the venture capital provided to these firms. Among publicly owned enterprises and collective enterprises "with supervising units," the proportion is even higher, with leading units providing 76.1 percent and 75.3 percent respectively of the firms' initial venture capital. In contrast, supervising agencies invested only 5 percent of the venture capital for enterprises listed as "collectives without an initiating unit." The latter firms received the largest portion of their capital—63.9 percent—from individual investors. Public enterprises and collective enterprises "with a supervising unit," by contrast, received only .8 percent and 1.4 percent respectively of their venture capital from individual investors.[31]

Despite the substantial role that government agencies and public institutions play in launching and funding spin-off enterprises, the property rights of parent agencies over these firms are not clearly defined or well secured. Several factors contribute to this.

First is the lack of legal recognition and protection of the ownership rights of individual public agencies and institutions. Official ownership categories do not recognize *individual* public agencies and institutions as a distinct category of owner, in contrast to private individuals, "the state," or "the collective." Chinese law has no official category of "agency-owned" or "unit-owned" enterprises. From a legal perspective, no differentiation is made between the property rights of individual subunits of the state and "the state" more broadly. Spin-offs are typically officially registered as "publicly owned" (*quanmin qiye*), a status that does not legally distinguish them from the traditional state-owned enterprises (SOEs). Nor does the category "collective enterprises" specifically recognize and protect the property rights of individual agencies. Company documents reflect this in their failure to explicitly state the ownership rights of parent agencies over subsidiaries. According to the rules and regulations of the Fangzheng Corporation, one of the most successful computer companies in China, for example, Beijing University is only recognized as having "sponsored" (*zhubande*) the company. While this recognizes a special role for the university, it is far from a firm statement of ownership.[32]

The ambiguous legal status of agency-owned enterprises is consistent with the state's ambivalence toward public institutions and government agencies running their own businesses. This is reflected in contradictory and vaguely defined policies. On the one hand, government policy has backed spin-offs by encouraging decentralization and financial self-sufficiency, with universities and research institutes in particular receiving explicit policy support for running high-tech businesses.[33] Following favorable policy statements by Deng Xiaoping during his "southern tour" to Shenzhen in 1992, there was an explosion of institution-run and agency-run businesses. On the other hand, the state launches periodic campaigns aimed at forcing government agencies and public institutions to cut ties with the businesses they sponsor.[34] While these crackdowns appear to have had limited success, they highlight the insecure status of this property form. From the perspective of parent agencies, the state has not only failed to provide a "credible commitment" to this property form, but periodically assumes a predatory attitude by pressuring agencies to sever their links with these enterprises.[35] Interestingly, unlike most predatory states, the Chinese state contributes to the insecurity of spin-off property rights, not through the threat of expropriation, but through its support of the autonomy of these enterprises from their parent units.

The second reason why the rights of the parent agency are unclear is that high-tech spin-offs are typically launched by employees who remain in their jobs while undertaking commercial activities outside the scope of their normal work responsibilities, but who often continue to use the offices, laboratories, and other institutional resources of the parent agency. Under these conditions, it is difficult to pinpoint precisely who had the original idea for launching the business venture—generally a key factor in determining property rights. Individual founders—scientists, professors, and technical staff—often contribute important ideas about how to commercialize a technology they may have personally developed. University administrators, institute directors, and department heads also contribute ideas to commercial ventures. The collective nature of the effort makes it difficult to distinguish between the investment of ideas, effort, skill, and knowledge by individuals and the contribution by the parent agency in terms of facilities, office space, and intangibles such as name recognition and political contacts. This method of launching a business venture also makes it difficult to determine when companies are effectively established. Under the umbrella of the parent institution, commercial ventures typically enjoy an incubation period that allows them to utilize the institution's resources and facilities while they work on product design, marketing strategies, and mobilizing capital. Spin-offs are often only officially registered after considerable research and development has been carried out, when their products are ready to be marketed, and in some cases even *after* services or products have begun to be marketed.[36] Spin-offs thus benefit from the institutional support of the parent agency in ways that are difficult to calculate.

A third factor contributing to the underspecified nature of spin-off property rights is the lack of well-developed labor, technology, and capital markets. The lack of such markets increases the cost of specifying the values of various inputs. For instance, the lack of a well-developed market for technology has added to the difficulty of specifying the value of the technological investments made by parent agencies. In Haidian District's high-tech zone, over half of the technology utilized to launch high-tech firms—technology that typically is made available by a university, research institute, or other institution—is reported to have been "freely invested." More than half of the technology utilized by new high-tech enterprises operating in China's high-tech zones nationwide in 1995 was not patented.[37] In interviews, informants often disregarded technology altogether in discussion of various forms of investment and often failed to recognize technology as a significant investment on the part of the parent institution. One company manager said he felt that his company's parent institution—an institute of the CAS—had no legitimate claim to company profits, because it had not invested any capital in the company, despite recognizing that the technology that had been key to the company's initial product had been provided by the institute.[38]

A final, although more elusive, factor that contributes to the underspecification of property rights is the ease with which individuals accept, and regard as normal, the fact that who gets what, who exercises what control, who can make what claims over the profits of a business, and so on, can be worked out in practice through negotiation rather than being determined a priori. Informants expressed an easy acceptance of the fact that property rights could be worked out over time, rather than being specified at the initiation of a business venture. Many said it does not make sense to try to specify things in too great detail in advance, given that the success of a commercial venture was not yet known, that the level of contribution of the participants was not known, and that other conditions could change. This attitude makes sense in a context where neither the legal system nor some equivalent external, state-backed mechanism is perceived as effective in providing a guarantee of formal contracts. However, this attitude, and the resulting habit of informality, diminishes reliance on legal norms and institutions, which in turn further contributes to the latter's ineffectualness.

Bargained Property Rights

Rather than being either clearly defined and protected legal property rights or rights guaranteed by local custom and norms, in the high-tech spin-offs, effective property rights are contested by a range of actors and worked out through a process of bargaining. The results of this process are shaped by the bargaining position of the various contestants, subject to certain institutional constraints.[39] Consequently, property rights in spin-offs vary considerably over time as the bargaining positions of parent units and spin-offs evolve. Parent agencies continuously face the possibility that the commercial ventures they spawn will really "spin off" and gain de facto autonomy. While relatively stable property rights arrangements may emerge over time, these are a *result* of the bargaining process, not its precondition. This process is akin to the competitive, or "spontaneous," emergence of institutions (in this case property) that come into existence and persist through arrangements worked out through individual bargains, without the guiding role of a centralizing force such as the state. It is also distinct from a process in which emerging property rights are determined by community norms and custom.[40]

BARGAINING OVER RESIDUAL INCOME

The right to the residual income of a resource is a key property right, in principle allowing "owners" to claim the income deriving from an asset and to utilize it as they wish, whether for reinvestment in the asset, expansion of facilities, donation to charity, or personal consumption. This right is said to be most fully exercised when the owner can decide to use the entire residual income on personal consumption.[41] Parent agencies exercise certain claims to the residual income of spin-offs, evident in their ability to extract a portion of the profits. In the case of high-tech spin-offs, they typically receive a percentage of the profits. Informants reported that enterprises turned over a range of 0–70 percent of their net profits to their parent institutions, the average being closer to 15–30 percent.[42] The Beida Fangzheng Group turned over Y10 million to Beijing University in 1992 out of a reported Y60 million in net profits. The Lian Xiang Company was reported to have turned over approximately 30 percent of net profits to its parent institution, the CAS Institute of Computer Technology, in 1992. A corporation affiliated with the China Youth League gave between Y1 and Y2 million annually out of gross profits of Y10 million. In some cases parent units claim the lion's share of spin-off profits. Managers at the Beijing Control Technic Development Company, established under the sponsorship of the Industrial Control Institute of the Ministry of Aeronautics and Aviation, complained that they were obliged to turn over 70 percent of company profits in the company's formative stage.[43] In other cases, parent agencies receive no fixed portion of company profits but are paid a "management" fee from the spin-off. These fees are generally justified on the grounds that parent units should be compensated for the temporary "loan" of their employees to affiliated companies, who remain technically employed by the parent unit while working in the spin-off.[44] In one case, a computer company paid the CAS Software Institute, its parent institution, Y6,000 annually for each of the 20 employees who had transferred from the company, a total of Y120,000 a year.[45]

Profit-sharing arrangements were often not specified in writing but were worked out informally. According to the general manager of a company affiliated with the national China Youth League (CYL), the amount of profits that his company transferred to the league was not "fixed" (*bu queding*) but "worked out through discussion" (*tongguo koutou lai anding*).[46] There was a general understanding of the terms between the corporation and the CYL, but specifics were in practice worked out informally. According to a top official in a university-affiliated computer company, the amount of profit that the company turned over to the school was not clearly set out but was determined through negotiations.[47]

In cases when written contracts were drawn up that specifically detailed how profits were to be divided, they were often ignored or violated in practice. In some cases, spin-offs turn over less than the amount written into the formal contract. The contract between a large computer company and its university affiliate specified that the company was to pay 33 percent of its gross profits to the school. Yet, in practice, the company was on average transferring only 10 percent of its profits to the university. In another case, the contract between a consulting company and its parent university specified that the company should pay 15 percent of its profits to the school. Initially, the company's profits were quite small, and the university appeared not to pay too much attention to it. However, when the company landed a large consulting job with the Beijing Broadcasting Corporation for Y1 million, the college president suddenly demanded that the school get a larger share of the profits. After a great deal of contention, the company manager succumbed to the pressure and agreed to hand over more than the 15 percent specified in the contract. Frequent violations of written contracts, or the lack thereof, means that parent agencies and their spin-offs are constantly negotiating and renegotiating profit-sharing and other terms.

The indeterminate nature of property rights over spin-offs is reflected in variability in the distribution of profits. Most companies experienced renegotiation in the terms of profit-sharing. With time the proportion of their profits that spin-offs turn over to their parent units tends to go down. For the Beijing Control Technic Development Company, a subsidiary of the Industrial Control Institute of the Ministry of Aeronautics and Aviation, this declined from 70 percent to 30 percent. Beida Fangzheng and Lian Xiang, similarly, were both able over time to reduce the ratio of their profits that they transferred to their parent institutions. In its initial years, Beida Fangzheng was reported to have turned over around 30 percent of company profits. This portion was reported to have dropped to 17 percent and 10 percent in 1993 and 1996 respectively.

The ambiguity of ownership rights is reflected in the sensitivity of the issue of profit distribution, which informants were typically hesitant to discuss. One strategy that parent agencies adopt to deal with this is to take profits in kind, rather than in cash transfers. Corporations affiliated with the China Youth League, for instance, contributed to various CYL projects, such as sponsoring Youth League events and helping with the construction of local cultural youth centers and other business projects, rather than transferring capital directly to the CYL. One project involved having CYL-affiliated corporations help selected villages (the project was said to involve 10,000 of China's poorest villages) build their local economies through investments in and joint ventures with local enterprises.[48] While these business arrangements were expected to be sound economic investments, they also served to promote the CYL's institutional connections nationwide.

BARGAINING OVER THE RIGHTS OF CONTROL AND UTILIZATION

For the firm, the rights of control and utilization include the right to determine what productive functions a firm performs and the contracts the firm enters into, including employment contracts, the right to make strategic decisions with regard to the future development of the firm, and the right to "unilaterally fill in the details of incomplete contracts with some agents, e.g. employees."[49] Perhaps the most critical of these is the right to appoint the agent in charge of managing a resource or enterprise. Short of being able to manage a resource directly themselves, owners exercise the right to appoint an agent to do so in their place. Identifying who exercises this right is thus key to identifying ownership over an asset, and the clarity of property rights is reflected in the extent to which this right is clearly specified. In the case of spin-offs, the rights of control and utilization are typically not clearly specified, and in practice they are contested by parent agencies and enterprises.

High-tech spin-offs typically lacked clearly defined procedures for selecting and appointing general managers. The ambiguous legal status of spin-offs makes it unclear who should exercise this right. While parent agencies typically exercised a degree of control over managerial appointments, this was based more on their institutional leverage than on their rights as owners. A parent institution's leverage over its subsidiaries rests on its institutional control over such matters as personnel appointments. Some parent units appeared to have minimal control over appointments, evident in their inability to fire managers even in the case of serious conflicts. This is illustrated in the case of You Quanzi, general manager of the Lian Xiang Company, described below. In other cases, parent institutions exercise fairly effective control over the selection and appointment of top company executives, evident in their ability to hire and fire managers.

Several factors limit the effective control of parent agencies over the appointment of managers. First are the periodic state campaigns aimed at "de-linking" government agencies and public institutions from their subsidiaries,[50] already mentioned above. Second is the informal power that the individual founders and managers exercise over these companies. Long-time managers in successful companies are often hard to displace, as the case of You Quanzi of the Lian Xiang Company as described below illustrates. In cases where general managers simply refuse to step down, parent agencies cannot count on legal recourse to make them do so. These individuals may have been among the original founders of the company and those who had the idea of launching the commercial venture. Often it is their hard work, skill, and efforts that account for the company's growth and success. Based on their unique role in developing these businesses, founder-managers exercise enormous personal power over these firms, and they often exhibit a proprietary attitude, viewing them as "their" firms. In most cases, the founders or groups of founders become the company presidents and general managers, and they often remain in those positions indefinitely.

In other cases, individual founders of a company may exercise informal power over managerial decisions without holding a formal leadership position. Wang Xuan, a professor of mathematics at Beijing University and a founder of the Beida Fangzheng Company, was recognized by informants as exercising enormous managerial power, even though he held no formal office in the company.[51] Informants reported that Wang Xuan had a great deal of influence in the selection of general managers,[52] even though internal Beijing University documents give the university the authority to appoint the general and deputy managers, based on the old communist bureaucratic principle of "authority over appointments at two subordinate ranks" (*xiaguan liangji*).

The autonomy of spin-offs over the selection of general managers has been enhanced by the Company Law passed in 1994, which advocated the adoption of enterprise "boards of directors" as a leadership system.[53] According to this law, boards of directors may exercise broad decision-making power and the authority to appoint top-level managers. Because they are self-selecting—board members select replacements for retiring members—this type of leadership system shifts authority from parent agencies to companies. In 1996, top executives of Beida Fangzheng wanted to introduce this system in order to strengthen the company's authority over personnel appointments at the expense of university administrators. The wide implementation of a system of boards of directors among government subsidiaries would significantly weaken the authority of parent agencies over the selection of top executives, undermining a key property right.

CONFLICT BETWEEN SPIN-OFFS AND
PARENT AGENCIES

The case of the Lian Xiang Company illustrates the difficulty that parent institutions can experience in controlling their subsidiaries, and how close spin-off enterprises can come to literally spinning off from their parent agencies and becoming de facto autonomous entities, particularly large, profitable, and successful companies.[54] Founded in 1984 by a group of 20 researchers of the CAS Institute of Computer Technology, Lian Xiang is one of China's top-ranking computer companies. The individual founders received Y 200,000 from the Institute of Computer Technology to help them launch the venture, but no subsequent financial support from the institute. The company's initial product was after-sales computer services, a product that relied primarily on the skill and know-how of the original founders, and that thus required relatively low capital investment. The company subsequently diversified into manufacturing and software development, largely on the basis of profits. Under the management of You Quanzi, one of the company's original founders, the company grew rapidly from a small commercial venture into a large, successful, and profitable firm.

From the time it began turning a profit, the arrangement was that Lian Xiang would turn over a certain portion of its profits to the Institute of Computer Technology.[55] However, in the late 1980s, following several years of rapid growth, You Quanzi, the general manager, is reported to have become unhappy with this arrangement, feeling that the institute's initial financial assistance of Y 200,000 did not justify its continuing claim to the same proportion of the company's profits. You is said to have complained to the institute and to have resisted turning over that much of the company's profits. The institute is reported to have rejected any change in the arrangements, and a major struggle ensued.

You pursued a variety of strategies in his battle with the institute. First, he questioned the institute's rights of ownership over the company and its right to unilaterally make demands on its profits. He claimed that he and the other individual founders had launched the company through their own efforts, relying largely on their individual skills for the products they sold, and that the institute had been of only marginal assistance through the small loan it had given them. Second, You utilized his contacts with the press to publicize the conflict and to generate public support for his position. He gave interviews to journalist friends who wrote articles sympathetic to his position. The institute, for its part, threatened to fire You—asserting its unquestioned ownership of the company. You, in turn, threatened to resign, and to ruin the company if he was fired. Many believed that You was still critical to the continued vitality of the company, whose success he was given credit for. Informants suggested that You had considerable means to damage its reputation and market standing by revealing the ongoing power struggles between the company and the institute. You Quanzi further pursued a bureaucratic strategy of going over the heads of his immediate superiors in the institute and appealing to *their* bosses—the administrative authorities at the level of the CAS. He is reported to have argued to CAS officials that the institute was no longer actively contributing to the company's growth and development and was simply a drain on the company's vitality.

In the end, You Quanzi got his way. He simply refused to hand over the level of profits demanded by the institute. The institute apparently lacked the will or ability to fire him and was unable to pressure him into compliance. Lian Xiang's commercial success and its market independence gave it de facto autonomy and deprived the institute of effective leverage. The company did not rely on the institute for human, technological, or capital resources. It did nearly all of its hiring in the market, rather than from CAS. Furthermore, CAS authorities are said not to have been able or willing to exercise significant bureaucratic or political clout to help the institute out. You Quanzi remained in his position as company manager. The institute backed down on its threat to fire him and acquiesced to a renegotiated profit-sharing arrangement that allowed the company to retain a greater portion of its profits.

The conflict between Lian Xiang and the Computer Technology Institute illustrates the conflict described above over property rights and who can legitimately claim ownership of a company. The institute claimed property rights based on its capital investment of Y 200,000; the fact that all the founding members of the company were institute employees at the time of its founding, and that many continued to be affiliated with CAS subsequently; the fact that the skills and know-how of these individuals—which had been critical to the company's initial products—had been acquired in their capacity as CAS employees; and the fact that the company advertised itself as a "CAS company" and had derived significant visibility and public trust from this identity, which the institute argued had been critical to Lian Xiang's success.

The company questioned the legitimacy of the institute's ownership claims. Company leaders contended that they had had the idea for launching the company and had taken the initiative in doing so. In their view, the institute had only "lent" the group Y 200,000, an amount that the company had more than paid back to the institute over the years and that certainly did not justify its continued claim to company profits. The founders had furthermore relied primarily on their own skills, technological knowledge, hard work, and experience to make the company successful.

Factors Shaping Bargaining Outcomes

The evidence presented above suggests that property rights over spin-offs are legally not well specified, that written contracts are often violated, and that they are effectively determined through contestation and bargaining. This raises the question of what factors shape bargaining outcomes. While it is difficult to get detailed knowledge of this sensitive process, several key factors emerge. The first is the extent to which spin-off enterprises develop independently of their parent agencies. Lian Xiang and Beida Fangzheng provide an interesting contrast in this respect. Beida Fangzheng (originally the Beijing University New Technology Company) developed in close symbiosis with Beijing University and continues to receive critical inputs from the university. From its inception, Fangzheng received considerable support from Beijing University in terms of capital investment, technology, personnel, and institutional support. Beida invested an initial Y 400,000 and subsequently helped to mobilize an additional Y 4 million, Y 1,500,000 from the university's own funds and Y 2,500,000 as a loan from a local farmers' collective, which the university helped to secure.[56] Beida provided the key technology that launched the company and was the basis of its core products for many years—technology that was the result of years of work by a large research team funded by the "748" project, aimed at developing technology to save Chinese characters in computer memory—

out of a large government research grant given to the university in 1974.[57] Because of the nature of the company's product, Beida has played a critical role in Fangzheng's marketing and distribution. Because its typesetting technology is targeted primarily at large publishing houses and newspapers, Beijing University's reputation and its institutional and political contacts have been critical in gaining a market for the company's product among the country's largest newspapers and publishing institutions. Company managers felt that without Beida's institutional backing, Fangzheng would never have been able to capture a market for its product. Beida has also been a continuing source of Beida Fangzheng's personnel— critical to the success of a high-tech enterprise. Roughly 90 percent of Fangzheng's employees are graduates of or former employees of Beijing University. These are some of the factors that help explain why Fangzheng employees tend to recognize as legitimate the university's claims of "ownership" over the company.[58]

Lian Xiang, by contrast, developed in a much more autonomous fashion. This commercial venture received relatively little financial support from its parent institution—the CAS Institute of Computer Technology— only the one lump sum of Y200,000.[59] It did not rely on the Computer Technology Institute for technology, developing its own R&D capabilities instead. The company's initial product of after-sales service for personal computers drew heavily on the skills and know-how of its individual founders rather than on "hard" technology provided by the parent agency. The sponsoring institute was therefore not viewed as having contributed critical technology. Furthermore, Lian Xiang has not relied on CAS for skilled personnel to the same extent that Fangzheng relied on Beijing University, but has developed more market-based hiring practices. Fewer than 10 percent of company employees have an affiliation with the CAS. The nature of the company's initial product, furthermore, allowed it to be highly self-reliant in terms of marketing and distribution. Because its customers were primarily individuals, small companies, and work units, Lian Xiang was not as reliant as Fangzheng on its parent institution in building up its market niche. As a consequence, Lian Xiang developed relatively independently of its parent agency, relying minimally on the latter for R&D, capital, institutional resources, personnel, or marketing support.

Initial contributions are, to an important extent, "sunk costs," which do not adequately secure property rights in the future. Parent agencies that make significant initial contributions of capital or technology but do not continue to be vital to the development of a company are likely to experience diminishing leverage. Beida not only made substantial initial contributions to Fangzheng but continued over the years to be the key source of resources, personnel, technology, and R&D resources for the company.[60] A research institute of the university—the Beijing University Computer Sciences Research Institute (formerly the Chinese Language Research Institute)—has served as Fangzheng's key R&D division. In the mid 1980s, when it had around 30 employees, the institute's operating costs and staff salaries were paid for by the university.[61] Furthermore, as recounted earlier, Fangzheng continues to hire nearly all of its personnel from the university and is dependent on the university for its skilled labor.[62]

A second key factor shaping property rights is the nature of the administrative apparatus available to the parent agencies for supervising and managing the spin-offs. Some parent agencies set up specialized administrative apparatuses to oversee affiliated business ventures, which enhances their ability to effectively manage these enterprises, and others do not. The CAS, for instance, initially took a very hands-off approach to the business ventures affiliated with its various institutes. Informants say that this explains the independence of many CAS-affiliated companies, such as Lian Xiang, which grew up with little administrative interference from the CAS. The CAS did establish a management company in 1992, the CAS Group (Zhongke jituan—short for Zhongguo kexue yuan jituan), which gave it more effective control over personnel, production, management, finances, etc. However, the Zhongke jituan was only put in charge of 22 out of a much larger number of affiliated firms. Many older CAS-affiliated firms, such as Lian Xiang, were already too independent and powerful to be easily brought under centralized control.

Beijing University, by contrast, took a more activist approach to management of university-affiliated firms from the start. And university administrators have taken a high profile in the management of university businesses. In response to the proliferation of university-affiliated enterprises after 1992, Beida established a Committee for the Management of University Enterprises (Beida xuexiao chanye guanli weiyuan hui), whose members include the university president, two deputy presidents, a member in charge of personnel, and a member in charge of finance. Below this committee is the Office for the Management of University Enterprises, directly in charge of managing the school's enterprises and implementing the policies of the University Management Committee with regard to personnel, finances, enterprise restructuring, and so on. The high profile of university leadership with regard to management of its enterprises and the existence of an administrative organ to carry out policy have facilitated the university's control over the burgeoning number of companies operating under its institutional umbrella. According to one informant, the management office's role is to "exercise the university's authority to manage its enterprises."[63] This includes implementing university policy regarding its enterprises, making appointments of top-level executives, making sure that enterprises transfer the agreed-upon portion of their profits to the university, helping enterprises keep abreast of changing regulatory policies, and deciding strategies for downsizing and mergers. For instance, it was the management office's responsibility to attempt to shut down the small, department-run enterprises that the university deemed to be inefficient. While the establishment of the management office strengthened the university's management of small and medium-sized enterprises and more recently established enterprises, it was clear that a company of the size, stature, and financial clout of Beida Fangzheng was beyond the control of this office and had to be supervised directly by top-level university officials. Beijing University has exercised relatively great influence over managerial appointments, having been able to remove more than one general manager.[64]

The physical and organizational characteristics of the parent agency are a third factor that comes into play in the shaping of property rights. The CAS's hands-off approach to its affiliated businesses is linked to its being a physically decentralized organization, which has no central campus, consisting of a large number of relatively autonomous institutes scattered through the city. These factors do not contribute to the institution's sense of unity and coherence as a community. They have made it more difficult for the CAS to exercise centralized management over affiliated companies, and have given it less incentive to do so. Beida, in contrast, and like most Chinese universities, is physically centralized, with a walled campus and a strong sense of institutional community. Partly as a consequence of these features, the university administration actively shapes and controls the university community, and it has taken a more activist approach to supervising university-affiliated businesses. According to informants, the political sensitivity of university student politics further contributes to the incentives for Beida and other universities to tightly regulate the university community, including its businesses. This suggests that the authority that parent agencies exercise over their subsidiaries is dependent on their institutional characteristics, rather than on strictly defined legal property rights.

A fourth factor affecting the control of parent agencies over spin-off enterprises is their power over personnel. The employees of subsidiary firms who transfer from the parent agency tend to remain formally employed by the latter while working for the company, which allows them to retain many of the privileges of public employment. This arrangement, however, gives parent units continued leverage over them. They control the personnel dossiers (*dang'an*) of spin-off employees, which affect employment status and benefits. The proportion of spin-off employees who transfer from the parent agency varies widely, as the examples above have shown. In 1996, 80 percent of Beida Fangzheng's new hires were graduates of, or employees who transferred from, Beijing University. By contrast, 80–90 percent of Lian Xiang's new employees were hired from "the outside"—that is, through market channels, not from the parent agency—a factor that would give them greater independence.

Other factors being equal, large, profitable, and successful companies enjoy greater relative autonomy and leverage vis-à-vis their parent institutions. Being an economic powerhouse gives a company bargaining leverage, especially when the parent institution is financially dependent on its spin-offs, not the other way around. As one company employee put it, the Institute of Computer Technology needs Lian Xiang much more than the company needs the institute.[65] Furthermore, as firms grow in size, complexity, technical sophistication, and product diversity, it becomes increasingly difficult for parent institutions to micro-manage them. Managers of large subsidiaries tended to state that they exercise considerable autonomy in day-to-day decision-making regarding production, marketing, investment decisions, and personnel management. In their view, administrators in the parent agency lack the necessary knowledge of these matters to influence managerial decisions. Finally, managers said that market competition reduced the intervention of higher levels, inasmuch as managerial decisions had to be made quickly under pressure of changing market conditions, something that did not allow for cumbersome bureaucratic intervention from above.[66]

The Benefits of Spin-off Enterprises

Despite the contested and bargained nature of their property rights, spin-off enterprises have contributed to the dynamism, entrepreneurship, competition, and growth of China's market economy. They have done so in at least five ways. First, spin-offs have facilitated the rapid transfer of resources—capital, personnel, technology, and institutional resources—from the state sector to more dynamic, innovative, and productive business enterprises. Within the high-tech sector, spin-offs have been an organizational strategy for restructuring China's R&D system and promoting the commercialization of technology. R&D institutes, institutes of higher learning, governmental agencies, and individuals have the incentive to market the resources available to them.[67] The fact that more than half of the capital invested in new high-tech firms comes from institutions is evidence of the effectiveness of spin-offs in shifting state-controlled resources to innovative business ventures.

Second, spin-offs have contributed to the level of entrepreneurship in the economy by lowering the risks to individuals of engaging in business, a key role of economic institutions. Employment in spin-off enterprises has allowed public employees to work in business enterprises without giving up the benefits and security associated with public employment. While they receive their salaries from the company, transferred personnel retain their "personnel links" with their parent unit, and in some cases continue to receive a salary from the parent unit as well.[68] This allows them to retain privileges associated with the status of state employee, which guarantees, among other things, their public employment benefits, public housing, state-guaranteed retirement pension, public health insurance, job security, and a host of other privileges associated with the status of state cadres.[69] Because the skilled personnel needed for high-tech companies are concerned with keeping their privileges, spin-offs have encouraged the shift of skilled personnel from the traditional state sector to more entrepreneurial and innovative activities.[70] By operating under the institutional umbrella of a public institution, spin-offs encourage individual scientists, engineers, and other skilled personnel to "jump into the sea" of business.

Third, spin-offs have contributed to the strengthening of hard budget constraints in the economy. Spin-offs are typically launched in order to resolve budget crises in the sponsoring agencies. Parent institutions are often financially dependent on their spin-offs, not the other way around. The limited fixed budgets of sponsoring agencies, particularly of R&D institutes and universities, constrain their ability to subsidize their commercial ventures in the event of failure. In some cases, the revenue of the spin-off enterprise may far exceed that of its sponsoring institution.[71] Not having the ability and the authority to extract additional revenue through taxes in order to subsidize failing enterprises, as local governments do, further limits soft budgets among spin-off enterprises. Spin-offs, furthermore, are not integrated into the state plan and are thus not guaranteed state-allocated materials and production inputs, state-guaranteed markets, or guaranteed salaries and benefits.[72]

Fourth, spin-offs have increased the level of competition in the economy by contributing to the growth in the number of commercial enterprises that must compete in the market to survive. The running of businesses by individual subunits of the state produces a relatively pluralistic ownership structure, which generally denies spin-offs the monopoly status enjoyed by traditional state-owned enterprises. In the high-tech sector, firms affiliated with universities, research institutes, national-level ministries, and so on, must compete against one another. The high level of investment in R&D by high-tech spin-offs is one indication of the competitive pressure under which they operate.[73]

Spin-offs, lastly, are more likely to contribute to the emergence of a new work culture than privatized state-owned enterprises, because they are new firms with new management, new management-worker relations, and the potential for establishing a new corporate culture and work ethic. Privatized state-owned enterprises, despite having the advantage of more clearly defined ownership, suffer from the persistence of old management, old management-worker relations, and the old work ethic.

Conclusions: Spin-offs and China's Dynamic Market Transition

Contrary to the proposition that clearly defined and secured property rights are critical to economic growth and dynamism, China's economy has experienced the proliferation of an enterprise type whose property rights are neither clearly defined nor well secured. Public institutions and state agencies of all types sponsor, invest in, and manage commercial ventures, but their property rights over these businesses are legally not well defined or secured; are attacked in state campaigns; and are challenged by the commercial ventures themselves, which often seek to operate autonomously and literally spin off to become independent firms. The proliferation of this type of enterprise in China's market transition points to a property-rights regime characterized by poorly defined and ill-secured property rights.

This chapter has argued that despite this, and in some ways on account of their fuzzy property rights, spin-off enterprises in China have contributed in unique ways to the transition from a centrally planned to a market economy. They have given individual and organizational actors the incentive to embark on commercial enterprises; they have facilitated the transfer of resources away from the old state sector to more dynamic enterprises; they have helped to harden budget constraints; they have contributed to the level of competition in the economy; and they have contributed to new, market-oriented management practices. Spin-offs have thus helped resolve specific organizational, institutional, and economic challenges associated with the transition from a centrally planned to a market economy. This suggests that the utility of particular property forms cannot be abstracted from the institutional and organizational context in which an economy operates. Mainstream theories that advocate the necessity of privatization in the postcommunist context are based on a view of market economies that fails to consider the institutional and organizational context of the societies in which these economic institutions operate.[74] Because of this, they are not well equipped to explain the paradox of China's economy, in which one of the most effective market transitions has been accompanied by neither systematic privatization nor the emergence of relatively well defined and protected property rights.

Chapter 11

Producing Property Rights: Strategies, Networks, and Efficiency in Urban China's Nonstate Firms

DAVID L. WANK

China's emerging market economy presents a puzzle: why such dynamic economic growth without the clarification of legal rights to private property? Since 1979, China's economy has grown about 10 percent annually, while the southeastern coastal region has been growing almost twice as fast. A main engine of growth has been the entrepreneurial nonstate economy, consisting of private and collective sector firms. Yet empirical research persistently portrays these firms as operating through ties to local government that do not conform to our own legal distinctions between public and private property.

Here I examine this puzzle from an analytic perspective different from that found in many recent studies. Drawing on the assumption of an ideal typical market, the market transition account views the ties to local government as evidence of poorly enforced legal property rights and an obstacle to the formation of a more complete market economy. The ties are said to reflect the inefficiency of firms, because they embody suboptimal incentives and higher transaction costs, resulting in lower rates of reinvestment in business.[1] But this neglects the crucial issue of how the institutions of an "incomplete" market economy can nonetheless create such economic dynamism.

A second perspective might be called the "traditional culture" account. It views economic relationships as norms of cooperation and authority rooted in traditional kinship and community institutions. These norms function as de facto property rights by stabilizing expectations in economic transactions.[2] In this account, legal property rights are of no apparent relevance, and the state's role and its policies in the emerging market economy are neglected. This potentially reductionist character is also seen in the market transition account: neither perspective sufficiently appreciates the institutionally jumbled commercial environment in which entrepreneurs must operate.

This chapter examines entrepreneurial strategies within this environment for clues about possible sources of market dynamism. This environment includes the haphazard observation of legal rights to property, changing state policies, ambiguous standards of legitimacy, and the commercial interests of local government agencies and agents. In this context, company operators cannot take for granted a single external institution to secure their property: instead they must help *produce* property rights through their own actions. They do so by creatively combining available institutional resources that stabilize expectations in their dealings with others.[3] Commercial operators can thus be considered Schumpterian entrepreneurs: their innovative strategies stimulate economic activity that would otherwise not occur.

I focus on the reasonably coherent strategies of entrepreneurs designed to produce stable expectations.[4] A strategy is a sequence of means toward an end: for entrepreneurs, the ultimate end is maximizing profit and security for their firms. Coherence occurs when diverse institutional elements such as state policies, social norms, and local government ties are successfully woven together such that entrepreneurial dealings with others further the profitability and security of their firms.[5] I use the term "reasonable" here to refer to the optimizing decisions and choices that reflect the readily available resources at hand. Such reasonably coherent strategies, as will be shown in this chapter, are expressed in networks.[6] While these networks may be suboptimal institutions from the perspective of economic theory, they are in fact the best available strategy for entrepreneurs who must cope with an emerging market economy that lacks strong legal institutions for enforcing property rights.

I describe, first, the institutions of an emerging market economy and show how networks are rational responses. Second, I describe how entrepreneurs' commercial strategies proceed through them. Third, I address the question of the economic efficiency of networks raised by the market transition account. This discussion suggests how entrepreneurial strategies serve to create market dynamism. Finally, I extend the discussion of how networks stimulate market dynamism in China by drawing brief contrasts with market economies in Eastern Europe.

My arguments are based on nineteen months of fieldwork from 1988 to 1995 in Xiamen, an old port city and now a special economic zone in Fujian

Province, along China's southeast coast.[7] Xiamen's nonstate sectors, including both the domestic and transnational sectors, have come to constitute the lion's share of local market activity, with commerce and services growing more rapidly than manufacturing.[8] This is owing to Xiamen's status as a special economic zone, making it a site of intensive commodity circulation between the domestic and international economies. Official statistics indicate about 15,000 domestic nonstate trading firms in Xiamen in 1989 when my main fieldwork was undertaken.[9] At the top end were private and collective trading companies (*maoyi gongsi*) that operated through clientelist ties with public units and government agents to trade interregionally and transnationally. At the bottom end were private shops (*getihu*) selling to one another and to retail customers in local markets. This chapter draws on a sample of 147 trading companies in the nonstate sector.[10]

As a special economic zone, Xiamen is not typical of China's market economy. What light can it shed on the nonstate sector of China's economy as a whole? As a special economic zone designed to take the lead in developing as a market economy, Xiamen has favorable economic policies, a good communications infrastructure, and ethnic advantages in attracting investment flows from speakers of the local Minnan dialect living outside the People's Republic, primarily in Taiwan, but also in Southeast Asia and Hong Kong. In such key respects as capitalization of firms, business volume, and the relative decline of the state sector, Xiamen embodies an extreme of market emergence. However, this does not correspond to the greater clarification of legal rights to property, as many of the same processes of blurring observed elsewhere in China are also seen in Xiamen. Thus, the local situation casts into sharp relief the aforementioned puzzle of China's emerging market economy.

The Institutional Environment

Business operators forge networks in response to institutional characteristics of their environment. The features of networks are responses to these characteristics. One characteristic is the enduring power of local government. In China in the 1980s, this included control over many public assets, such as land and administratively priced commodities, that constituted the best profit opportunities. Although this aspect of local government power has eroded by the 1990s, local governments have acquired greater administrative control over the market economy in their jurisdictions through new regulatory, taxation, and licensing powers. Thus, commercial firms are still dependent on local government in many aspects of their operation, although the emphasis has shifted over time from obtaining profit opportunities to reducing uncertainty.

Clientelism enables entrepreneurs to manage their dependence on local government by creating alliances to enhance business opportunities. They refer to higher-ranking patrons with greater discretionary power as "hard" (*ying*) and seek to forge ties with such officials to stimulate business. They also value the connectivity (*lianluo*) of officials. This refers to the extent that an official is linked to others in the government, providing access to information across the functional boundaries of bureaucratic jurisdictions and levels. Greater connectivity enhances access to information and communication. Access hinges on strategies of reciprocity. Reciprocity can involve quid pro quo exchange of commercial wealth for official discretion; these are idiomatically called money connections (*jinqian guanxi*). Reciprocity can also be less blatantly instrumental discharges of obligations rooted in affective bonds of kinship and familiarity, called emotive connections (*ganqing guanxi*). The mix of money and emotion in any single relation and the content of the exchange is contingent on the specific relationship between the exchange parties and the type of business involved.

A second institutional characteristic is the haphazard enforcement of legal rights to private property. This stems in part from the self-serving manner in which local governments enforce laws and regulations. Officials often put pressure on entrepreneurs for payoffs and shares in their firms, while successful private companies can be forced to sell out to local governments. Uncertainty in regard to legal rights is exacerbated by the lack of impartial courts to enforce legal rights to private property. Even after almost two decades of reform, the courts are viewed as easily influenced in any but the most petty cases. Furthermore, given the perception that "officials shield one another" (*guan guan xianghu*), private company operators are unwilling to press charges in court when malfeasance involves officials and public units.

Particularism helps compensate for the weakness of legal definitions in determining the relational statuses of exchange parties. Social distinctions between insider (*neiren*) and outsider (*wairen*) play a prominent role. One distinction is family/nonfamily, with the strongest obligations being those considered family. Another obligation is linked to the idiom of "sameness" (*tong*). Those who perceive similar characteristics among themselves, such as schoolmates (*tongxue*), colleagues (*tongshi*), and compatriots (*tongxiang*), feel enhanced obligations. Other distinctions are between familiar (*shou*) persons and strangers (*sheng*). The perception of relative statuses gives rise to use of money and emotive ties to achieve a more favorable relative position by manipulating insider-outsider distinctions. Manipulation is expressed in such typical idioms of the "art of guanxi" (guanxixue) as doing "favors" (renqingwei), "concern" (guanxin), and giving "special treatment" (teshu youdai) and "consideration" (zhaogu) to others.[11]

A third characteristic is ambiguity over what constitutes legitimate activity. In the early 1980s, the very notion of private business was controversial, and state policy discriminated against private firms by, for example, restricting their access to state bank loans and denying them the right to use mechanized transport. In the latter half of the 1980s, there was much debate over specific practices: were business commissions a legitimate incentive or an illegitimate kickback; were the operators of cooperative firms heroes for using private capital to solve public problems (e.g., unemployment) or scoundrels exploiting public status for private gain? In the 1990s, the accounting of assets in the corporatization of state firms has given rise to new debates. Given these ambiguities, the propensity is for commercial strategies to push at the boundaries of what is formally permitted. This is reflected in the entrepreneurial argot of business by such terms as "exploiting loopholes" (zuan kongzi) and "walking on the edge of the policy" (zou zai zhengce de bianshang). Business involves not so much doing what is explicitly legal but rather doing what is not expressly forbidden. The risks are greater but profits can be much higher. The perception that "if you operate within the bounds of the policy, you will never become rich" is widespread.

Networks allow entrepreneurs to cope with these environmental ambiguities by creating a corresponding ambiguity in their firms' legal structures. In the early and mid 1980s, networks enabled entrepreneurs to cope with the discrimination against the private sector. Through such practices as "red-hatting" (dai hong maozi), privately operated firms came to enjoy legal public status, helping them attract customers and bypassing discriminatory legislation against legally private firms. In the 1990s, the utility of this ambiguity has increasingly centered on matters of taxation, "pocket-swapping" (huan koudai—the shifting of public assets to legal private ownership), and socializing risk to enhance private gain in a process referred to as "private consumption of gain and public absorption of losses" (siren chi li, guojia chikui). Networks obscure the legal status of a firm, keeping regulatory agencies off guard and unsure of how to treat it. This reduces entrepreneurs' accountability, giving them greater freedom of action.[12]

In sum, networks enhance entrepreneurs' expectations in dealing with state agents and others by enabling them to better channel state power toward business enhancement, achieve a reasonable degree of enforcement through popular norms, and enhance freedom of action from government agencies.

Entrepreneurial Strategies

In the uncertain environment of the emerging market economy, business is largely about the forging and enhancing of supportive ties with others. The specific kind of ties forged and the legal type of firm in which strategies proceed are contingent on the social status of specific entrepreneurs. Broadly speaking, two strategies are pursued. One is forged from below, in that the entrepreneurs who pursue it hold no formal office in government and strive to develop connections with officialdom. The other is forged from above, in that its operators are current officials who use the power of their positions to enhance their connections. While the means of each strategy differ somewhat, they both establish networks for private gain with the local government that transgress the formal borders of public and private, and of state and society. In this section I describe the two strategies as they appeared in the 1980s and the trends of change observed through the mid 1990s.

STRATEGIES FROM BELOW

Nonofficials seek ties with public agencies and officials to enhance access to public resources controlled by local governments. Their strategies are pursued through cooperative (*minban jiti*) and private (*siying*) firms. The state policies that launched these firms opened up opportunities for private (i.e., nonofficial) holders of capital by prohibiting current officeholders from running them.

In the mid 1980s, links to local governments were forged through "people-run collectives" (*minban jiti*). These are enterprises established with private capital and privately managed that are usually attached to government agencies at the district level and below, or to collective enterprises. They proliferated in the mid 1980s as a state initiative to stimulate private enterprise without expanding the legal scope of the private sector, an ideologically contentious issue at the time. New regulations enabled four or more persons who were legally unemployed to pool their own capital to found cooperative firms. These firms are legally owned by a sponsoring public unit, but partners can transfer their shares freely to the other partners. The operators make business decisions independently of their public sponsors. For example, while regulations may stipulate that after-tax profits be divided among an accumulation fund, a welfare fund, wages, and dividends, it is the operators who decide on the proportions, subject only to the provision that dividends not exceed 15 percent of the value of a firm's shares.[13]

Running a cooperative firm in the 1980s had many advantages relative to private shops (*getihu*), which were restricted by the aforementioned policy. Although many limitations on private shops were removed by the mid 1980s, key ones remained, such as a limit of seven employees and a ceiling of Y100 in the amount of receipts. This hindered the growth of private firms. Public legal status for cooperative firms let operators bypass such restrictions and enjoy tax holidays. Also, in the ideological atmosphere of the time, private business was suspect, and red-hatting let entrepreneurs represent themselves as public firms, ensuring better treatment from government agencies and inspiring confidence in consumers.

Cooperative firm operators also found that they could profit from their firms' public status by selling affiliations to private operators, leading to the proliferation of subcontracting arrangements, colloquially termed "hanging on" (*guakao*). The transportation industry is a case in point. Regulations in the 1980s required private taxis to be sponsored by a public transportation firm. Cooperative transportation firms could serve as sponsors. The average monthly sponsorship fee paid by private taxis was Y1,000, and larger firms sponsored dozens of taxis.

Many operators of cooperative companies also lease out subsidiaries, which in turn are subleased by the lessee, generating profits all along the subcontracting chain. I found subcontracting by Xiamen's larger firms to be so multilayered that their operators had little idea of the exact number of other firms, shops, and outlets attached to their companies.

The promulgation of the Private Enterprise Interim Regulation in 1988 opened up additional strategies. This regulation permitted single-owner, joint-stock, and incorporated private companies with fewer formal restrictions. For example, there were no limits on the number of employees or the amount of receipts, leading to the emergence of 185 privately owned trading companies in Xiamen's urban districts within a year of the policy being announced. Some of these were formed by private shopkeepers (*getihu*) who had been in business since the early days of market reform and had accumulated enough capital to establish a private company. Others were formed by low- or middle-ranking cadres who resigned their posts in the late 1980s to set up private companies under the Interim Regulations. Many of these later entrants to entrepreneurship were descended from families that had belonged to the prerevolutionary bourgeoisie and received start-up capital from relatives overseas.

Despite the wholly private legal status of these companies, their operators immediately began forging links to local government. They sought the participation of officials in their firms by giving them positions as advisors, shareholders, and board members. Called "backstage bosses" (*houtai laoban*) or "backers" (*kaoshan*), these officials assist the companies by providing timely information on the supply and demand of scarce resources, ensuring lower tax bills, preventing harassment by government agencies, and helping in other ways.[14]

Licenses to run both cooperative and private firms were also obtained via networks, a process idiomatically called "getting hold of authority" (*gaodao quanli*). This is because licenses can be scarce, particularly in the first stages of policy implementation, when the state is testing out the new policy. Yet it is precisely at this early stage that holding a license confers the greatest business advantage, because there are fewer regulations and local governments eagerly support the policy to ensure its success.

Entrepreneurs obtained these licenses through networks in several ways. Some small private shopkeepers from low social backgrounds who had limited ties to officialdom did so by becoming members of the "preparatory committee" (*choubei hui*) set up to familiarize selected entrepreneurs with a new policy to ensure its smooth implementation. Such committees were established as preludes to the formal launching of both the cooperative policy in the mid 1980s and the private enterprise policy in the late 1980s. Members of such committees were among the first to be authorized to run the new types of enterprise. To ensure membership, these entrepreneurs actively participated in the Self-Employed Laborers' Association (Geti laodongzhe xiehui), the mandatory state-run association for private proprietors, which brought them into close contact with the Industry and Commerce Bureau officials who supervised it. Since the Industry and Commerce Bureau also helps establish the preparatory committees and then issues the new business licenses, the entrepreneurs were then able to prevail on supervisory officials for inclusion on preparatory committees.[15]

Other entrepreneurs used kinship ties to officials to get licenses. Many cooperatives founded in the mid 1980s had a son or daughter of a city government official among the original partners. The ties of these offspring not only secured enterprise licenses for the partnership but supported the subsequent business as well.

STRATEGIES FROM ABOVE

Officials may obtain privileged access to scarce public resources and shift public resources to private ownership by various means. Characteristic vehicles for this strategy are branch (*neilian*) and leased (*zulin*) firms. The operation of the former is restricted to current officeholders by state policy, while opportunities to operate the latter in practice heavily favor their former public managers.

Branch firms appeared in the early 1980s as part of a state effort to compensate for the perceived shortcomings of overcentralization in the planned economy by developing new lateral flows of information and resources. Public agencies and enterprises were encouraged to bypass the hierarchical channels of the planned economy by establishing branches elsewhere to obtain their own resources and outlets. Inland public units established branches in marketized coastal locales such as Xiamen to generate income. The operators of these companies enjoy user rights to orchestrate firms' assets and limited income rights to set their salaries and those of employees, but have no transfer rights.[16]

Unlike running a private or cooperative firm, running a branch or leased firm is an opportunity almost exclusively for current or recently resigned cadres. Branch firm operators are officials from geographically distant public concerns sent to Xiamen to give those entities a presence in Xiamen's special economic zone. Some of the most entrepreneurial officials that I encountered in Xiamen were branch company operators who had previously managed rural manufacturing enterprises owned by township and county governments. They had lost their positions during the retrenchment of rural public industry in the early 1980s and were given the opportunity to run a branch firm as consolation. Many had taken "internal retirement" (*neitui*) and received no wages, although they were still formally government cadres.

Their long years of public service had left them with rich and profitable networks in government. Some used their networks for the practice of official profiteering (*guandao*). In the 1980s, with the two-tier price system, goods procured at administrative prices could be resold at market prices for a profit. Indeed, a number of branch companies were little more than conduits for transferring administratively priced commodities controlled by parent units to the special economic zone, where demand is high. This practice is especially prevalent in the construction industry, which is characterized by booming demand and administrative control of key resources such as lumber and cable, resulting in scarcity of and high prices for these commodities. Another way is what is called pocket-swapping. This practice is facilitated by the geographic distance of branch firms from their parent units, making monitoring lax and giving entrepreneurs much freedom of action. Firm operators invest heavily in real estate and other fixed assets, such as cars and machinery, which they then resell at low prices to affiliated private firms operated by family members.[17] Others give sweetheart contracts to affiliated private firms to reduce their tax bills by padding their expenditures. Yet another way of using prior networks for business is called "pulling over connections" (*ba guanxi la-guolai*). This involves the total shift of a branch firm's supplier and customer base to an affiliated private firm, an increasingly common practice by the late 1980s as the status of private business rose. A case in point is a firm in the seafood trade owned by a village government along the coast. It was founded in 1983 by the former manager of a rural fishing boat factory, who used his prior ties with fishing boat captains to obtain fresh fish for sale to luxury hotels throughout China. The firm's public status was an asset during the first few years in purchasing from rural fishing collectives and selling to joint-venture luxury hotels. However, by the late 1980s, the operator was confident enough to begin shifting the business to a private company established by his son in 1988. This eventually bankrupted the firm, but by then the operator had secured its commercial potential in the private firms of his offspring.

The practice of leasing (*zulin*) collective trading companies began in the mid 1980s as a state effort to turn the money-losing subsidiary collectives established in great numbers in the late 1970s and early 1980s—the so-called May 7 enterprises—into profitable firms.[18] Many state units had established May 7 enterprises to create jobs for unneeded employees and the unemployed offspring of employees.[19] To turn the firms around, leaseholders were given legal income and user rights to the firms for the leases' duration, usually three to five years. The policy intention was to create greater entrepreneurial incentives for operators without privatizing transfer rights, which was ideologically problematic at the time.[20]

The operation of leased firms is through networks, beginning with the leasing process itself, which appears to consist largely of bid-rigging. According to regulations, firms are to be leased to nonofficials through open and fair bidding. But a number of the lessees I talked to said that bidding was rigged, for reasons discussed later in this chapter. In some instances, the lessees were told the amounts of the other bids, enabling them to submit the highest, while in other cases, the auction was never publicized, and the lessee's bid was the only one.

Other practices that confound the formal legal boundaries of public and private property also occur in leased firms. Owing to its legal structure, in which transfer rights belong to the leasing public units, while income and control rights are in the hands of the lessee for a specified period, this type of firm is an especially prime site for the practice of "private consumption of benefits and state absorption of losses." It is easy for operators to allocate business risk and overhead depreciation to the firms while assigning profits to themselves. For example, a loan can be obtained from the state bank in the name of the public firm for a business venture. If the venture is successful, the operator reaps the profit, and if it fails, he or she can declare bankruptcy and default on the loan, leaving the bank and the public owner to fight over responsibility for the debt and the firm's remaining assets.

The practice of private consumption of gain and public absorption of losses can even be written into leasing contracts. The case of a firm that traded in such restricted construction goods as lumber and cable is illustrative. The firm was founded in 1983 by a senior cadre from the forestry bureau of a rural administrative region, who used the substantial ties acquired during the course of a career as long as the history of the People's Republic to obtain highly restricted lumber for sale. In 1985, his firm was investigated for irregularities, and he resigned and retired to his rural village. However, the new manager lacked the old cadre's ties and could not obtain lumber. The forestry bureau officials pleaded with the cadre to come back and run the firm. The cadre agreed, but not before negotiating a lease contract with extremely favorable conditions. He eliminated his business risk by having three clauses inserted in the contract voiding it if he became sick and unable to work, if public construction bureaus stopped selling materials to him at the lower administrative price, and if state policies changed to oppose the policy of leasing. These clauses were so broad as to let him legally abandon the firm whenever he wanted, leaving its public owner to shoulder outstanding liabilities.

Another practice is the undervaluation of public assets when determining the leasing price. This low valuation is called "favor value" (*renqing jia*), because it is forthcoming only in the context of a personal tie between the lessee and officials in the sponsoring public unit. The low charge for private user rights boosts the profits accruing to the firm operator via private income rights. For example, in leased firms, the leasing fee rarely reflects the firm's income producing potential. In the late 1980s, monthly leasing fees for district-level collective trading firms were about Y 3,000 for firms with assets worth at least several hundred thousand yuan and capable of earning profits many times the lease fees. Furthermore, many lessees subcontract out the less profitable assets of leased firms, an income potential not reflected in the leasing fee. One lessee, for example, subleased three retail counters in a leased firm for Y 1,000 a month each, generating a Y 3,000 profit, which covered the monthly lease, while the operator concentrated on more profitable wholesale trade.

The Evolution of Strategies

The strategies and networks that transgress legal property boundaries have evolved over time. One trend occurs as a firm's capital accumulates. By the late 1980s, wealthy trading firms had shifted to the more expansive network strategy of enterprise groups (*qiye jituan*). These consist of from three to several dozen firms linked by overlapping ownership and management ties embedded in kinship and friendship. These firms are diversified not only in terms of business lines but also in the legal status of

constituent firms. Many of them include legally private, leased, cooperative, and even branch companies.

This diversification among legal property rights lets entrepreneurs
more readily shift assets to avoid detection and obscure their origins
through such practices as pocket-swapping. Various practices such as
transfer pricing, in which a component firm is overcharged for services or
goods purchased by another firm in the group, facilitate tax evasion by
representing taxable income as expenditures. Private firms in one's group
are also convenient for holding real estate or other assets purchased by a
public firm in the group. Similarly, a public firm can procure certain restricted commodities, such as construction materials, for private units in
the group. This diversification also gives entrepreneurs greater freedom of
action in responding to sudden policy changes. For example, when I first
began fieldwork in summer 1988, policies were vigorously promoting
private business. In the excitement of the propaganda buildup to the new
policy, even cooperative operators were enthusiastic about being seen as
private. Some that I met that summer told me that their firms were really
private because they had provided their own start-up capital. In the fall, an
economic rectification campaign was launched that targeted deviant commercial practices, and optimism about private business evaporated. When
I subsequently met these operators, they insisted that their firms were
really public because they were legally owned by public units. In other
words, the operators played off different criteria to represent the status of
their firms as private or public, depending on which was more advantageous in a given policy climate.

The second evolutionary trend is the adaptation of strategies to new
opportunities created by policy changes. This can be seen in the response
to a new state policy, the 1994 Company Law (Gongsi fa), which established a legal framework for the corporatization of state enterprises. Ownership was vested in corporations defined as "legal individuals" (*faren*),
while their operators were the "legal individual's representative" (*faren
daibiao*). In these new corporations I heard of practices reminiscent of my
earlier observations, except that the scale was far greater. Many corporations were vehicles for diverting public property from state enterprises
through the practices I had observed earlier, giving rise to the state's
identification of yet another economic crime—pilfering (*toudao*).[21]

Corporatization in the 1990s appears to be proceeding along the two
routes apparent in the 1980s. Strategies from below have occurred when
the wealthiest cooperative companies take advantage of the law to corpo-
ratize. This course is illustrated by the career of an entrepreneur who was
an unemployed youth when he first began business in 1980 with a small
sundries stall. By ingratiating himself with officials of the Self-Employed

Laborers' Association, he became one of the first entrepreneurs in Xiamen authorized to run a cooperative, and by the mid 1980s he was running one of the wealthiest nonstate firms in Xiamen. In 1994, his company was reputedly the first private company to make a public stock offering under the Company Law, raising Y25 million, and it now deals mostly in real estate and public works projects all over China.

Strategies from above involve high-ranking officials who resign their posts to establish private firms and then use their *guanxi* to establish partnerships (*hezi*) with public units. For example, a high-ranking officer in the People's Liberation Army resigned in 1993 when he heard from an acquaintance that a coal mine in Shanxi Province was seeking cash to upgrade its equipment. He obtained a Y6 million bank loan by tapping personal ties with former comrades-in-arms who had returned to their native villages, where, as former soldiers, they occupied leading positions in village and township governments: they let him use land under their jurisdictions as collateral for the loan. He thereupon founded a private company and entered into a public-private partnership with the state mining enterprise to export coal; receipts totaled Y400 million in 1994. In 1995, the partnership became a corporation, and many assets were intentionally undervalued and then transferred to the new corporation.

It is striking how the various entrepreneurial strategies adopted in the nonstate economy of the late 1980s mostly by smaller local firms are moving up the state hierarchy to encompass larger state-sector enterprises and higher-level officials at the city and provincial levels in the 1990s. Rather than heralding a further step toward greater clarification of legal rights to property, it seems, corporatization has stimulated the spread of network strategies to higher levels of the state structure.[22]

In sum, the various strategies and their evolution show how property rights are produced, not by any single institution, but by entrepreneurial strategies that integrate various elements in their institutional environment into courses of action. These mixes include factors as varied as state policies, local government administration, entrepreneurs' social statuses, and popular ethics and norms. They are productive because they enhance entrepreneurs' expectations in interactions with others, stimulating economic activity that would otherwise be unlikely to occur.

Efficiency Considerations

Are the strategies I have described a stimulant or an obstacle to the emerging market economy? Do they create commercial dynamism or suboptimal outcomes? Answers to these questions are critical in evaluating the economic performance of networks in China's emerging market economy. My claim is that the strategies are efficient because they stimulate commercial activity that would otherwise not occur. This contrasts sharply with the market transition account, which views the networks as inefficient because the performance of firms is less than would be the case if legal rights to property were more completely observed.[23] In this section I shall seek to show that the answer to these questions largely reflects the definition of efficiency held by the analyst, and that the market transition definition, implicitly or otherwise, overlooks institutional sources of dynamism in networks.

The different definitions of efficiency just noted accord with Harold Demsetz's distinction between comparative efficiency and so-called nirvana efficiency.[24] In nirvana efficiency, existing economic activity is gauged as a deviation from an ideal typical market of completely enforced legal property rights with zero transaction costs. This definition is implicit in the market transition perspective, and by its standards existing situations are always inefficient. This is doubtless useful for making policy suggestions to improve on existing conditions, but it does not really explain how China's market economy is able to flourish in the context of such suboptimal arrangements.

Comparative efficiency, the definition that informs this chapter, refers to making choices among realistically possible alternatives. It reveals the utility of different arrangements, suggesting why one becomes the basis of strategies and organization and others not.

THE EFFICIENCY OF NETWORK STRATEGIES IN LEASED FIRMS

With respect to the practices of leased firms, the nirvana and comparative efficiency definitions generate very different conclusions about the efficiency of networks. As already noted, collective trading firms are leased to private individuals through an auction that allocates firms (or rather their legal income and user rights) among a pool of bidders. There are basically two possible auction arrangements. An open auction is characterized by competitive, sealed bids, and the lease is awarded to the highest bidder based on price alone. A rigged auction is one in which the lessee is secretly determined by the public authority and allocation proceeds through favoritism. What appears to have mostly occurred in my sample of 23 leased firms is leasing through rigged auctions. Eighteen of their operators were their former public managers, while the other five were former officials or their offspring from the parent public units. Several operators told me that they had been told the amounts of the other sealed bids ahead of time, ensuring that their bid would be the highest.

The two definitions of efficiency shed very different light on the consequences of rigged auctions for efficiency. By the logic of nirvana efficiency, rigging auctions hinders the performance of leased firms in several ways. First, it prevents more potentially talented operators from assuming control of firms.[25] Second, operators who receive control of firms through favoritism lack sufficient incentives to develop them, inasmuch as they do not bear full business risks. Taken together, these factors constitute a drag on the firms' profit potential and reduce rates of reinvestment. Also by the nirvana logic, rigged auctions are inequitable, inasmuch as they favor those with political power.

Examining the motives and perceptions held by the actors in the leasing process suggests that a rigged auction is more efficient and equitable than an open auction in certain key respects. First, while leasing often prevents operators with higher levels of human capital such as education from assuming the helm, in an emerging market economy, where information channels for supply and demand are few, the social capital of operators from the pre-market-reform era is at least as important. This can be seen in the case of the aforementioned lumber trading firm. When the original manager, the senior cadre in his late fifties, was replaced by a younger manager in his thirties, the firm's fortunes plummeted. Although the younger manager had a college degree in enterprise management, he lacked personal ties such as those the senior cadre had forged during his long career. The senior cadre had worked his way up from a lumberyard worker to a leading position in the western Fujian Forestry Bureau. He knew public lumber mill supervisors throughout Fujian and had ties to the bureau's provincial and national levels. The younger manager had never worked in a lumberyard and lacked comparable ties. Not surprisingly, he was unable to get lumber for sale. Given the restricted nature of this commodity, trading in it was branded as profiteering, and so it could only be procured through personal ties. As the firm's fortunes plummeted, the bureau beseeched the senior cadre to return. The value of his social capital is evident in the favorable leasing contract he then negotiated.

Personal ties also stimulate firms' performance. Turning unprofitable firms into profitable ones, which is the goal of leasing, is facilitated by favorable administrative decisions, which are more likely to be forthcoming in personal ties between firm operators and parent public unit officials. These ties reduce uncertainties stemming from the ambiguous character of the decisions. For example, several informants told me that in the leasing policy's early stage, the Xiamen city government decreed that a firm's existing public employees should be kept on after the firm was leased. While this stipulation was intended to protect the employees' livelihood, it worked at cross-purposes with the goal of enhancing the firms' performance. As mentioned above, many of the firms were originally set up as May 7 firms to provide jobs for the parent public units' redundant and problem workers and their unemployed offspring. Such employees were in general not suited to doing the harder work demanded by the operators once the firm was leased out. Lessees who were known to parent unit officials worked with them to get around the stipulation. For example, many public units transferred the employees back to the parent unit just before the auction.

Personal ties also enhance flows of capital to the leased firm, stimulating its performance. As can be seen in the above example of the lumber firm, goods for sale were only forthcoming in the context of personal ties. Access to bank loans is another important consideration. Legally, a lessee is a private person and should apply for a bank loan as such, in which case it is difficult to get one because of discrimination against private borrowers. However, if the lessee is known to parent unit officials, they will guarantee the loan or even let the lessee take out a loan in the name of the parent public unit. In short, rigged auctions ensure that the firm is allocated to an operator with the personal ties that can overcome many of the institutional difficulties of the emerging market economy.

While nirvana logic would see a rigged auction as inequitable because it entails the use of office for private gain, the leasing of firms in rigged auctions arguably creates more public benefits than would occur in open auction.[26] The lessee selected by rigged auction has close personal ties to the parent public unit, which can stimulate the transfer of firm profits to the public unit. For example, operators make side payments above the low lease value, held down to reduce the tax bill, to the parent unit. While some of this money undoubtedly goes into the pockets of parent unit officials as personal income, some also enters the unit's extra-budgetary funds, which can be used to provide such public benefits as higher salaries, holiday bonuses (*guojie fei*), and new housing. For example, the senior ex-cadre operating the lumber trading company has contributed to the pension fund of the forestry bureau and underwritten the cost of a research institute to find new uses for lumber by-products, several of which led to new commercial ventures by the bureau, which employed its personnel. Presumably these income flows from the leased firm back to the public unit would be reduced if the operator had no personal ties with the parent unit.

The preceding discussion has highlighted aspects of efficiency, as well as equity, that reflect realistically possible decisions. In an environment that differs significantly from the ideal typical market, rigged auctions stimulate performance and profit sharing in a leased firm that would not occur in their absence. Rather than hindering the emergence of a more complete market economy, they stimulate the emergence of a market economy by helping to institute new kinds of commercial calculations in the evolution away from a centrally planned economy.

ENFORCEMENT IN NETWORKS

The viewpoint of nirvana efficiency maintains that networks lack effective enforcement mechanisms relative to legal property rights.[27] With legal property rights, enforcement is externalized in the court system, whereas networks increase transaction costs, since entrepreneurs must bear more of the costs in terms of payoffs and much time spent in face-to-face interaction. Certainly, in a theoretical sense, a recourse to law and the court system is less costly. But in an environment where courts are considered corrupt and the self-serving enforcement of laws by local state agents is pervasive, networks that emphasize particularistic identities and personal obligations might actually be considered more effective. Therefore it is necessary to examine what kinds of enforcement possibilities can proceed in networks. In first- and second-party enforcement, the personal ethics and social norms of face-to-face interaction play a large role, while third-party enforcement also invokes the institutions of community and the state.

First-party enforcement consists of sanctions imposed by a person on him- or herself in dealings with others. These sanctions stem from the personal honor system of "upright conduct" (*zuoren*). It is frequently heard in the business world that "one must understand how to conduct oneself in society" (*yao dongde zenme zuoren chu shi*). For example, in discussing the issue of bureaucratic corruption, one entrepreneur said, "Some businesspeople blame all their problems on bureaucratic corruption. But this is wrong. It is not a question of whether officials are honest or dishonest. . . . If you know how to conduct [*zuoren*] yourself, you can work things out." In first-party enforcement, the effective sanctions are ethical imperatives. One imperative is propriety (*li*). This stresses the observation of the rituals and etiquette that conform to the relative statuses in social interaction. A closely related imperative is reciprocity (*bao*), which emphasizes the need to repay a gift or favor. Adherence to these ethics, which are diffused among the population, as well as canonized in the Confucian classics, is inculcated by prior socialization.[28] Sanctioning is through the feelings of shame produced by nonobservation. Such feelings of shame are indicated by the popular idiom of "loss of face" (*diu lian*). Thus, the aforementioned operator of the lumber firm might have been generous in his contributions to his former public unit partly because of the memories of the kindness and warm feelings shown to him by his former colleagues.

Second-party enforcement involves an understanding between two persons. Failure by either to uphold his or her end of the understanding can lead to sanctions by the aggrieved party. Enforcement is expressed in the idiom of *guanxi*. It consists of manipulating the ethics described above to create feelings of obligation in others, inducing them to provide support toward achieving self-interested goals. Sanctioning occurs in the dyadic interaction. One sanction is when the offended individual also stops honoring his or her end of the contract and withdraws support. In high-affect relationships, the sanction is to diminish emotional closeness. In more instrumental money connections, the sanction is reducing or halting material rewards. A second sanction, closely linked to the first, is reduced support in future interactions. Such processes may also help explain why the operator of the lumber firm was generous to his former public unit: perhaps its officials manipulated their ties with him to increase the payments.

There are several processes of third-party enforcement in networks. One is rooted in the community that surrounds dyads. A community in this definition consists of persons who know others by reputation (*mingyu*) and have the possibility of face-to-face encounters. Sanctioning is more diffuse but highly effective. One sanction is that malfeasance in a dyad will become known to the wider community, negatively affecting the reputation of the malefactor. This reduces the likelihood of future cooperation, not only in the dyad, but also for potential future interactions in the community. This is reflected in a young tax official's explanation to me of his willingness to give special attention (*teshu youdai*) to businesspeople introduced by mutual friends. "Xiamen is a small place and everybody knows one another," he said. "You must realize that you will live here for your entire life. You must pay attention to your reputation. If you do not show sufficient spirit of helping others then you will find it difficult to live here. No one will support you when you need it." In extreme cases, sanctioning can be through social ostracism.

Another process of third-party enforcement is linked to state agencies. Some are appendages of the Communist Party's United Front Bureau, representing such societal and occupational groups as the Xiamen Chamber of Commerce (Xiamenshi shanghui) and the Young Factory Director and Manager Association (Qingnian changzhang jingli xiehui). Some private and cooperative firm operators have pushed the chamber to lobby on their behalf in conflicts with administrative bureaus, and others use it to enforce contracts. For example, several firm operators had experienced disputes over ownership rights and responsibilities in business partnerships with public units and sought the intervention of the chamber on their behalf.[29] Other organs are the various distributive, manufacturing, and administrative units in the government that are the business partners or direct sponsors of nonstate firms. Operators prevail on these units to intercede on their behalf in disputes and when harassed by other agencies. For example, after two different departments of the Tax Bureau separately tried to tax a leased firm, one treating it as a collective firm and one as a private firm, the operator asked his sponsoring unit to negotiate with the Tax Bureau on his firm's behalf.

Another type of third-party enforcement proceeds with reference to the state's legal and regulatory apparatus. However, the sanctioning mechanism is not formal recourse to the apparatus but rather fear that it might be invoked. It proceeds by the entrepreneur giving gifts and favors to an official so that he or she will actively intervene to prevent investigation of the firm's activities. The sanctioning mechanism here is not simply the dynamics of *guanxi* but also the official's fear that investigation of the firm could implicate (*lianlei*) him or her in its dubious activities. An illustrative example is the aforementioned branch firm operator, who bought four luxury condominiums, which he registered as the legal property of family members. Whenever officials from his sponsoring township government visit Xiamen, the entrepreneur lavishly entertains them. This increases the likelihood that the officials will shield the firm from investigation during regulatory campaigns. Officials are motivated to do so not only by norms of reciprocity but also from fear that, as recipients of the operator's largesse, they might be seen as condoning any wrongdoing that is uncovered, and punished accordingly.

In yet another manifestation of third-party enforcement, the popular categories of insider and outsider inform perceptions of the utility of the state's legal apparatus for enforcement. As already mentioned, the court system is perceived as corrupt, with decisions going to those best able to influence the judges. Also, going to court exposes one's affairs to scrutiny by government agencies, which is risky given the ambiguity of many commercial practices. Hardly any entrepreneurs in Xiamen had ever used the court system to enforce contracts, and several told me that they would consider doing so only if the person involved were an outsider and the court were geographically distant from Xiamen. Outsider status is important because, with minimal expectations of future cooperation, there is no potential sacrifice of it in taking the party to court. Geographic distance is also important. Taking a party to court is a sign that interpersonal relations have failed, and so an entrepreneur who initiates court proceedings is revealing his or her failure to solve the problem through personal ties. Such a person is likely to be tagged as someone who cannot conduct themselves properly in society (*budongde zenme zuoren chushi*) because they do not understand the dynamics of personal relations, a damning reputation when so much business is conducted through just such ties. Recourse to a geographically distant court will thus better preserve an entrepreneur's reputation (*mingyu*) in his or her home base, inasmuch as news of the legal action is less likely to reach Xiamen.[30]

PATTERNS OF REINVESTMENT

Finally, let me consider the issue of reinvestment. The nirvana efficiency concept views the lack of clear legal enforcement as weakening property rights and increasing transaction costs. One result is the drain of business capital through unproductive payoffs to officials, reducing reinvestment in firms. Also, entrepreneurs are said to respond to official predation by using profits for personal consumption. The evidence for such suboptimal investment is said to be the small size of firms, which is assumed to indicate undercapitalization.[31]

My findings from Xiamen, dovetailing with research on Chinese enterprises in Taiwan and overseas, shows how reinvestment does not proceed in unitary corporate strategies but rather through interfirm networks.[32] In other words, profits are not reinvested with an eye to developing a single bounded firm into a multilayered, hierarchical corporation but rather to promote a more organizationally diffuse enterprise group of small firms connected by particularistic ties of kinship. The advantages of such network strategies in the context of China's emerging market economy have already been discussed. The point I would like to make is that the notion of nirvana efficiency rests on such concepts as "too small," "undercapitalized," and "suboptimal reinvestment," which are ambiguous, because it is not clear what the alternatives are. The strategy of enterprise groups suggests that much more reinvestment probably occurs than is recognized by the concept of nirvana efficiency. While any particular unit in a network may seem small, this is often part of the entrepreneurial strategy of "wearing a small hat" (*dai xiao maozi*): this minimizes the profile of each component of the group, masking the much larger wealth accumulation contained in the network. This strategy further enhances the entrepreneur's sense of security and willingness to reinvest.

A more relevant indicator of efficiency, in my view, is patterns of reinvestment. In the context of uncertain legal property rights, speculative forms of trade might be preferable to manufacturing or service ventures because the turnover is quicker and wealth more readily concealed, making the firm less subject to predation by officials. Therefore, if entrepreneurs perceive great uncertainties and high transaction costs, they are unlikely to diversify out of speculative trade. However, there is much diversification in the firms in my sample. For example, of 100 private and cooperative firms, 46 have diversified out of commerce, 20 into manufacturing, 19 into services, and 7 into both. Many initially accumulated capital in speculative activities and then shifted to manufacturing and service ventures. This suggests that stable expectations, arising from the previously described enforcement processes, do exist in the emerging market economy despite the lack of clearly defined legal rights to property.

Transnational capital flows are an even more relevant indicator. When uncertain property rights create high transaction costs, one might expect an increase of capital flight and the stagnation of the domestic economy. This does not appear to be the case in Xiamen. A number of entrepreneurs I met no longer thought of emigrating, because business opportunities in China seem better than elsewhere. While many held foreign passports, this was as a means of escape should the authorities investigate their businesses, rather than a vote of no confidence in the domestic economy. To the extent that entrepreneurs emigrate, they stay abroad long enough to establish foreign residence or nationality and then return, bringing their financial capital with them. Their new legal statuses as foreign nationals or overseas Chinese (*huaqiao*) or Macao and Taiwan compatriots (*tongbao*) lets them establish enterprises that fall under policies that are in some respects more favorable than those for domestic enterprises in regard to taxes and access to state bank loans. The process of funneling money out of the country and then back in again under these advantageous statuses, called "round tripping," accounts for some of the huge amount of foreign investment flowing into China.[33] In short, capital flight, which is usually seen as indicating uncertainty, reappears as foreign investment. This is simply part of a broader process of creating confidence and stable expectations. It is part of a strategy of shifting among legal property rights and policies to find the legal status that provides the best returns and most stable expectations.

In sum, definitions of efficiency that ignore the context in which means and ends are devised shed less light on how existing arrangements promote economic activity than the alternative concept of comparative efficiency. The latter emphasizes the utility of strategies that, while far from theoretically optimal arrangements, are nevertheless the best possible arrangement for meeting the practical opportunities and challenges of the emerging market economy.

Conclusions: China and Eastern Europe Compared

By way of conclusion, let me address a question raised by the analysis I have presented here: Why do clientelist networks appear conducive to a vibrant commercial economy in the Chinese context but much less so in postcommunist economies in Eastern Europe? The networks that I have described are similar to what analysts of Eastern Europe's market transitions variously refer to by such names as *nomenklatura* privatization, hidden privatization, and political capitalism.[34] In Eastern European market economies, Kazimierz Z. Poznanski observes,

> control over capital is put in private hands, with the majority of assets made available to the Communist authorities, the party, and/or state. In the transfer, private owners are forced into a patron-client relationship with the political leadership. As a consequence, both access to and exit from production are made conditional on loyalty to the political establishment. At the same time, this support for the "super-structure" becomes essential to private owners for securing access to capital means.[35]

These ties are widely seen as a cause for the relatively poor performance of Eastern European economies.

The key issue is why network strategies appear to stimulate commercial dynamism in one situation (China) but not in another (Eastern Europe). One possible reason for the difference lies in the different state-society contexts in which networks function, a difference attributable to different state policies of reform.[36] This context is more conducive in China to connecting government officials and entrepreneurs at the local level, enhancing communication and negotiation and thereby stabilizing expectations.

A number of scholars have commented on China's more gradual reform process.[37] Whereas the Russian and other Eastern European programs conceived of reform as the dismantling of communist-era bureaucratic controls on the economy in order to release market forces, the Chinese project sought to decentralize control rather than dismantle it per se. Therefore the Chinese bureaucracy maintains a high degree of institutional continuity and structural integrity. Increased decentralization notwithstanding, Wei Li observes, "the Chinese system is not realistically in imminent danger of the disintegration that has befallen the Communist countries in Eastern Europe and the Soviet Union."[38] When looking at the more local levels of the national bureaucracy, the degree of cohesion is even more remarkable: as Andrew Walder puts it, "what strikes the researcher is not its fragmentation but its degree of integration."[39] Of particular relevance to my argument is Susan Shirk's insight that the relatively greater hierarchical integrity of the Chinese state has kept patron-client ties intact, facilitating communication, negotiation, and loyalty. The key point is that the particularistic process of Chinese policy implementation gives lower-level officials modest amounts of power, which they can then dole out to their supporters, creating lower-level support for central policies. In other words, patron-client ties have advanced rather than obstructed the market reform process and development of a commercial economy. Extending this insight to clientelist networks in the nonstate economy suggests an explanation for China's superior economic performance.

Variations in bureaucratic integrity could have several consequences for comparative efficiency. In regard to allocation, there might be several consequences. First, the Chinese reform process has to a greater extent left intact the prior social networks linking officials and citizens. Thus, while all postcommunist economies have a relative lack of effective legal instruments, in China's market economy, popular instruments are better able to compensate in creating stable expectations. Patron-client ties remain relatively intact, heightening the function of social networks as sanctioning mechanisms in exchanges. Thus, relative to Eastern European economies, clientelist networks are better able to reduce transaction costs. The evidence from Xiamen suggests that significant rates of reinvestment are occurring along the networks linking firm operators with state agents and others in the social environment.

More specifically, variations in states' bureaucratic integrity could also produce differences in the efficiency of enforcement via third-party sanctioning. In Eastern Europe, the dismantling of state control structures has led to the rise of mafia-style criminal gangs, which flourish where central states are weak, selling protection to businesspeople.[40] Reportedly, even small retail stores post guards with automatic weapons to prevent extortion by criminals.[41] Gangs have reemerged in China too, but they seem to operate more within limits defined by local governments and do not approach the scale of gangs in Eastern Europe. For example, Ole Bruun notes the rise of secret societies and criminal gangs in Chengdu City that seek to extort protection money from private shopkeepers. But many proprietors refuse to pay. Also, these criminal elements appear to operate at the sufferance of local authorities.[42] Thus, the Chinese bureaucracy plays a relatively larger role in enforcement of property rights via the third-party enforcement described in the preceding section.

Although both Eastern European gangs and the local Chinese bureaucracy enforce property rights in ways that deviate from a standard legal system, there are important differences between the enforcement possibilities they offer. First, mafias are criminal gangs, usually operating with less legitimacy than government. Consequently, they have shorter time horizons and demand larger sums from firms with little concern for their ongoing viability.[43] By contrast, local governments have a long-term interest in promoting private business in their jurisdictions as ongoing revenue sources. Thus, in China, third-party enforcement is enacted by an organization with a longer time horizon, reducing transaction costs. This difference is also suggested by the comments of other observers. The economist Anders Aslund writes that the Russian mafia "behave like robbers . . . [without] an interest in the survival of local enterprises. As a result, Russian entrepreneurs often find it impossible to collaborate with gangster syndicates."[44] In regard to China, Susan Young avers that ad hoc levies by local governments, while burdensome, have "probably been a major factor in the growth of private business. They certainly have not been so heavy as to prevent it, and they have given local officials a direct incentive to support it."[45]

Second, there might be variations in the capacity of firm operators to obtain enforcement. As illegitimate organizations, criminal gangs function in secrecy, and membership is often opaque to the local communities they operate in. In Russia and Eastern Europe, opaqueness is further enhanced by the ethnic character of gangs, such as the Chechen gangs that sell protection in urban marketplaces for agricultural produce. Ethnicity creates solidarity within the group by organizational closure to the outside. In contrast, government agents in China often reside in the communities they administer, while street-level officials in southern Fujian are often native, a reflection of the need for local dialect speakers to interact with citizens in fulfilling administrative tasks. Their social networks in the community overlap with those of the businesspeople over whom they wield authority. Therefore, Chinese entrepreneurs have lower costs in getting effective third-party sanctions to protect property rights, such as disciplining officials who transgress community-based perceptions of the amount of legitimate payoffs.

Thirdly, the greater bureaucratic integrity of the Chinese state also means that local officials are more likely to be disciplined from above by their superiors when they exceed accepted payoff levels. Such attempts can be seen in the ongoing anti-corruption drives launched by the state, which have disciplined increasingly higher levels of officials during the course of the past two decades. These campaigns have sought to define illegitimate behavior for officials and identify and punish transgressors. Presumably such disciplining would be less likely to occur in the Eastern European state structures, which have seen greater shifts in personnel, and where presumably lines of communication between locales and the center have been disrupted, with Russia again being an extreme example of this.

In sum, a process of transformation in which political reform proceeded more slowly than market reform gave Chinese entrepreneurs advantages in forging networks across local state-society borders to enhance business and stimulate the economy. Chinese entrepreneurs often faced local agents they knew, and in some cases had known for decades, whereas their Eastern European counterparts were less likely to have such an advantage. Chinese entrepreneurs were also presumably more able than their Eastern European counterparts to hold on to stable expectations in the institutional jumble of the postcommunist economy, because, given the greater integrity of the state structure, popular norms and hierarchical authority were better able to operate as enforcement mechanisms in interactions between state agents and commercial operators. The juxtaposition of the Chinese and Eastern European reform experiences also underscores the crucial point that strategies that produce property rights are highly constrained by the institutional context. Entrepreneurs do not choose as they please but rather are limited by factors beyond their control, such as the structural integrity of the state, the content of state policies, and the available local enforcement agencies.

Reference Matter

Notes

CHAPTER 1   *Walder and Oi, Property Rights in the Chinese Economy*

1. See, e.g., Maxim Boycko, Andrei Shleifer, and Robert Vishny, *Privatizing Russia* (Cambridge, Mass.: MIT Press, 1995).

2. See Jeffrey D. Sachs, *Poland's Jump to the Market Economy* (Cambridge, Mass.: MIT Press, 1993); Olivier Blanchard, Rudiger Dornbusch, Paul Krugman, Richard Layard, and Lawrence Summers, *Reform in Eastern Europe* (Cambridge, Mass.: MIT Press, 1991); and Merton J. Peck and Thomas J. Richardson, *What Is to Be Done? Proposals for the Soviet Transition to the Market* (New Haven, Conn.: Yale University Press, 1991).

3. See Peter Murrell, "Evolutionary and Radical Approaches to Economic Reform," *Economics of Planning* 25, 1 (1992): 79–95; and David Stark, "Path Dependence and Privatization Strategies in Eastern Europe," *East European Politics and Societies* 6, 1 (Winter 1992): 17–54.

4. Such critics might also have pointed out that very different institutions have evolved in the rapidly growing economies of East Asia. See, e.g., Chalmers Johnson, *MITI and the Japanese Miracle: The Growth of Industrial Policy, 1925–1975* (Stanford, Calif.: Stanford University Press, 1982); Alice Amsdem, "A Theory of Government Intervention in Late Industrialization," in Louis Putterman and Dietrich Rueschemeyer, eds., *State and Market in Development: Synergy or Rivalry?* (Boulder, Colo.: Westview Press, 1992), pp. 53–84; Robert Wade, *Governing the Market: Economic Theory and the Role of Government in East Asian Industrialization* (Princeton, N.J.: Princeton University Press, 1990); Kiren Aziz Chaudhry, "The Myth of the Market and the Common History of Late Development," *Politics and Society* 21, 3 (Sept. 1993): 245–74; Paul Streeten, "Markets and States: Against Minimalism," *World Development* 21, 8 (Aug. 1993): 1281–98; and Peter Evans, *Embedded Autonomy: States and Industrial Transformation* (Princeton, N.J.: Princeton University Press, 1995). But see also Gernot Grabher and David Stark, "Organizing Diversity: Evolutionary Theory, Network Analysis, and Post-Socialism," in David Stark and Gernot Grabher, eds., *Restructuring Networks in Post-Socialism* (Oxford: Oxford University Press, 1997), pp. 1–32.

5. See Peter Murrell, "Can Neoclassical Economics Underpin the Reform of

Centrally Planned Economies?" *Journal of Economic Perspectives* 5, 4 (Fall 1991): 59–76.

6. See David Stark, "Recombinant Property in East European Capitalism," *American Journal of Sociology* 101 (Jan. 1996): 993–1027; and David Stark and László Bruszt, *Postsocialist Pathways: Transforming Politics and Property in East Central Europe* (Cambridge: Cambridge University Press, 1998).

7. See esp. János Kornai, "The Affinity Between Ownership Forms and Coordination Mechanisms: The Common Experience of Reform in Socialist Countries," *Journal of Economic Perspectives* 4, 3 (Summer 1990), pp. 131–47; id., *The Road to a Free Economy: Shifting from a Socialist System: The Example of Hungary* (New York: Norton, 1990); and id., *The Socialist System: The Political Economy of Communism* (Princeton, N.J.: Princeton University Press, 1992).

8. Many economists' reasoning was based, not on a dynamic theory of moves from one kind of system to another, but on a comparison of two static theoretical equilibria, a contrast between the observable flaws of command economies with an equilibrium model of a market economy. See the discussion by Thomas G. Rawski, "Implications of China's Reform Experience," *China Quarterly*, no. 144 (Dec. 1995): 1150–73, at 1157–59, reprinted in Andrew G. Walder, ed., *China's Transitional Economy* (Oxford: Oxford University Press, 1996), pp. 188–211. Institutionalists from whatever discipline have produced appealing general statements, usually illustrated with factual examples of path dependence and the importance of social networks, but have yet to articulate clear theories about paths of change, the network properties of economies, or the conditions under which a given path of change will lead to rapid economic growth.

9. See William A. Byrd and Qingsong Lin, "Why Industrialize? The Incentives for Rural Community Governments," in William A. Byrd and Qingsong Lin, eds., *China's Rural Industry: Structure, Development, and Reform* (New York: Oxford University Press, 1990), pp. 358–87; Jean C. Oi, "Fiscal Reform and the Economic Foundations of Local State Corporatism in China," *World Politics* 45 (Oct. 1992): 99–126; Christine Wong, "Interpreting Rural Growth in the Post-Mao Period," *Modern China* 14 (1988): 3–30; and Christine Wong, "Fiscal Reform and Local Industrialization: The Problematic Sequencing of Reform in Post-Mao China," *Modern China* 18 (1992): 197–227.

10. See Victor Nee, "Peasant Entrepreneurship and the Politics of Regulation in China," in Victor Nee and David Stark, eds., *Remaking the Economic Institutions of Socialism: China and Eastern Europe* (Stanford, Calif.: Stanford University Press, 1989); id., "Organizational Dynamics of Market Transition: Hybrid Forms, Property Rights, and Mixed Economy in China," *Administrative Science Quarterly* 37 (Mar. 1992): 1–27; and id. and Sijin Su, "Institutions, Social Ties, and Commitment in China's Corporatist Transformation," in John McMillan and Barry Naughton, eds., *Reforming Asian Socialism: The Growth of Market Institutions* (Ann Arbor: University of Michigan Press, 1996), pp. 111–34.

11. Some see the associated property rights as vaguely defined: e.g., Martin Weitzman and Chenggang Xu, "Chinese Township–Village Enterprises and Vaguely Defined Cooperatives," *Journal of Comparative Economics* 18, 2 (Apr. 1994): 121–45.

12. See Nan Lin, "Local Market Socialism: Local Corporatism in Action in Rural China," *Theory and Society* 24, 3 (June 1995): 301–54.

13. For the first view, see Thomas G. Rawski, "Progress Without Privatization: The Reform of China's State Industries," in Vedat Milor, ed., *Changing Political Economies: Privatization in Post-Communist and Reforming Communist States* (Boulder, Colo.: Lynne Rienner, 1994), pp. 27–52, and for the second, see Jeffrey D. Sachs and Wing Thye Woo, "Structural Factors in the Economic Reforms of China, Eastern Europe, and the Former Soviet Union," *Economic Policy* 18 (1994): 102–45. Louis Putterman provides a clear and thoughtful review of these disagreements in "The Role of Ownership and Property Rights in China's Economic Transition," *China Quarterly*, no. 144 (Dec. 1995): 1047–64, reprinted in Andrew G. Walder, ed., *China's Transitional Economy* (Oxford: Oxford University Press, 1996), pp. 85–102.

14. A notable exception is Jiahua Che and Yingyi Qian, "Insecure Property Rights and Government Ownership of Firms," *Quarterly Journal of Economics* 113, 2 (May 1998): 467–96.

15. See David Stark, "Privatization in Hungary: From Plan to Market or from Plan to Clan?" *East European Politics and Societies* 4, 3 (Fall 1990): 351–92; and Nee, "Organizational Dynamics of Market Transition."

16. See Harold Demsetz, "Toward a Theory of Property Rights," in id., *Ownership, Control, and the Firm: The Organization of Economic Activity* (Oxford: Blackwell, 1967), 1: 104–16.

17. See, e.g., Armen Alchian and Harold Demsetz, "Production, Information Costs, and Economic Organization," *American Economic Review* 62, 5 (Dec. 1972): 777–95. Xiao Geng, a student of Demsetz's, has pursued this agenda in his research on the Chinese economy. See Xiao Geng, *Chanquan yu Zhongguo de jingji gaige* [Property rights and China's economic reforms] (Beijing: Zhongguo shehui kexue chubanshe, 1997).

18. See Louis Putterman, "Ownership and the Nature of the Firm," *Journal of Comparative Economics* 17, 2 (June 1993): 243–63, and the representative collection of articles reprinted in Louis Putterman and Randall Kroszner, eds., *The Economic Nature of the Firm: A Reader*, 2d ed. (New York: Cambridge University Press, 1996).

19. This point is elaborated in Jean C. Oi, *Rural China Takes Off: Institutional Foundations of Economic Reform* (Berkeley and Los Angeles: University of California Press, 1999).

20. See Christine P. W. Wong, "Ownership and Control in Chinese Industry: The Maoist Legacy and Prospects for the 1980s," in U.S. Congress, Joint Economic Committee, *China's Economy Looks Toward the Year 29* (Washington, D.C.: GPO, 1986), pp. 571–603.

21. See Kornai, *Socialist System*, pp. 62–227.

22. See ibid., pp. 474–564.

23. The more accessible statements of the different positions are to be found in Gary Jefferson and Thomas G. Rawski, "Enterprise Reform in Chinese Industry," *Journal of Economic Perspectives* 8, 2 (Spring 1994): 47–70; Wing Thye Woo, Wen Hai, Yibiao Jin, and Gang Fan, "How Successful Has Chinese Enterprise

Reform Been? Pitfalls in Opposite Biases and Focus," *Journal of Comparative Economics* 18, 3 (June 1994): 410–37; and the summary of the debate in Andrew G. Walder, "China's Transitional Economy: Interpreting Its Significance," in id., ed., *China's Transitional Economy*, pp. 7–8.

24. There is, of course, considerable variation in practice. Almost all rural industrial enterprises operate under some kind of arrangement referred to as contracting, but one would have to examine the terms of these contracts closely to discover whether they are, in fact, incentive schemes for hired managers, similar to arrangements in reformed public firms, or more akin to partnerships. Our definition of "contracting" here is more restrictive than that used colloquially in China. See Oi, *Rural China Takes Off*, ch. 2.

25. This definition sets aside the pervasive informal practices through which owners of private enterprises create alliances and partnerships with individual officials as part of an effort to reduce their risk and enhance their opportunities. See David L. Wank, *Commodifying Communism: Business, Trust, and Politics in a Chinese City* (Cambridge: Cambridge University Press, 1999).

26. When a state-sector firm establishes a joint venture with a foreign partner, or when it spins off new firms under its ownership, it moves assets into forms of ownership that resemble the contracted, leased, or even private forms. Parts of the old state sector therefore have adopted complex property forms. The "shareholding cooperatives" analyzed in three of the chapters in this volume also contain complex allocations of rights; Eduard Vermeer's Chapter 6 shows that there is such wide variation in such allocations across shareholding forms that they cannot easily be characterized along this continuum.

27. See Yuanzheng Cao, Yingyi Qian, and Barry Weingast, "From Federalism, Chinese Style, to Privatization, Chinese Style" (paper, Stanford University, Dec. 1997).

28. This same trend has been observed in Zouping County, Shandong, another area known for its corporatist practices in the 1980s. See Jean C. Oi, "The Evolution of Local State Corporatism," in Andrew G. Walder, ed., *Zouping in Transition: The Process of Reform in Rural North China* (Cambridge, Mass.: Harvard University Press, 1998), pp. 35–61. See also Oi, *Rural China Takes Off*.

29. See Yuan Jian, "Creating Property Under Market Socialism: Development of Private Industry in Rural China" (Ph.D. diss., Yale University, 1994).

30. Barry Naughton, *Growing Out of the Plan: Chinese Economic Reform, 1978–1993* (Cambridge: Cambridge University Press, 1995).

31. See Oi, "Fiscal Reform and the Economic Foundations of Local State Corporatism in China."

32. See also the studies of the southern Jiangsu region in Byrd and Lin, eds., *China's Rural Industry*; the study of a central Hebei county in Marc Blecher and Vivienne Shue, *Tethered Deer: Government and Economy in a Chinese County* (Stanford, Calif.: Stanford University Press, 1996); and the study of central Shandong in Walder, ed., *Zouping in Transition*.

33. See also the following studies of the littoral regions of Wenzhou and coastal Fujian: Yia-Ling Liu, "Reform from Below: The Private Economy and Local Politics in the Rural Industrialization of Wenzhou," *China Quarterly*, no.

130 (June 1992): 293–316; Kristen Parris, "Local Initiative and National Reform: The Wenzhou Model of Development," *China Quarterly*, no. 134 (June 1993): 242–63; and Nee, "Peasant Entrepreneurship and the Politics of Regulation."

34. Oi, *Rural China Takes Off*, examines sources of collective funding in chs. 3 and 4.

35. As the reforms progressed, it became financially feasible for increasing numbers of individuals to mount substantial investment efforts; this was not possible at the outset of the reforms more than a decade earlier. See Oi, *Rural China Takes Off*, ch. 3.

36. Barry Naughton, "Implications of the State Monopoly over Industry and Its Relaxation," *Modern China* 18 (Jan. 1992): 14–41; and id., "Chinese Institutional Innovation and Privatization from Below," *American Economic Review* 84 (May 1994): 266–70.

37. See also Naughton, *Growing Out of the Plan*, pp. 311–19.

38. See also Shu-min Huang and Stewart Odend'hal, "Fengjia: A Village in Transition," in Andrew G. Walder, ed., *Zouping in Transition: The Process of Reform in Rural North China* (Cambridge, Mass.: Harvard University Press, 1998), pp. 86–114.

39. See also David Wank, "Bureaucratic Patronage and Private Business: Changing Networks of Power in Urban China," in Andrew G. Walder, ed., *The Waning of the Communist State: Economic Origins of Political Decline in China and Hungary* (Berkeley and Los Angeles: University of California Press, 1995): 153–83.

40. See, e.g., Jan Winiecki, "Why Economic Reforms Fail in the Soviet System: A Property Rights-Based Approach," *Economic Inquiry* 28, 2 (Apr. 1990): 195–221; and see the longer discussion of this point of view in Andrew G. Walder, "The State as an Ensemble of Economic Actors: Some Inferences from China's Trajectory of Change," in Joan Nelson, Charles Tilly, and Lee Walker, eds., *Transforming Post-Communist Political Economies* (Washington, D.C.: National Academy Press, 1998): 432–52. This view of the inherent political limits of economic reform under single-party rule is lucidly explicated in Steven M. Goldstein, "China in Transition: The Political Foundations of Incremental Reform," *China Quarterly*, no. 144 (Dec. 1995): 1105–31; reprinted in Walder, ed., *China's Transitional Economy*, pp. 143–69.

41. See also Andrew G. Walder, "The Quiet Revolution from Within: Economic Reform as a Source of Political Decline," in id., *Waning of the Communist State*, pp. 1–24.

42. One such analysis of officials as economic actors is Yingyi Qian and Barry R. Weingast, "Federalism as a Commitment to Preserving Market Incentives," *Journal of Economic Perspectives* 11, 4 (Fall 1997): 83–92.

43. See William A. Byrd, *The Market Mechanism and Economic Reforms in China* (Armonk, N.Y.: M.E. Sharpe, 1991); Naughton, *Growing Out of the Plan*; and Rawski, "Implications of China's Reform Experience."

44. Developments in Zouping County, Shandong, parallel those in Wuxi; see Oi, "Evolution of Local State Corporatism," in Walder, ed., *Zouping in Transition*.

45. This does not imply that the property regimes alone are responsible for

growth; we simply point to the fact that rapidly growing regions vary in their property arrangements.

46. See Elemér Hankiss, *East European Alternatives* (New York: Oxford University Press, 1990); and Jadwiga Staniskis, " 'Political Capitalism' in Poland," *East European Politics and Societies* 5, 1 (Winter 1991): 127–41.

47. Susan Whiting's Chapter 8 in this book, and her own forthcoming book, are efforts in this direction.

48. See esp. Rawski's spirited arguments in his "Implications of China's Reform Experience."

49. See also Wank, *Commodifying Communism*, ch. 7.

CHAPTER 2   *Ruf, Collective Enterprise and Property Rights*

I thank Maris Gillette and Rubie Watson, not only for offering helpful comments on an earlier draft, but also for their support and encouragement.

1. The word "private" itself has a complex history in the English language. It may sometimes convey ambiguous meanings, which limits its analytical utility. For example, in the term "private enterprises" the distinction drawn is often from "state" rather than "public." See Raymond Williams, *Keywords: A Vocabulary of Culture and Society* (New York: Oxford University Press, 1983).

2. Harold Demsetz, "Toward a Theory of Property Rights," in Eirik Furubotn and Svetozar Pejovich, eds., *The Economics of Property Rights* (Cambridge, Mass.: Ballinger, 1974); János Kornai, *The Socialist System: The Political Economy of Communism* (Princeton, N.J.: Princeton University Press, 1992), pp. 63–83.

3. Christine Wong, "Fiscal Reform and Local Industrialization: The Problematic Sequencing of Reform in Post-Mao China," *Modern China* 18, 2 (Apr. 1992): 197–227; Jean Oi, "Fiscal Reform and the Economic Foundations of Local State Corporatism in China," *World Politics* 45, 1 (Oct. 1992): 99–126.

4. William Byrd and Lin Qingsong, eds., *China's Rural Industry: Structure, Development, and Reform* (Oxford: Oxford University Press, 1990); Andrew Walder, "Local Governments as Industrial Firms: An Organizational Analysis of China's Transitional Economy," *American Journal of Sociology* 101, 2 (Sept. 1995): 263–301.

5. See, e.g., Bronislaw Malinowski, *Coral Gardens and Their Magic* (London: Allen & Unwin, 1935); Max Gluckman, *The Judicial Process Among the Barotse of Northern Rhodesia* (Manchester: Manchester University Press, 1955); Edmund Leach, *Pul Eliya: A Village in Ceylon. A Study of Land Tenure and Kinship* (Cambridge: Cambridge University Press, 1961); David Nugent, "Property Relations, Production Relations, and Inequality: Anthropology, Political Economy, and the Blackfeet," *American Ethnologist* 20, 2 (1993): 336–62.

6. It would be unfair to characterize managerial corporatism in Qiaolou as simple nepotism. As I argue, not all kin of the Party secretary who governed the village enjoyed the same privileged economic benefits and political power, and those who did enjoy such privileges are not all his kin.

7. Martin Weitzman and Chenggang Xu, "Chinese Township-Village Enter-

prises as Vaguely Defined Cooperatives," *Journal of Comparative Economics* 18, 2 (Apr. 1994): 121–45.

8. Township and village enterprises in China have taken a wide variety of forms, including not only collective ownership and operation but also contract management and private proprietorship. The organization and management of Qiaolou, specifically, was in many respects similar to local-government-run business corporations described elsewhere in China. See Jean Oi, "The Role of the Local State in China's Transitional Economy," *China Quarterly*, no. 144 (Dec. 1995): 1132–49; Walder, "Local Governments as Industrial Firms."

9. Material for this study was collected during eight months of fieldwork in Qiaolou village during 1990–91. Additional observations were made during a return visit in the winter of 1994–95. The original research was supported by the Committee on Scholarly Communication with China, and the Wenner-Gren Foundation for Anthropological Research. That work was part of a larger collaborative research project directed by Myron Cohen, funded by the Luce Foundation and involving scholars from Columbia University and the Shanghai and Sichuan Academies of Social Sciences, the latter of which graciously sponsored my work in China.

10. There were, in addition, two brick factories and a distillery owned by the township government. Note that while none of Qiaolou's major enterprises had been leased out, the village committee had issued fixed fee contracts to individual families for operation of two electrically powered grain-processing machines owned by the village.

11. The conditions under which this research was conducted restricted my access to most written documentary sources, including village archives and enterprise accounts. Regrettably, I can offer no specific quantitative data on investments, output, costs, revenues, or other fiscal flows, all of which are pertinent to an understanding of enterprise property rights.

12. Domestic expenditures, along with land tenure, inheritance, betrothal payments, and reproductive rights, reflect the structuring of property rights within and between individual families. While these relationships may influence management practices in village enterprises, a comprehensive analysis of such issues lies beyond the scope of this study.

13. Women had few officially recognized property rights during the early twentieth century. By established practice, daughters could expect to receive a dowry (*jiazhuang*) when they married, but its value was usually less than that of their brothers' entitlement share of the natal family estate. Dowry, moreover, was regarded as "conjugal property" (*fangchan*), belonging to the conjugal branch (*fang*) unit of husband and wife. Women did, however, have (informally recognized) rights to "private room money" (*sifangqian*), usually cash or jewelry they received from their natal family and relatives at their marriage.

14. Unlike the formal and state-recognized family head, always the senior male, family managers could be either male or female, and in Qiaolou most have been the senior woman married into a family. Family managers controlled most use of family property, including the revenues derived from it. They not only

supervised the day-to-day activities of family members, assigning tasks to various individuals, but also controlled a family's budget. It was they who maintained family accounts, made most investment and expenditure decisions, and distributed income and other resources.

15. Notions of shareholding rights were well developed in late imperial China, and were a principal idiom through which membership was defined in a range of social organizations. See, e.g., P. Steven Sangren, "Traditional Chinese Corporations: Beyond Kinship," *Journal of Asian Studies* 43, 3 (May 1984): 391–415; Patricia Buckley Ebrey and James Watson, eds., *Kinship Organization in Late Imperial China, 1000–1940* (Berkeley and Los Angeles: University of California Press, 1986); Myron Cohen, "Shared Beliefs: Corporations, Community, and Religion Among the South Taiwan Hakka During the Ch'ing," *Late Imperial China* 14, 1 (1993): 1–33.

16. The principal institutional landowners in 1940s Qiaolou included three separate ancestral associations (Qingminghui) and a vegetarian religious society (Qingfutang). Two nearby temples owned much larger landholdings, but these were located elsewhere in the township. Membership in such organizations was restricted, generally through an idiom of kinship. Managers of these corporate property-holding institutions were elected on a rotating basis. While they supervised the use of this land and the revenue it generated, they had no authority to sell or transfer such property.

17. The "Sixty Articles" of 1962 stipulated that land in each production team's area belonged to the team itself as a collective unit, yet general guidelines for land use, as well as rights of transfer of land, were controlled by state authorities. See Mark Selden, *The Political Economy of Chinese Development* (Armonk, N.Y.: M.E. Sharpe, 1993), p. 189. In the 1970s, the Meishan County government appropriated several acres of land in northern Qiaolou, on which an asphalt "ring road" was constructed around the township market settlement. No compensation or remuneration was extended to local brigades and teams that lost land. Note, however, that Qiaolou brigade authorities could also transfer land and other assets from one production team to another, redraw team borders, or even disband teams.

18. Selden, *Political Economy*, pp. 188–90.

19. Myron Cohen, "Family Management and Family Division in Contemporary Rural China," *China Quarterly*, no. 130 (June 1992): 357–77. Individual families continued to enjoy limited property rights to "private plots" (*ziliudi*) throughout the Maoist era, exercising decision-making authority over crop selection, inputs, labor allocation, product distribution, marketing (when permitted), and consumption. Families also held limited transfer rights over "private plots," at least insofar as they could determine how they would be distributed among sons in family partition (*fenjia*) settlements. However, state authorities did sometimes appropriate "private plots," reducing their permissible size during radical periods of mobilizational collectivism.

20. Collectivized agriculture encouraged economies of scale within families. Workpoints earned by each individual laborer were publicly noted, but accumulated tallies were administratively recorded by family household. At year's

end accounting, the collective total of a family's workpoint earnings was converted into cash and goods (most crops), which were redistributed by the production team to each head of household. Larger families thus had greater earning potential for both cash and foodstuffs. Indeed, more families attained joint organizational form during the collective era than in the decades before or since. Nevertheless, the complexity of such units rendered them vulnerable to partition, and the long-term viability of any particular family unit depended largely on the abilities and skills of its domestic manager.

21. Such concerns also affected the control of property rights to collective property at the brigade or village level. One of the accusations directed against Qiaolou's previous Party secretary, a "poor peasant" from a minor descent group in the village, who resigned at the height of the Cultural Revolution for reasons of "ill health," was that he had acted improperly by allocating the house of a former "landlord" to his eldest daughter on the occasion of her marriage. Some cynics in the village complained that it was the finest dowry ever seen in Qiaolou.

22. Richard Latham, "The Implications of Rural Reform for Grass-Roots Cadres," in Elizabeth Perry and Christine Wong, eds., *The Political Economy of Reform in Post-Mao China* (Cambridge, Mass.: Harvard University Press, 1985): 157–73; John Burns, "Local Cadre Accommodation to the 'Responsibility System' in Rural China," *Pacific Affairs* 58, 4 (1986): 607–25; Tyrene White, "Political Reform and Rural Government," in Deborah Davis and Ezra Vogel, eds., *Chinese Society on the Eve of Tiananmen: The Impact of Reform* (Cambridge, Mass.: Harvard University Press, 1990), pp. 37–60.

23. The Party secretary said he feared that privatization of agriculture would foster disparities of wealth between families, which might threaten social and political stability. He argued that a revitalized collective enterprise sector, offering guaranteed wage labor and social welfare benefits to village families, would provide a "safety net" (*anquan wang*) for those adversely affected by agricultural decollectivization.

24. A portion of the income each family earned from agricultural workpoints was deducted for brigade funds before procurement payments from the state were redistributed to production teams.

25. In addition to the brigade construction team, Qiaolou had made several earlier attempts at nonagricultural collective enterprise in the 1970s, including a rapeseed oil press and an agricultural machine repair station. The former, little more than a wooden beam manually pressed into a metal drum filled with rapeseed, was abandoned after only a few years. The machine repair station, which employed demobilized soldiers returned to the brigade, proved more successful. But these skilled laborers were soon "called up to the commune" for work at its machine station, an indication of the rights commune officials commanded over labor during the Maoist era.

26. The saplings were purchased and transplanted from a neighboring brigade that had pioneered orange cultivation in the commune. A leading cadre from that village suggested to me, in the company of several prominent Qiaolou men, that those who had adopted orange cultivation ought to pay his village a

fee for appropriating the intellectual property rights of this innovation. Other villages and families in the area quickly followed this profitable new sideline, leading to local market saturation and falling returns on orange harvests. Yet Qiaolou's transport team gave the village favorable access to road and rail shipping, enabling orchard managers to market their produce as far away as Gansu, Beijing, Heilongjiang, and even the Soviet Union and Japan.

27. The political capital of the long-incumbent Party secretary, who was respected as a reliable administrator, was critical in attracting state support for collective village industrialization in Qiaolou.

28. A limited number of additional Y 100 shares were sold to selected families in other villages of the township. While these "outsiders," as registered members of other villages, had no residential claims to membership in the Qiaolou collective, they did have kinship (mostly marital) ties to Qiaolou. These supplemental shares offered outside investors a fixed rate of interest reportedly several points higher than that offered to depositors at the township credit cooperative or state-run banks in the county seat. Those willing to defer any claims to these interest payments indefinitely were offered jobs in the brick factories.

29. Two leading village officials were appointed by the county Party committee rather than locally elected to their posts: the secretary of the village Party branch and his deputy, whom he nominated. The current Party secretary has had a notably long incumbency, having been a political leader in Qiaolou since the early 1950s and Party chief since the mid 1960s. It was he who drafted the first slate of (unopposed) candidates for village office when elections were established in 1982. Since then, the incumbent administrative committee members have drafted candidate slates in subsequent elections every four years, usually renominating themselves.

30. The Party secretary, e.g., was the official manager of the transport team. His deputy, who is also his elder brother's son, has managed a brick factory and the distillery. The village accountant has also served as distillery manager in the past, while the village head has been manager of a brick factory and the zinc refinery. The village security chief has been a manager of the village orchard. These local officials, in consultation with the Qiaolou Party secretary, have selected the men (and the few women) who served on enterprise management committees.

31. The Qiaolou Party secretary also frequently loaned village trucks and drivers to officials in the township government, a practice that brought the village added benefits or favors, such as preferential access to township-managed irrigation water during the critical agricultural periods.

32. See Selden, *Political Economy.* It is noteworthy that the Qiaolou Party secretary, who received little formal education and has limited literacy skills, is an avid and careful reader of the official publication *Fa Zhi* (Legal system), a news periodical in which new laws, directives, and policies are discussed and elaborated.

33. Such analogies were frequently voiced in Qiaolou, particularly by the village managerial elite, including the Party secretary. The same expression, *da jiating*, was used generally to describe extended family organizations, which as noted above were based on corporate shareholding principles.

34. It might be noted that Qiaolou officials spoke much more frequently of villagers' shares in collective enterprises than did villagers themselves. Among the latter, complaints about the obligatory character of share purchases were not uncommon, particularly in the case of families that had earned relatively less income from village jobs than their neighbors.

35. Wages were generally based on a graduated workpoint system, with ranks for employment seniority, labor skills, and technical expertise. Two exceptions were clay diggers (paid piecemeal, by the cartload) and office staff (who effectively received fixed monthly salaries). Although staff workers themselves characterized their earnings as "wages" (*gongzi*), their incomes have been steady and sometimes several times higher than those of production workers, which are subject to fluctuation or even suspension when enterprises fail to turn a profit.

36. These meetings, which can be quite rambunctious and were sometimes punctuated by loud emotional outbursts, solicit information and suggestions from enterprise managers, but final decisions are ultimately determined by the Party secretary.

37. It should be noted that, unlike some local officials in other regions reported to have aggrandized themselves or their families through their positions, Qiaolou's Party secretary has derived little direct or immediate personal economic gain from the success of his efforts. He has continued to live modestly compared with some of his neighbors. Yet other Qiaolou cadres, as well as growing numbers of enterprise staff, have in recent years rebuilt their family homes, often on a conspicuous scale, with formidable walled courtyards.

38. See, e.g., Yunxiang Yan, *The Flow of Gifts: Reciprocity and Social Networks in a Chinese Village* (Stanford, Calif.: Stanford University Press, 1996). In the mid 1990s, the daughter of a wealthy and powerful Qiaolou village councilman committed suicide, reportedly to protest a dowry she regarded as shamefully low in value. Her death prompted her father's retirement from office and a minor realignment of village leadership.

39. Monthly salaries for drivers, whose hours were long, and whose work was sometimes dangerous, were more than half the average annual per capita income in the village in 1991. Moreover, drivers had ample opportunities to engage in profitable private trading and transport activities while away from the village. The only Qiaolou man popularly regarded as having "made his fortune" (*fale cai*) was one of the village's first truck drivers, the only child of the Party secretary. He subsequently broke with his father and moved to the county seat of Meishan, where he ran his own private long-distance trucking company.

40. Of the distillery's four full-time workers, two were nephews of the Party secretary, a third was related by marriage to both him and the village accountant, while the fourth was the patrilineal nephew of Qiaolou's only Korean War veteran (an affine and childhood friend of the Party secretary who formerly served as brigade security chief and production team leader). Indeed, some villagers saw the distillery as a family-run (*jia ban de*) enterprise operated by patrilineal kin of the Party secretary.

41. This man had been personally groomed for a leadership position by the

Qiaolou Party secretary, who arranged a village-funded scholarship to support his enrollment in a cadre training school. Formerly employed for several years as a township head elsewhere in Meishan, he later became one of Qiaolou's most important personal contacts in the county government.

42. For studies of the influence of affect (*ganqing*), human sentiment (*renqing*), and particularistic social connections (*guanxi*), see Morton Fried, *The Fabric of Chinese Society* (New York: Praeger, 1953); Yan, *Flow of Gifts*; David Wank, "Bureaucratic Patronage and Private Business: Changing Networks of Power in Urban China," in Andrew Walder, ed., *The Waning of the Communist State* (Berkeley and Los Angeles: University of California Press, 1995), pp. 153–83; and Andrew Kipnis, *Producing Guanxi: Sentiment, Self, and Subculture in a North China Village* (Durham, N.C.: Duke University Press, 1997).

43. Rubie Watson, "Corporate Property and Local Leadership in the Pearl River Delta, 1898–1941," in Joseph Esherick and Mary Backus Rankin, eds., *Chinese Local Elites and Patterns of Dominance* (Berkeley and Los Angeles: University of California Press, 1990), pp. 239–60.

44. The quality of the soil in the area of the No. 2 Brick Factory was not as suitable for kiln firing as that near the No. 1 Brick Factory. The clay had a high content of tiny stones, which often caused bricks to explode during the firing process. Many of those that did survive the kiln were considered second-rate owing to their pebbles and numerous air holes.

45. Qiaolou's collective orchards, however, continued to bring in good revenues, largely through their economy of scale and the ability of village leaders to arrange railway transport and to ship large numbers of fruit crates to the rail depot at short notice, using vehicles from the village truck team. While not as capital-intensive as the industrial factories, Qiaolou's orchards were one of the most important collective village enterprises.

46. Once again, the political contacts available to village authorities were instrumental in creating this new venture. The Party secretary had asked one of the Chengdu scholars who accompanied me in Qiaolou to arrange an introduction with potential investors and technical specialists in the provincial capital.

47. The refinery, like its predecessor, the No. 2 Brick Factory, paid a fixed and largely nominal use fee to the villager group (*cunmin xiaozu*), or former production team, whose land it occupied.

48. Room and board were provided free of charge by Qiaolou for urban technical staff whose presence was necessary at the refinery site. Their transportation to and from the village was also paid for from village funds. An early point of conflict in the partnership focused on these travel reimbursements, which included expenses questioned by Qiaolou authorities.

49. The Qiaolou refinery was apparently aided in establishing new supply and marketing contacts by county authorities. The county did not invest directly in the refinery, although it did authorize low-interest loans from state banks. It has, however, provided administrative support for the enterprise. The nameplate on the refinery gate identified the enterprise as the "Meishan Zinc Refinery," implying an affiliation with the Meishan County government.

50. Future production plans included the manufacture of racing-style bicycle seats. Marketing managers in Qiaolou believed that the uncomfortable character of standard bike seats would make their new product very popular.

51. These "shares," like those issued to Qiaolou villagers for other collective enterprises, could not be sold but could be transferred to descendants.

52. Qiaolou's deputy Party secretary had previously worked on management committees for both earlier brick kilns, as well as in the distillery. He had held his political post since the mid 1980s, after replacing his predecessor (who was himself the patrilineal nephew of Qiaolou's previous Party chief).

53. Several years earlier, he had contracted operation of one of Qiaolou's two electrically driven grain-processing machines as a proxy for his younger brother, who himself acknowledged that he lacked the "face" (*mianzi*), "status" (*diwei*), and "connections" (*guanxi*) to obtain such a contract.

54. Note that the distillery was the one major collective enterprise in Qiaolou that had not been financed through the sale of "shares." Investment capital for the facility came entirely from revenues generated by the brick factories.

55. Although in this case, as well as in the one that follows, the principals involved described their arrangements as "contracting" (*chengbao*), the terms of the agreements seem to convey rights and powers generally associated with "leasing" (*zulin*). In both instances, the "contractors" paid a one-time fee for facility use and retained all profits after taxes. The distillery contractor created a storm of controversy when he dismissed the six Qiaolou men with whom he had worked for a decade and hired a new crew of his choosing, mainly friends and associates from nearby villages.

56. Violent entrepreneurs have often arisen on the frontiers of capitalism where centralized state control has been weak. See Anton Blok, *The Mafia of a Sicilian Village, 1860–1960: A Study of Violent Peasant Entrepreneurs* (Prospect Heights, Ill.: Waveland Press, 1974). The growing presence of such organizations in both China and Eastern Europe has been an issue of concern to many observers. In Meishan County, those who participate in "shadowy" or illicit business relations were popularly referred to as "people of society" (*shehuishang de ren*). Many have joined associations based on idioms of sworn brotherhood, organizations often likened to the "Elder Brothers Society" (*Gelaohui*) of the past. Some have reportedly engaged in armed violence.

57. Qiaolou residents continued to use the terms "village" (*cun*), "brigade" (*dadui*), and "collective" (*jiti*) interchangeably, in contrast to vernacular practice in other local villages where the latter two terms have fallen into disuse. The village office building, e.g., is still referred to as the "brigade building" (*dadui lou*). Since it is strongly associated with the collective and its leadership, the allegedly forced appropriation of space in the structure by an organization of private investors represented a direct challenge to the Qiaolou corporate elite.

58. I offer this assessment tentatively, for without access to village and enterprise accounts and records, it is difficult to reconstruct a precise history of fiscal management.

59. The investment priorities and venture plans of young adults were often at

odds with those of their parents, and they have occasionally clashed. Note also that formal family partitions (*fenjia*) now regularly occur soon, if not immediately, after a son's marriage, a trend widely noted throughout China.

60. This is similar to trends in urban areas, particularly along the eastern coast where the phrase "diving into the sea" (*xiahai*) has become a euphemism for leaving the security of state work units to seek one's own fortune in private business. Perhaps not surprisingly, the metaphor has not gained currency in the hills of Baimapu.

61. Shortly before Lunar New Year 1995, this man was married in grand fashion to a woman from a neighboring county whom he had met at school. His wedding was one of the largest and most elaborate in memory.

CHAPTER 3   *Chen, Property Rights in Southern Fujian*

1. Calculated from data in *Zhongguo tongji nianjian, 1995* [Statistical yearbook of China, 1995] (Beijing: Zhongguo tongji chubanshe, 1995), pp. 85, 375.

2. Eirik G. Furubotn and Svetozar Pejovich, eds., *The Economics of Property Rights* (Cambridge, Mass.: Ballinger, 1974), p. 3; Andrew G. Walder, "Corporate Organization and Local Government Property Rights in China," in Vedat Milor, ed., *Changing Political Economies: Privatization in Post-Communist and Reforming Communist States* (Boulder, Colo.: Lynne Rienner, 1994), pp. 53–66; and id., "Evolving Property Rights and Their Political Consequences," in David S. G. Goodman and Beverley Hooper, eds., *China's Quiet Revolution: New Interactions Between State and Society* (New York: St. Martin's Press, 1994), pp. 3–18.

3. See, e.g., János Kornai, *The Socialist System: The Political Economy of Communism* (Princeton, N.J.: Princeton University Press, 1992), pp. 63–83.

4. Jean Oi, *State and Peasant in Contemporary China: The Political Economy of Village Government* (Berkeley and Los Angeles: University of California Press, 1989); id., "The Fate of the Collective After the Commune," in Deborah Davis and Ezra Vogel, eds., *Chinese Society on the Eve of Tiananmen: The Impact of Reform* (Cambridge, Mass.: Council on East Asian Studies, Harvard University, 1990), pp. 15–36; id., "Fiscal Reform and the Economic Foundations of Local State Corporatism in China," *World Politics* 45, 1 (Oct. 1992): 99–126; Andrew G. Walder, "The County Government as Industrial Corporation," in id., ed., *Zouping in Transition: The Process of Reform in Rural North China* (Cambridge, Mass.: Harvard University Press, 1998), pp. 62–85.

5. Victor Nee, "A Theory of Market Transition: From Redistribution to Markets in State Socialism," *American Sociological Review* 54, 5 (Oct. 1989): 663–81; id., "Social Inequalities in Reforming State Socialism: Between Redistribution and Markets in China," *American Sociological Review* 56, 3 (June 1991): 267–82; id. and Rebecca Matthews, "Market Transition and Societal Transformation in Reforming State Socialism," *Annual Review of Sociology* 22 (1996): 401–35.

6. Nan Lin, "Local Market Socialism: Local Corporatism in Action in Rural China," *Theory and Society* 24, 3 (June 1995): 301–54.

7. The name Jinjiang will be used throughout this chapter to denote the current administrative divisions of both Jinjiang City and Shishi City. Unless

otherwise indicated, the statistical data referring to Jinjiang also combine Jinjiang City and Shishi City.

8. Wu Luhe, Lin Zhenping, and Yu Daowang, "Jinjiang shi xiangcun chengshihua de fazhan yu qishi" [The development and revelation of Jinjiang's urbanization in the countryside], *Zhongguo nongcun jingji* [China's rural economy] 2 (1995): 56–60.

9. While per capita GNP is higher in Jinjiang than in the Shanghai suburbs and Suzhou, its per capita GVIO is much less. According to Chinese statistical measures, GNP counts only the newly created value in the process of producing goods and services and excludes the value of inputs of intermediate goods and services. It focuses on the value added in the production process. GVIO refers to the total volume of industrial products sold or available for sale in value terms that reflect the total achievements and overall scale of industrial production. GVIO, calculated from the original value of the products, is very much determined by the industrial structure of the locality. In addition, Jinjiang receives more contributions from the tertiary sector (e.g., commerce and services) than do the Shanghai suburbs, which in turn increases the gap in per capita GNP between these two regions.

10. For a comparative study of the property rights transformation in Jinjiang and the Yangtze Delta, see Chih-jou Jay Chen, *Markets and Clientelism: The Transformation of Property Rights in Rural China* (London: Routledge, forthcoming).

11. See, e.g., Yia-Ling Liu, "Reform from Below: The Private Economy and Local Politics in the Rural Industrialization of Wenzhou," *China Quarterly*, no. 130 (June 1992): 293–316; Kristen Parris, "Local Initiative and National Reform: The Wenzhou Model of Development," *China Quarterly*, no. 134 (June 1993): 242–63; Susan Young, *Private Business and Economic Reform in China* (Armonk, N.Y.: M. E. Sharpe, 1995), pp. 96–97.

12. To protect the anonymity of the villages and my interviewees, I have changed the names of all the villages, enterprises, and people mentioned in this chapter. Real names are used for administrative divisions above the village level (e.g., township and county) and for public figures at the national level.

13. Of the 26 villages in Chendai township, 7 are recognized by the government as belonging to the Hui (Muslim) minority. In 1994, the Hui community accounted for 28% of the population and 40% of the industrial output in Chendai. For a study on the prosperous economy and ethnic revitalization in Chendai's Hui community, see Dru C. Gladney, *Muslim Chinese: Ethnic Nationalism in the People's Republic* (Cambridge, Mass.: Council on East Asian Studies, Harvard University, 1991), pp. 261–92, and id., "Economy and Ethnicity: The Revitalization of a Muslim Minority in Southeastern China," in Andrew G. Walder, ed., *The Waning of the Communist State: Economic Origins of Political Decline in China and Hungary* (Berkeley and Los Angeles: University of California Press, 1995), pp. 242–66.

14. Of the ten villages with production values exceeding Y 100 million, five are Hui villages and the rest, including Yangcun, are Han villages.

15. Information from fieldwork, Apr. 1995. See also *Zhongguo guoqing congshu: baixianshi jingji shehui diaocha, jinjiang juan* [Chinese national conditions: A

socioeconomic survey of 100 counties and cities: Jinjiang book] (Beijing: Zhong-guo dabaike quanshu chubanshe, 1992), p. 31.

16. *Jinjiang shi zhi* [Jinjiang municipal gazetteer] (Shanghai: Sanlian Shu-dian, 1994), p. 306. Before the commune and brigade were replaced by township and village in 1984, the township- and village-run enterprises were termed commune- and brigade-run enterprises. In this chapter, for convenience, township and village are also used to denote their predecessors, the commune and the brigade.

17. *Zhongguo guoqing congshu*, p. 31.

18. Calculated from data in ibid., p. 50; *Suzhou shi shehui jingji tongji ziliao, 1949–1985* [Statistical materials on society and economy in Suzhou Munici-pality, 1949–1985] (Suzhou: Statistical Bureau of Suzhou City, 1986), p. 5.

19. Information from fieldwork, Sept. 1995. See also *Jinjiang shi zhi*, p. 304.

20. Since wearing a "Chairman Mao" pin was then an overwhelming fashion nationwide, production of such pins, even by private factories masquerading as collectives, was thought patriotic and deserving of special treatment from the government. See Gao Mingqun, ed., *Shishi shanggong wenhua yanjiu* [Research on the commercial and industrial culture in Shishi] (Xiamen: Xiamen University Press, 1995), pp. 299–301.

21. *Zhongguo guoqing congshu*, p. 31.

22. In 1971, a work team was sent to Shishi to clean up "underground black factories." As a result twelve private factories were torn down and five owner-proprietors were jailed. In 1975, Chen Yonggui, then the vice-premier, inspected Fujian and criticized the market activities of Shishi as showing "everything but a Kuomintang flag." In 1977, in a national campaign to clean up "the restoration of capitalism," the factory production and commodity markets in Shishi experi-enced an unprecedented setback when more than 150 private owner-proprietors were arrested and charged with "speculation" (*toujidaoba*). See Guo Biliang, *Shishi: Zhongguo minban tequ* [Shishi: A people-run special zone in China] (Fu-zhou: Fujian renmin chubanshe, 1993), pp. 10–70; *Zhongguo guoqing congshu*, pp. 538–40.

23. The Third Plenum of the Eleventh Central Committee of the CCP in 1978 announced that products from sideline activities could be sold directly to end-users. In effect, with this change, local government gave official sanction to the return of individual entrepreneurship and of private production and commerce. The central government did not permit rural residents to transport and sell selected goods until 1984.

24. Information from fieldwork, Sept. 1995. See also *Zhongguo guoqing cong-shu*, p. 470.

25. Similar practices were also found in Wenzhou during the early reform period. See Liu, "Reform from Below."

26. Since a single collective license was shared by ten or more factories, all the official documents, such as bank accounts, invoices, and stamps, were also shared. For example, the outside buyers remitted fees or payments to the shared bank account for the factory involved to receive.

27. For the laws and regulations regarding individual and private enterprises

in the reforms, see *Zhongguo siying jingji nianjian* [Almanac of China's private economy] (Hong Kong: Jingji daobaoshe, 1994), pp. 1–42. See also Willy Kraus, *Private Business in China* (Honolulu: University of Hawaii Press, 1991), pp. 16–24; Young, *Private Business*, pp. 105–11.

28. Township records, obtained from fieldwork, May 1995.

29. Author's field interview, Mar. 1995.

30. In Wenzhou, at least in the late 1980s, few private enterprises were willing to be identified as "private," but preferred to be called "local collective enterprises" or "partnership enterprises." See Liu, "Reform from Below," p. 302. This preference did not appear in Jinjiang during my interviews, probably because after fifteen years of reforms, people feel more secure about private ownership.

31. See, e.g., *Zhongguo yanhai touzi huanjing zonglan: Shishi* [A comprehensive review of investment environments in China's coastal cities: Shishi] (Shanghai: East China Normal University Press, 1989), p. 16; *Shishi shi shehui jingji tongji nianjian* [Statistical yearbook of social and economic statistics, Shishi City] (Shishi: Economic Bureau of Shishi City, 1994), pp. 81–85.

32. The central government did not officially approve the new joint-household (*lianhu*) ownership forms until 1984, but the Jinjiang County government had issued a regulation mandating similar arrangements at the end of 1980. The category of "joint-household enterprise" first appeared in the internal statistical materials of Jinjiang in 1981. State statistical materials did not list such a category until 1984.

33. *Zhongguo guoqing congshu*, p. 390.

34. The data, drawn from the survey on "Economic Development and Women's Work in Jinjiang," are kindly provided by Yu-hsia Lu, Institute of Sociology, Academia Sinica. The survey was conducted in two villages in Jinjiang in August 1995. The author served as a survey supervisor in the field. This research employed a systematic sampling method to select 50 households each from one village in Chendai township and one village in Jinjiang township. The questionnaire was used to interview housewives regarding their family members' working conditions, family businesses (if any), share of housework, and personal background.

35. Author's interview, Mar. 1995.

36. The role of the township government in the company's development deserves closer examination. What happened to the role of the township government and its original investment when the company was transformed into a foreign joint venture? Unfortunately, the information is not complete as this report is being written. One of the author's speculations is that the original investment from the township was taken as a loan, instead of a share. A loan involved in a project was usually termed an "investment" (*touzi*). It is possible that the township "invested" in this firm by offering a loan, to be repaid after a certain period.

37. See Maurice Freedman, *Lineage Organization in Southeastern China* (London: Athlone Press, 1958); Myron L. Cohen, "Lineage Organization in North China," *Journal of Asian Studies* 49, 3 (Aug. 1990): 509–34. For lineage and kinship relations in rural villages in the reforms in Fujian and Guangdong, see

Anita Chan, Richard Madsen, and Jonathan Unger, *Chen Village Under Mao and Deng* (Berkeley and Los Angeles: University of California Press, 1992); Yuen-fong Woon, "Social Change and Continuity in South China: Overseas Chinese and the Guan Lineage of Kaiping County, 1949–87," *China Quarterly*, no. 118 (June 1989): 324–44; Huang Shu-min, *The Spiral Road: Change in a Chinese Village Through the Eyes of a Communist Party Leader* (Boulder, Colo.: Westview Press, 1989).

38. For discussions of lineages and collective property in traditional South China, see Maurice Freedman, *Chinese Lineage and Society: Fukien and Kwangtung* (London: Athlone Press, 1966); Jack Potter, "Land and Lineage in Traditional China," in Maurice Freedman, ed., *Family and Kinship in Chinese Society* (Stanford, Calif.: Stanford University Press, 1972), pp. 121–38; and James L. Watson, "Chinese Kinship Reconsidered: Anthropological Perspectives on Historical Research," *China Quarterly*, no. 92 (Dec. 1982): 589–622.

39. The Quanzhou Maritime Museum has been collecting and compiling local genealogies in southern Fujian since the late 1980s. A research fellow confirmed that most of the genealogies were burned during various campaigns, but on the other hand quite a few were concealed and successfully preserved. Most of these recovered genealogies were maintained by old local gentry or retired cadres, whose social prestige and political position enabled them to conceal their lineage genealogies, despite some risks involved.

40. Zhuang Jinghui, "Chendai dingshi huizu hanhua de yanjiu" [Research on Han assimilation of the Ding lineage in Chendai], *Haijiaoshi yanjiu* [Research on maritime history] 34 (1993): 93–107.

41. For more detailed descriptions of the ethnic politics and economic prosperity in Chendai's Hui villages, see Gladney, *Muslim Chinese*, pp. 261–92, and "Economy and Ethnicity."

42. In August 1995, a lineage delegation from Taixi, a town on the west coast of Taiwan, visited its ancestral hometown for the first time since 1949. This lineage delegation, which the author joined, received such an enthusiastic reception in Chendai that a number of members burst into tears. According to one Taiwanese lineage member, "The reception was so intense and honorable that it could only happen to Lee Teng-hui [the president] in Taiwan."

43. According to a 1987 census of overseas Chinese, those who originated from Jinjiang number 944,500, of which 651,700 (70%) reside in the Philippines, 95,000 (10%) in Indonesia, 75,000 (8%) in Malaysia, and 45,000 (5%) in Singapore. Between the 1950s and the 1980s, about 270,000 people had emigrated from Jinjiang to Hong Kong. Also, more than a million Taiwanese residents are descendants of Jinjiang emigrants. See *Jinjiang shi zhi*, pp. 1184–1224.

44. *Quanzhou shi huaqiao zhi* [Annals of Quanzhou overseas Chinese] (Beijing: Zhongguo shehui chubanshe, 1996), pp. 295 and 300. These statistics on overseas Chinese include those living in Hong Kong and Macao, but exclude those in Taiwan.

45. A coastal village in Xiamen also shows a similar pattern of overseas connections. See Huang, *Spiral Road*, pp. 25–40.

46. *Zhongguo guoqing congshu*, p. 382.

47. According to a statistical record, the foreign remittances from overseas Chinese to Jinjiang from 1950 to 1980 reached a low between 1959 and 1962. However, the lowest offering in 1962 still amounted to more than ¥20 million, around one-third of the average amount in other years.

48. Thanks to ceaseless support from overseas relatives and fellow villagers, even during the national famine of 1959–62, Jinjiang escaped the starvation that struck other rural regions across China. Most aid from abroad was delivered in the form of such foodstuffs as rice, wheat flour, and cooking oil.

49. *Quanzhou shi huaqiao zhi*, p. 295. See also *Jinjiang shi zhi*, pp. 1209–15. When I conducted field research in Jinjiang in 1995, I was amazed by the fact that *every* school I visited in the countryside had a number of memorial tablets on which the benevolence of donations from overseas fellow villagers was recorded and praised.

50. In September 1979, the State Council formally promulgated the "Regulations on External Processing and Assembling and Small- and Medium-Sized Compensatory Trade." The processing and compensation trades are called *sanlai yibu* ("three comings-in and one compensation"), referring to the processing of imported materials (*lailiao jiagong*), the processing and assembling of supplied materials, parts, and components provided by overseas firms (*laiyang jiagong* and *laijian zhuangpei*), and the compensation trade (*buchang maoyi*), in which the foreign investors provide equipment, technology, and management support in return for exported output. The materials, parts, and production equipment imported into China, and the finished goods exported, are free from duties.

51. *Zhongguo guoqing congshu*, p. 157.

52. All special trade arrangements required government approval, but a division of control over foreign trade and investment had been delegated to the local authorities, particularly in Fujian and Guangdong. Local governments sometimes took orders and subcontracted the business to local enterprises. In most cases, the business was first acquired by local enterprises through their social ties. Then local governments would sign the contracts with foreign parties on behalf of local enterprises and transmit the foreign remittances to the local producers in renminbi. Through their mediating role, local governments were entitled to receive a fixed amount of compensation and were able to control foreign exchange.

53. *Jinjiang shi zhi*, p. 1219; *Zhongguo guoqing congshu*, p. 384.

54. From 1984 to 1988, in Jinjiang there were 154 joint ventures, but none of them were wholly foreign-owned enterprises. See *Jinjiang shi zhi*, p. 306.

55. Australia, Department of Foreign Affairs and Trade, East Asia Analytical Unit, *Overseas Chinese Business Networks in Asia* (Canberra: Australian Govt. Pub. Service, 1995), pp. 219–27. For a related study on diaspora investors in China, see Constance Lever-Tracy, David Ip, and Noel Tracy, *The Chinese Diaspora and Mainland China: An Emerging Economic Synergy* (London: Macmillan; New York: St. Martin's Press, 1996).

56. Approximately 2% of Hong Kong's residents are Hokkien; 90% are Cantonese, with their ancestral origins in Fujian's neighboring Guangdong Province.

57. In practice, the foreign parties had to remit the investment payment to local banks to verify the arrival of foreign capital, but in fact the capital was sometimes provided by local enterprises beforehand.

58. See, e.g., Jean Oi, "Fiscal Reform," and "The Role of the Local State in China's Transitional Economy," *China Quarterly*, no. 144 (Dec. 1995): 1132–49; Nan Lin, "Local Market Socialism"; Chih-jou Jay Chen, *Markets and Clientelism*.

59. *Zhongguo quoqing congshu*, pp. 31, 393.

60. Guo, *Shishi*, pp. 25–27.

61. *Jinjiang shi zhi*, p. 304; Guo, *Shishi*, pp. 41–44. The policy was reconfirmed the next year by the prefecture and provincial authorities. See *Quanzhou shi xiangzhen qiye zhi* [The annals of township and village enterprises in Quanzhou] (Quanzhou: Quanzhou wanbao, 1993), p. 18.

62. In Central Document No. 1 of 1984, the government openly approved new ownership forms such as joint-household enterprises (*lianhu*) and joint ownership by different administrative units (*lianying*). It stated that governments at all levels should encourage collectives and peasants to pool their funds and jointly establish various kinds of enterprises based on voluntary participation and mutual benefit. See "Zhonggong zhongyang guanyu 1984 nian nong-cun gongzuo de tongzhi" [Circular of the Central Committee of the CCP on agricultural work during 1984], in *Zhongguo nongye nianjian, 1984* [Agricultural yearbook of China, 1984] (Beijing: Nongye chubanshe, 1985), p. 2.

63. *Zhongguo guoqing congshu*, pp. 393–94.

64. On July 13, 1985, the evening news report of the Chinese Central TV Station broadcast "An open letter from the CCP Central Committee Discipline Inspection Commission to the Jinjiang Prefectural CCP Committee and the Jinjiang Administrative Office," which was reprinted in newspapers across the country on July 14. For example, see *Renmin ribao* [People's daily], July 14, 1985; and *Fujian ribao* [Fujian daily], July 14, 1985.

65. In fact, the "counterfeit drugs" were canned comestibles such as *yin er* (silver ear), a type of semi-transparent white fungus believed to be highly nutritious. The problem was that local manufacturers labeled the products "medicine for lowering blood pressure" or "flu and cold relief" so that they could be prescribed by medical institutes to their patients, whose medical costs would be fully paid by the state.

66. According to an investigation report, among the 57 enterprises charged with producing "counterfeit drugs," 45 were located in Chendai. During 1983–84, the output value of "counterfeit drugs" in Chendai amounted to Y 20 million. See *Fujian ribao*, July 13, 1985. Another source reports that more than 200 enterprises were shut down in the aftermath of the crackdown. See *Zhongguo guoqing congshu*, p. 395.

67. The management fee could be seen as payment for use of the village label. But the underlying norm is that each firm has to contribute to the village, and the amount of the remittance is primarily determined by the firm's scale rather than its registration title. The fee is collected once or twice a year, generally as a lump-sum payment. For bureaucratic convenience, the payments from large firms were categorized as land and building fees, not management fees.

68. Basically the terms and treatment of land contracting discriminated between villagers (including overseas villagers and relatives) and outsiders, but in any case, village cadres retain the power to make the final decision over the terms of the contract. The village can retain all the income from residential land but has to share the rent payment of industrial land with the township government. In an earlier work, Oi points out that the reforms up to the mid 1980s have transformed the primary function of village government from implementing government policies and managing agricultural production to being the general contractor of collective property. See Jean Oi, "Commercializing China's Rural Cadres," *Problems of Communism* 35 (Sept.–Oct. 1986): 1–15.

69. Yangcun combined management fees with land rent for enterprises registered as village-run. The basic terms were similar to those in Hancun, although Hancun categorized the land rent as village management income rather than enterprise remittances. The charge for a household factory was relatively low (say Y 500 per year), but once the factory exceeded the land quota of a household, it was asked to contribute a much higher rent for land use.

70. According to law, land belongs to the state, and what the villagers purchased was actually the "use right" (*shiyongquan*). But in practice, local residents used the term "sell" for the transaction. The land purchased is allowed to be traded to other villagers, but not outsiders, at a mutually agreed price.

71. The income shared with the township mainly derives from payments of village enterprises (including 35 enterprises entitled joint ventures). Since Yangcun village developed early and has a large number of enterprises, it has maintained the "custom" of sharing part of its enterprise remittances with the township. The flow of money between township and village governments should not be seen as part of the revenue-sharing system between higher levels of government. Villages are not part of the national fiscal system and do not receive any allocation from the national budget.

72. The township shared part of the expenditure on infrastructure maintenance (e.g., roads, parks, and street lights).

73. Hancun village has overseas-donated funds for the elders (Y 1,500,000), for education (Y 250,000), for farmland irrigation (Y 2,500,000), and for Party members (Y 100,000). In 1993, Yangcun established an endowment of Y 1,500,000 to subsidize the wages of schoolteachers.

74. See Walder, "Corporate Organization and Local Government," p. 59.

CHAPTER 4   *Guo, Local Government and Property Rights*

1. Louis Putterman, "The Role of Ownership and Property Rights in China's Economic Transition," *China Quarterly*, no. 144 (Dec. 1995): 1047.

2. Based mainly on my field research in 1992, with some data updated in 1996.

3. The "state" in this chapter specifically refers to the higher, policy-making levels of government, from which state financial subsidies emanate.

4. For example, "*de facto* private agriculture" as used by Putterman in "Role of Ownership and Property Rights in China's Economic Transition," 1048; "land

reprivatised *de facto*," used by János Kornai in "The Affinity Between Ownership Forms and Coordination Mechanisms: The Common Experience of Reform
in Socialist Countries," *WIDER* [World Institute for Development Economics
Research of the United Nations University], 1990, p. 7.

5. "Zhonggong zhongyang guanyu 1984 nongcun gongzuo de tongzhi"
[CCP central circular about rural work in 1984], in *Xinshiqi nongye he nongcun
gongzuo zhongyao wenxian xuanbian* [Selected important documents on agriculture and rural affairs in the new era] (Beijing: Zhongyang wenxian chubanshe,
1992), p. 224. In the same year, the land contract in poverty-stricken areas was
allowed to extend up to 30 years; see "Zhonggong zhongyang, guowuyuan
guanyu bangzhu pinkun diqu jinkuai gaibian mianmao de tongzhi" [CCP center and State Council circular on speeding up economic development in poor
areas], in ibid., p. 297.

6. "Zhonghua renmin gongheguo tudi guanlifa" [Land Administration Law
of the People's Republic of China], revised in December 1988, in *Zhonghua
renmin gongheguo fagui huibian, 1988* [Collected laws and regulations of the PRC,
1988] (Beijing: Falü chubanshe, 1990), pp. 623–37.

7. "Zhonggong zhongyang guowuyuan guanyu 1991 nongye he nongcun
gongzuo de tongzhi" [CCP center and State Council circular about agriculture
and rural work in 1991], in *Xinshiqi nongye he nongcun gongzuo zhongyao wenxian
xuanbian* [Selected important documents on agriculture and rural affairs in the
new era] (Beijing: Zhongyang wenxian chubanshe 1992), pp. 633–34.

8. "Land Administration Law of the People's Republic of China" (1986), in
The Laws of the People's Republic of China, 1983–86 (Beijing: Foreign Languages
Press, 1987).

9. "Nongcun renmin gongshe gongzuo tiaoli xiuzheng cao'an" [Regulations
on the work of the rural people's communes, revised draft], in *Nongye jitihua
zhongyao wenjian huibian, 1958–81* [Collected important documents on agricultural collectivization, 1958–81], vol. 2 (Beijing: Zhonggong zhongyang dangxiao
chubanshe 1981), pp. 628–49.

10. Collective property also used to include major farm implements and livestock.

11. Compensation for requisition of cultivated land is three to six times the
average annual output value of the requisitioned land for the three years preceding such requisition; see "Land Administration Law of the People's Republic
of China" (1987), p. 263.

12. See, e.g., Robert F. Ash, "The Agricultural Sector in China: Performance
and Policy Dilemmas During the 1990s," *China Quarterly*, no. 131 (Sept. 1992):
545–76. This reflects the general situation that apparently led to the adjustment
of the central policy in 1984 to extend the land contract to fifteen years; see
"Zhongyang shujichu nongcun zhengce yanjiushi jieshi youguan tudi chengbao
de jige wenti" [Central Party Secretariat Rural Policy Research Office explains
land contract issues], in Du Xichuan and Xu Xiuyi, eds., *Zhongguo tudi guanli falü
daquan* [Compilation of Chinese land administration laws and regulations] (Beijing: Zhongguo guoji guangbo chubanshe 1990), p. 166.

13. The Jinguan township land management officer calls the land contract the "three-land system" (*santian zhi*) because it includes the grain-ration land (*kouliang tian*) cultivated for basic food supply, taxed land (*gongyu liang tian*) cultivated for levies of agricultural tax and state procurement, and collective levies land (*jiti tiliu tian*) cultivated to pay collective fees. This is a local interpretation, although it is similar to the officially defined, "two-land system" (*liangtian zhi*), which is divided into "subsistence land" (*kouliang tian*) and "responsibility land" (*zeren tian*). See Li Zheng, "1989 Zhongguo nongye jingji tizhi gaige zongshu" [Summary of China's rural economic reform in 1989], in *Zhongguo jingji tizhi gaige nianjian, 1990* [China's economic reform yearbook, 1990] (Beijing: Gaige chubanshe, 1990), p. 441.

14. Zhou Haibo, "Special Revenue Sources and Their Impact on Yunnan Finances," *Chinese Economic Studies* 29, 4 (July–Aug. 1996): 82–90.

15. There are two harvests a year in grain production, which doubles land use and increases land income. But with tobacco production, the land only yields one crop a year.

16. This coincided with the promulgation by the central government in 1993 of the Agricultural Law, which emphasized and specified the individual grower's rights of decision-making in production (*shengchan jingying quan*) and rights to residual income (*chanpin chufen quan, chanpin shouyi quan*); see FBIS-CHI-93–133 (July 2, 1993): 17–18. However, the real reason that the county government changed its policy with respect to tobacco production may well be related to the fiscal reform in 1994, which adjusted sharing of tobacco revenues between higher and lower levels of government. In 1996, a tobacco quota (and subsequently the tobacco-growing area) was once again assigned by the county government, apparently under local budget constraints following the fiscal reform. But this time no coercive measures were taken, and as a result only 10% of the quota was achieved (my interviews in the summer of 1996).

17. Putterman, "Role of Ownership," p. 1052.

18. This seems to be a common phenomenon of the transitional reforms in the former socialist countries, as Kornai discusses in "Affinity Between Ownership Forms and Coordination Mechanisms," p. 11.

19. This view was clearly revealed to me during my household interviews in 1992.

20. Although state procurement still exists in Yongning, it has been reduced since 1979, and the fulfillment of procurement quotas is not compulsory. However, because the state procurement quotas are linked to the state supply of production materials at subsidized prices, peasants in Yongning prefer to sell grain to the state if they have a surplus.

21. In all Yongning hamlets, the contribution to collective funds is an annual flat fee of Y 2 per person with contracted land, which is three times less than in Jinguan. The difference lies mainly in the use of the collective funds. In Jinguan, much of the collective fund is used to pay for irrigation, maintenance of public facilities (roads and ditches), and sometimes the village schoolteachers' salaries. In Yongning, there is no fee charged for irrigation, and much of the communal

construction is funded by the government, which also pays the hamlet school-teachers; the only use of the collective fund in Yongning is to pay the wages of the hamlet leaders.

22. "Nongcun renmin gongshe gongzuo tiaoli xiuzheng cao'an," 1962 (cited n. 9 above), p. 634.

23. "Land Administration Law of the People's Republic of China," 1987, p. 266.

24. The average Han Chinese peasant residence in Jinguan consists of a house, a detached kitchen, and a small garden plot. The Mosuo residence has four buildings plus a large garden plot.

25. The lack of pressure on land resources also contributes to the nonenforcement of rules regarding residential sites.

26. *Zhongguo tongji nianjian 1992* [Statistical yearbook of China, 1992] (Beijing: Zhongguo tongji chubanshe, 1993).

27. Jinguan Township statistics, 1991.

28. Yongning Township statistics, 1991.

29. According to a township enterprise administration official, the difference between state-owned and township enterprises is based on two criteria: the source of investment capital and the nature of employment. Enterprises with investment capital from the state and workers recruited under the quota of state plans are state enterprises; all others are categorized as township enterprises.

30. Jean C. Oi, "The Role of the Local State in China's Transitional Economy," *China Quarterly*, no. 144 (Dec. 1995): 1132–49; Andrew G. Walder, "China's Transitional Economy: Interpreting Its Significance," *China Quarterly*, no. 144 (Dec. 1995): 964–79.

31. The "eight minority regions/provinces" consist of five ethnic minority autonomous regions and three provinces with large ethnic minority populations. The five autonomous regions are Inner Mongolia, Xinjiang (Uighur), Guangxi (Zhuang), Ningxia (Hui), and Tibet; and the three provinces are Yunnan, Guizhou, and Qinghai.

32. *Dangdai Zhongguo de Yunnan* [Contemporary China: Yunnan] (Beijing: Dangdai Zhongguo chubanshe, 1991), p. 407.

33. Ibid. However, the tax situation may have changed after the 1994 fiscal reform.

34. The power station in Yongning is a collective enterprise, and owing to lack of funds, its equipment has been poorly maintained. In the winter of 1992–93, the township's electricity supply was interrupted, but the township government did not undertake any serious repair work. As one of the cadres said: "Soon the repair work will go beyond the means of the collective enterprise, and the state [i.e., the next higher level of government] will have to do something to save the power station."

35. This was abandoned farmland once appropriated for use by urban school graduates in the early 1970s.

36. The social basis of this relation has been called a "legacy of communist central planning," in that the state monopolizes crucial resources and the horizontal information channels are weak. See David Wank's unpublished paper

"Exchange and Power in China's Market Economy: A Partial Theory of Post-Communist Institutional Transformation" (1996), p. 8.

37. This phenomenon is also described as the "symbiotic relationship between enterprises and government." See Dorothy J. Solinger, "Urban Entrepreneurs and the State: The Merger of State and Society," in Arthur L. Rosenbaum, ed., *State and Society in China: The Consequences of Reform* (Boulder, Colo.: Westview Press, 1992), p. 129.

38. In contrast to the behavior of the Jinguan township government, according to a county official in the township enterprise administration, the Ninglang county government (under which Yongning township is administered) has contracted out a number of *xianshu qiye* (county-owned enterprises) that were not profitable.

39. Jinguan township enterprise statistics, 1996.

40. One evolved from the old Jinguan construction firm, and the other emerged from former village-run enterprises.

41. For instance, the financial subsidy to the Yongning township government from the county government specifically designates funds for "official entertainment" (i.e., banquets and similar expenses).

42. See Jean C. Oi, "Fiscal Reform and the Economic Foundations of Local State Corporatism in China," *World Politics* 45, 1 (Oct. 1992): 99–126.

43. In Yunnan province, 102 out of 127 county-level administrations were in financial deficit at that time; see *Dangdai Zhongguo de Yunnan*, p. 709.

44. Earmarked for local economic construction in general.

45. Earmarked for education and health programs.

46. Earmarked for developing agricultural capital construction.

47. *Lao-shao-bian-qiong* stands for "old revolutionary base, ethnic minority, border region, and poverty-stricken areas."

48. The monthly interest rate paid on such loans provided by the Bank of Agriculture is 0.74%, of which 0.5% is subsidized out of central government finances.

49. My interview with the county government poverty-alleviation office in 1996.

50. Known as *fanxiao liang*, this is grain that local authorities can sell to residents at the lowest state-subsidized price.

51. Corn is a high-yield crop, and the Ninglang County government subsidizes the cost of chemical fertilizer in order to encourage the peasants to grow corn to increase grain output.

52. Ninglang was first classified as a state poverty-stricken county in 1985, and this status was renewed in 1994 when the state redefined the poverty line. The national plan is to eliminate poverty by the year 2000, as stated in "Guojia baqi fupin gongjian jihua" [National eight-seven strategic plan for poverty alleviation], *Kaifa yu zhifu*, no. 4 (1994): 3–21. A further adjustment of the poverty line is not foreseen, and the poverty status of Ninglang is unlikely to change until that happens.

53. As to why the local leadership in the minority area does not maximize its gains by taking advantage of state subsidies and developing local enterprises,

the answer may be found in many historical, social, and environmental factors that are not central to the argument of this chapter.

54. Douglass North, "Economic Performance Through Time," *American Economic Review* 84, 3 (June 1994): 359–68.

55. Also see Andrew G. Walder, "Local Governments as Industrial Firms: An Organizational Analysis of China's Transitional Economy," *American Journal of Sociology* 101, 2 (Sept. 1995): 2–3.

56. See Victor Nee, "A Theory of Market Transition: From Redistribution to Markets in State Socialism," *American Sociological Review* 54, 5 (Oct. 1989): 663–81.

57. "Shichang guanbuliao shizhang" ("The market cannot override the mayor") was a popular saying in Yunnan among the local cadres I came across in 1996.

CHAPTER 5   *Kung, Property Rights in Village Enterprises*

I thank Jean Oi and Andrew Walder for detailed comments on earlier drafts; Scott Rozelle, conference participants, and two reviewers for useful comments; the Hong Kong University of Science and Technology for funding (grant no. DAG94/95.HSS05), Shouying Liu and researchers at the Development Research Center of the State Council for helping organize the survey and interviews; and the Wuxi Municipal Government and many village officials there. Any errors and views expressed are the sole responsibility of the author.

1. William A. Byrd and Alan Gelb, "Why Industrialize? The Incentives for Rural Community Governments," in William Byrd and Lin Qingsong, eds., *China's Rural Industry: Structure, Development, and Reform* (New York: Oxford University Press, 1990), pp. 358–88; Jean C. Oi, "Fiscal Reform and the Economic Foundations of Local State Corporatism in China," *World Politics* 45 (Oct. 1992): 99–126.

2. See the sources cited in n. 1 above.

3. As will be subsequently shown, because village authorities are prohibited from selling the village's land to private individuals, they retain ownership over this particular factor input. But that does not necessarily render privatization incomplete. Ownership, according to economic theory, is defined by the rights to claim residual profits—net of the marginal product of labor and nonlabor costs of production—rather than by ownership of the factors of production. See Armen Alchian and Harold Demsetz, "Production, Information Costs, and Economic Organization," *American Economic Review* 62, 5 (Dec. 1972): 777–95.

4. See, e.g., the comparative study of four counties in Byrd and Lin, eds., *China's Rural Industry*, chs. 1 and 2, and Policy Research Unit, Wuxi Municipal Committee, "Huaxi cun jingji shehui fazhan diaocha" [An investigation of social and economic development in Huaxi village], *Zhongguo nongcun jingji* [China's rural economy] 3 (1996): 37–41.

5. The important roles of cadres in obtaining the much needed "critical inputs" for township and village enterprise development have indeed been identified in the literature on TVEs. See inter alia Byrd and Gelb, "Why Industrial-

ize?"; Chang Chun and Wang Yijiang, "The Nature of the Township-Village Enterprise," *Journal of Comparative Economics* 19, 3 (Dec. 1994): 434–52; and Victor Nee, "Organizational Dynamics of Market Transition: Hybrid Forms, Property Rights, and Mixed Economy in China," *Administrative Science Quarterly* 37 (Mar. 1992): 1–27.

6. Although most enterprises undergoing privatization tend to be small, the trend appears unabated over the near and medium term. In Zhucheng County, Shandong Province, for example, over 90% of the small state-owned and collective concerns, among them township and village enterprises, have recently been privatized. Zhucheng is an experimental zone for ownership reform of state and collective enterprises, and the Zhucheng experience was reportedly endorsed by China's vice-premier Zhu Rongji (see *Ming Pao Daily News* [Hong Kong], May 24, 1996).

7. The village accountant was asked to fill out a questionnaire covering many aspects of the village economy, ranging from basic socio-demographic and migration data to more specific data about both nonagricultural enterprises and farm institutions. Structured, in-depth interviews were also conducted with both the Party branch secretary, or *cun shuji*, who is responsible for the overall management of village enterprises, and the village chief, or *cunzhang*, who bears responsibility for agricultural production.

8. Table 5.1 refers to the absolute size of these township economies, however, and does not adjust for population size.

9. As the village Party secretary of Yinzheng village remarked, local leaders are involved rather in managing the village economy as a whole.

10. The actual number should be fourteen, if we count the answers given respectively by the village Party secretary in Chenxu village, who indicated that he and the accountant were the "overseers" (*guanlizhe*) of the village economy, and the Party branch secretary in Xiaoxing village, who answered "yes" to the question, since he was also the manager of one enterprise there. This leaves Shengan as the only village where the few senior village cadres were actually involved in the day-to-day management of their three enterprises. In terms of enterprise output value, this village is ranked in the bottom third among the sixteen sample villages in Wuxi, which is perhaps an important reason why cadres there are at the same time also managers of the village enterprises.

11. As one Bingkou village cadre put it, the relationship between the village Party secretary and enterprise managers is basically one of "superior and subordinates."

12. This is analogous to the "moral economy" thesis advanced by James C. Scott in *The Moral Economy of the Peasant: Subsistence and Rebellion in Southeast Asia* (New Haven, Conn.: Yale University Press, 1976). The constraining effect of "fairness" on institutional choice in the post-Mao context in fact had a historical parallel during the period of China's collectivized agriculture, when jobs were scarce (especially during agricultural slack seasons) and thus had to be rationed among members of the production team, who would otherwise be eager to supply more labor than allowed, in order to earn more workpoints and therefore higher incomes. See the analysis in James K. Kung, "Egalitarianism, Sub-

sistence Provision, and Work Incentives in China's Agricultural Collectives," *World Development* 22, 2 (Feb. 1994): 175–88, esp. 180.

13. Zhu's de facto power was partially confirmed by the village accountant, who remarked that "enterprise managers are usually allowed to make their own decisions for small investments, simply by informing [*dage zhaohu*] Mr. Zhu, but for investments that have strategic implications, they would need Mr. Zhu's approval."

14. This is one reason why nominal owners of TVEs "assign" control rights to their agent, the township and village government, according to Chang and Wang, "Nature of the Township-Village Enterprise."

15. Indeed, this particular function is so important that when we attempt to ascertain the relationship between the control variable, on the one hand (1 = ownership and control are not separated, 0 = otherwise), and the bundle of rights assigned to the enterprise manager, on the other hand (e.g., credit provision, party responsible for enterprise investment decisions, etc.), the only variable that turns out to have a statistically significant relationship with the control variable is credit provision (-0.59, 2% two-tailed significance).

16. See Joseph E. Stiglitz and A. Weiss, "Credit Rationing in Markets with Imperfect Information," *American Economic Review* 71, 3 (June 1981): 393–419.

17. The finding that cadres play an important role, especially in obtaining credits for village enterprises and in job allocation and determining the total wage bill, is supported by the statistically significant relationship between the last two variables, the employment level and overall wages ($-.54$ at 3% level of two-tailed significance).

18. It may be argued that if villagers were not perceived as the owners of these enterprises, this norm, basically reflecting their preference, would be unlikely to have such a significant bearing on managerial income, as would be the case in a private enterprise.

19. Only one cadre in our sample had difficulty telling who the owner of village enterprises was.

20. When answering this question, the Party branch secretary of Yinzheng village deliberately crossed out the word *zhengfu* (government) after the adjective *cun* (village) and remarked that the village was not part of the government apparatus. In point of fact, the lowest unit of local government to which the fiscal revenue-sharing system applies is the township, not the village.

21. Instituted in 1958 under Mao to promote rapid industrial development at the lowest possible cost in urban growth, *hukou* is a household registration system aimed at restricting peasant migration to towns and cities. Backed by restricted access to employment, housing, and education in urban areas, and by the rationing of cheap food and other products there, the *hukou* system effectively limited rural-urban migration prior to the rural reforms.

22. This is a classic example of the "weapons of the weak." See James C. Scott, *Weapons of the Weak: Everyday Forms of Peasant Resistance* (New Haven, Conn.: Yale University Press, 1985).

23. See, e.g., Byrd and Gelb, "Why Industrialize?"; Barry Naughton, "Chinese Institutional Innovation and Privatization from Below," *American Economic*

Review 4, 2 (May 1994): 266–70; and Nee, "Organizational Dynamics of Market Transition."

24. Barry Naughton, "Implications of the State Monopoly over Industry and Its Relaxation," *Modern China* 18 (Jan. 1992): 14–41.

25. There is the usual caveat that the figures employed here are in current prices. Given the enormous difference in output value between the three periods in question, we would expect the results of F-tests for inequality to be statistically significant, which indeed turns out to be so (Table 5.5).

26. This retention of ownership over land enables the village authorities to receive fixed rental payments, and in some instances even management fees, from those who now own these basically private enterprises.

27. The latter objective function is perhaps less important in Qianxiang because the ratio of nonlocal enterprise workers to total enterprise workers is relatively high, 52.7%, implying that villagers are basically fully employed there (author's survey, 1995). If true, this would most certainly facilitate privatization.

28. The usual accounting procedure for arriving at an enterprise's net asset value is to deduct liability from its gross asset value.

29. As pointed out earlier in the chapter, ownership depends, not on legally owning the factor inputs used in production (they can be leased), but on entitlement to the right to claim residual profits.

30. In Qianxiang village, for example, rental payments in 1995 were set at Y 10,000 per mu. With seven mu of land designated for industrial use, the village authority obtained Y 1.4 million simply by renting out spaces to the private enterprises—an amount, according to the village Party secretary, that far exceeded what they used to get from the same enterprises before they became private.

31. Xinkaihe reportedly charges the same rate as Qianxiang and had, moreover, rented out three times as much land to private enterprises in 1995—25.5 mu.

32. In Xinkaihe village, for example, a management fee is levied at 0.5% of enterprise sales revenue and an education surcharge at 0.3%. In addition, 10% of enterprise profits will be levied as a contribution to the catchall category of "social expenditure" (*shehuixing kaizhi*), and a surcharge is also levied on a per worker basis for welfare expenditures for the elderly.

33. The cadre in Weihua village made similar remarks.

34. In connection to this point, the village Party secretary in Yinzheng also remarked that factory work in the beginning did instill a sense of pride in the enterprise workers, particularly because it was a time when not everybody had yet had the chance of getting nonfarm employment; at least that was the case in a small village like his, where the progress of rural industrialization was below the average level attained by the more prosperous villages in Wuxi.

35. In some villages, privatization is confined to enterprises with a net asset value not exceeding the stipulated amount. In Hongmin village, for example, Y 1 million is the upper limit. What this practice reflects, clearly, is the constraint the private entrepreneur will likely face in raising funds for buying out the capital value required by privatization.

36. Although an enterprise may have loans outstanding to its customers, business partners, etc., at the time of ownership change, these loans are often defaulted on and thus have to be written off (author's fieldwork, 1995). In recent years, intensified competition and tight credit control have manifestly led to rising debt-to-capital ratios among many township and village enterprises. Unable to pay their business partners, they become indebted to one another—a problem similar in nature to what has long afflicted the state-owned enterprises (so-called triangular debts, or *sanjiao zhai*). See, e.g., Ji Yongmao, "Xiangzhen qiye zhaiwu lian de xingcheng ji qi jietuo duicha" [The formation and resolution of township and village enterprises' chain debts], *Guancha, yanjiu, shiyan* [Observations, research, and experiments] 4 (1996): 54–56.

37. Such is the case, for instance, with the gearwheel factory in Xinkaihe village. In "decollectivizing" this enterprise, the original enterprise manager put in 30% of the capitalized value, and the functional managers and workers each accounted for 30%, with the remaining 10% chipped in by the enterprise business partners (*guanxihu*).

38. Even though an open bidding scheme had reportedly been adopted in some villages in the privatization process, the incumbent enterprise manager was invariably the one being offered the contract.

39. Oliver Williamson, *Markets and Hierarchies: Analysis and Antitrust Implications* (New York: Free Press, 1975).

40. Alchian and Demsetz, "Production, Information Costs, and Economic Organization."

41. Moreover, given that detecting shirking in a team context is always expensive, a would-be team member—the person who claims that she will work harder than the one she is replacing—will have the same incentives not to honor her promise once she is given the job.

42. See Harvey Leibenstein, "Allocative Efficiency vs. X-Efficiency," *American Economic Review* 56, 3 (June 1966): 392–415.

43. Based on my fieldwork in 1995, I am not aware of any major social consequences of layoffs in Xinkaihe, as most of the redundant workers were subsequently employed by the village's other, presumably "collective," enterprises.

44. Alchian and Demsetz, "Production, Information Costs, and Economic Organization."

45. Ibid.

46. That said, it should be borne in mind that the shirking problems noted above were not endemic from the beginning; after all, the collectively owned village enterprises had been a powerful engine driving rural economic growth prior to the emergence of competition by private enterprises. The institutional rigidities posed by the property rights nature of village enterprises have become severe only since China's village economy became more competitive.

CHAPTER 6   *Vermeer, Shareholding Cooperatives*

I thank the Dutch-Israeli Developmental Research Foundation for its support of a survey conducted in Shandong and Hebei in 1995 with Zhang Xiaoshan and

Yuan Peng of the Rural Development Institute, Chinese Academy of Social Sciences; and Zhang Xiaoshan also for his helpful comments.

1. Tian Zhen, "Gufen hezuozhi: Xiangzhen qiye gaige yu fazhan de biran xuanze" [The shareholding cooperative system: The necessary choice for reform and development of TVEs], in Han Jun and Zhang Qingzhong, eds., *Zhongguo nongcun gufen hezuo jingji: Lilun, shijian, zhengce* [China's rural shareholding cooperative economy: Theory, practice, policies] (Beijing: Jingji Guanli, 1993), pp. 385–92.

2. Fu Chunsheng et al., eds., *Zhongguo xiangzhen qiye jingying zhengce fagui daquan* [Compendium of policies and regulations for TVE management] (Beijing: Zhongguo Tongji, 1993).

3. The survey covered Zhoucun County and Zunhua Municipality, and included interviews with managers, technicians, workshop heads, accountants, and workers in each visited enterprise (all but three with more than 75 employees), yielding 159 effective respondents from 20 industrial enterprises in Zhoucun and 12 in Zunhua. For details, see E. B. Vermeer, "Experiments with Rural Share-holding Cooperatives: The Case of Zhoucun District, Shandong Province," *China Information* 11, 2 (1996): 75–107.

4. The SSB includes many small SHC enterprises in "rural partnerships" (*nongcun lianying qiye*) and larger ones in "collective enterprises" (*jiti qiye*), but never in "shareholding enterprises" (*gufenzhi jingji qiye*). The first belong to the private/cooperative economy, the second to the collective economy, and the third (a product of the Company Law) fall into a category by themselves. In 1994, the SSB began to distinguish between *xiang-* and *cun-*managed SHC enterprises.

5. Joseph R. Blasi, *Employee Ownership: Revolution or Rip-off?* (Cambridge, Mass.: Ballinger, 1988); John Case, "ESOPs: Dead or Alive?" *Inc.*, June 1988, pp. 94–100.

6. Yuan Peng, "Gufen hezuozhi yu xiangzhen qiye zhidu zhuangxin" [SHCS and renewal of the TVE system], *Zhongguo nongcun jingji* [China's rural economy] 12 (Dec. 1995): 48–52.

7. Liu Jiang, ed., *Zhongguo nongye quanshu: Shandong juan* [Compendium of China's agriculture: Shandong volume] (Beijing: Zhongguo Nongye, 1994), pp. 500–501.

8. Zhang Luoxiong and Wang Qiang, "Nongcun gufen hezuo qiye de fazhan qingkuang ji zhengce jianyi" [The development of the rural SHC enterprises and a policy proposal], *Zhongguo nongcun jingji* 6 (1993): 8–13.

9. Ministry of Agriculture, "Regulations on the contract management responsibility system in TVEs," Apr. 4, 1990, rule 19.

10. Ministry of Agriculture preliminary regulations for rural SHCs, Feb. 12, 1990, in Nongyebu Zhengce Tizhi Gaige Fagui Si, ed., *Nongye fa quanshu* [Complete documentation of agricultural laws] (Beijing: Zhongguo Nongye, 1994), pp. 73–79.

11. *Nongmin ribao* [Farmers' daily], May 18, 1992.

12. Until 1989, Wenzhou maintained the 35% tax rate on private enterprises. See Yu Guoyao, Wen Tiejun, and Zhang Xiaoshan, eds., *Jiushi niandai chanquan zhidu de duice yanjiu: Zhongguo nongcun gufen hezuo jingji zhuanji* [Research into

policies regarding the property rights system in the 1990s: Special collection on China's rural SHC economy] (Beijing: Zhongguo Shangwu, 1994), p. 22.

13. Yuan, "Gufen hezuozhi" (cited n. 6 above).

14. *Zhongguo nongcun jingji* 11 (1992): 3–7.

15. See, e.g., Zhang and Wang, "Nongcun" (cited n. 8 above).

16. The examples I visited in Dalian in 1996 had a strong collectivist character. For an interesting subdivision of such asset-holding companies, see Mu Yongtai and Tan Wei, "Laiyangshi gufen hezuozhi de shijian yu qishi" [Practice and inspiration drawn from the SHCS in Laiyang Municipality], *Zhongguo nongcun jingji* 7 (1993): 47–51.

17. Ministry of Agriculture, "Guanyu tuixing he wanshan xiangzhen qiye gufen hezuozhi de tongzhi" [Circular on promotion and perfection of the SHCS for TVEs], in Liang Yi et al., eds., *Xiangzhen gufen hezuo qiye zujian yu yunzuo* [Establishment and application of township and village SHC enterprises] (Beijing: Zhongguo Jingji, 1993), pp. 306–11.

18. Zhou Jianqiu, "Gufen hezuozhi shi shixian he fazhan gongyouzhi de zhongyao xingshi" [SHCS is an important form for realizing and developing a public ownership system], *Zhongguo nongcun jingji* 12 (1992): 36–41.

19. Yu, Wen, and Zhang, eds., *Jiushi niandai* (cited n. 12 above), pp. 3–7, 13–18.

20. Guo Wei, "Lun nongcun gufen hezuozhi" [About the rural SHCS], *Nongye jingji wenti* [Problems of agricultural economy] 5 (1995): 33–38.

21. Ibid., 33.

22. Average turnover per employee was Y 43,512, and pretax profits per employee amounted to Y 4,077. These figures were Y 8,105 and Y 1,152 respectively above the average for all TVEs. See *Zhongguo qiye guanli nianjian, 1994* [Yearbook of China's enterprise management, 1994] (Beijing: Zhongguo Qiye, 1994), pp. 253–55, and id., *1995*, pp. 232–33, 362–63.

23. Yao Zhiji, "Dui xiangzhen qiye zhidu gaige de sikao" [Thoughts about the TVE system reform], *Nongye jingji* [Agricultural economy] 3 (1995): 39–40.

24. A synopsis of part of the debate may be found in *Zhongguo jingji kexue nianjian, 1994* [Yearbook of China's economic science, 1994] (Beijing: Zhongguo Tongji, 1994), pp. 158–59.

25. Luo Ning and Xiao Mingdi, "Zichan pinggu zhongzai de wenti jiqi duice" [Existing problems and remedies in asset evaluation], *Jingji yanjiu cankao* [References for economic research] 175 (1994): 46–49.

26. *Guowuyuan gongbao* [State Council bulletin], Nov. 15, 1991, asset evaluation rules, par. 4, art. 21–23.

27. Yu, Wen and Zhang, eds., *Jiushi niandai*, pp. 3–7, 13–18, 23; Han Yuanqin et al., "Nongmin gufen hezuo qiye yanjiu baogao" [Research report on farmers' SHCs] (CASS Agricultural Economy Institute, Beijing, Mar. 1994), p. 30.

28. Interviews with Zunhua municipal officials and with Mr. Yun, Zhoucun Accountants' Affairs Office, Sept. 1995.

29. See next note.

30. In 1994, China's township and village SHCs (excluding Guangdong) had fixed assets with an original value of Y 113 billion and liquid (gross) assets totaling Y 131 billion. If fixed assets are corrected for depreciation, the net value

of fixed and liquid assets was only 5% more than the reported total share value of Y 99 billion. Reported 1994 profits were Y 42.3 billion before taxes and Y 25.6 billion after taxes, which gives an average return on shares of 25.7%. Township SHCs gave lower returns (24%) than village SHCs (28%). For 1993, data were given only for pretax profits; they were lower in 1993 (33%) than in 1994 (42%). However, when corrected for inflation with the rural cost-of-living index of 1.126 in 1993 and 1.234 in 1994, real yields declined from 8 to 2%. See Zhongguo xiangzhen qiye nianjian bianji weiyuanhui [China's Rural Enterprise Yearbook Editorial Committee], *Zhongguo xiangzhen qiye nianjian, 1994* [China's rural enterprise yearbook, 1994] (Beijing: Nongye chubanshe, 1994), pp. 362–63, 366–67, and id., *1995*, pp. 232–37.

31. The different types of shareholders and shares in the SHC enterprise and their rights deserve some fuller explanation. Company statutes stipulate the amount and types. As for shareholders, the Ministry of Agriculture's 1992 Circular no. 24 mentioned five types: (1) township- and village-held *collective shares*; (2) *enterprise shares*, based on its accumulated assets (part could be distributed to individual employees as *employee preferred shares*, which are nontransferable and noninheritable); (3) shares held by other units, so-called *social legal person's shares*, on the basis of a (past) investment; (4) *ordinary individual shares*, owned by employees (or outsiders, then called *social individual shares*) who have contributed capital, materials, or technical skills; and (5) *foreign shares*. More recently, "enterprise shares" have been abolished and distributed to employees. There are two types of shares: common (risk-bearing) shares and preferred shares. The latter (sometimes called "empty shares" [*xugu*]) pay fixed dividends, which come before any other distribution of net profits, and their claim to residuals is prior to that of common shareholders, but their holders are not entitled to any of the other rights of common shareholders who have purchased their shares. See Zang Rihong and Cha Zhenxiang, eds., *Nongcun gufen hezuozhi qiye kuaiji hesuan yu caiwu guanli* [Accounting of budgets and financial management in rural SHC enterprises] (Beijing: Zhongguo Nongye, 1995). Some company charters have ruled that preferred shares may be converted into ordinary shares within a given period. In the early years, preferred shares were sometimes given free to the employees. More recently, employees have received such shares only as additions to purchased shares. Shares may be sold at a discount or with a bonus preferred share, but usually are sold at face value.

32. *Zhongguo nongye nianjian, 1994* [Agricultural yearbook of China, 1994] (Beijing: Nongye 1995), p. 129.

33. Han Yuanqin et al., "Nongmin," hold such valuation of state policies to be incorrect. A report by the Production Office of the Structural Reform Committee, *Zhongguo Tigai Yanjiuhui Yanjiu Baogao*, no. 5 (June 20, 1995), notes the dilemma but does not take a stand.

34. Yu, Wen, and Zhang, eds., *Jiushi niandai*, pp. 3–7, 13–18, 23; Han Yuanqin et al., "Nongmin," p. 30.

35. Yu, Wen, and Zhang, eds., *Jiushi niandai*, pp. 148–49.

36. Interview with Bi Jinxian, head of Wangcun *zhen* government, Aug. 29, 1995.

37. Average holdings of managers and common workers differed by a factor of 6 in Zunhua (Y35,800 and Y6,000 respectively) and a factor of 4 in Zhoucun (Y14,170 and Y3,540 respectively). In Zunhua, workshop heads, technicians, and accountants formed an intermediate layer of stockholders, with averages of from Y10,000 to Y12,000. In Zhoucun, these three categories owned little more than the common workers; technicians and workshop heads averaged less than Y5,000 and accountants about Y6,500. It should be noted that some of the largest shareholder-managers (one with over Y1,000,000 in shares) refused to be included in our sample. Because of our small sample size, the few large shareholder-managers had a great effect on the Zhoucun and Zunhua averages.

38. Art. 6 of the State Council rules on rural collective enterprises, dated June 3, 1990, states: "Provided the collective ownership form is not changed, rural collective enterprises may absorb investment that is put into shares."

39. "Because individual shares cannot be sold, transferred, mortgaged or circulated, they are not ordinary private property, but a form of socialist private property," notes Shi Yueqin. "Guanyu Shenzhenshi Henggangzhen gufen hezuozhi de kaocha baogao" [Investigation report of the SHCS in Henggang town in Shenzhen], *Nongye jingji* 10 (1995): 28–29.

40. "According to regulations, the collective should own half of the shares.... Some places convert the collective assets at current market value to create a share fund, and allow employees to buy shares. This belies the principle of one-man one-share. Other places distinguish between two types of allocated shares, one on the basis of capital and another per person. This is wrong, too.... The SHCS is characterized by the equal combination of labor and capital, and should have one share per employee in order to stimulate the workers," states Shi Yueqin. "Dui nongcun jiti qiye tuixing gufen hezuozhi jige juti wenti de renzhi" [Understanding of some concrete problems in the promotion of the SHCS for rural collective enterprises], *Nongye jingji* 11 (1995): 23–24.

41. The sequence of profit distribution, after compensation for losses, is as follows: (1) 10% of after-tax profits to the public accumulation fund, as required by law; (2) the common welfare fund for collective employee welfare; (3) priority shareholders; (4) public accumulation fund, according to company regulations and decision of the shareholders' meeting; (5) ordinary share dividends (Zang and Cha, eds., *Nongcun gufen* [cited n. 31 above], pp. 6, 257–59).

42. Zhoucun ruled that 50 to 60% of profits should be retained by the enterprise for reinvestment, 10% should go to welfare, and 30 to 40% should be distributed as dividends (to a maximum of 20% of the nominal share value). Malanyu *zhen* (in Zunhua) ruled that this ratio should be 4:2:4. Zunhua County had ruled that about 25% should be retained, 30% distributed as a cash dividend, 30% paid as a stock dividend, and 15% allocated to employee bonuses and welfare. Interviews with municipal officials, Sept. 1995.

43. Wenzhou ruled that 15% should be retained in the public accumulation fund, 50% should be distributed in stock dividends, 10% should go to welfare, and a maximum of 25% should be paid in cash dividends (including interest). Some places in Wenzhou allowed share capital to be paid back to investors before taxes (this went at the expense of tax revenues). See Yu, Wen and Zhang,

eds., *Jiushi niandai,* pp. 3–7, 13–18, 23; Han Yuanqin et al., "Nongmin," p. 30; Zhoucun interviews.

44. In principle, no dividend should be paid if there are no profits. However, shareholders may decide to distribute a maximum of 6% of the nominal share value from the public accumulation fund, as long as it does not drop below 25% of the registered capital. See Zang Rihong and Cha Zhenxiang, eds., *Nongcun gufen hezuozhi qiye kuaiji hesuan yu caiwu guanli* [Accounting of budgets and financial management in rural SHC enterprises] (Beijing: Zhongguo nongye chubanshe, 1995).

CHAPTER 7   *Lin and Chen, Local Elites as Officials and Owners*

1. Calculated from data in *Zhongguo tongji nianjian, 1995* [Statistical yearbook of China, 1995] (Beijing: Zhongguo tongji chubanshe, 1995), pp. 85, 375.

2. *Zhongguo nongye nianjian, 1985* [Agricultural yearbook of China, 1985] (Beijing: Nongye chubanshe, 1986), p. 2.

3. See "Company Law of the People's Republic of China," in *PRC Year Book, 1995* (Beijing: PRC Year Book Ltd., 1996), pp. 138–87.

4. Art. 21, in ibid., p. 140.

5. Art. 81, in ibid., p. 147.

6. Information from fieldwork conducted by the second author, 1996. See also Xie Zifen and Ling Yaochu, *Xiangzhen qiye yunxing jizhi yanjiu* [Research on the operating mechanisms of township and village enterprises] (Shanghai: Shanghai Academy of Social Sciences, 1994).

7. See, e.g., Yu Zuomin, "Zongjingli de baogao" [Report of the CEO] (Daquizhuang: mimeographed, 1988); "Daqiuzhuang jueqi de mimi" [The secrets of the rise of Daqiuzhuang] (Daquizhuang: mimeographed, 1988); "Sishinian de zhuiqiu" [Forty years' pursuit] (Daquizhuang: mimeographed, 1988); and "Shijian he gouxiang" [Implementation and conceptualization] (Daquizhuang: mimeographed, 1989).

8. All figures are based on reports produced by Daqiuzhuang or verbal reports by the various officers and informants interviewed. There has not been any external validity check, and the figures can only be seen as rough estimates.

9. This section is based on a personal interview with Liu Wanmin, June 1994.

10. See Nan Lin and Mai-shou Hao, "Getting Rich First: The Story of Daqiuzhuang: A Case Study of Rural Development in China" (MS, Department of Sociology, Duke University, Durham, N.C., 1991); Nan Lin, "Local Market Socialism: Local Corporatism in Action in Rural China," *Theory and Society* 24, 3 (June 1995): 301–54.

11. A fifth group was later created for the agricultural sector.

12. See Nan Lin, "Local Market Socialism," n. 90.

13. See ibid., and Nan Lin and Mai-shou Hao, "Getting Rich First."

14. One report suggested that he uncovered corruption and intended to report on Yu (*New York Times,* Mar. 31, 1993), but this cannot be confirmed from other sources.

15. *Shijie ribao* [World journal], May 7, 1993.

16. *Renmin ribao* [People's daily], Aug. 28, 1993.

17. Interview with Wei Zongjin, the newly appointed Party secretary of the town, June 1994.

18. The central command system only reaches down to the town level, where all officials are directly appointed from the county government.

19. *Renmin ribao* (overseas ed.), Feb. 22, 1994.

20. The name Daqiuzhuang Agricultural-Industrial-Commercial United Corporation was changed to Daqiuzhuang General Corporation in the early 1990s.

21. All workers since the mid 1980s have been from outside the village; all Daqiuzhuang residents had become managers by then.

22. All the original shares were apparently bought back for their original cash values.

23. From the description of the Company Law, both these systems (the limited liability companies and the joint-stock limited companies) fit the description of the joint-stock limited system, in that individual shares are issued, all shares are of equal value, and total assets exceed the minimal requirement. The variation is that one system allows shareholders to come from outside the company, whereas the other only distributes shares to insiders.

24. The figures given and the claims made do not coincide. They are presented here to indicate the economic scale and the effort entailed.

25. In 1993, Group J produced 170,000 tons of steel. In 1994, it produced 360,000 tons, and in 1995, 600,000 tons (even excluding a new factory, which produced 100,000 tons, it still increased production by 140,000 tons). In 1995, it made a profit of Y120 million.

26. It is not clear to us what the General Group proposed to do with profits from sales of the collective shares over time. We doubt that it would have returned the money to the town or county.

27. Group Y is also exploring another method: the joint-stock system. For the bigger, more profitable enterprises, the joint-stock method would be used to absorb more cash and technology. For example, the group's steel plate plant attracted twelve outside companies as customers, who contributed Y230,000,000 of the total of Y660,000,000 yuan to establish a second thin-plate steel plant with a production goal of 120,000 tons per month. Another company, the JinMeng Steel Tube Plant, has amassed assets of Y120,000,000 in cooperation with an Inner Mongolian company. This system has no individual shares.

28. As of May 1996, the Big Four had not yet committed to any formal plan regarding payment of the debts left by the fifth group. In interviews, group officials all demurred about any such plan.

29. Ostensibly, it could be argued that the elites of the groups represented the street committees, and therefore the collectives. But the reality is that they controlled the collective shares representing the enterprise, rather than the street committee. It is clear to everyone in Daqiuzhuang that the Big Four, not the street committee or the Party, controlled the streets, the population, and the land. The elite identified themselves first and foremost as leaders of the Big Four, and only secondarily as directors of street committees and Party secretaries.

CHAPTER 8 *Whiting, Regional Evolution of Ownership*

1. For a definition of property rights, see Chapter 1 of this volume.

2. Promotion, status, and job security were among the top priorities of leaders in two sets of village surveys, as shown by Scott Rozelle, "Decision-Making in China's Rural Economy," *China Quarterly*, no. 137 (Mar. 1994): 99–124.

3. Space limitations preclude a full treatment of the incentive structure of local officials. For a detailed analysis, see Susan H. Whiting, *Power and Wealth in China's Rural Industry: The Political Economy of Institutional Change* (New York: Cambridge University Press, forthcoming).

4. Under the incentive structure outlined above, local officials might be expected to prefer collective enterprises, all else being equal. While the township government was paid taxes and fees by all rural enterprises, as the owner of township-run collectives, it also received profit remittances from these firms. Furthermore, as owner, the local government faced lower information costs in extracting revenue from these firms.

5. John M. Litwack, "Legality and Market Reform in Soviet-Type Economies," *Journal of Economic Perspectives* 5, no. 4 (Fall 1991): 78.

6. Douglass C. North, *Institutions, Institutional Change and Economic Performance* (New York: Cambridge University Press, 1990), p. 6. See also Donald C. Clarke, "Regulation and Its Discontents," *Stanford Journal of International Law* 28, no. 2 (1992).

7. Yang Chungui, "Make an Effort to Grasp the Dialectics of Socialist Modernization—Studying Comrade Jiang Zemin's 'Correctly Handle Several Major Relationships in the Socialist Modernization Drive,'" *Renmin ribao* [People's daily], Nov. 6, 1995, trans. in FBIS-CH-95-241 (Dec. 15, 1995): 17.

8. See also Victor Nee, "The Emergence of a Market Society: Changing Mechanisms of Stratification in China," *American Journal of Sociology* 101, no. 4 (Jan. 1996).

9. A vast secondary literature has emerged on the Wenzhou model; among the best accounts are He Rongfei, ed., *Wenzhou jingji geju* [The structure of the Wenzhou economy] (Wenzhou: Zhejiang renmin chubanshe, 1987); Zhang Renshou and Li Hong, "Wenzhou moshi" [The Wenzhou model], in Zhang Liuzheng, ed., *Zhongguo nongcun jingji fazhan tansuo* [An exploration of China's rural economic development] (Beijing: Zhongguo jingji chubanshe, 1990), pp. 88–179; and Zhang Renshou and Li Hong, *Wenzhou moshi yanjiu* [Research on the Wenzhou model] (Beijing: Zhongguo shehui kexue chubanshe, 1990). For a full set of references, see Whiting, *Power and Wealth.*

10. *Songjiang xianzhi* [Gazetteer of Songjiang County] (Shanghai: Shanghai renmin chubanshe, 1991); and *Yueqing sishi nian* [Forty years in Yueqing] (Yueqing: Yueqing xian tongjiju, 1989).

11. For a more detailed treatment of this issue, see Whiting, *Power and Wealth.*

12. Zhang and Li, *Wenzhou moshi yanjiu* (cited n. 9 above), p. 32; and *Yueqing sishi nian* (cited in n. 10 above), p. 107.

13. These guises included household firms affiliated with collectives (*guahu*), joint-household firms (*lianhu*)—considered a type of cooperative (*hezuo jing-*

ying), individual household firms (*getihu*), private partnerships (*siren hezuo qiye*), and shareholding cooperative enterprises (*gufen hezuo qiye*), as well as individual and private firms that falsely registered as collectives.

14. Reports indicate that private entrepreneurs who remained in business through the mid 1980s were unwilling to increase their investments beyond a limited scale. See, e.g., Zhang Gensheng et al., "Wenzhou moshi yu ruogan zhengce wenti" [The Wenzhou model and several policy issues], in Lin Bai et al., eds., *Wenzhou moshi de lilun tansuo* [A theoretical exploration of the Wenzhou model] (Nanning: Guangxi renmin chubanshe, 1987), pp. 20–35.

15. The other two tracks developed regulations governing household enterprises affiliated with township- and village-run collectives and shareholding cooperatives respectively.

16. This action was preceded in April by a constitutional revision recognizing the legitimacy of private enterprise. For the revised text of the constitution, see "Zhonghua renmin gongheguo xianfa xiuzheng'an" [People's Republic of China constitutional revisions], in *Zhongguo nongye nianjian, 1989* [Agricultural yearbook of China, 1989] (Beijing: Nongye chubanshe, 1989), p. 538. For the regulations, see "Zhonghua renmin gongheguo siying qiye zhanxing tiaoli" [Provisional regulations for private enterprise], *Jingji ribao* [Economic daily], June 29, 1988, p. 2.

17. See State Council document, 1989, #60, "Guanyu dali jiaqiang chengxiang geti gongshanghu he siying qiye shuishou zhengguan gongzuo de jueding" [Decision regarding vigorously strengthening tax collection work in urban and rural individual industrial and commercial enterprises and private enterprises], *Guowuyuan gongbao* [State Council bulletin], no. 16 (Sept. 20, 1989): 626–29.

18. Central Committee document, 1989, #11, "Guanyu jinyibu zhili zhengdun he shenhua gaige de jueding" [Decision regarding advancing rectification and deepening reforms], in Guojia tigaiwei bangongting, *Shiyijie sanzhong quanhui yilai jingji tizhi gaige zhongyao wenjian huibian* [Compendium of important documents on economic system reform since the Third Plenum) (Beijing: Gaige chubanshe, 1990), 3: 598–99.

19. Yang, "Dialectics of Socialist Modernization" (cited n. 7 above), p. 17.

20. Gao Kuanzhong, "Wending he fazhan nongcun geti, siying jingji de ruogan wenti tantao" [An inquiry into several questions on stabilizing and developing the rural individual and private economies], in Nongyebu jingji zhengce yanjiu zhongxin [Ministry of Agriculture Economic Policy Research Center], *Zhongguo nongcun: Zhengce yanjiu beiwanglu* [Rural China: Policy research memorandum] (Beijing: Nongye chubanshe, 1991), 2: 310–20. Informant 174 indicated that researchers at the Zhejiang Academy of Social Sciences reached the same conclusion.

21. Informant 149.

22. Gao, "Wending he fazhan nongcun geti, siying jingji de ruogan wenti tantao" (cited n. 20 above).

23. Informant 171.

24. Informants 148, 149, 155, 169.

25. Based on 1991 county-level data from *Zhejiangsheng tongji nianjian, 1992*

[Zhejiang province statistical yearbook, 1992 (Beijing: Zhongguo tongji chuban-she, 1993)] for all counties in Zhejiang Province (where Yueqing County is lo-cated), the scale of working capital loans in each county was positively cor-related with the share of collective industry in the county and negatively correlated with the share of private industry. Correlation coefficients are .36 and −.31 respectively.

26. A 1989 survey reported that access to capital was the biggest problem facing 63% of private entrepreneurs during the start-up period, and that it continued to be the biggest problem facing 56% of the entrepreneurs even once they became established. Subsequent surveys supported these findings. See Zhonggong zhongyang nongcun yanjiushi [Central Committee Rural Policy Research Office], "Dui baijia nongcun siying qiye diaocha de chubu fenxi" [An initial analysis of a survey of one hundred rural private enterprises], *Nongye jingji wenti* [Problems of agricultural economy], no. 2 (1989): 18–23. See also the findings of a survey commissioned by the All-China Federation of Industry and Commerce reported by Agence France-Presse, Oct. 21, 1994, reproduced in *China News Digest*, Oct. 23–25, 1994. Findings from a sample of rural enterprises in Zhejiang and Sichuan studied in 1989 offer further confirmation of the prob-lems private enterprises faced in gaining access to capital. The median size of loans was ¥123,700 for township enterprises, ¥43,000 for village enterprises, and ¥18,000 for private enterprises, while the mean size of loans was ¥299,649, ¥218,873, and ¥58,996 respectively (Per Ronnas and Zhang Gang, "The Capital Structure of Township Enterprises" [MS, Stockholm, 1993], cited in Jiahua Che and Yingyi Qian, "Understanding China's Township-Village Enterprises" [MS, Stanford University, Nov. 1995], p. 21).

27. Informants 149, 158, and 159.

28. Informant 158.

29. Private banks have only recently begun to develop on a new basis. The main focus here is on the allocation of credit through the state banking system; a complete discussion of alternative sources of credit is beyond the scope of this chapter. On the experience in Wenzhou, see Yuan Enzhen, ed., *Wenzhou moshi yu fuyu zhi lu* [The Wenzhou model and the road to affluence] (Shanghai: Shanghai shehui kexueyuan chubanshe, 1987), pp. 98–122; and Zhang and Li, *Wenzhou moshi yanjiu* (cited n. 9 above), pp. 128–45. On nonstate financial institutions, see On-kit Tam, "A Private Bank in China," *China Quarterly*, no. 131 (Sept. 1992): 766–77; id., "Capital Market Development in China," *World Development* 19, 5 (1991): 511–32; Thiagarajan Manoharan, "Credit and Financial Institutions at the Rural Level in China," in E. B. Vermeer, ed., *From Peasant to Entrepreneur: Growth and Change in Rural China. Papers Originating from the Second European Conference on Agriculture and Rural Development in China, Leiden, January 14–17, 1991* (Wageningen, Neth.: Pudoc, 1992), pp. 183–216.

30. Informants 149 and 156.

31. Informant 169. See also He, *Wenzhou jingji geju* (cited n. 9 above).

32. "[V]oluntary, cooperative operations in industry and commerce . . . have emerged in quite a few places," noted a 1983 State Council document, "Guanyu chengzhen laodongzhe hezuo jingying de ruogan guiding" [Several

regulations regarding cooperative ventures among laborers in cities and towns], in Nongmuyuyebu zhengce yanjiushi [Policy Research Office, Ministry of Agriculture], *Nongcun shiyong fagui shouce* [Handbook of commonly used rural laws and regulations) (Beijing: Falü chubanshe, 1987), p. 724.

33. He, *Wenzhou jingji geju,* pp. 69–75. Informants 164 and 165.

34. Informant 247.

35. Zhonggong zhongyang [Central Committee], "Dangqian nongcun jingji zhengce de ruogan wenti" [Several questions regarding current rural enterprise policy], in *Nongcun shiyong fagui shouce* (cited n. 32 above), pp. 68–83.

36. "Rugu de zijin huo qita caiwu *reng shu geren suo you*" [emphasis added] ("Guanyu chengzhen laodongzhe hezuo jingying de ruogan guiding" [cited n. 32 above], p. 724).

37. Profits were to be divided among dividends, labor compensation, and enterprise accumulation and welfare funds, with the relative weights of the last three items to be decided by the members of the cooperative (ibid., p. 725). The issue of the proper distribution of profits, including the acceptability of paying dividends on assets, was established in Central Committee document, 1983, #1, ch. 4.

38. A precursor can be found in mutual aid teams and lower-level agricultural producers cooperatives prior to 1955.

39. Wenzhou Municipal Government document, 1987, #79, "Guanyu nongcun gufen hezuo qiye ruogan wenti de zhanxing guiding" [Provisional regulations on several questions regarding rural shareholding cooperatives]. The term "accumulation fund" refers to assets that could not be liquidated or claimed as the personal property of the investors; however, it is important to note that this portion of the assets did *not* belong to the local government but rather to the firm as a collective entity. Later regulations clarified that in the event of the dissolution of the firm, that portion of the assets accounted for under the accumulation fund could be applied to a variety of uses at the discretion of the owners. However, that portion of the assets could not be liquidated or distributed to either the individual owners or the workers. The approved uses for such assets included developing a new enterprise, investing in an existing enterprise, developing agriculture, or establishing an independent welfare and insurance fund for firm employees. Wenzhou Municipal Government document, 1990, #5, "Rizhuan 'guanyu gufen hezuo qiye guifanhua ruogan zhengce guiding de baogao'" [Notice of the approval and transmission of "Report regarding several policy regulations on the standardization of cooperative stock enterprises"], in Yueqingxian tizhi gaige weiyuanhui [Yueqing County System Reform Commission], *Gufen hezuo jingji wenjian huibian* [A collection of documents on the cooperative shareholding economy] (n.p., 1991), pp. 28–33.

40. Ministry of Agriculture document, 1990, #14, "Nongmin gufen hezuo qiye zanxing guiding" [Provisional regulations on rural shareholding cooperatives], *Guowuyuan gongbao,* no. 4 (Mar. 23, 1990): 121–28.

41. Ministry of Agriculture document, 1992, #24, "Guanyu tuixing he wanshan xiangzhen qiye gufen hezuozhi de tongzhi" [Notice regarding promoting and improving the cooperative shareholding system in rural enterprises], in

Zhongguo xiangzhen qiye nianjian bianji weiyuanhui [China's Rural Enterprise Yearbook Editorial Committee], *Zhongguo xiangzhen qiye nianjian, 1993* [China's rural enterprise yearbook, 1993] (Beijing: Nongye chubanshe, 1993), pp. 134–36.

42. This corresponds to the concept of ambiguous property rights analyzed by David Li; however, in Yueqing, this framework was ultimately rejected by most private investors in favor of the more explicit shareholding cooperative framework. See David D. Li, "A Theory of Ambiguous Property Rights in Transition Economies," *Journal of Comparative Economics* 23, 1 (Aug. 1996): 1–19.

43. Clarke, "Regulation and Its Discontents," p. 305. This problem is also discussed in Du Yan et al., "Zhongguo nongcun gaige shiyan qu 1989 nian bannian gongzuo baogao" [1989 mid-year work report on China's rural reform experimental zones], *Fazhan yanjiu tongxun* [Development research bulletin], no. 125 (Oct. 30, 1989): 1015–44. See also Nongyebu jingji zhengce yanjiu zhongxin, *Zhongguo nongcun* (cited n. 20 above), esp. 1: 371–85.

44. Informants 146 and 147. These two formerly fake collective enterprises had been founded with private investments and were later taken over by a township and a village respectively—with the original investors receiving compensation only for the value of their initial investments and not for the full value of the firm at the time it was taken over.

45. See State Council document, 1989, #60, in *Guowuyuan gongbao* (cited n. 17 above).

46. For the local regulations applying to Wenzhou, see Zhejiang Province Industrial-Commercial Administrative Management Bureau document, 1989, #21, "Guanyu qingli 'jia jiti' he dui hezuo jingying qiye ruhe dengji guanli de tongzhi" [Notice regarding cleaning up "fake collectives" and how to manage registration of share-holding cooperatives], in *Gufen hezuo jingji wenjian huibian* (cited n. 39 above), pp. 52–54.

47. Informant 159. In February 1992, Deng Xiaoping's "southern tour" (*nanxun*) marked a significant liberalization of policy toward *siying qiye* in Yueqing and elsewhere.

48. Yueqing County can approve transactions involving up to 3 mu, Wenzhou Municipality up to 5 mu, and Zhejiang Province up to 10 mu. Informant 243.

49. Informant 148. See also Yueqingxian [Yueqing County], "Guifanhua gufen hezuo qiye ruogan zhengce buchong guiding de tongzhi" [Notice on several supplemental policy regulations for standardization of shareholding cooperatives], in Yueqingxian tizhi gaige weiyuanhui, *Gufen hezuo jingji wenjian huibian* (cited in n. 39 above), pp. 55–59.

50. Informant 235.

51. These include both the relevant production bureau (*chanpin guikou guanli bumen*) and the local economic commission (*difang jingwei*). See State Council, "Gongye chanpin shengchan xukezheng shixing tiaoli" [Implementing rules for production permits for industrial products], in *Nongcun shiyong fagui shouce* (cited in n. 32 above), pp. 773–76.

52. See Wenzhou Municipal Government document, "Guanyu nongcun gufen hezuo qiye ruogan wenti de zanxing guiding" [Provisional regulations

regarding several questions concerning rural cooperative shareholding enterprises], art. 19; and Wenzhou Municipal Government document, 1989, #35, "Guanyu gufen hezuo qiye guifanhua ruogan wenti de tongzhi" [Notice regarding several questions concerning the standardization of cooperative shareholding enterprises], in Yueqingxian tizhi gaige weiyuanhui, *Gufen hezuo jingji wenjian huibian* (cited n. 39 above), p. 25.

53. Zhao Shunpeng, "Yueqing gufenzhi qiye shiqinian fazhan toushi" [A perspective on seventeen years of development of the shareholding system in Yueqing] (MS, Yueqing tigaiwei [Yueqing System Reform Commission], 1996), pp. 3–4.

54. Informants 151, 155, 156, 236, 237, 239, and 240. By contrast, a private enterprise owner complained in 1992 about the absence of such support from the town industry office (informant 149).

55. Informant 164.

56. Ibid.

57. Informants 149, 152, and 247. See also Yueqingxian, "Guifanhua gufen hezuo qiye ruogan zhengce buchong guiding de tongzhi" (cited n. 49 above), pp. 56–59.

58. Informant 247.

59. As noted in Table 8.1, the output of shareholding cooperatives is reported explicitly for Yueqing County. For Songjiang County, the output of shareholding cooperatives in which the township or village is the dominant shareholder is included under township- or village-run collectives respectively.

60. See also the reference to Li Peng's dissatisfaction with the handling of shareholding cooperatives in Liu Xirong, "Guanyu fazhan gufen hezuo jingji de jige wenti" [Several questions regarding the development of the cooperative shareholding economy], in Yueqingxian tizhi gaige weiyuanhui, *Gufen hezuo jingji wenjian huibian* (cited n. 39 above), p. 5.

61. Wenzhou Muncipal Government document, 1989, #35, "Guanyu gufen hezuo qiye guifanhua ruogan wenti de tongzhi" (cited n. 52 above).

62. Liu, "Guanyu fazhan gufen hezuo jingji de jige wenti" (cited n. 60 above).

63. Moreover, most of the relevant tax privileges were to be phased out after 1994.

64. "Guanyu gufen hezuo qiye guifanhua ruogan wenti de tongzhi" (cited in n. 52 above); and id., "Gufen hezuo qiye shifan zhangcheng" [Model charter for shareholding cooperatives], in Yueqingxian tizhi gaige weiyuanhui, *Gufen hezuo jingji wenjian huibian* (cited in n. 39 above), pp. 60–65.

65. For a more detailed analysis of the early development of commune and brigade enterprises, see Whiting, *Power and Wealth.*

66. Wang Xiaolu, "Capital Formation and Utilization," in William A. Byrd and Lin Qingsong, eds., *China's Rural Industry: Structure, Development, and Reform* (New York: Oxford University Press, 1990), p. 229.

67. State Council document, 1979, #170, "Guanyu fazhan shedui qiye ruogan wenti de guiding (shixing cao'an)" [Regulations regarding several questions about the development of commune and brigade enterprises (provisional draft)], in Zhongguo xiangzhen qiye nianjian bianji weiyuanhui [China's Rural

Enterprise Yearbook Editorial Committee], *Zhongguo xiangzhen qiye nianjian, 1978–87* [China's rural enterprise yearbook, 1978–87] (Beijing: Nongye chubanshe, 1989), p. 428. This document was circulated on July 3, 1979. For a concise summary of the historical background of township- and village-run collectives, see William A. Byrd and Lin Qingsong, "China's Rural Industry: An Introduction," in id., eds., *China's Rural Industry*, pp. 9–11.

68. Central Committee document, 1983, #35, "Guanyu shixing zhengshe fenkai jianli xiang zhengfu de tongzhi" [Announcement regarding the implementation of the separation of party and government and the establishment of the township government], in Zhongguo nongye kuaiji xuehui Chongqing fenhui and Chongqingshi caizhengju zhengce yanjiushi [China Rural Accountants' Association Chongqing Branch and Chongqing City Public Finance Bureau Policy Research Office], *Xiangzhen caizheng shouce* [Handbook on township finance] (Chengdu: Sichuan kexue jishu chubanshe, 1987), pp. 1–3.

69. Wang, "Capital Formation and Utilization," in Byrd and Lin, eds., *China's Rural Industry*, p. 229.

70. Informant 97.

71. State Council document, 1979, #170 (cited n. 67 above), directed agricultural banks to set aside funds for low-interest loans to commune- and brigade-run enterprises. See also Agriculture Bank of China document, 1979, #202, "Zhongguo nongye yinhang nongcun shedui qiye daikuan shixing banfa" [Provisional methods for making loans to rural commune and brigade enterprises], in *Zhongguo xiangzhen qiye nianjian, 1978–87* (cited n. 67 above), pp. 487–88.

72. For additional detail on the conditions for loans to rural collectives, see Susan H. Whiting, "Market Discipline and Rural Enterprise in China," in John McMillan and Barry Naughton, eds., *Reforming Asian Socialism: The Growth of Market Institutions* (Ann Arbor: University of Michigan Press, 1996).

73. Qiu Jicheng, "Xiangzhen qiye—shequ (zhengfu) guanli moshi de jiben xiansuo" [Township and village enterprises—the basic threads of the community (government) management model], *Fazhan yanjiu tongxun*, no. 104 (Dec. 1988): 744–68.

74. Although complete data on the sources of working capital are not available, incomplete data suggest that bank loans accounted for an even larger share of capital in that category. See Whiting, "Market Discipline."

75. Informant 99.

76. Informants 83, 96, and 106. See also Xu Heping, "Zhongshi danbao shencha quebao zhaiquan luoshi" [Take seriously the investigation of guarantors, ensure the fulfillment of creditors' rights], *Shanghai nongcun jinrong* [Shanghai rural finance], no. 1 (1992): 42–43.

77. Informants 56, 68, and 70.

78. Informant 97.

79. Fewer than 10% of firms surveyed could control the selection of the manager. See Qiu, "Xiangzhen qiye—shequ (zhengfu) guanli moshi de jiben xiansuo" (cited n. 73 above).

80. Du Haiyan, *Zhongguo nongcun gongyehua yanjiu* [Research on rural industrialization in China] (Hubei: Zhongguo wujia chubanshe, 1992); Du Yan,

"Xiangzhen gongye qiye jingying de shichang huanjing" [The market environment in which rural industrial enterprises operate], *Fazhan yanjiu tongxun*, no. 49 (Feb. 28, 1987): 272–73; Barry Naughton, *Growing Out of the Plan* (New York: Cambridge University Press, 1995).

81. According to Gary H. Jefferson, John Zhiqiang Zhao, and Mai Lu, "Reforming Property Rights: Chinese Industry" (MS, Brandeis University, Apr. 10, 1996), only 16% of firms surveyed in 1991 could control the selection of the manager.

82. Particularly relevant here is a study by Hongyi Chen and Scott Rozelle, "Local Leaders, Managers, and the Organization of Township and Village Enterprises in China" (MS, Stanford University, Jan. 1995).

83. Loren Brandt and Xiaodong Zhu, "Soft Budget Constraints and Inflation Cycles: A Positive Model of the Post-Reform Chinese Economy" (MS, University of Toronto, Oct. 22, 1995), p. 10.

84. Ibid., p. 11. This is a comprehensive assessment based on credit data drawn from all the state-run commercial banks, rural and urban credit cooperatives, and trust and investment companies.

85. Barry Naughton, "China's Macroeconomy in Transition," *China Quarterly*, no. 144 (Dec. 1995): 1097 (emphasis added).

86. See also Brandt and Zhu, "Soft Budget Constraints and Inflation Cycles," who point out that deposits in specialized banks declined at the peak points in the most recent inflation cycles (p. 13).

87. See, e.g., Central Committee document, 1989, #11, "Guanyu jin yibu zhili zhengdun he shenhua gaige de jueding" [Decision regarding advancing rectification and deepening reforms], in *Shiyi jie sanzhong quanhui yilai jingji tizhi gaige zhongyao wenjian* [Compendium of important documents Since the Third Plenum of the Eleventh Central Committee] (Beijing: Gaige chubanshe, 1990), 3: 594–605, which criticizes township- and village-run enterprises for competing with key state-run enterprises for energy and raw materials.

88. Nongmuyuyebu [Ministry of Agriculture], "Guanyu kaichuang shedui qiye xin jumian de baogao" [Report regarding creating a new situation for commune and brigade enterprises], in *Zhongguo xiangzhen qiye nianjian, 1978–87* (cited n. 67 above), p. 423.

89. Informants 1, 3, 37, 76, 103, 192, and 195.

90. Informant 39.

91. Informant 52.

92. Informants 89, 94, and 114.

93. Central Committee, "Resolution on Several Questions About Speeding up Agricultural Development," as translated in Byrd and Lin, eds., *China's Rural Industry*, p. 10. See also State Council document, 1979, #170 (cited n. 67 above).

94. Barry Naughton, *Growing Out of the Plan*, p. 147.

95. Shanghai jiaoqu nongcun gufen hezuozhi yanjiu ketizu [Research group on rural shareholding cooperatives in the Shanghai suburbs], "Shanghai jiaoqu nongcun gufen hezuo ruogan wenti yanjiu" [Research on several issues regarding rural shareholding cooperatives in the Shanghai suburbs], *Caijing yanjiu* [Financial research], no. 6 (1993): 24–30.

96. There were 1,666 industrial enterprises: 404 township-run; 871 village-run; 27 team-run; 15 joint household-run; and 349 private (informant 111).

97. Informants 89 and 94.

98. Even as of 1996, the political debate continued over the political status of shareholding cooperatives in cases in which private individuals or corporate entities other than the local government owned the majority of shares. A front-page editorial in *Jingji ribao*, Mar. 29, 1996, defended these firms against charges that they were private and not public in nature and that they represented the privatization of public assets.

99. Central Committee document, 1987, #5, "Ba nongcun gaige yinxiang shenru (zhaiyao)" [Deepening rural reforms (abstract)], in *Zhongguo xiangzhen qiye nianjian, 1978–87* (cited n. 67 above), pp. 518–21.

100. Li Huigen, Wu Hongbin, and Xiong Shiping, "Shanghai jiaoqu nongcun gufen hezuozhi shidian qingkuang de diaocha" [Investigation into the situation of rural share-holding cooperative experiments in the Shanghai suburbs], *Caijing yanjiu* [Financial research], no. 6 (1993): 31–35.

101. Zhonggong Chuansha xianwei zhengce yanjiushi [Chuansha County Party Committee Policy Research Office], "Guanyu Chuansha yinran jixie chang shixing gufen hezuozhi de diaocha he sikao" [An investigation into and reflections on the implementation of the cooperative shareholding system in the Chuansha Printing and Dyeing Machinery Factory], *Chuansha diaoyan* [Chuansha investigation and research], no. 7 (Apr. 20, 1991): 1–11.

102. Informant 2. This client accounted for 80% of sales in 1989. In 1990, orders by the same client were cut by 70% (falling from Y16 million to Y4.8 million).

103. Technically, the shares were held by the township *jingji lianheshe* (economic conglomerate), which was essentially run by the township Party secretary (informant 23). The Chuansha County Party Committee Research Office's investigation (cited n. 101 above), p. 2, indicated that Y500,000 was only a portion of the township's investment in the firm. An additional Y1.56 million in township investment was treated as an interest-bearing loan, with interest to be accounted for as a cost to be paid out of pretax earnings. This arrangement was explicitly intended to minimize the risk to the township if the enterprise should perform poorly. Indeed, in the first two years under the cooperative stock system, interest payments on the "loan" and dividend payments on township shares exceeded the level of profit remittances the township would have received under the old system.

104. At the same time, an additional Y500,000 in existing township investment was converted into shares held by the township (informant 24). This preserved the township's majority control of voting shares.

105. However, the combined payment of interest and dividends on employees' shares could not exceed 30% of the shares' face value in this experiment.

106. Since these interest payments could have been deducted as costs, they would have constituted a means of paying private owners out of pretax profits (informant 154).

107. Zhonggong Chuansha xianwei zhengce yanjiushi, "Guanyu Chuansha

yinran jixie chang shixing gufen hezuozhi de diaocha he sikao" (cited n. 101 above).

108. Chen Jianguang, "Xiangzhen qiye gufen hezuozhi wenti tansuo" [An exploration of questions on the cooperative share-holding system in rural enterprises], in Zhongguo xiangzhen qiye nianjian bianji weiyuanhui [China's Rural Enterprise Yearbook Editorial Committee], *Zhongguo xiangzhen qiye nianjian, 1995* [China's rural enterprise yearbook, 1995] (Beijing: Nongye chubanshe, 1995), pp. 342–44.

109. As the report "Research on . . . Rural Shareholding Cooperatives in the Shanghai Suburbs" (cited n. 95 above) put it, the experiments broke through "the old method of 'the collective builds the factory; the farmers do the work, and when they have money, they put it in the bank' [*jiti ban chang, nongmin zuogong; nongmin youqian, cunru yinhang*]" by directly attracting funds from employees, local residents, and society more broadly.

110. Such shares accounted for only about 10% of all employee-held shares as of 1992. See Li, Wu, and Xiong, "Shanghai jiaoqu nongcun gufen hezuozhi shidian qingkuang de diaocha" (cited n. 100 above), pp. 31–35.

111. "Shanghai jiaoqu nongcun gufen hezuo ruogan wenti yanjiu" (cited n. 95 above).

112. Informant 214. Note that shareholding cooperatives were treated in the context of speeding up economic development and not in the context of increasing enterprise autonomy or improving enterprise efficiency.

113. As of August 1996, according to informant 214, the interest rate paid was approximately 11%, while the dividend rate was 25% on average, which contributed to the unsustainability of this model.

114. Informant 217. See also Songjiang County government document, 1994, #31, "Guanyu gongye shengchan jingji zerenzhi buchong yijian" [A supplemental opinion on the economic responsibility system for industrial production] (mimeographed, Mar. 16, 1994); and Songjiang County government document, 1995, #101, "Guanyu gongye shengchan zerenzhi jiuwu niandu buchong yijian" [A supplemental opinion on the 1995 industrial production responsibility system] (mimeographed, June 16, 1995).

115. Songjiang County executive, "Zai woxian qiye gaizhi gongzuo huiyishang de jianghua" [Speech at the work conference on enterprise reform] (mimeographed, Aug. 15, 1996).

116. Guowuyuan yanjiushi diaochazu [State Council Research Office Investigation Group], "Zhejiang Wenzhou shixing gufen hezuo qiye de qingkuang" [The situation surrounding the implementation of shareholding cooperatives in Wenzhou, Zhejiang] (mimeographed, Sept. 8, 1989).

CHAPTER 9   *Lin and Zhang, Backyard Profit Centers*

We thank Andrew Walder and Jean Oi for comments and suggestions that have helped sharpen the focus of this chapter.

1. Song Defu, ed., *Dangdai Zhongguo de renshi guanli* [Personnel management in contemporary China] (Beijing: Dangdai Zhongguo chubanshe, 1994), 2: 430–33.

2. For a discussion of the profit-seeking entities sponsored by organizationally independent *shiye danwei*, see Chapter 10 in this volume.

3. Under the pre-reform system, the term *gongsi* was mainly used in the names of commercial organizations (e.g., *baihuo gongsi*, "department store"). Nearly all industrial organizations were called *gongchang*, or factories. Because most of the economic entities set up by state agencies in their backyards in the early 1980s were engaged in commercial activities, they were referred to, along with many similar organizations set up by nonstate parties, as *gongsi* to indicate the nature of their business. However, after 1989, this usage gradually vanished, probably because of the difficulty of ascertaining the nature of the increasingly diverse economic activities carried out by various organizations using this term in their names. Since the enactment of the Company Law (Gongsi fa) in January 1994, *shiti* has been the most widely used term to refer to state agencies' backyard profit centers.

4. Fei Kailong and Zuo Ping, eds., *Dangdai Zhongguo de gongshang xingzheng guanli* [Industrial and commercial administration in contemporary China] (Beijing: Dangdai Zhongguo chubanshe, 1991), p. 164.

5. *Zhongguo gongshang bao* [Industrial and commercial news of China], Sept. 11, 1989.

6. There are two borderline cases in this regard: (i) school-run enterprises under the Education Department, and (ii) welfare enterprises employing handicapped persons under the Civil Administration Department. Although these departments are not in charge of economic activities, they have been given formal permission to set up and run these two types of enterprises.

7. Wang Sibin and Wang Hansheng, eds., *Jiequ jingji, zhengfu, yu shehui* [Government, economy, and society in an urban district] (Beijing: Shehui chubanshe, forthcoming).

8. Because of this, the salaries and benefits received by their employees are not necessarily in line with those of the employees in their sponsoring agencies.

9. In official statistics, extra-budgetary funds are further divided into three categories: (i) various surcharges levied or controlled by the finance departments of local governments; (ii) various fees collected by state agencies; and (iii) retained profits and depreciation and maintenance funds of state-owned enterprises, which are partially controlled by the supervising agencies of these enterprises. While (iii) accounts for the largest share of extra-budgetary funds, (ii) has the largest and fastest growing number of items and is most open to discretionary uses. Starting from 1994, (iii) is no longer included in official statistics on extra-budgetary funds. See Deng Yingtao, Yao Gang, Xu Xiaobo, and Xue Yuwei, *Zhongguo yusuan wai zijin fenxi* [An analysis of China's extra-budgetary funds] (Beijing: Zhongguo renmin daxue chubanshe, 1990).

10. Guojia tongji ju, *Zhongguo tongji nianjian, 1994* [Statistical yearbook of China, 1994] (Beijing: Zhongguo tongji chubanshe, 1994), p. 221.

11. Deng et al., *Zhongguo yusuan wai zijin fenxi*.

12. Guowuyuan fazhi ju, *Zhonghua renmin gongheguo fagui huibian 1989.1–12* [A collection of laws and regulations of the People's Republic of China, Jan.–Dec. 1989] (Beijing: Zhongguo fazhi chubanshe, 1990), pp. 198–200; Guowu-

yuan fazhi ju, *Zhonghua renmin gongheguo xin fagui huibian* [A collection of new laws and regulations of the People's Republic of China] (Beijing: Zhongguo fazhi chubanshe, 1995), 2: 194–96.

13. The measure was modified and finalized in 1988. Among the major modifications are a stipulation on the percentage (no less than 50%) of spending surplus for administrative purposes and a more detailed classification of the terms of contract. See Sifa bu and guwuyuan fazhi ju, eds., *Zhonghua renmin gongheguo xingzheng fagui xuanbian* [Selected administrative laws and regulations of the People's Republic of China] (Beijing: Falü chubanshe, 1991), 1: 564–65.

14. Sifa bu lushi si, Jianshe bu tigai fagui si, eds., *Zhonghua renmin gongheguo fangdichan fagui huibian* [A collection of real estate laws and regulations of the People's Republic of China] (Beijing: Zhongguo jiancha chubanshe, 1992), pp. 354–62.

15. Ibid., pp. 353–54.

16. Ibid., pp. 354–62.

17. Song Defu, ed., *Dangdai Zhongguo de renshi guanli*, 2: 143.

18. Ibid.

19. Guojia tongji ju shehui tongji si, *Zhongguo laodong gongzi tongji ziliao, 1949–1985* [Labor and wage statistics of China, 1949–1985] (Beijing: Zhongguo tongji chubanshe, 1987), p. 165.

20. Bianxie zu, ed., *Zhongguo xingzheng gaige da qushi* [Mega-trends in China's administrative reforms] (Beijing: Jingji kexue chubanshe, 1993).

21. He Guang, ed., *Dangdai Zhongguo de laodongli guanli* [Labor force management in contemporary China] (Beijing: Zhongguo shehui kexue chubanshe, 1990), p. 475.

22. Ibid., p. 57.

23. Under the policy during the Cultural Revolution, each family could only keep one child from being sent to the countryside after middle school.

24. He, ed., *Dangdai Zhongguo de laodongli guanli*, p. 60.

25. Ibid.

26. A complementary measure was to allow unemployed urban residents to undertake private economic activities in the capacity of "self-employed individuals" (*getihu*). See Fei and Zuo, eds., *Dangdai Zhongguo de gongshang xingzheng guanli*.

27. Ibid., p. 346.

28. Authors' interviews.

29. Chen Ruisheng et al., eds., *Zhongguo gaige quanshu: Zhengzhi tizhi gaige juan* [An encyclopedia of China's reform: Reform of the political system] (Dalian: Dalian chubanshe, 1992), p. 21.

30. Guojia tongji ju, *Zhongguo tongji nianjian, 1986* [Statistical yearbook of China, 1986] (Beijing: Zhongguo tongji chubanshe, 1986), p. 129.

31. Guojia jingji tizhi gaige weiyuanhui zonghe guihua he shidian si, *Zhongguo gaige kaifang shidian* [A handbook on important events in China's reform and opening] (Guangzhou: Guangdong renmin chubanshe, 1993), pp. 478–83.

32. *Zhongguo xingzheng* [Public administration in China] (monthly), Dec. 1987, pp. 42–45.

33. Ibid.

34. He, ed., *Dangdai Zhongguo de laodongli guanli*, p. 346.

35. *Zhongguo gongshang bao*, Sept. 11 1989.

36. Joseph Cheng and Xie Qingkui, *Dangdai Zhongguo zhengfu* [Government in contemporary China] (Hong Kong: Cosmos Books Ltd., 1991), p. 266.

37. Chen et al., *Zhongguo gaige quanshu: Zhengzhi tizhi gaige*, p. 25, p. 493.

38. Kang Shizhao, ed., *Zhongguo gaige quanshu: Wenhua tizhi gaige juan* [An encyclopedia of China's reform: Reform of the cultural administration system] (Dalian: Dalian chubanshe, 1992).

39. Wang and Wang, eds., *Jiequ jingji*.

40. Bianxie zu, ed., *Zhongguo xingzheng gaige da qushi*, pp. 824–30.

41. Investigation task force, "Guanyu Beijing shi dangzheng jiguan yu suo-ban jingji shiti tuogou gongzuo qingkuang de zongjie baogao" [Report on the work to delink agency-sponsored economic entities from their sponsoring Party and government agencies in Beijing] (Beijing Municipal Government internal document, photocopied, 1994), p. 5.

42. *Renmin ribao* [People's daily], July 5, 6, 1995.

43. Investigation task force, "Guanyu jiancha jingji shiti gongzuo de zongjie baogao" [Report on the investigation into agency-sponsored economic entities] (Beijing Municipal Government internal document, photocopied, 1995), pp. 2–3.

44. Ibid.

45. Fei and Zuo, eds., *Dangdai Zhongguo de gongshang xingzheng guanli*.

46. Wang and Wang, *Jiequ jingji*.

47. Such input need not be financial. Regulatory favors can be valued and priced accordingly. In our fieldwork, we have repeatedly heard about what are called *gangu* (dry shares)—rewards in the form of company shares given for the "services" provided by state agencies or agents.

48. Authors' interviews.

49. Wang and Wang, *Jiequ jingji*.

50. Authors' interviews.

51. In two of the backyard profit centers where we conducted our interviews, the attempts by their former leaders to delink their organizations from their sponsoring agencies were defeated by the latter through a reappointment of the leadership teams.

52. *Zhongguo gongshang bao*, Sept. 11, 1989.

53. Investigation task force, "Guanyu jiancha jingji shiti gongzuo de zongjie baogao" (1995), p. 3.

54. Wu Jinglian, "China's Economic Reform: Retrospect and Prospect" (paper presented at the Chinese Economic Reform Workshop, Division of Social Science, Hong Kong University of Science and Technology, May 1995).

55. *Renmin ribao*, Aug. 17 1989.

56. Guojia tongji ju, *Zhongguo tongji nianjian, 1995*, p. 526.

57. *Zhongguo gongshang bao*, July 15, Sept. 26 and 28, 1995; Feb. 24, 1996.

58. *Beijing wanbao* [Beijing evening news], Aug. 22, 1994.

59. See, e.g., *Qiyejia bao* [Entrepreneur news], Apr. 8, 1993.

60. *Jingji xinxi bao* [Economic information daily], Mar. 29, 1995.

61. Investigation task force, "Guanyu jiancha jingji shiti gongzuo de zongjie baogao" (1995), p. 5.

62. Authors' interviews.

63. This figure is calculated from the survey data set. It should be noted that in calculating the income shares, we treat all the salary components authorized by the financial authority as coming from budgetary funds. This may not always be true, in that many state agencies, especially those categorized as *shiye danwei*, do not get full allocation of budgetary funds for salary payment and have to use their off-budget funds to make up the gap between the authorized salary bill for their employees and the budgetary funds allocated. Thus the figure reported here should be seen as a conservative estimate.

64. These figures are computed from various tables on "nonproduction" fixed asset investment by state agencies in *Zhongguo tongji nianjian* [Statistical yearbook of China] (Beijing: Zhongguo tongji chubanshe, 1986–93). The investment figures reported here do not include the capital used by state agencies to purchase commercial housing, which is a parallel source of housing provision to their employees. A major measure adopted in the urban housing reforms since the mid 1980s is to let state agency employees sublet, or purchase the use rights of, housing constructed or purchased by their work units from the housing market. The rent and price in these arrangements are set below market price, and the difference is made up by the agencies from slush funds.

65. Deng et al., *Zhongguo yusuan wai zijin fenxi*, pp. 126–29.

66. See, e.g., *Renmin ribao*, May 28, Sept. 2, and Nov. 19, 1988; Nov. 17, 1989.

67. Investigation task force, "Guanyu jiancha jingji shiti gongzuo de zongjie baogao" (1995), p. 4.

68. Deng et al., *Zhongguo yusuan wai zijin fenxi*.

69. Ibid.

70. Authors' interviews.

71. *Renmin ribao*, various issues, July and Aug. 1991.

72. *Zhongguo gongshang bao*, Sept. 11, 1989.

73. *Renmin ribao*, Sept. 3, 1988.

74. *Zhongguo gongshang bao*, Sept. 11, 1989.

75. *Renmin ribao*, Sept. 26, 1989.

76. A Beijing University study completed prior to the campaign reveals that each and every department or agency in the district government of a northern provincial capital had set up and run profit-seeking operations in its backyard. See Wang and Wang, *Jiequ jingji*.

77. Investigation task force, "Guanyu jiancha jingji shiti gongzuo de zongjie baogao" (1995), p. 5.

78. Since the mid 1980s, various units in the People's Liberation Army have also set up large numbers of profit-seeking entities (see, e.g., *Renmin ribao*, July 14, 16, and 23, 1998; *Far Eastern Economic Review*, Aug. 6, 1998, pp. 68–69). But it appears that they were not targeted by the three nationwide cleanup campaigns.

79. Authors' interviews.

80. Authors' interviews.

81. Investigation task force, "Zongjie baogao," 1994, 1995 (cited nn. 41 and 43 above).

82. See, e.g., nn. 70–71.

83. See, e.g., *Renmin ribao*, Aug. 17, 1989; *Zhongguo gongshang bao*, Sept. 11, 1989; and Guowuyuan fazhi ju, *Zhonghua renmin gongheguo xin fagui huibian 1993.1–12* [A collection of new laws and regulations of the People's Republic of China, Jan.–Dec. 1993] (Beijing: Zhongguo fazhi chubanshe, 1994), pp. 1294–97.

84. Investigation task force, "Guanyu jiancha jingji shiti gongzuo de zongjie baogao" (1995), pp. 3–7.

85. Guojia xinxi zhongxin xinxi bu, *Laws and Regulations of China* (Beijing: Guojia xinxi zhongxin, 1996), CD ROM, GD 96–02, Sept. 11, 1992.

86. For discussions of this issue in different organizational settings, see Susan L. Shirk, *Competitive Comrades: Career Incentives and Student Strategies in China* (Berkeley and Los Angeles: University of California Press, 1982), and Andrew Walder, *Communist Neo-Traditionalism: Work and Authority in Chinese Industry* (Berkeley and Los Angeles: University of California Press, 1986).

87. In the 1993 Beijing University–*Zhongguo qingnian bao* survey mentioned above, e.g., 87.8% (n = 600) of the responding state agency employees regarded their incomes as being at below-average levels in the society, and 63.2% (n = 598) of them claimed that their incomes had experienced relative decline in comparison with those of other social groups during the previous few years.

88. This is substantiated by, e.g., Wang and Wang, *Jiequ jingji*; *Renmin ribao*, Aug. 7, 1994; *Jingji ribao* [Economic daily], Apr. 24, 1995; authors' interviews; and Chapter 10 in this volume.

89. See, e.g., Mancur Olson, *The Logic of Collective Action* (Cambridge, Mass.: Harvard University Press, 1965), and Russell Hardin, *Collective Action* (Baltimore: Johns Hopkins University Press, 1982).

CHAPTER 10   *Francis, Bargained Property Rights*

1. For a statement by a modern theorist, see Richard Posner, *Economic Analysis of Law* (2d ed., Boston: Little, Brown, 1977). For this perspective with regard to market transitions in Eastern Europe and Russia, see David Lipton and Jeffrey Sachs, "Creating a Market Economy in Eastern Europe: The Case of Poland," *Brookings Papers on Economic Activity*, no. 1 (Spring 1990): 75–147; Ellen Comisso, "Property Rights, Liberalism, and the Transition from 'Actually Existing' Socialism," *East European Politics and Society* 5, 1 (Winter 1991): 162–88; and Olivier Blanchard, Rudiger Dornbusch, Paul Krugman, Richard Layard, and Lawrence Summers, *Reform in Eastern Europe* (Cambridge, Mass.: MIT Press, 1991). For an institutional approach that argues for the efficiency of well-clarified property rights, see Douglass North, *Institutions, Institutional Change and Economic Performance* (Cambridge: Cambridge University Press, 1990), and id. and Barry Weingast, "Constitutions and Commitment: The Evolution of Institutions Governing Public Choice in Seventeenth-Century England," *Journal of Economic History*, no. 49 (Dec. 1989).

2. Carol Rose, "The Comedy of the Commons: Custom, Commerce, and Inherently Public," *University of Chicago Law Review* 53, 3 (Summer 1986): 711–81.

3. For diverse viewpoints see, among others, Kuan Chen, Hongchang Wang, Yuxin Zheng, Gary H. Jefferson, and Thomas Rawski, "Productivity Change in Chinese Industry: 1953–1985," *Journal of Comparative Economics* 12 (Dec. 1988): 570–91; Gene Tidrick and Jiyuan Chen, eds., *China's Industrial Reforms* (New York: Oxford University Press, 1987); and Christine P. W. Wong, "Between Plan and Market: The Role of the Local Sector in Post-Mao China," *Journal of Comparative Economics* 11 (Sept. 1987): 385–98. For a property rights perspective, see Geng Xiao, *Property Rights Arrangements and Industrial Productivity in China*, Research Paper Series: Enterprise Behavior and Economic Reforms, World Bank, No. Ch-RPS #11, Sept. 1991; and id., *The Impact of Property Rights Structure on Productivity, Capital Allocation, and Labor Income in Chinese State and Collective Enterprises*, Program in Applied Econometrics Discussion Paper No. 32 (Los Angeles: Department of Economics, UCLA, 1990).

4. Yia-ling Liu, "Reform from Below: The Private Economy and Local Politics in the Rural Industrialization of Wenzhou," *China Quarterly*, no. 130 (1992): 293–316; Kate Xiao Zhou, *How the Farmers Changed China: Power of the People* (Boulder, Colo.: Westview Press, 1996).

5. Jean Oi, "Fiscal Reform and Economic Foundations of Local State Corporatism in China," *World Politics* 45 (Oct. 1992): 99–126; Andrew Walder, "Local Governments as Industrial Firms: An Organizational Analysis of China's Transitional Economy," *American Journal of Sociology* 101, 2 (1995): 263–301; id., "Corporate Organization and Local Government Property Rights in China," in Vedat Milor, ed., *Changing Political Economies: Privatization in Post-Communist and Reforming Communist States* (Boulder, Colo.: Lynne Rienner, 1994), pp. 53–66; and id., "The County Government as an Industrial Corporation," in Andrew Walder, ed., *Zouping in Transition: The Process of Reform in Rural North China* (Cambridge, Mass.: Harvard University Press, 1998), pp. 62–85.

6. Walder, "Local Governments as Industrial Firms," and "Corporate Organization and Local Government Property Rights."

7. Martin L. Weitzman and Chenggang Xu, "Chinese Township-Village Enterprises as Vaguely Defined Cooperatives," *Journal of Comparative Economics* 18 (Apr. 1994): 121–45.

8. Harold Demsetz, "Towards a Theory of Property Rights," *American Economic Review* 57, 2 (1967): 347–59. One of the earliest works that makes a case for social norms and tradition as a basis for property rights is E. Adamson Hoebel, "Fundamental Legal Concepts as Applied in the Study of Primitive Law," *Yale Law Review*, no. 51 (1942): 951–66.

9. This chapter is based on the results of two research trips in 1993 and 1996. In 1993, interviews were conducted with six high-tech spin-off firms. These ranged in size from around 100 employees to 1,400, the largest being Lian Xiang, with 800 employees in Beijing, 300 in the rest of China, and 300 in Hong Kong. The oldest company was established in 1984, one was established in 1992, and the others were established in the mid to late 1980s. The 1996 interviews were conducted with informants from eight parent agencies, including universities,

university departments, the China Youth League, a Beijing municipal government department, and a business school, and with managers and employees of three individual spin-off firms. In addition to the formal interviews, I gained important insights from informal discussions with friends who were former employees of spin-off firms.

10. For a description of the changing budgetary system and increases in the proportion of extra-budgetary revenue, see *Zhongguo yusuanwai zijin guanli lilun yu shijian* [Theory and practice in the management of China's extrabudgetary revenue] (Harbin: Heilongjiang Publishing House, 1992).

11. For instance, the operating budgets of the 117 institutes of the Chinese Academy of Sciences are reported to have been cut 70% since the initiation of the post-Mao reforms. See "Dozens of High-Tech Firms Started by University Researchers," *Science*, Oct. 15, 1993.

12. The Chinese term most frequently used is *jingji shiti*, or "economic entity." See, e.g., "Geji renmin yinhang yu suoban jingji shiti" [The various levels of the People's Bank of China and its economic entities], *Renmin ribao* [People's daily], Aug. 30, 1993. For the use of this term in a government document, see Investigation Task Force, "Guanyu Beijing shi dangzheng jiguan yu suoban jingji shiti tuogou gongzuo qingkuang de zongjie baogao" [Report on the work to delink agency-sponsored economic entities from their sponsoring Party and government agencies in Beijing] (Beijing Municipal Government internal document, photocopied, 1993); and id., "Guanyu jiancha jingji shiti gongzuo de zongjie baogao" [Report on the investigation into agency sponsored economic entities] (Beijing Municipal Government internal document, photocopied, 1995). For analysis of spin-offs in other national contexts, see David Ellerman, "Spinoffs as a Restructuring Strategy for Post-Socialist Enterprises" (paper presented at conference on "Commercializing High Technology: East and West," May 11–13, 1995, Stanford University); David Bernstein, "Spin-offs and Start-ups in Russia: A Key Element of Industrial Restructuring," in Michael McFaul and Tova Perlmutter, eds., *Privatization, Conversion, and Enterprise Reform: Selected Conference Papers* (Stanford, Calif.: Center for International Security and Arms Control, May 1994).

13. Cheng-Tian Kuo, "Privatization Within the Chinese State" (paper presented at the 1994 Annual Meeting of the American Political Science Association, New York, Sept. 1–4, 1994). For analyses of the commercial activities of the Chinese military, see Thomas Bickford, "The Chinese Military as Entrepreneurs," *Asian Survey*, May 1994; Maria Christina Valdecanas, "From Machine Guns to Motorcycles," *China Business Review* 22, 6 (Nov.–Dec. 1995): 14–18; and "State Business: Privatization Fever Sweeps Asia," *Far Eastern Economic Review*, Feb. 23, 1995. The People's Liberation Army has been one of the most active institutions in the market and has built up an impressive business complex. See Solomon M. Karmel, "The Chinese Military's Hunt for Profits," *Foreign Policy*, no. 107 (Summer 1997): 102–13.

14. The Shanghai Islamic Association helped set up the Light and Power Trading Company, which specializes in import-export business with Islamic countries. See "Religious Circles Enter Market Economy," FBIS-CHI-93-057 (Mar. 26, 1993): 30–31.

15. These are similar to incentives described by William A. Byrd and Alan Gelb, "Why Industrialize? The Incentives for Rural Community Governments," in William Byrd and Qingsong Lin, eds., *China's Rural Industry: Structure, Development, and Reform* (New York: Oxford University Press, 1990).

16. For an analysis of commercial activities undertaken by individuals or small groups of officials, see Chapter 11 in this volume.

17. For an overview of spin-off enterprises in China's high-technology sector, see Shulin Gu, *Spin-off Enterprises in China: Channeling the Components of R&D Institutions into Innovative Businesses*, UNU/INTECH Working Paper No. 16 (Maastricht, Neth.: United Nations, 1994). For an overview of the development of high-tech zones in China, see Erik Baark, "China's High-Tech Zones in Historical Perspective" (paper presented at the 48th Annual Meeting of the Association for Asian Studies, Honolulu, Hawaii, Apr. 11–14, 1996); id., "China's New High Technology Development Zones: The Politics of Commercializing Technology, 1982–1992," *Washington Journal of Modern China* 2, 1 (1994): 83–102; Shulin Gu, *A Review of Reform Policy for the S&T System in China: From Paid Transactions for Technology to Organizational Restructuring*, UNU/INTECH Working Paper No. 17 (Maastricht, Neth.: United Nations, 1995).

18. One of the earliest high-tech spin-offs was established in Haidian District in 1980. Cheng Chunxian, a research professor at the Institute of Physics of the Chinese Academy of Sciences (CAS), created a technological development project now called the Beijing Huaxia Guigu (China-Silicon Valley) Information System Corporation Ltd. See Gu, *Spin-off Enterprises in China*, p. 7.

19. *Zhongguo Beijing xinjishu chanye kaifa shiyan qu yanjiu baogao* [Report on Beijing's new technology and production experimental zone] (Beijing: Research Group on China's Beijing New Technology and Enterprise Experimental Zone, 1995).

20. Gu, *Spin-off Enterprises in China*.

21. "High Anxiety: Doing Business with China Is Never Easy: Beijing's Entry into the Satellite Market," *Far Eastern Economic Review*, Aug. 18, 1994, pp. 46–49; "Out of Line: U.S. Tries to Prise Open China's Telecom Sector," ibid., Dec. 1, 1994, pp. 64–65.

22. Examples of research institutes outside of Beijing that have set up successful businesses include the Institute of Optical Technology of Wuhan City, the Cell Biology Institute of the Shanghai Academy of Sciences, and the Zhejiang Institute of Mechanical and Electrical Engineering Design in Zhejiang Province.

23. For an overview of the reforms of China's science and technology system, see Gu, *Review of Reform Policy for the S&T System in China*.

24. An initial goal of China's S&T reforms was to create a market for technology in which industrial users of technology would pay R&D institutes for the transfer of product and process technologies, technological consulting services, and contracts for the development of production technology. Spin-offs represent a more fundamental institutional reform, which alters the organizational relationship between R&D and entrepreneurship. Other mechanisms used, such as the direct merger of R&D institutes with existing enterprises and the transfor-

mation of entire R&D institutes into profit-making enterprises, had not proved that effective. See Gu, *Spin-off Enterprises in China*, p. 2, for further elaboration.

25. However, as Erik Baark has pointed out, the launching of the Torch Program and the increasing number of high-tech zones also reflected the goal of the central and local governments to better control and regulate the growing number of high-tech spin-offs. This is evident in a tightening of the requirements regarding formal licenses targeting enterprises that had spontaneously "spun off." See Baark, "China's New High Technology Development Zones," and Gu, *Spin-off Enterprises in China*.

26. In 1983, Beijing's technology zone had 11 new technology enterprises. In 1993, the number had increased to 3,000. Gu, *Spin-off Enterprises in China*, p. 11.

27. Ibid., p. 25.

28. Ibid., p. 27.

29. Ibid.

30. Enterprises listed as publicly owned reported that only .8% of venture capital came from loans from sources other than individuals or their supervising institutions. This percentage was only 1.4% for collectives with leading units. Gu Shulin believes, however, that banks are beginning to play a more important role in financing enterprise development, particularly within high-tech zones (Gu, *Spin-off Enterprises in China*, p. 47).

31. *Zhongguo Beijing xinjishu chanye* (cited n. 19 above). In the case of public enterprises 56.6% of the capital was invested by a "leading organ," while 19.5% was borrowed by the enterprise from a "leading organ." In the case of collective enterprises with a supervising unit, 61.6% of the capital came from originating unit funds, while 13.7% was in the form of a loan to the enterprise. See ibid., p. 28.

32. See "Beijing Beida Fangzheng Jituan Gongse zhangcheng" [Charter of the Beijing Beida Fangzheng Group Corporation] (internal university document), art. 2.

33. "Li Peng on Trading Autonomy for Research Groups," Beijing Xinhua News Agency, Mar. 12, 1993; FBIS-CHI-93-046 (Mar. 12, 1993): 11. "Colleges Developing High-Tech Industry," Beijing Xinhua News Agency, Mar. 28, 1993; FBIS-CHI-93-059 (Mar. 30, 1993): 66.

34. "Guanyu zhuanfa guojia jingmaowei 'Guanyu dangzheng jiguan yu suoban jingji shiti tuogoude jueding' de tongzhi" [Announcement regarding transmitting the Commission of Economics and Commerce's "Decision regarding de-linking Party and government organs from their economic entities"] (Office of the Party's Central Committee, Office of the State Council, Document, 1993, #17). For a description of the results of this campaign in Beijing, see "Guanyu Beijing shi dangzheng jiguan yu suoban jingji shiti" and "Guanyu jiancha jingji shiti gongzuo de zongjie baogao" (both cited in n. 12 above).

35. David Weimer, ed., *The Political Economy of Property Rights: Institutional Change and Credibility in the Reform of Centrally Planned Economies* (Cambridge: Cambridge University Press, 1997).

36. Managers of one company commented casually that their company had

been set up just as development of the principal technology was completed (author's interviews, PRC, 1993). However, I thank Pete Suttmeier for stressing that there is not a clear line between "basic" research and the commercialization stage, and that the latter presents a serious technological challenge as well (personal communications).

37. *Zhongguo Beijing xinjishu chanye* (cited n. 19 above). In response to the question regarding ownership of the technology utilized by a spin-off, respondents reported that only 16.3% belonged to the leading organ, while 37.4% was said to belong to the enterprise as a collective, 21.4% belonged to individual enterprise employees, and 16% was said to belong to the public. See ibid., p. 30.

38. This manager denied that the company's parent institution exercised any proprietary claim over the company, since it had not provided any capital, despite the fact that the technology from which the company's key initial products were derived had come from the institute. This could suggest that technology is simply not viewed as a significant form of investment. Or it could mean that the technology is not viewed as belonging to the institute, even though it was developed by institute personnel, and perhaps was seen as belonging more to the researchers themselves. Author's interviews, PRC, 1993.

39. This is not to imply that bargaining does not also occur in situations in which property rights are relatively more clearly defined in legal terms. On bargaining in a "Western" context, see William A. Klein, "The Modern Business Organization: Bargaining Under Constraints," *Yale Law Journal* 91, 8 (July 1982): 1521–64. It does indicate that the relative lack of legal clarification and the absence of traditional custom together contribute to the lack of specification of property rights.

40. Robert Sugden, "Spontaneous Order," *Journal of Economic Perspectives* 3, 4 (Fall 1989): 85–97.

41. Eirik Furubotn and Svetozar Pejovich, "Property Rights and Economic Theory," in Furubotn and Pejovich, eds., *The Economics of Property Rights* (Cambridge, Mass.: Ballinger, 1974).

42. One informant said that spin-offs often had to pay a proportion of their net profits comparable to the amount they paid to the state in taxes, although the amounts are in practice often lower (author's interviews, PRC, 1993).

43. According to one manager in this company, "the institute didn't trust us, so they took all our profits" (author's interviews, 1993).

44. Author's interviews, PRC, 1996.

45. In this case the initial capital had been invested entirely by individual founders of the company and a foreign joint partner (author's interviews, PRC, 1993).

46. The general manager said that the corporation would provide ¥1–2 million annually, out of gross profits of roughly ¥10 million in 1996 (author's interviews, 1996).

47. Author's interviews, PRC, 1993.

48. According to the general manager of the corporation, the China Youth League had selected 10,000 extremely poor villages and sought to pair each

village with an enterprise, some of which belonged to its corporation (author's interviews, 1996).

49. Louis Putterman, "Ownership and the Nature of the Firm," *Journal of Comparative Economics* 17, 2 (June 1993): 243–63, at 246.

50. "Guanyu dangzheng jiguan yu suoban jingji shiti tuogoude jueding" (see n. 34 above).

51. Although he does not hold a top executive position in the Fangzheng Corporation, Wang Xuan was its chief advisor in 1996, chairman of the board of Founder (Hong Kong) Ltd., and director of the Computer Institute of Beijing University (author's interviews, 1996). See also Shi Lihong, "Wang Xuan: High-Tech Guru Speaks," *China Daily*, Apr. 10, 1996, p. 10, for an interview with Wang Xuan.

52. This is the same principle that applies in state-owned enterprises, where supervising bureaus exercise nominal authority over the appointment of the enterprise-level and deputy-level positions. In the traditional SOEs, this included the positions of Party secretary, deputy Party secretary, and enterprise manager and deputy manager.

53. *Zhongguo gongsifa yuanli yu shiwu* [Principles and practice of China's company law] (Chengdu: Sichuan Publishing House, 1994).

54. This account is based on interviews conducted in 1993 and 1996 with both present and past employees of Lian Xiang, and with journalists who were involved in the case.

55. I was unable to find out the specific amount that was transmitted from the company to the institute.

56. Author's interviews, PRC, 1993.

57. According to one of the three original founders of the company, this grant was sponsored by the Ministry of Planning, under the name "748 Project," which indicated the month and year that the project was initiated—August 1974. Originally, there were only 4 people working on this project, but in 1977 Beida received an additional research grant funding the establishment of a Chinese Character Information Processing Research Department (Hanzi xinxi chuli yanjiu shi), which employed 20–30 people, all of them directly employed by the university (author's interviews, 1996).

58. Author's interviews, PRC, 1993 and 1996.

59. Ibid.

60. The question of how innovative enterprises continue to be after they have been "spun off" is a crucial one, but it is beyond the scope of this chapter. This issue is addressed by some of the excellent work being done that evaluates the success of China's science and technology reforms. See Erik Baark, "Technological Entrepreneurship and Commercialization of Research Results in the West and China: Comparative Perspectives," *Technology Analysis and Strategic Management* 6, 2 (1994): 203–14; and Richard P. Suttmeier, "China's Strategy for High Technology: Reform, R&D, and the Search for 'Complementarity Assets' " (MS).

61. This institute was subsequently renamed and transformed again, becoming the Fangzheng Technology Research Institute, with a staff of around 100 in

1996. It is now largely funded by the Fangzheng Group. According to one informant it receives close to Y 10 million a year from Fangzheng.

62. According to one informant 60–70% of Fangzheng's employees were from Beida in 1996 (author's interviews, 1996).

63. Author's interviews, PRC, 1996.

64. A disadvantage of this system, as pointed out by one informant, is that the management committee overseeing high-tech spin-offs lacks specialized knowledge of the computer and electronics industry, making the selection process subject to bureaucratic and political influences (author's interviews, PRC, 1993).

65. Author's interviews, PRC, 1993.

66. The CEO of CITIC made the same claim for the decision-making process of his corporation, saying that CITIC management was autonomous in its decision-making and not subject to interference from the State Council, its nominal "owner" (informal discussion, Brown University, May 1995).

67. For further discussion of this point, see Suttmeier, "China's Strategy for High Technology"; Denis Fred Simon, ed., *The Emerging Technological Trajectory of the Pacific Rim* (Armonk, N.Y.: M. E. Sharpe, 1995); Nathan Rosenberg, Ralph Landau, and David Mowery, eds., *Technology and the Wealth of Nations* (Stanford, Calif.: Stanford University Press, 1992).

68. "Guanyu Beijing shi dangzheng jiguan" (cited n. 12 above). According to this report (p. 3), only the occasional employee of an agency-sponsored enterprise continues to receive a salary from the supervising unit. However, there are still large numbers who retain their "personnel links" with the sponsoring agency, allowing them to retain their cadre status.

69. Author's interviews, 1993 and 1996. For more elaboration of personnel management in spin-off enterprises, see Corinna-Barbara Francis, "Reproduction of *Danwei* Institutional Features in the Context of China's Market Economy: The Case of Haidian District's High-Tech Sector," *China Quarterly*, no. 147 (Sept. 1996): 839–59.

70. By contrast, employees who are hired by spin-off firms from outside the parent institution are generally employed on the basis of a labor contract and do not enjoy the same benefits and job security as personnel who transfer from the parent institution. They may be laid off owing to poor performance or downsizing by the enterprise, but are able to maintain their public employee status through the institutional innovation of local "skilled personnel employment exchange centers" (*rencai jiaoliu zhongxin*). Author's interviews, PRC, 1993 and 1996. For further discussion of the personnel and benefits arrangements in spin-off enterprises, see Francis, "Reproduction of *Danwei* Institutional Features."

71. The companies set up by the Shanghai Institute of Cell Biology are reported to have contributed Y 7 million to the institute's budget in 1993, for instance, compared to the Y 2 million that it received from the Chinese Academy of Sciences ("Dozens of High-Tech Firms Started by University Researchers" [cited n. 11 above]).

72. In "Local Governments as Industrial Firms" (cited n. 5 above), Andrew Walder argues that this is one of the strengths of ownership by local as opposed

to higher levels of government, but traditional SOEs no longer enjoy the extensive state-backed guarantees that they used to. Many of them are handing out IOUs to their employees and forcing them into extended unpaid "vacations."

73. On the whole, high-technology spin-offs invest more in R&D than the average industrial firm. The average ratio between expenditures on technological development and turnover by high-tech spin-offs was between 5% and 9% between 1990 and 1992. This is much higher than the average for industrial enterprises in China, which was 1%. See Gu, *Spin-off Enterprises in China*, p. 13.

74. See David Stark, "Path Dependence and Privatization Strategies in East Central Europe," *East European Politics and Societies* 6, 1 (Winter 1992): 17–54, at 19.

CHAPTER 11   *Wank, Producing Property Rights*

I am grateful to Jean Oi and Andrew Walder for insightful comments on successive drafts of this chapter, and to Nan Lin, Susan Young, and other participants at the conference from which this volume stems, for numerous helpful suggestions.

1. Ding Lu, *Entrepreneurship in Suppressed Markets: Private-Sector Experience in China* (New York: Garland Publishing, 1994); Victor Nee, "Organizational Dynamics of Market Transition: Hybrid Forms, Property Rights, and Mixed Economy in China," *Administrative Science Quarterly* 37 (Mar. 1992): 1–27.

2. Nan Lin, "Local Market Socialism: Local Corporatism in Action in Rural China," *Theory and Society* 24, 3 (June 1995): 301–54; Martin L. Weitzman and Chenggang Xu, "Chinese Township-Village Enterprises as Vaguely Defined Co-operatives," *Journal of Comparative Economics* 18, 2 (Apr. 1994): 121–45.

3. I follow Harold Demsetz's definition of property rights as "an instrument of society . . . that . . . help[s] a man form those expectations that he can reasonably hold in his dealings with others. These expectations find expression in the laws, customs, and mores of a society." See Harold Demsetz, "Toward a Theory of Property Rights," in *Ownership, Control, and the Firm* (Oxford: Blackwell, [1967] 1988), pp. 104–16.

4. This chapter extends David Stark's analysis of these institutionally plural environments and of commercial action as "bricolage." See David Stark, "Recombinant Property in East European Capitalism," *American Journal of Sociology* 101, 4 (Jan. 1996): 993–1027.

5. I see institutions as the cognitive categories and social norms that construct relationships, while strategies are the actions of people who are constrained by institutions but can maneuver within those constraints to develop relationships that further their interests. Such manipulation is not the action of a fully rational actor but rather the partially unreflective routines and improvisations of a competent person. Such action is akin to what Pierre Bourdieu calls the "habitus."

6. These networks have also become an institutional element of the emerging market economy.

7. For a description of Xiamen City and discussion of the fieldwork and

sample, see David L. Wank, *Commodifying Communism: Business, Trust, and Politics in a Chinese City* (Cambridge: Cambridge University Press, 1999).

8. Although not apparent in published local statistics in the late 1980s, officials at the time told me that the total value of goods and services produced by the domestic and foreign nonstate sector had surpassed that of the state sector. Such a figure was not realized in the national economy till the 1990s.

9. At the time it was impossible for a foreign or overseas Chinese firm to obtain a license for commerce. Thus the licensed trading concerns were, by legal definition, entirely domestic. However, by the late 1980s, the distinction between domestic and international was also becoming blurred. This trend is only tangentially mentioned in this chapter.

10. The sample is composed of 24 branch, 30 cooperative, 23 leased, and 70 private firms.

11. For more general discussion of these idioms during market reform, see Mayfair Mei-hui Yang, *Gifts, Favors, and Banquets: The Art of Social Relationships in China* (Ithaca, N.Y.: Cornell University Press, 1994).

12. Stark, "Recombinant Property," terms this process "organizational hedging."

13. While it is difficult to know which collective-sector trading firms are cooperatives and which are fully socialized, city government statistics suggest that there were 441 cooperative firms in the late 1980s.

14. Another private business link with government occurred in the realm of perceptions. Companies with Y 500,000 in registered capital are licensed by the city-level Industry and Commerce Bureau and authorized to use the words "Xiamen City" and "company" (*gongsi*) in their name, creating an impression of affiliation with the city government. Companies with Y 50,000 in registered capital are licensed by district-level bureau branches and lack such authorization, but some nevertheless created the impression of public affiliation by designating themselves using terms applicable to public enterprises, such as "business department" (*jingyingbu*).

15. Licenses for cooperative firms were usually issued by labor service companies (*laodong fuwu gongsi*) and for private firms by the Industry and Commerce Bureau.

16. Branch firms can also be state-sector enterprises, although this chapter is not concerned with them. By the late 1980s, there were about 500 such firms in Xiamen, mostly corporations conducting foreign trade.

17. Many branch operators buy real estate and register it in the name of family members. As purchase of a house or condominium in Xiamen confers on the owner a permanent residence permit, these operators have been able to bring their families to Xiamen.

18. In theory, leasing differs from contracting (*chengbao*) in the greater income and user rights that entrepreneurs acquire in the former, but in practice there is little difference. In Xiamen, the term "leasing" is applied to trading firms, and "contracting" to manufacturing and service firms.

19. They were called May 7 enterprises after a speech by Mao Zedong that exhorted citizens to combine productive labor with other activities. These enter-

prises constituted a quarter of the urban collective industrial labor force in the early market reform era.

20. At the time of my fieldwork, there were 205 collective trading firms sponsored by district and other levels of local government that had been leased in the mid 1980s. This figure is my own estimate, based on interviews at government agencies and published local statistics.

21. During the first half of the 1990s, it is officially estimated, Y 100 million (U.S.$12 million) was pilfered daily. According to another official estimate, in 1993, China had U.S.$416 billion in state assets, while another U.S.$57 billion had been illegally privatized. See "China's Vanishing Assets: State Prepares Crackdown on 'Pilferers,'" *International Herald Tribune*, Apr. 26, 1996, p. 11.

22. Some analysts, such as Jean Oi and Andrew Walder, see property rights reform as the devolution of legal property rights to public actors in the lower bureaucracy. This chapter suggests that this devolved control over resources also stimulates a parallel upward penetration of the state by the networks of nonstate entrepreneurs. See Jean C. Oi, "The Fate of the Collective After the Commune," in Deborah Davis and Ezra F. Vogel, eds., *Chinese Society on the Eve of Tiananmen: The Impact of Reform* (Cambridge, Mass.: Council on East Asian Studies and Harvard University, 1990), pp. 15–36; Andrew G. Walder, "Corporate Organization and Local Government Property Rights in China," in Vedat Milor, ed., *Changing Political Economies: Privatization in Post-Communist and Reforming Communist States* (Boulder, Colo.: Lynne Rienner, 1994), pp. 53–66.

23. The inefficiencies of networks transgressing state-society boundaries are more explicitly stated in the literature on East European economies cited in n. 34.

24. Harold Demsetz, "Information and Efficiency: Another Viewpoint," *Journal of Law and Economics* 12, 1 (Apr. 1969): 1–22.

25. For example, a trio of foreign advisors to the Russian government maintain that giving government officeholders shares in publicly owned firms "reduces the likelihood that control over assets will shift to managers with skills needed to restructure firms. . . . To the extent that management turnover is essential for efficient resource allocation, giving equity to politicians can entrench the old human capital and thereby reduce efficiency" (Maxim Boycko, Andrei Shleifer, and Robert Vishny, *Privatizing Russia* [Cambridge, Mass.: MIT Press, 1995], p. 59).

26. "Giving politicians equity is obviously extremely unfair. . . . Like corruption, *nomenklatura* privatization rewards arbitrary grabbing of control rights and openly acknowledges that politicians are not acting in the public interest" (ibid., p. 59).

27. According to the aforementioned Russian government advisors, side-payments by entrepreneurs to officeholders attempt to create investment incentives by precluding officeholders from interfering in their firms. But side-payments are ultimately inefficient inasmuch as they lack enforcement mechanisms. "The arbitrary element of a politician's control rights, which enables him to collect bribes, does not constitute a legal right that a court would protect or that he can surrender through a contract enforceable in court. In practice this

means that the politician can come back and demand another bribe from the manager, or another politician can also demand a bribe" (ibid., p. 51).

28. For example, in the Confucian classic *Li Ji* [The Book of Rites], propriety is linked with reciprocity. "And what the rules of propriety value is reciprocity. If I give a gift and nothing comes in return, that is contrary to propriety; if the thing comes to me, and I give nothing in return, that also is contrary to propriety" (quoted in Yunxiang Yan, *The Flow of Gifts: Reciprocity and Social Networks in a Chinese Village* [Stanford, Calif.: Stanford University Press, 1995], p. 124). According to Yan, popular diffusion of this ethic is reflected in the common proverb "Propriety upholds reciprocal interactions" (*Li shang wanglai*).

29. For a more detailed description of entrepreneurial strategies in regard to the Chamber of Commerce, see David L. Wank, "Private Business, Bureaucracy, and Political Alliance in a Chinese City," *Australian Journal of Chinese Affairs* 33 (Jan. 1995): 55–71, at 60.

30. For a similar discussion, see Lucie Cheng and Arthur Rosett, "Contract with a Chinese Face: Socially Embedded Factors in the Transformation from Hierarchy to Market, 1978–1989," in Tahirih V. Lee, ed., *Contract, Guanxi, and Dispute Resolution in China* (New York: Garland Publishing, 1997), pp. 192–96.

31. For example, Victor Nee writes that private business operators "are reluctant to make long-term investment in the growth of their enterprise because, in the absence of legal protection of private property rights and possible hostility directed against them in future political campaigns, they worry about possible appropriation of their assets" (Nee, "Organizational Dynamics," p. 14).

32. See, e.g., Gary G. Hamilton, ed., *Business Networks and Economic Development in East and Southeast Asia* (Hong Kong: University of Hong Kong, Centre of Asian Studies, 1991).

33. In 1995, foreign investment in China was valued at U.S.$38 billion, second only to the U.S.$60 billion in the United States, and far more than the U.S.$5.8 billion in Malaysia, the second largest recipient in Asia ("Not Quite So Sparkling China," *Economist*, Mar. 1–7, 1997, p. 30).

34. See, e.g., Jeffrey Sachs, "Spontaneous Privatization: A Comment," *Soviet Economy* 7, 4 (Oct.–Dec. 1991): 317–21; and Jadwiga Staniszkis, " 'Political Capitalism' in Poland," *East European Politics and Societies* 5, 1 (Winter 1991): 127–41.

35. Kazimierz Z. Poznanski, "A Property Rights Perspective on the Evolution of Communist-Type Economies," in id., ed., *Constructing Capitalism: The Reemergence of Civil Society and Liberal Economy in the Post-Communist World*, pp. 71–96 (Boulder, Colo.: Westview Press, 1992), at pp. 76–77.

36. In chapter 7 of *Commodifying Communism*, I further argue that differences in state policies are an important but insufficient explanation for variations in the performance of economic networks in China and Eastern Europe. Differences in institutional culture are also crucial.

37. See, e.g., Susan L. Shirk, *The Political Logic of Economic Reform in China* (Berkeley and Los Angeles: University of California Press, 1993).

38. Wei Li, *The Chinese Staff System: A Mechanism for Bureaucratic Control and Integration*, China Research Monograph 44 (Berkeley: Institute of East Asian Studies, University of California, 1994), p. 1.

39. Andrew G. Walder, "Local Bargaining Relationships and Urban Industrial Finance," in Kenneth G. Lieberthal and David M. Lampton, eds., *Bureaucracy, Politics, and Decision Making in Post-Mao China* (Berkeley and Los Angeles: University of California Press, 1992), p. 310.

40. Anton Blok, *Violent Peasant Entrepreneurs: The Mafia of a Sicilian Village* (Oxford: Blackwell, 1974); Diego Gambetta, *The Sicilian Mafia: The Business of Private Protection* (Cambridge, Mass.: Harvard University Press, 1993).

41. "Management Brief," *Economist*, Sept. 6–12, 1997, p. 67.

42. "Some suggested that the police cooperated with the gangs, obtaining assistance from them in tracing hard criminals *in exchange for granting them a certain freedom to extort* from the private sector" [emphasis added], observes Ole Bruun, *Business and Bureaucracy in a Chinese City: An Ethnography of Private Business Households in Contemporary China*, China Research Monograph 43 (Berkeley: Institute of East Asian Studies / Center for Chinese Studies, University of California, 1993), p. 181.

43. Gambetta, *Sicilian Mafia*, p. 33.

44. Anders Aslund, *How Russia Became a Market Economy* (Washington, D.C.: Brookings Institution, 1995), p. 169.

45. Susan Young, *Private Business and Economic Reform in China* (Armonk, N.Y.: M.E. Sharpe, 1995), p. 53.

Index

Accumulation fund: of Qiaolou collective enterprises, 35, 283n24; Wenzhou regulations on, 179, 185, 314n39
Administrative expenditure contract system (*xingzheng kaizhi baogan zhi*), 208–9, 322n13
Administrative fees (*guanli fei*): in Qiaolou, 30, 31, 35; on Jinjiang enterprises, 56–57, 67, 294n67, 295n69; as mutual benefit, 82, 87–88, 299n37; on Jinguan enterprises, 82–83, 84; on Yongning enterprises, 85; versus taxes, 87; on Daqiuzhuang corporations, 159; on private versus collective enterprises, 183; on backyard profit centers, 210, 217; on spin-offs, 235, 330n45
Administrative responsiblity system, 88, 91–92, 172, 311nn2,4. *See also* Incentives
Agency theory, 6–7
Agricultural Law (1993), 297n16
Agriculture Bank, 177, 181, 189
Aid to developing areas fund (*zhiyuan bufada diqu zijin*), 90, 299n44
Aid to work as relief (*yigong daizhen*), 90, 299n46
Alchian, Armen, 116
Arbitrage practice, 215–16
Asian Games (1990), 218
Aslund, Anders, 271
Assets: and risk deposit measure, 163–64; of Yueqing versus Songjiang's collective sector, 175; of shareholding cooperatives, 179, 180, 185, 314nn37–39; of fake collectives, 180, 315nn42,44; of local collectives, 187
Asset valuation: of net assets of private

enterprises, 115, 303nn28,35; of TVEs for SHC conversion, 133–34, 138–39; and share value, 134–35, 144, 306–7n30; for limited liability conversion, 164
Auctions, *see* Rigged auctions

Baark, Erik, 329n25
Backyard profit centers: property rights relations in, 203–4, 214–15, 223, 323nn47,51; shared gains from, 204–5, 222; agency affiliations of, 205–6, 321n6; extra-budgetary status of, 206, 321n8; funds contributed by, 206–7, 217–19, 321n9, 324nn63,64; factors leading to, 207–13, 223–24, 322nn13,23,26; investigations of, 213, 215, 217, 218, 219–20, 232; formation of, 213–14; profit-making methods of, 215–17; central policy on, 221; economic inefficiencies from, 224–25; categories of, 228–29, 327nn13,14; terms for, 321n3; of People's Liberation Army, 324n78. *See also* High-tech spin-offs; Spin-off enterprises
Ba guanxi laguolai (pulling over connections), 256–57
Baiting the hook practice, 218
Bao (reciprocity), and propriety, 264, 336n28
Bargaining process: over ambiguous property rights, 233–34, 330n39; over residual income, 234–36, 330nn42,43, 330nn45,46,48; over control/use rights, 236–38; Liang Xiang Company in, 238–40, 331n54; factors shaping outcome of, 240–44, 331nn57,61, 332nn62,64,66

Library of Congress Cataloging-in-Publication Data

Property rights and economic reform in China / edited by Jean C. Oi
   and Andrew G. Walder.
      p.   cm.
   Includes index.
      ISBN 0-8047-3456-9 (cloth : alk. paper). — ISBN 0-8047-3788-6
   (pbk. : alk. paper)
      1. Right of property—China.   2. Government ownership—China.
   3. Privatization—China.   I. Oi, Jean C.   II. Walder, Andrew
   George.
   HB711.P736   1999
   333.3'0951—dc21   99-11806

∞   This book is printed on acid-free, recycled paper.

Original printing 1999
Last figure below indicates year of this printing:
08   07   06   05   04   03   02   01   00   99